Brad Gerhard

SHANE WHITE is the Challis Professor of History at the University of Sydney. Specializing in African American history, he has authored or coauthored five books and collaborated on the website Digital Harlem. His work has won prizes from the American Historical Association and the Organization of American Historians. He lives in Sydney. *Prince of Darkness* is the winner of the 2016 New York City Book Award and the 2015 Society for Historians of the Early American Republic Best Book Prize.

Additional Praise for *Prince of Darkness*

"Hamilton's story is gripping; so, too, is his puzzling near-disappearance from the historical record. White does an excellent job drawing out the facts of Hamilton's life and supplementing them with details from the history of Wall Street and of other African American New Yorkers of the era." —*Library Journal*

"Like Mr. Hamilton himself, Shane White makes the impossible possible. Only the indispensable historian of black New York could have brought the Prince of Darkness back to life. He makes smudgy newspapers and dusty court records pulse with the ambition, treachery, and hilarity of a different age of boom, bust, and dubious racial progress. A great read about a one-of-a-kind who nevertheless has much to tell us about Gotham and U.S. history."
—David Waldstreicher, The Graduate Center,
City University of New York

"Superb scholarship and a sprightly style recover an unaccountably overlooked life." —*Kirkus Reviews*

"Examines the colorful, complex life of the man who, in the nineteenth century, was reportedly the wealthiest black man in the United States."
—*Essence*

"Compelling . . . *Prince of Darkness* tells the complex story of race and wealth in antebellum New York, with a mysterious and sometimes purposefully ambiguous character at its center. From the islands of the Caribbean to Gotham, Hamilton welded together grit and intellectual agility that propelled him into unimaginable wealth. Unlike his African American contemporaries, Jeremiah Hamilton was less concerned with respectability politics or racial uplift. The Prince of Darkness was a man who wanted to be rich, and nothing would stand in his way."
—Erica Armstrong Dunbar, author of *A Fragile Freedom: African American Women and Emancipation in the Antebellum City*

"White details [Hamilton's] incredible life, marriage to a white woman, and contentious presence on Wall Street, in the process revealing the ways that historians reconstruct the past. An engaging look at an extraordinary man."   —*Booklist*

"A fitting tribute to a man who had all but been forgotten."
                    —*Perspectives on History*, American Historical Association

"In *Prince of Darkness*, Shane White employs the superb skills of an accomplished historian to narrate the compelling story of a New York Hamilton who commanded front page news attention in his day and faded into obscurity in the years that followed. I highly recommend this important new book."
                    —Earl Lewis, president for The Andrew W. Mellon Foundation
                    and coauthor (with Heidi Ardizzone) of *Love on Trial*

"A well-told, stereotype-busting tale about a nineteenth-century black financier who dared to be larger than life, and got away with it!"
                    —Elizabeth Dowling Taylor, author of *A Slave in the White House*

PRINCE

of

DARKNESS

THE UNTOLD STORY OF
JEREMIAH G. HAMILTON,
WALL STREET'S FIRST
BLACK MILLIONAIRE

SHANE WHITE

Picador
———
St. Martin's Press
New York

This one is for
Mac White

And for friends:
Stephen Garton, Glenda Sluga and Chris Hilliard

picadorusa.com • picadorbookroom.tumblr.com
twitter.com/picadorusa • facebook.com/picadorusa

Picador® is a U.S. registered trademark and is used by St. Martin's Press under license from Pan Books Limited.

For book club information, please visit facebook.com/picadorbookclub or e-mail marketing@picadorusa.com.

Photograph of Adelaide Morris Hamilton Krizek is provided courtesy of Elisabeth Mantello and is used with permission.

Designed by Letra Libre, Inc.

The Library of Congress has cataloged the St. Martin's Press edition as follows:

White, Shane, author.
Prince of darkness : the untold story of Jeremiah G. Hamilton, Wall Street's first black millionaire / Shane White.
    p. cm.
ISBN 978-1-250-07056-2 (hardcover)
ISBN 978-1-4668-8071-9 (e-book)
1. Hamilton, Jeremiah G., ?—1875. 2. African American capitalists and financiers—Biography. 3. Millionaires—United States—Biography.
4. African Americans—Social conditions—19th century. 5. Finance—United States—History—19th century. 6. United States—Social conditions—19th century. 7. United States—Race relations—History—19th century. I. Title.
HG172.H36W45 2015
332.6092—dc23
[B]   2015011416

Picador Paperback ISBN 978-1-250-09981-5

Our books may be purchased in bulk for promotional, educational, or business use. Please contact your local bookseller or the Macmillan Corporate and Premium Sales Department at 1-800-221-7945, extension 5442, or by e-mail at MacmillanSpecialMarkets@macmillan.com.

First published by St. Martin's Press

First Picador Edition: October 2016

10 9 8 7 6 5 4 3 2 1

CONTENTS

INTRODUCTION

INVISIBLE MAN

I t was still dark when the reporter slipped into the Halls of Justice on Centre Street, an architectural disaster known on account of its misguided inspiration as the Egyptian Tombs, or simply the Tombs, and glanced at the previous night's watch returns. His eye fixed on the entry for a small-time crim who preyed mostly on other blacks in and around the Five Points, by the early 1840s the best-known slum in the world. In truth, there were scores of black con men just like him, living off their wits and a glib tongue. At regular intervals an irresistible white mark would come into view and be taken down. In this case, the black man and a couple of confederates had lured some dupe from out of town into a rum cellar and filched twenty-five dollars from his pocket. Next morning the victim raised hell. The Points was rife with stool pigeons and informers, and someone always talked. Late the previous night the police had gone straight to a well-known haunt to arrest the three black men. Not that the reporter was much concerned with the humdrum details of the crime or the arrest. What had caught his fancy was that this African American had taken the name John Jacob Astor. He had his lead item for the next day's paper.[1]

The white John Jacob Astor epitomized fabulous wealth. Born in what would later become Germany, he had arrived in the United States soon after the Revolution and amassed his fortune initially in the fur trade and later in real estate. He bought up large tracts of Manhattan and made a killing as the city expanded. By the 1840s Astor was worth a fantastic sum, somewhere between ten and twenty million dollars. For all his later patronage of the arts and culture, there was a crassness to the man. Contemporaries skewered him for, among other things, hazarding "the opinion that a man possessing five hundred thousand dollars *can* be comfortable!" Astor was one of the earliest individuals to whom contemporaries attached the novel description "millionaire." By the 1840s, the word, first used by Lord Byron in 1816, was well on its way to becoming an American label. Partly this was because a million dollars was worth only a fraction of a million pounds sterling, but mostly it was a result of the dynamism of the American economy. John Jacob Astor, whose very name, according to Herman Melville, "rings like unto bullion," was the archetypal millionaire, the energetic if slightly uncouth embodiment of New York capitalism.[2]

The idea of a black John Jacob Astor appealed immediately to the reporter. Police roundsmen had considerable latitude in the way they wrote their copy. A lively and often-irreverent take on the business before the city's courts became one of the signature features of most antebellum New York newspapers, particularly the *Herald,* this man's employer. Editors welcomed humor, often a very broad humor, and a black Astor had potential. In this instance the writer exercised restraint. All he had to do was insert an exclamation mark mid-sentence—". . . seeing the name of John Jacob Astor! John Owen, and Thomas Lowrie, charged with high way robbery." The piece's italicized caption—*"What's in a Name?"*—telegraphed to readers that there was a joke.[3] And the joke worked because a black John Jacob Astor was an oxymoron.

The reporter's quip would lose little of its punch over the rest of the century. Most white Americans viewed African Americans as irrelevant to economic progress, a people left floundering off to one side of capitalism's onward rush. Few would have disagreed with the comment of one irritated letter writer to the *Morning Courier and New-York Enquirer:* "Negroes are a blotch of the darkest hue on the character of the 'first commercial city.'"⁴ White Americans struggled especially with the very idea of a wealthy black man, associating all African Americans with slavery and poverty. Nevertheless, within a decade of the *Herald* reporter's story, New York had its first publicly acknowledged black millionaire. In a March 1852 issue of *Frederick Douglass' Paper,* the black intellectual and activist James McCune Smith referred to Jerry Hamilton as "the only black millionaire in New York."⁵ Although McCune Smith scorned him for his single-minded pursuit of the dollar, he and other members of the black intelligentsia such as Frederick Douglass had to concede the degree of Hamilton's success. He thus became not just the first African American, but also one of the earliest Americans, to be labeled a millionaire. At his death, twenty-three years later, dozens of newspapers from as far afield as Ohio, Louisiana, Missouri, Texas and California acknowledged that Hamilton was the richest colored man in the country—as one of them put it, he had "accumulated a colossal fortune of nearly two millions ($2,000,000) dollars."⁶

Jerry Hamilton, better known as Jeremiah G. Hamilton, was a broker, a black man whose very existence flies in the face of our understanding of the way things were in nineteenth-century New York. Although a pioneer, far from being some novice feeling his way around the economy's periphery, he was a Wall Street adept, a skilled and innovative financial manipulator. Unlike later black success stories, such as Madam C. J. Walker, the early-twentieth-century manufacturer of beauty products often assumed to be the first African American millionaire, who would make their fortunes selling goods to black consumers, Hamilton cut a swath through the lily-white New York business world of the middle decades of the nineteenth century. In this domain his depredations soon earned him the nickname "Prince of Darkness." Others, with even less affection, simply called him "Nigger Hamilton."

No one will ever erect a statue honoring Jeremiah Hamilton—he was not a saint; indeed, he was at least as aggressive and ruthless as most antebellum businessmen. Rumors of counterfeiting and scams against insurance companies dogged him until he died, partly because even the more far-fetched stories often had elements of truth to them. Not that the ethics or business practices of many of his contemporaries could bear too much scrutiny, but Hamilton was the one saddled with the title "Prince of Darkness." Wall Street was never going to be a level playing field for the trailblazing African American. Yet for all that, brokers and merchants generally were more interested in the color of the black man's money than his skin. Not that Hamilton gave a damn one way or the other: he simply brushed aside all obstacles placed in his way, or connived to get around them, and carried on amassing his fortune.

The black man cut a familiar figure downtown in the city's financial quarter. In 1836, according to the *Courier and New-York Enquirer,* he was "well known in Wall street." Four years later, a *Herald* writer described him, backhandedly, as "a 'highly respectable' colored gentleman of some celebrity in Wall Street," and a *New York Sun* reporter identified him as being "commonly known as the colored broker of Wall st."[7] Any reader of New York newspapers in the 1830s and 1840s could scarcely avoid coming across stories mentioning Hamilton—there were scores of articles and thousands of words detailing various incidents and controversies in which he was involved. Not only did his picaresque comings and goings make him grist for the mill of the newly invented penny press, but he also was acquainted with several of the editors and, on occasion, found himself drawn into their internecine strife. The iconoclastic firebrand Mike Walsh acknowledged in the *Subterranean:* "We do not know much of Hamilton, beyond his newspaper reputation." Walsh then settled a few of his own scores by adding: "But it requires very little discernment to see that he is far ahead, both in talent and *character* to the miserable wretches of the Sun and the Herald."[8]

Yet, for all his celebrity, Hamilton retained an aura of mystery. Although no one was certain where he came from, those claiming to be in the know persisted in whispering startling stories about a murky past. Shrewd judges agreed that the story of Jeremiah Hamilton's life, told properly, would make riveting reading. Some even hinted they might tell it. James Gordon Bennett, acerbic editor of the *New York Herald,* almost admiringly admitted in 1836: "Jerry Hamilton is one of the most remarkable men of his race and we shall give a historical sketch of his life and adventures one of these days."

He never did, more is the pity. A consideration of the black broker by perhaps the most astute newspaperman of the century could not have been anything but a revelation. Seven years later, a hostile Moses Beach, editor of the *New York Sun,* dismissed Hamilton as little more than "a walking forgery." Even he had to admit, though, that it was regrettable "the world could not have his full history."[9] Beach, content as he often was with name-calling, never supplied any such accounting. This too was unfortunate, for he knew more than enough to pen a revealing sketch of the elusive black broker.

Hamilton encouraged the mystery surrounding him and his past. After all, in a society as sensitive about race as antebellum New York, there was little point in someone with his appearance trying to fade into Wall Street's background. At different times and to different people he intimated that he came from Richmond, Virginia, or from somewhere in the Caribbean, perhaps Haiti or Cuba or even Puerto Rico. An easy charm deflected too close a scrutiny of his studied vagueness about the past. However, he was decidedly leery when anyone did start prying into his history, particularly into any of his business dealings. In October 1841, the *Sunday Flash* announced: "We're preparing a sketch of Jeremiah G. Hamilton for the Gallery of Rascalities and Notorieties series." This teaser was part advertisement, more the opening move of an extortion attempt. Anyone threatened with such a public shaming knew that the editor usually would be amenable to negotiate whether or not he published. Blackmail was a lucrative sideline for many antebellum tabloids. A worried Hamilton dispatched Benjamin Day, his best friend and founder of the *New York Sun,* to sort things out with the *Sunday Flash.* As the phlegmatic newspaperman discovered, the forthcoming article was about to blacken Hamilton's character, charging him "with all sorts of offences." Unruffled, Day simply called in a favor, and the editor of the *Flash* spiked the piece—it never appeared in print.[10] There were things that Hamilton did not want anyone to know about his life and that no one ever will know.

His celebrity was at its height in the 1830s, 1840s, and into the 1850s, tapering off in the last decades of his life. After a flurry of obituaries in 1875, the black millionaire was very soon forgotten. There was no context in which to remember him. Hamilton was part of no one's usable past. He was always too unusual a figure to fit comfortably into any history of Wall Street. More importantly, the black broker and the city's race leaders disdainfully had avoided one another—he was never going to feature in any African New Yorker story of racial struggle and survival. Remarkably quickly, Hamilton was relegated to the waste bin of history—and there, until now, he has stayed.

American historians have not noticed Hamilton's prominence in his lifetime and have evinced almost no interest in him. Since the beginning of the twentieth century, only four authors have mentioned his name in their published works. And these most fleeting of references are mostly mistaken or misleading. One writer, describing gold rush steamers and the Accessory Transit Company in the 1850s, reported that Hamilton, whom he never questioned was anything but white, "was said in the press to be a son-in-law of [Cornelius] Vanderbilt."[11] Two more recent historians of the New York draft riots of 1863 referred very briefly to an abortive attack on Hamilton's house on the second night of violence. For the first, Hamilton "was actually a white man, but he had spent nearly all his life in the West Indies, and his deeply tanned complexion made his neighbors believe he was black." The second described Hamilton as a "West Indian broker."[12] Most revealing of all, the editor of a recent compilation of James McCune Smith's writings reprinted from *Frederick Douglass' Paper* the article in which the black intellectual referred to Hamilton as the "only black millionaire in New York." Glossing this statement, he darted off on a tangent: "As McCune Smith probably knew, the wealthiest blacks in the country in 1850 were southern 'black masters'—light-skinned cotton and sugar planters in Louisiana, Mississippi, and South Carolina, who were accepted as whites because of their wealth and proslavery principles."[13] Perhaps. But McCune Smith's reference to the situation in New York was not an accident: his twenty-first-century editor's remarks are a small but telling sign of how implausible Jeremiah Hamilton's existence still appears to historians.

And there, of course, is the rub. What fascinates about these fleeting glimpses of Hamilton is that the authors had no idea who they were dealing with. There was no reason why they should. All of the usual tools historians rely on, such as biographical dictionaries and various reference books, would have been of no help. Each had stumbled across Hamilton at a particular moment in time, be it some point in the 1850s or July 1863. He was peripheral to their interests, and, perhaps led astray by assumptions, they interpreted the sources in front of them. So, for the record: Hamilton's relationship with Cornelius Vanderbilt may have been a tad tortured, but he was not his son-in-law; Hamilton was not "white," whatever that might have meant; and Hamilton's dark complexion was not acquired thanks to a West Indian suntan, nor did that tanned visage fool his New York neighbors into thinking him black. No matter how inconvenient it is for accepted views of nineteenth-century New York, Jeremiah Hamilton was a wealthy African American who lived and worked in the city for just over forty years. Furthermore, the only way to come to any sort of understanding of the man is to piece together all, not just one or two, of the scattered fragments and shards left of his life. He needs to be considered whole.

To be honest, I continue to be astounded at Hamilton's *complete* absence from the telling of the American story. There are so many books and articles written about American history, making it one of the densest historiographies in the world. As well, over the last half-century historians have devoted a large proportion of their efforts to recovering the African American past. On any given subject, you can usually find several dissertations, an article or two, and often a book. The recently completed eight-volume reference work *African American National Biography* (2008) contains an entry for each of more than 4,100 African Americans, providing a handy guide to the way blacks have been rewritten into that American story over recent decades. There is no mention of Hamilton.[14] Perhaps most damning of all, Jeremiah Hamilton did not even have a Wikipedia page until 2013, when someone put one up, borrowing from a 2,000-word piece I wrote for the *New York Times* website.

Is it possible to recover the story of someone who, for well over a century, became all but invisible? This is a rather different enterprise than writing about a Thomas Jefferson or even a John Jacob Astor. Unlike the case with the Founding Fathers or other "Great Men," no venerable institution coveted and collected any of Jeremiah

Hamilton's papers. To be sure, acquisition policies have changed: nowadays, libraries, historical societies and even individual collectors would pursue avidly any correspondence or account books of a nineteenth-century black broker that happened to turn up. But this is all a century too late. There are no letters to or from Hamilton, no diaries or ledgers concerning him in any of the repositories historians habitually haunt. No accounting of the way authors have written, and not written, history should neglect ease of access to the sources as a contributing factor.

Sometimes it is the small things that bring home how different it is writing about Jeremiah G. Hamilton as opposed to, say, Alexander Hamilton. He was proud of that "G"—it formed the centerpiece of a very elaborate signature that he affixed with some care to a variety of documents. After years of searching, I still do not have any idea what the "G" stands for. On no official or other document does Hamilton supply his middle name. Even on his death certificate, where the form made it clear that the "full name of deceased" should be written in, someone entered only "Jeremiah G. Hamilton."

Or, another instance: As best I can work out, there is no known image of Hamilton. Not an oil painting, a sketch done for a newspaper by an artist, or even a photograph. In truth, he almost certainly did have photographs taken, and quite likely commissioned a painting, but if any likenesses have survived they are probably catalogued somewhere under "miscellaneous" or as "subject unknown."

Consequently, determining what he looked like is difficult, dependent on contemporary newspaper descriptions that are both sparse and spare. A Port-au-Prince merchant, in an 1828 letter published in the *Commercial Advertiser,* pronounced Hamilton "a dark mulatto," a rare comment about his skin color. The then-twenty-year-old was about five feet six and a half inches tall with "short woolly hair." Fifteen years later, a witness in a court case thought Hamilton's lips and nose were "something like" those of a Negro. At that time, he also had an enviably flourishing set of dark whiskers.[15] None of this is particularly helpful—or distinguished him from any number of African American men walking the streets of New York at the time.

There were, however, a couple of features that did set him apart. Fastidious about his dress and a little bit showy, he sported ostentatiously "the largest diamonds." Diamonds, of any size, would have been enough to mark him off from most New York men. As well, after Hamilton's death a writer in *Harper's Bazaar* remembered that he had "a peculiarly shrill voice, and without the slightest effort, always made himself heard." When he spoke to someone his words were audible in every corner of the room whether he intended them to be or not, a characteristic that, given his penchant for telling it like it was, probably did not endear him to some of the citizenry.[16]

And, judging by the spiteful comment it generated, one detail of his appearance differentiated the black man from almost every other New Yorker. As soon as he had moved there permanently in the early 1830s, he shaved his head and acquired "a wig of fine flowing black hair." For forty years Hamilton roamed his city resplendent in a hairpiece—it became his signature trait, an idiosyncrasy that contributed further to the mystery surrounding the black man. At his death, he was still flaunting "a fine black long haired wig."[17] The hairpiece tantalized other New Yorkers—what could it signify? When Moses Beach labeled Hamilton a "walking forgery," he was referring, in part, to Hamilton's wig; what it concealed would become an issue in a controversial libel trial in 1843. I must confess that I am almost as tantalized by the bewigged Hamilton as were his contemporaries, although my curiosity is centered on something readily apparent to them—how he looked in what must have been an eye-catching hairpiece.

The nature of the research required to recover the elusive Jeremiah Hamilton's past is also rather different from that employed by most historians writing about better-documented and better-known Americans. It bears a closer resemblance to the strategies employed over the last half-century by social and cultural historians.[18] My major sources are not personal papers but antebellum New York City's public record. Newspapers, court cases and government files provide many clues about how Hamilton behaved as he contended with the Wall Street financial community and his fellow New Yorkers. But lacking commentary from Hamilton, it is more difficult to discern his thoughts about these dealings. Sometimes imaginative reading of sources can be revelatory, although often, all that the historian can attempt is an indirect and imprecise teasing out of what happened. Nevertheless, even if at times Hamilton's thinking stays unknowable, the interactions between this black man and Wall Street still can tell us much that is new about New York.

My attempt at rescuing the life of Jeremiah G. Hamilton from history's oblivion relies on two main sources. The first is New York newspapers. Dozens of titles, weeklies as well as dailies, were published in New York before the Civil War. Although it may seem old-fashioned, reading newspapers discolored with age—reveling in their feel, smell and appearance—remains, to my mind, one of the pleasures of being an historian. Not for much longer. Commercial enterprises have digitized and made searchable more and more nineteenth-century American newspapers; nowadays historians sitting in their office can do in minutes what once involved travel and took months. To be sure, something also has been lost, but it would be foolish to deny that a revolution has occurred in the way we find out about the past. When I started searching for Hamilton this process was in its infancy and only a couple of New York newspapers were incompletely digitized. Consequently, I have used this technology mainly for checking or following up on things discovered elsewhere. Almost all of the material in this book was drawn from more than three decades of doing history the way I was taught, of sitting down in a library and reading long runs of the full gamut of New York newspapers, not just sampling or dipping into one or two of the better-known titles. This has enabled me to take advantage of the different coverage from the whole range of these newspapers, for they were anything but clones of one another. Revealingly, in the 1830s and 1840s, editors and reporters, fascinated by the city's grittiness, detailed facets of African American life to a surprising extent, and I have used many of their stories in this book.

These were indeed glory days for the New York press. The great newspapers, particularly the *Sun*, the *Herald* and the *Tribune*, did more than just record what had happened during the previous day; they, and their editors, actively shaped what was about to happen. This was particularly so in the milieu in which Jeremiah Hamilton moved. Wherever possible I have done my best to convey a sense of this liveliness, to show how the newspapers, and their editors, were part of my story, not just a source to be credited perfunctorily in the footnotes.

The second major source on which I rely is the New York legal system. Although it is often unacknowledged, courts and trials played a central role in African American life in the nineteenth century. After the completion of the Tombs in 1838, the majority of the city's legal dramas took place in this preposterous-looking edifice. Here was where a procession of black men and women were accused, and usually convicted, of a whole litany of crimes. But it was also the place where African Americans who had been robbed or beaten up on the street sought justice, where New York blacks congregated and rioted in support of captured fugitives contesting their re-enslavement, where African Americans mounted challenges to Jim Crow segregation on public transport and much more besides. Admittedly there were few other options, but African Americans had not yet given up on the legal system. Fortunately, antebellum New York's legal records, although incomplete, are extensive, much more so than those of most American cities. The District Attorney's Indictment Papers, held by the Municipal Archives of the City of New York, are remarkable and voluminous. A disproportionate number of these files involve African Americans. As well, the New York County Clerk's office, located in the same building as the Municipal Archives, also houses tens of thousands of files, products of business litigation. Far fewer of these cases involved African Americans, but some did. Sooner or later, even the most respectable of New York blacks had his or her day in court as a litigant or merely as a witness and left a paper trail in these records. These still-underused archives are crucial for the writing of any more inclusive history of African New Yorkers.[19]

Jeremiah Hamilton was sui generis, typical of nothing. Nevertheless, his predilection for relying on the courts to sort out his affairs was an extreme example of what was common practice among African Americans of his time. Filed away in these archives, and mostly unread for more than a century and a half, are well in excess of fifty legal cases—some criminal, some civil—to which Hamilton was a party. In several more his name surfaced in testimony for some reason or other. He had more justification than most when he boasted, as he once did to someone he bumped into on a New York street, that "he knew as much law as any lawyer."[20] Much of this book is based on material drawn from the records generated by his serial court appearances.

In effect, then, I have dragged a fine-meshed seine through an ocean of water, trawling through thousands of law cases, well over 100,000 pages of New York newspapers, and much else besides, in order to recover whatever evidence remains of Jeremiah G. Hamilton's life and world.

My ambition for *Prince of Darkness* was always to do more than just tell Hamilton's story. Writing about the experiences of a man who shunned other African Americans but whom whites scorned as black provides the opportunity to understand anew race relations in a crucial period of the city's history. Jeremiah Hamilton made his fortune in the years after slavery ended in the state, just as New Yorkers were pioneering the development of segregationist practices. The strange result was a startling disjuncture between the financial world, where the black broker relished his predatory role, pursuing aggressively whatever edge he could find in his dealings with white businessmen, and his everyday existence on New York streets ruled by an unforgiving and demeaning racial etiquette. At work Hamilton was, to borrow Tom Wolfe's term, a Master of the Universe.[21] For the rest of the day and night he was barely a second-class citizen. Ironically, for all the distance Hamilton put between himself and other African Americans, to white New Yorkers seeing him about town, he remained just another "nigger." It was an impossibly schizophrenic way of living.

The forgotten story of Jeremiah Hamilton serves to remind us that African Americans too were actors in the history of American capitalism, not just slaves and some white man or woman's capital investment. Overwhelmingly, those writing about the years after slavery ended in the North, elaborating on the views of antebellum whites themselves, have agreed on a story in which the newly free blacks were left to one side of the American economy, a dwindling and beleaguered minority in dynamically expanding centers such as New York. To be sure, there were successful black businessmen, but usually they were confined to service-sector niche markets, most famously as restaurateurs such as Henry Minton in Philadelphia and Thomas Downing in New York. According to the consensus, the recently freed blacks engaged with the burgeoning marketplace in only the most tentative of fashions. And yet, for all the obvious merits of such a sensible view, there is a danger that the orthodoxy blinds us to an individual's achievement, in this instance a black broker on Wall Street trading commodities and buying and selling shares and real estate. In such a case, are we able to discern what faces us in the historical record, or, in some banal postscript to Ralph Ellison's masterpiece, will we look straight through what to us is an invisible man?

Jeremiah Hamilton's unique position in New York presents any writer with an opportunity for coming to a new understanding of the way the nineteenth-century city worked. He offers a way to reconsider subjects that are seen, without too much thought, as being quintessentially white, totally segregated from the African American past. Most obviously this is the case with Wall Street, the Stock Exchange and the Great Fire, but it is also true of the penny press revolution of the 1830s and many other topics. Far too often, historians treat African Americans as if white segregationists had succeeded, as if blacks lived in their own separate world, physically and culturally removed from everyone else. In effect, African Americans become segregated for a second time in the telling of their history, easily marginalized from the main American story, relegated to the footnotes. Hamilton trampled all over such black and white distinctions, and anyone telling his story today must be similarly disdainful of racial shibboleths.

In the end, though, it is Hamilton who stands alone in the limelight. His was a dramatic life, cinematic in its vividness. It included incidents of derring-do, a trial that was the talk of the town, and more than the occasional angry confrontation about business ethics or his lack of them. In all this, Hamilton never took one backward step. He was not a forgiving man. If you crossed him, he returned the favor and always added a few percent for interest. It was one thing for a Cornelius Vanderbilt, or any other white man, to be this aggressive, rather another for the so-called Prince of Darkness to behave in such a fashion. He often rubbed people the wrong way, though he never seemed to care too much. Hamilton could also be charming, as silkily smooth as any other hustler trying his luck on Wall Street. A wise person did not trust him very far at all. He had learned in a hard school that books should be balanced, accounts for the most part settled, and the law treated as simply something to be taken advantage of or got around. This African American was as at home in courtroom or East River waterfront, New York Society Library or Delmonico's. He could tell you which railroad stocks were a good buy, converse about Francis Bacon's philosophical treatises or Henry Fielding's *The History of Tom Jones, A Foundling* (1749), stitch up a deal to sell a refitted steamboat to Cuba, dash off an article for the *New York Sun,* and arrange to scuttle an overinsured ship. Most remarkably of all, he was a black man who became rich while living out the American nightmare of race.

The Prince of Darkness was an extraordinary figure, and I have lived with him now for too many years. My telling of the untold story of Jeremiah G. Hamilton, Wall Street's first black millionaire, begins in 1828, the year in which he first got under the skin of a New York businessman.

ONE

HAITI, 1828

Jeremiah Hamilton's story is a New York one, but the first act opens some 1,530 miles to the south. On February 27, 1828, the brig *Ann Eliza Jane,* with the twenty-year-old Hamilton on board, slipped past Fort Islet and anchored quietly in Port-au-Prince Harbor. The sleek vessel, with two square-rigged masts and flying the American flag, had taken just over a fortnight to sail down from New York. Two days later, the dockworkers began unloading her cargo of provisions, completing the job on March 3.[1] Such a sight was common enough—there was a profit to be made in the provisioning trade, and New York and New England merchants were not shy when it came to making money. In 1825, 374 American vessels had sailed to the Haitian capital, carrying 39,199 tons of beef, hams, dried codfish, flour, soap, naval stores, tobacco and the like. A little over a decade before the *Ann Eliza Jane* arrived in Port-au-Prince, Paul Cuffee, the great African American sea captain and merchant of New Bedford, Massachusetts, had doubled his investment of $5,000 on a single business venture to Haiti by selling fish, oil and shingles in the tropical port and then buying coffee and sugar to take back on the return voyage.[2]

At first glance, such details appear to illustrate little more than normal trade between countries, but almost nothing involving the fledgling black republic of Haiti was normal. The country was an oddity, a pariah among the slaveholding societies of the New World. Its tumultuous history over the previous third of a century had inaugurated a new era of freedom in the Americas, and that very past—indeed, Haiti's continued existence as a nation—disconcerted governments with Caribbean interests. In the late eighteenth century Saint-Domingue, as Haiti was then known, was the most profitable colony on the planet, exporting more sugar than Jamaica, Cuba and Brazil combined and growing half of the world's supply of coffee. Although the French possession was only about the size of Massachusetts, it generated more money for France than did all thirteen American colonies for England.[3] Its colonists extracted immense wealth from the blood and sweat of the roughly half a million slaves they compelled to work their land in a system of plantation slavery as brutal and exploitative as any created in the New World. Saint-Domingue was a charnel house where every year between 5 and 10 percent of the slave population died and had to be replaced. In 1790 alone, more than 40,000 fresh African slaves were unloaded from the slave ships, put on the block and sold. As the country's leading modern historian noted pithily: "It was cheaper to let slaves die and buy more from Africa, so that is what the planters did."[4]

The Haitian Revolution, sparked by a slave revolt in 1791, fueled by the burning of the city of Cap François on June 20, 1793, and stoked by the egalitarian rhetoric of the French Revolution, turned on its head this ordered and hierarchical world.[5] Over the ensuing dozen years, the slaves and free people of color defeated the French, shucked off their rule, and abolished the institution of slavery. In 1804 they founded the independent nation of Haiti. It is hard to overestimate the impact that the Haitian Revolution's shockwaves had as they reverberated around the Atlantic world, inspiring slaves everywhere and horrifying those who profited from their enslavement. The violent overthrow of slavery, let alone the spectacle of former slaves organizing themselves into a nation, was something entirely new and profoundly unsettling for the accepted view of the way societies should function. As a writer in the London *Times* acknowledged, "a Black State in the Western Archipelago is utterly incompatible with the system of all European colonization."[6] Unsurprisingly, France, Spain, Great Britain and the United States—hardly coincidentally, all slaveholding powers—refused to recognize the new nation, but, as one historian has written, they "took no concerted measures to rid the world of the anomaly of a free, black nation."[7] Their own rivalries, being played out on European and American battlefields, allowed Haiti some much-needed respite, for the country's early years were characterized by considerable internal upheaval as well.

By the 1820s, Haiti had become a symbol of the consequences of emancipation for both supporters and opponents of ending slavery in the United States. On the one hand, some antislavery supporters, most especially the growing free African American populations living in New York, Philadelphia, Boston, and elsewhere in the North, invested almost-utopian hopes in the hemisphere's other, and black, republic, and many dreamed of moving there. During the mid-1820s the Haitian government subsidized the cost of the passage to the Caribbean nation for some 6,000 African Americans, and the total number emigrating may have been as high as twice that figure.[8] To be sure, few stayed in Haiti for long, but, nevertheless, the fact that so many willingly abandoned one republic for the other eloquently revealed much about black expectations of, and aspirations for, racial justice in the first half of the nineteenth century. The example of the Haitian Revolution mattered to African Americans, and they showed how it did so in often-surprising ways. Some twenty years later, near the middle of the century, John Benwell, an English traveler, visited the impressively large house of a former slave in Charleston. The sumptuous décor included many "good oil paintings," nearly all family portraits of one sort or another, but the "most prominent in position" was a likeness of Toussaint Louverture, the Saint-Dominguan revolutionary leader who also had started life as a slave.[9] For many African Americans, the very idea of Haiti offered inspiration, the reassuring possibility of an alternative society based on equality and in which blacks were expected to become leading citizens. On the other hand, for many more white Americans, Haiti epitomized the dangers of emancipation, demonstrating conclusively that interfering with slavery would lead to a bloodbath and chaos. The security of the United States, and particularly the safety of southern white slaveholders, required isolating the contagion of liberty and dissipating the specter of slave revolt. Needless to say, of these two groups, the latter was more important politically.

Consequently, the United States maintained a policy of refusing to recognize Haiti even as American merchants, or at least northern ones, pursued trade opportunities there. And the former colony, no longer tied to a European power, did present an opportunity. Although Haiti was nowhere near as wealthy or productive as Saint-Domingue once had been, the Caribbean nation was still some way from becoming the byword for poverty and underdevelopment that it would be in the twentieth century. With freedom, plantation-style agriculture gave way to mixed farming—understandably, the inhabitants refused to be exploited in the same fashion as when they were enslaved—but Haitians still needed American goods and produced agricultural surpluses, particularly coffee, to trade. What made Haiti even more valuable was that it was one of very few locations in the Caribbean where Americans could do business unhindered by the restrictions imposed by the mercantilist policies of European powers. Americans, for example, were unable to trade legally with British West Indian ports until after an agreement was signed with Great Britain in 1830.[10] Southern merchants may have shunned Port-au-Prince in an attempt to pretend that a black republic did not exist, but for those in the North, Haiti was becoming a significant commercial interest.

And yet, for all the potential profit to be made from Haiti, participating in the lucrative provisioning trade was merely the cover story for the *Ann Eliza Jane*'s voyage; the expedition's real, and illegal, purpose involved the self-enclosed and provincial world of Port-au-Prince itself. Haiti's capital had a population of about 35,000, and by the 1820s it no longer impressed European eyes. James Franklin, a British traveler writing in 1828, thought that for a stranger approaching from the sea, the city "has an odd appearance, exhibiting nothing but dilapidation and decay." As far as Franklin and other visitors were concerned, such deterioration resulted inevitably from the inhabitants' temerity in overthrowing European rule and ending slavery. Although Port-au-Prince had "stood unrivalled in the point of elegance and splendour in the time of the French," the Revolution had transformed everything, and now "it is only remarkable for ruins and every species of filth and uncleanliness." When Charles Mackenzie, the British Consul General and a black man, arrived in 1826, he deprecated the wooden buildings, seldom more than two stories tall, and thought the city had "a paltry appearance." The few public edifices he characterized as "insignificant in appearance," and almost all of them were linked with "some scene of bloodshed" from the Revolution, associations that Mackenzie found "quite sickening." Summing up, James Franklin remarked: "Upon the whole nothing can be said in favour of the city of Port au Prince."[11]

Not every onlooker viewed the city with the same disapproval as these dyspeptic Englishmen nostalgic for Empire's civilizing touch. On board the *Ann Eliza Jane* Jeremiah Hamilton waited, impatient to get ashore. He was fluent in French as well as English, had short woolly black hair and looked little more than a kid, really. In New York whites categorized him as black—or, more likely, given what most thought of as his pretensions, as a "nigger"—but in Haiti, where racial descriptors were more nuanced than the simple binary "black" or "white," he was a mulatto, or, in one local merchant's description, a "dark mulatto."[12] Even though Port-au-Prince had become something of a backwater, this voyage was young Hamilton's break, his chance to begin making it big in the big time.

Every morning Hamilton disembarked from the *Ann Eliza Jane* and set off into the city. Tropical rains had made the no-longer-maintained roads a morass, impassable to carriages, forcing him to shoulder his way through the locals on foot. The canvas awnings jutting out from building facades shaded crowds of men and women who, to outsiders, invariably seemed idle: Charles Mackenzie, after perambulating the city, suspected disdainfully that "there is no part of the world where more time is literally 'whiled away' than in Haiti."[13] We know little of how or where Hamilton spent his hours ashore—although probably he tried to make it look like he too was whiling away his time, waiting for his ship to leave. Always fastidious about his appearance, the black visitor found a washerwoman to launder his clothes; at least once a day he visited the counting house of Squire and Alvaret, Port-au-Prince merchants, and every evening he returned to the vessel.[14] We do know, however, his purpose in spending his days wandering through the city—Hamilton, to use the trade's argot, was shoving very large quantities of spurious or counterfeit Haitian coin.

When it came to counterfeiting, the United States was at the cutting edge, a world leader—one scholar of the subject aptly titled his study *A Nation of Counterfeiters*. Some seven decades ago now, St. Clair McKelway, the *New Yorker* writer, opined wryly that "the idea of money is older than the idea of counterfeit money, but older, perhaps, by no more than a few minutes."[15] Coming first perhaps still held some residual meaning for antebellum Americans, but forged notes were so common that they had good cause for wondering whether the "real thing" was really more important than the fake. What made it all so much more complicated was that American currency was not issued by a central authority: in 1830, there were 321 separate banks disgorging a blizzard of paper currency. At any one time in the decades leading up to the Civil War, somewhere between 10 and 40 percent of the American notes in circulation were bogus, and historians nowadays incline toward the higher figure.[16] Encountering counterfeit money in everyday transactions simply became an expected part of American life. Meeting a new demand, entrepreneurs created a plethora of counterfeit detectors: there were at least seventy-two different titles published in the antebellum era, the best-known of which was the twice-weekly *Thompson's Bank Note Reporter,* with a circulation of some 100,000 in 1855.[17] Allan Pinkerton, of detective agency fame, recalled, "It was a popular remark among men of business at that time, that they preferred a good counterfeit on a solid bank to any genuine bill upon the 'shyster' institutions," and the evidence from newspapers and court cases suggests that he had a point. Certainly, most Americans followed the early-nineteenth-century merchant John Neal's advice that "if you buy the devil, the sooner you sell him, the better" and did their level best to unload whatever counterfeit bills had ended up in their own pocketbooks.[18] Antebellum America was a time and place that could have coined the phrase "caveat emptor." The New World wrinkle on the familiar Old World adage, though, was that Americans had to be wary not only of the goods being purchased, but also of the money used in the transaction.

If Americans were the experts in the field, the fragile Haitian economy was particularly vulnerable to counterfeiting. The government had debased and alloyed the country's coin, or, in other words, lowered its silver content, until, as one American writer commented, "the coins which pass in that country for 20 cents, might be made here for less than three cents."[19] On top of this, in 1825 the French had coerced the Haitian government into agreeing to hand over a massive indemnity of 150 million francs to compensate for losses incurred during the Revolution. Paying the French government (or, in reality, the French bank that had lent, at high interest and with ruinous charges, the 30 million francs needed for the initial installment) sucked dry the Haitian treasury, as repayments had to be made in francs, not the watered-down local currency. France ruthlessly strong-armed Haiti into the category of a debtor nation, and the country became, as one scholar has written, "an unlucky pioneer of the woes of postcolonial economic dependence."[20] Day by day foreign powers were strangling the Haitian economy. In late 1827 and 1828 rumors were rife of a regular conduit from New York dumping "a great deal of spurious coin" and "counterfeit bills to an immense amount" in Port-au-Prince. And there was always the nagging suspicion, too, that these outside interests—be they the French government or American counterfeiters—were almost as motivated by the damage that their activities wreaked on the Haitian financial system as by the actual money they made. Certainly, Haitian authorities had long viewed counterfeiting as most likely driven by outsiders and as a criminal infringement of their sovereignty. Article 95 of a law decreed on August 4, 1817, made it clear that "whoever shall have counterfeited or altered money of legal currency in Hayti, or participated in the emission of said counterfeit, or altered money, or to their introduction on the Haytien territory, shall be punished with death."[21] Jeremiah Hamilton's big opportunity entailed rolling dice with the executioner.

Counterfeiters had been unloading bogus notes in Haiti for a while, but forging the country's coin seems to have been a more recent development. A consortium of prominent New York merchants—unfortunately never named—put up the money for Hamilton's venture. Rumors of a conspiracy had first surfaced in the fall of 1827, when word came back to New York of a man, also unnamed, making inquiries in Canada looking for someone "to assist in coining Haytien money."[22] There were plenty of counterfeiters in the United States, but generally they forged banknotes— Americans had pioneered in making paper currency the essential form of money, contrasting markedly with the situation in Britain, where coin fulfilled this function. In the 1820s, Cogniac Street, a dirt road winding out of a town called Dunham just across the Canadian border, was the counterfeiting capital, the place where you could find the most skilled forgers. Almost everyone living in the settlement was involved in some way in manufacturing spurious money, and, for the most part, the legal authorities left the counterfeiters alone. With seeming impunity, they made their deliveries of packages of forged notes to New York and elsewhere in the United States. Although the terms "koniacker" or "coneyacker" have long since disappeared from the language, in the first half of the nineteenth century they were commonly accepted slang for a counterfeiter.[23] The chances are that the counterfeit coin stowed away on the *Ann Eliza Jane* had been minted on Cogniac Street and then transported down to New York City.

The underwriters of Hamilton's expedition wanted their names kept secret, and in that at least they succeeded. We also have no idea how the consortium of merchants knew of Jeremiah Hamilton and why—other than that he was a young black man on the make—they picked him to be their front man. Similarly, it is not clear how Hamilton, or his backers, chose the *Ann Eliza Jane* from the myriad vessels in New York Harbor. What we do know is that Hamilton arrived in New York from Port-au-Prince in mid-January and soon after chartered the brig from its owner, Paul R. Jehovitch. On January 24, 1828, the black man engaged Elisha T. Davis, originally from Boston, to take command of the vessel, and the ship's owner advanced the captain a month's wages of $50 on February 8. Apparently, then, the twenty-year-old black man chartered the vessel—although while on board he "called himself the owner of the vessel"—but the actual owner, Jehovitch, assumed responsibility for meeting the running costs and for filling the hold with cargo for Port-au-Prince. Later on Hamilton mentioned, in an aside to the editor of the *Commercial Advertiser,* "that the business [of counterfeiting Haitian money] was frequently carried on," and the smoothness of the whole operation smacked of the involvement of experienced heads.[24] The people behind the venture knew what they were doing: certainly, the *Ann Eliza Jane* was not chosen at random.

Her owner, Jehovitch, had turned up in New York around 1820 and within a few years established a reputation as a "respectable merchant," particularly known for his Mexican connections. In July 1827, Jehovitch advertised in the *New York Evening Post* on behalf of the State of Vera Cruz, calling for tenders from parties interested in contracting to dig a canal from Vera Cruz to Alvarado. His office at 33 South Street became a nerve center, a place to find out what was going on in the Spanish-speaking Caribbean. Little more than a year earlier, on a Sunday in March 1826, when two business associates from Vera Cruz arrived in New York, Jehovitch escorted them to Gabriel Collet's nearby establishment at 42 Broad Street, as "that was the only boarding house that I know of where Spaniards put up and associate together." He was a fixer, a facilitator—he knew people and did favors. As was also true of many other New York businessmen at this time, Jehovitch's "respectability" could not bear too close a scrutiny. In early 1828, John Duer, the U.S. Attorney for the Southern District of New York, charged Jehovitch with conspiring to scuttle the *General Vittoria,* supposedly en route to Tampico, in order to defraud the insurance company underwriting the voyage. Although Duer failed to secure a conviction, during the course of the trial witnesses testified that at the beginning of 1828 several insurance companies owed Jehovitch some $17,000, or in excess of $4 million in today's dollars, for earlier claims, and that this money was used to purchase the *Vittoria* for $5,300 and to pay the captain almost as much for running her aground. The trial revealed to everyone that Jehovitch was stretched financially, that if the *Vittoria* did not sink—and, as it happened, they did not proceed with their plan to wreck her—the merchant faced ruin.[25] A near-bankrupt ship owner, not averse to being on the wrong side of the law, made a sensible choice for the counterfeiters.

Ironically, what undid the counterfeiting venture was that its bogus coins were too good to be true. A Haitian clerk at Squire and Alvaret, where Hamilton had been depositing money, checked and discovered that, compared to the genuine item, the counterfeit coins had too much silver in them. On March 5, 1828, the conspirators were tipped off that the game was up and the authorities about to descend upon them. Hamilton, instructed by locals involved in the conspiracy to leave Port-au-Prince immediately, momentarily panicked, returned to the *Ann Eliza Jane* and tried to jettison the remaining counterfeit coin out of the window of the vessel's main cabin into the harbor, before abandoning ship and going into hiding. Shortly afterward, General Labou, a captain, and a guard of six armed soldiers marched down the dock, arrested Captain Davis and searched the *Ann Eliza Jane* from stem to stern. Hamilton had made a poor job of getting rid of the evidence: the Haitian authorities uncovered 1,600 quarter dollars hidden near the vessel's rudder head and another 1,600 coins in one of the cabin lockers used by the steward to store plates and dishes. Davis and the confiscated coin were taken to Labou's house, where the general "counted and examined the money, and found it to be spurious." The captain was then marched back to his impounded ship and left there under guard. A few days later, divers recovered counterfeit quarters by the bucketload—in excess of 2,000 of the coins that Hamilton had dumped out of the cabin window—from underneath the vessel.[26]

Locals gave Hamilton, now a fugitive, considerable assistance. According to one unfriendly account that did not surface for several months, some of the conspirators brushed him off with thirteen doubloons and told him to disappear. With a malicious relish, this writer added the damning detail that Hamilton immediately had visited his washerwoman, who was black, very poor, and could ill afford to be cheated, and reclaimed his clothes by paying her with counterfeit money. Other blacks secreted Hamilton near the harbor while he awaited a New York–bound vessel. For several days, the disguised fugitive employed a couple of locals to row him about in the river while they pretended to be fishing. Finally, after twelve days of lurking about Port-au-Prince, Hamilton boarded a ship and escaped from the city.[27]

Toward the end of March, a Haitian court sentenced Hamilton, in absentia, to be shot summarily if and when he was caught anywhere in the country. Soon after, the president of Haiti offered a $300 reward for Hamilton and had the proclamation to this effect read all over the island.[28] On May 8, 1828, a court condemned the *Ann Eliza Jane* and sequestered its cargo for five years, but the latter was "to be given up during that time, if claimed in person by Jeremiah Hamilton." Unless the Haitian president or court rescinded the death sentence for Hamilton, this was a case of your money for your life. The authorities were convinced, almost certainly correctly, that Elisha Davis, the *Ann Eliza Jane*'s captain, had no knowledge of the counterfeit cargo on board and released him. Once it became clear that his ship was not going to be returned to him, he collected together certified copies "of all the proceedings relating to the vessel and cargo in the Haytien Courts" and, on May 15, 1828, sailed for New York as a passenger on board the brig *Gleaner*.[29]

By early June, news of what had occurred in Port-au-Prince had filtered back to Wall Street. On June 19, the *Commercial Advertiser* broke the story—and it was a big story. The editor reprinted a letter from a Port-au-Prince businessman that not only recounted many details of the failed counterfeiting expedition, but also emphasized what remained the central concern of most American merchants— their reputation with the local authorities. "Such a base act," he wrote, "causes the Haytiens to look at all of us with a suspicious eye—especially the whites, who, they say, sent this base villain out to defraud their government." The editor agreed: "The character of our merchants in the St. Domingo trade is suffering. What course shall we take?"[30]

Jeremiah Hamilton responded by firing off a letter to the *New York Evening Post*, the *New York Morning Courier* and other newspapers, disputing particulars of the *Advertiser*'s account. His version of the facts underlined that others were involved both in New York and in Port-au-Prince. When word had leaked in the Haitian capital that they had been discovered, Hamilton wrote, "after a consultation with my friends, I *condescended* at their *instigation* to assume the whole responsibility upon myself." If he had not done so, "Messrs——would have been exposed, would have lost upwards

of $30,000 due to them, and their fate would have been death."
Hamilton's sacrifice had saved the Port-au-Prince businessmen: "I
extricated them, and hope they will make good their promises." Furthermore, he continued: "I did intend this morning to publish the
names of some of the most respectable merchants in the city, that
have been and still are engaged in that business [counterfeiting], but
for the present I will postpone it, knowing it will do me no good, and
on the contrary will ruin them, as they have stated to me." As well
as this, Hamilton visited the *Commercial Advertiser*'s premises and
requested to have a private conversation with the editor. According
to the newspaperman, it was obvious that the black man "had been
sent by some one behind the curtain" to uncover "the precise information in our possession."[31]

There was a precedent for a black man behaving in this fashion and trying to influence press coverage. A couple of years earlier,
in 1824, the black actor James Hewlett, star of the African Grove
theater in New York from 1821 to 1823 who, after whites had
forced the black troupe out of business, scraped together a living
for some eight years by staging his one-man show for white audiences, published a letter in the *National Advocate* eloquently challenging Charles Matthew's willfully cruel caricature of the "Negro
Theater" on the London stage and on several occasions dropped by
the newspaper's office in order to talk to its editor, Mordecai Noah.
Both James Hewlett and Jeremiah Hamilton enjoyed, indeed craved,
the limelight. There was, however, one essential difference between
the black actor and the black businessman: Hewlett was trying to
drum up free advertising and attention in order to sell tickets for his
shows, but Hamilton, much as he loved rubbing shoulders with editors and reporters and seeing his own words in print, was attempting
to make the story of derring-do in Haiti disappear.[32] This was the
first time Hamilton had had to deal with the press, and the incident
marked the beginning of the black man's long-term fascination with
newspapers—both the mechanics of the way they were put together
and produced and their power to shape opinion and influence the
business world.

Far from quieting the *Advertiser*'s editor, Hamilton's heavy-
handed intervention whetted the newspaperman's curiosity and left

him determined to reveal the identity of the persons behind that "curtain." The next day the editor "went out to investigate the matter," calling on, among other places, the office of the U.S. District Attorney and the Custom House. He was intrigued by the broader ramifications of the affair, how Hamilton's venture fitted into a larger pattern. If the counterfeiters had been successful, "the vessel was to have been placed with him [Hamilton] for owner, under the Haytien flag." The black man had concealed $5,000 worth of bogus coin in his trunk—it is not clear whether this was all the counterfeit money carried on the *Ann Eliza Jane* or not—and if he had succeeded in passing it off, Hamilton's cut would have been $2,000. Elisha Davis, the captain, told the editor that Jehovitch and Hamilton had had an agreement that the "vessel was to be transferred to the latter on Hamilton's paying the consignees at Port-au-Prince what the vessel cost here [in New York]." His conversations around town convinced the *Advertiser*'s editor that he had uncovered the beginnings of an ongoing conspiracy involving prominent New York businessmen and a black man, operating the *Ann Eliza Jane* under a Haitian flag.[33]

The *Commercial Advertiser* editor's investigation into what had occurred both in New York and in Port-au-Prince and his breaking of the story on June 19, 1828, set off a flurry of interest elsewhere: as a writer in the *New York Gazette* summed up, the case of the *Ann Eliza Jane* had "caused some excitement in this city, and been the subject of animadversion in several papers." Other editors promptly reprinted the *Advertiser*'s material along with anything new that they had managed to dig up, added their own commentaries, and jostled for the moral high ground. When William Coleman of the *New York Evening Post* pointed out that the Haitian government had devalued the country's coinage to the point where the value of the silver content of an individual coin made up barely more than 10 percent of its face value, thus creating the most inviting of targets for counterfeiters, and suggested that, as a consequence, Haitian officials should shoulder at least some of the responsibility for their own troubles, the editor of the *New York Spectator* immediately slammed what he termed "the moral philosophy of the Post." Evidently, the *Spectator*'s editor continued feverishly, the *Post* expected readers to infer that "there was therefore no iniquity in the transaction," or, in other words, Coleman was simply blaming the victim.[34] The inevitable explanations and retorts kept the pot bubbling: editorial bickering and sniping were a well-established and only intensifying feature of the cutthroat New York newspaper world.

Yet for all of the thousands of words expended on the affair, writers paid remarkably little attention to the fact that the other country involved was Haiti. Although racial views were then hardening and journalists increasingly used the word "nigger" almost as a matter of course, in this particular case references to the racial makeup of the Caribbean's newest nation were, by contrast, guardedly opaque: one writer in the *Commercial Advertiser,* worrying about the impact of the incident on trade, cautioned that "the people of St. Domingo not being the most enlightened in the world, know not how to distinguish between the guilty and the innocent—the honorable and the dishonorable." A *Daily Advertiser* reporter even preemptively dismissed race as a factor, claiming sarcastically that "we can conceive of no justification for such a traffic as this, unless it is that the island is peopled and governed by blacks and it is of no importance how much they are cheated." This writer's tone probably irritated some, but a chorus of pressmen acknowledged that Hamilton had caused an embarrassing ruckus. No one argued with the editor of the *Commercial Advertiser*'s use of the label "foul transaction" or disputed the claim of "an infamous fraud" printed in the *National Gazette,* and few doubted that Hamilton's venture had damaged the reputation of New York merchants in Port-au-Prince, and probably elsewhere in the Caribbean.[35] Other than the occasional disparaging racist aside, though, the white newspapers conveyed little sense that the world's only black republic was in any way special or different. However, for one segment of New York opinion Haiti was anything but just another country.

Historians are held captive by their sources. Uncovering the range of black views on any given subject in America's past, indeed often finding even a solitary black voice, usually presents a challenge. This is particularly so for the seventeenth, eighteenth, and early nineteenth centuries, a time span for which historians typically have to rely on chance descriptions of black actions, occasional opinions or even snatches of conversation from slaves or free blacks found buried in newspapers, letters, diaries, court records and the like. Such fragments, valuable as they may be, are embedded in their contexts, framed, selected and shaped by the purposes of their white authors. Over the last half-century or so, historians have also hunted down rare items penned by blacks ranging from letters to autobiographies, but even these documents are often mediated by white hands. Spurred on by the challenge of what eventually turned out to be not insuperable interpretive difficulties, scholars have imaginatively exploited this material, often reading against its grain, pieced together their hard-won shards of evidence, and revealed black life in a detail once thought impossible. And yet, although historians have managed adroitly to make the best of the lopsided sources left to them, the situation is far from perfect. That is why the founding of the early black newspapers, written by blacks for other blacks to read, making it much easier for any interested contemporaries and, well over a century and a half later, historians, to plumb African American opinion, is such an important event.

Jeremiah Hamilton and the *Ann Eliza Jane* had set sail for Port-au-Prince on the cusp of this change, one of the far-reaching developments then beginning to reshape black life in the United States. Some ten months earlier, on March 16, 1827, Samuel Cornish and John Russwurm published the inaugural edition of *Freedom's Journal,* the first African American newspaper. They editorialized on the front page of that momentous issue: "We wish to plead our own cause. Too long have others spoken for us." Partly, they sought a platform that would enable them to correct some of the more egregious slurs about blacks published as a matter of course in the newspapers, aspersions that had infuriated African Americans at least since the first days of the new nation: "Too long has the publick been deceived by misrepresentations, in things which concern us dearly." But mostly, they wanted to advocate causes that would benefit the race. Almost every Friday for two years, Russwurm (Cornish resigned after some six months) put out another edition, condemning white editors for their racism, attacking property requirements for black voters in New York State and the continued existence of slavery in the South, and, at least initially, dismissing the plans of the much-vaunted American Colonization Society. To be sure, dourly earnest entreaties for blacks to refrain from dancing and the like can become rather wearing to our eye, but *Freedom's Journal*'s four pages (after the first year this was increased to eight) remain a lively enough read, displaying a sprightliness at least partly attributable to the sheer novelty of its perspective. The advertisements from black-run grocery stores, pharmacies and boarding houses, the announcements of funerals and marriages, the many articles about how to celebrate—cautiously—the end of slavery in the state, and the myriad of other items besides made known entirely fresh details of the texture of everyday life of African Americans going about their business. Even the closest and most attentive reader of the white press would have had the greatest of difficulty in discerning any trace of what was readily apparent on every page of the black newspaper.[36]

No subject crystallized the differences between *Freedom's Journal* and the white press as clearly as the treatment of Haiti. In their stirring editorial on the front page of the inaugural issue, Russwurm and Cornish had announced: "The Haytiens, in declaring their independence, and their determination to maintain it, have done so in the face of the universe." That "in the face of the universe" was a call to arms, a plea for solidarity. Haiti's international isolation delivered grist for *Freedom's Journal*'s mill—the paper's ambitious remit included "whatever concerns us as a people"—and, in the case of Russwurm, one of the earliest pan-Africanists, took on a personal edge. While at Bowdoin, where he was the Maine college's first black student, Russwurm had written an admiring twenty-two-page essay titled "Toussaint L'Overture, the Principal Chief in the Revolution of St. Domingo." At his graduation in September 1826, Russwurm had delivered a widely reported address on "The Condition and Prospects of Hayti," and for much of that last year at Bowdoin he had expected to emigrate and settle on the island once he had completed his education.[37] Well aware of the overwhelming hostility of their fellow Americans, as well as that of every other power with an interest in the Caribbean, to the very existence of the black republic, the fledgling editors championed Haiti at every turn. In the first year of publication, they printed a six-part series on the history and present condition of Haiti and a three-part series detailing the life and times of the revolutionary hero Toussaint Louverture. Russwurm and Cornish believed that the futures of both African New Yorkers and Haitians were tied to those of people of African descent throughout the world, a connection that the movement of blacks to and fro between the United States and Haiti over the previous three decades had rendered less some abstract idea and more a palpable reality. Importantly, and symbolically, W. R. Gardiner, one of the black newspaper's earliest distributors, advertised as such in only the second issue, resided in Port-au-Prince.[38] That the first black republic supplied the first black newspaper's first foreign agent should come as no real surprise.

It also should come as no surprise that, from the moment the story surfaced, John Russwurm deplored the news of Hamilton's expedition to Haiti. In the June 27, 1828, issue of *Freedom's Journal,* Russwurm reprinted three of the key articles from the *Commercial Advertiser, Morning Courier,* and *Daily Advertiser,* resulting in an unusually extensive coverage of events in which he devoted almost the entirety of the news content of that week's paper and more than a page of newsprint to Hamilton's activities. By the time of publication of the next issue on July 4, the hard-pressed editor had found time to pen his own acerbic response to matters. He began by noting that the seizure of the *Ann Eliza Jane* in Port-au-Prince had "caused considerable discussion among the mercantile men of our city" and that an unknown "man of colour" was "the principal Agent in this most nefarious business." For Russwurm and his readers, the nub of the issue was simple and self-evident: "We are really sorry that any man of Colour would *condescend* to be the agent of a set of men, whose constant aim has been to vilify the government of Hayti, and ruin its currency by frequent ventures of *spurious* coin." As far as the indignant editor was concerned, "Hayti, whether acknowledged or not by the United States, is a sovereign and independent state," and there was no difference between counterfeiting its coin and trying to debase the currency of the United States. "Where is the man of Colour," Russwurm asked, "who does not wish the laws of Hayti could reach the being, who now fearlessly walks our streets?" Jeremiah Hamilton—although not named, everyone knew whom the writer castigated—was "an object of contempt to all but his kind patrons and copartners in this most wicked attempt." Indeed, the editor warned, "justice does not always slumber": Haitian laws could not touch him in this case, but "he will find at the end of his career" that "a good name—a fair name—and an honest name—are what all his riches and kind *condescension* cannot purchase."[39]

A few weeks later, Russwurm printed a subscriber's extraordinarily hostile letter about Hamilton in the pages of *Freedom's Journal*. The writer referred to "the Base villain, who was sent out to Hayti, as the tool of the merchants in New York," "the man who is at present condemned to death, and his body to be given over to the surgeons for dissection," as being unworthy of anyone's time or effort, "were it not that he is still admitted to contaminate with his presence, the parlours of some of the most respectable families our city can boast of." Indeed, "he was seen a few evenings since, with some respectable young ladies, promenading the battery." Furthermore, "this person is still to be seen traversing the mercantile section of our city, during business hours." The angry correspondent demanded to know if Hamilton was "so insensible to feeling to imagine for an instant that he is forgotten or that he does not excite disgust and indignation in the mind of every one seeing him" and was "at a loss to define why he is so tolerated unless it is the remaining cash given him to effect his escape from the Bullet Ball." He concluded "that it would be extremely inconsistent in us not to hold such a man from our community to public contempt, thereby manifesting our disapprobation of such proceedings." The letter was signed MEN OF COLOUR.[40]

By November the whole affair was no longer news and had blown over everywhere but in the black newspaper. Murmurs that Russwurm was pursuing his prey intemperately—and it would not be surprising if Hamilton had started, or at least encouraged, them— must have gotten back to the offices of *Freedom's Journal*. The black editor acknowledged this dissenting view—"the foolish idea having entered the brains of a few, that we entertain a personal pique against the individual implicated"—before dismissing it out of hand. Indeed, to demonstrate his own rectitude, Russwurm published the translation of a letter addressed to him, recently arrived via Baltimore, from a "respectable" individual in Port-au-Prince. The merchant praised "Freedom's Journal, which took such an active part in exposing that notorious fellow (Hamilton,) who attempted to defraud our government." Expansively, he continued, "I will assure you that the Haytiens in general have highly approved of the Editor's conduct, and have expressed a wish that he should have a more full account, and publish it in his paper." For Russwurm, this was all very gratifying. According to *Freedom's Journal*'s informant, Haitians, just like the black editor, wanted the names of the expedition's backers, and they wanted Hamilton's blood, for, as the writer ended his letter, "justice does not sleep."[41]

But, of course, it does—all the time. *Freedom's Journal* would contain only one more sentence on the whole affair. In the issue of December 5, 1828, under the head "The Mouse Trap," Russwurm wrote: "We cannot descend to answer the *'Mouse Trap'*, unless its author, JEREMIAH HAMILTON of *Haytien-Spurious-Coin* renown, will *condescend* to avow himself as such." Although the editor seemed certain enough of Hamilton's identity as the author, he sniffed: "Anonymous letters and publications we always consider beneath our notice."[42] Nevertheless, and assuming Russwurm was correct in his assumption, the title of "The Mouse Trap" tantalizes. It was almost certainly a reference to Act 3 of William Shakespeare's *Hamlet,* in which the prince gives the title of "Mousetrap" to the play within the play that reveals to all who killed his father, the king. Perhaps for Hamilton the endgame of the counterfeiting expedition, played out in New York, seemed a staged drama and he alluded to other guilty parties yet to be revealed?

The final wash-up of the whole affair was rather more certain. By the middle of 1829 the brig's owner, Paul Jehovitch, having lost the *Ann Eliza Jane* and her cargo to the Haitian authorities, was insolvent, and in September the Recorder, a municipal officer of New York City, was busy assigning the meager remnants of his estate for the benefit of his creditors.[43] At this point the broker's shadowy figure slipped beneath history's notice, and he was not heard from again. About the same time another of the main protagonists in the imbroglio also exited the New York stage. For eighteen months John Russwurm had struggled by himself to bring out *Freedom's Journal.* Although it had over 800 subscribers, and at least two or three times that number of readers, a combination of unpaid subscriptions and advertisers only settling their accounts in the most dilatory of fashions meant that the black newspaper had long been a losing financial proposition. In March 1829, John Russwurm published the final issue of *Freedom's Journal,* and by the end of the year he had left the United States and settled in Liberia.

For Jeremiah G. Hamilton the consequences of the counterfeiting expedition were mixed. He was now under a death sentence in Haiti—indeed, the word was that after the firing squad had finished its job his corpse was not to be buried but turned over to tyro surgeons in order for them to practice their scalpel work. The execution of a Frenchman caught in Port-au-Prince with counterfeit coin near the end of 1828 underlined the seriousness of this threat.[44] As best as I can tell, Hamilton never visited the country again. Neither was he persona grata with many New York blacks. Russwurm had warned him in the pages of *Freedom's Journal* that, in the end, no matter how much he was worth, his name or reputation could not be purchased. On that point the editor had been correct—or at least partially so: misremembered, exaggerated, and distorted versions of the Haitian escapade accreted to Hamilton's name and would remain cemented to it for the rest of his life and beyond. Almost seventy years after the event, and more than a score after Hamilton's death, Charles Haswell, a New York antiquarian, could remember, vaguely, that the black man "had been engaged in a venture to pass off a large amount of counterfeit coin in one of the West India islands." However, whether the meanings attached to Hamilton's name were clear, or even mattered at all, was another issue entirely. Throughout his career, stories in the press would identify Hamilton with descriptions such as "notorious character," "the well known Wall street stock jobber," or "colored gentleman, of some celebrity in Wall street," and it is not at all apparent that anything distinguished any of these labels.[45] In the New York business world that Hamilton aspired to join, admonitions about reputation were beginning to look dated, relics of a time when honor had been all-important. Perhaps for an outsider on Wall Street, in this case a black man trying to break in, simply having name recognition assumed more importance than whether that name was a good one or not. Certainly Hamilton was indifferent to black opinion—even at this early stage, he was playing for a much larger audience than African Americans, and for the rest of his life he would have very little to do with other blacks. By the end of 1828, then, Jeremiah Hamilton, barely into his twenties, had begun to establish his name and to make his mark on the world, if perhaps not quite in the way in which he had anticipated when the year had commenced.

Finally, the single most important result of the whole disastrous episode concerned Hamilton's reputation not with black or white New Yorkers generally, but with a very select group of merchants. Voluble as Hamilton was in the press and around town, on one crucial point—the identity of his financial backers—he remained silent. Although several times he had seemed on the verge of naming names—and even those threats seem to have been little more than maneuvering for position, a reminder to his backers of the cards that he held—he did nothing of the sort. Jeremiah Hamilton was clearly a young black man on the rise, and a number of very powerful white businessmen who had underwritten the counterfeiting enterprise now owed him for keeping his mouth shut and their names out of the newspapers.

TWO

MOVING TO NEW YORK

T he great black activist and autobiographer Frederick Douglass famously reminded his fellow Americans that "genealogical trees do not flourish among slaves."[1] Although not intended as such, this aphorism could be taken as a caution to would-be biographers of almost any nineteenth-century African American, a warning of the inevitable difficulties of writing about not just the protagonist's ancestry but also the years before he or she started making an impact on the world. Authors all too quickly run out of biographical facts, are forced to flesh out their narratives with context and conjecture, and find their prose getting entangled in a thicket of "perhaps," "probably," and "the chances are . . ." That, put simply, is the nature of the beast. In the case of Jeremiah Hamilton, the long silences about his life in the historical record are made even more difficult to penetrate by his penchant for periodically reinventing both his persona and his past.

Jeremiah Hamilton yearned for the big stage; New York was always going to be his destination. And with good reason, for the city provided him with the largest compass for action he could find in the Americas. By the late 1820s and early 1830s, New York had put all rivals into the shade and become the most dynamically alluring city in the hemisphere. Spurred on by the completion in 1826 of the Erie Canal linking New York to the agricultural emporium of the west and rapid improvements in transatlantic communication, the population of the metropolis mushroomed, growing from some 120,000 individuals in 1820 to over 200,000 by 1830. Throughout these years scores of scribbling European travelers trooped through New York as part of their American sojourns, and it was a rare one who did not comment on the "forest of masts" along the wharves or was not impressed by the tumult and bustle of the commercial streets.[2] As well, although the city was anything but a racial paradise, New York State had ended slavery, finally, on July 4, 1827. Not that this overly concerned Hamilton, who never paid much attention to legal or moral niceties. He was always more interested in the prospects for making money.

For all the attractions of New York, Hamilton had some concerns about locating there, and it remains unclear when he settled permanently in the city. What seems to have occurred is that in the immediate aftermath of the failed counterfeiting expedition in 1828, Hamilton, still a little too notorious, spent a few years to-ing and fro-ing between New York and elsewhere. He left traces—mostly unmet promissory notes and court appearances over unpaid debts— that show he was in New York, for instance, in June 1829, June–July 1830, November 1830 and January 1831.[3] Hamilton flitted about the fringes of the port city's economic life, putting together deals in the coasting trade and trying to establish himself as a broker. Subsequent accounts of his life, most notably his obituaries but also the stories he himself told later in the 1830s, made it sound as if he had been an instant success, but this was not the case. No matter who his important business friends were, the young black man—and it should be remembered that in 1830 or 1831 he was still in his early twenties—struggled for a number of years.

Hamilton probably made his final move to New York City in 1833. One of the more authoritative of his obituaries, in the *New York Tribune,* stated that he came to the city in that year. As well, in very early 1836, Hamilton swore in an affidavit that he lived now in New York, "having his store and office permanently there and such has been the case for at least three years."[4] This fits with other evidence. On February 16, 1833, the brig *Prince Edward* docked in New York from Matanzas, Cuba, with four passengers on board, including Hamilton, described in the vessel's manifest as a twenty-four-year-old merchant. On his arrival he replied perfunctorily to the routine queries asked everyone, about the country to which he belonged and the country in which he intended to become an inhabitant, with the same answer—New York.[5]

Perhaps Hamilton's response was casual and unthinking, but regardless, it still contained an essential truth: Jeremiah Hamilton was going to reinvent himself as a New Yorker, and much of the rest of this book will be about how he achieved his goal. But that was the future—the brig's port of departure, Matanzas, also raises the issue of Hamilton's past. There is considerable uncertainty about the black man's origins, mostly as a result of Hamilton's deliberate obfuscation. Quite possibly, though, Hamilton was born and had spent some of his youth in Matanzas, a port on the north coast some fifty miles east of Havana, or elsewhere in the Spanish possession of Cuba.

Or maybe not. When Jeremiah G. Hamilton first arrived in New York in very late 1827 or early 1828, seemingly he came from out of nowhere. At the height of the newspaper fracas sparked by the exposure of the Haitian counterfeiting conspiracy in late June and early July 1828, John Russwurm underlined the mystery of Hamilton's past when he reported in *Freedom's Journal* that "a man of colour, hitherto little known, has been dragged from obscurity as the principal Agent in this most nefarious business." Disconcertingly, and for all his contacts in the black world, the African American newspaper pioneer had to admit that "we know but little concerning the individual" then squirming in New York's limelight. The *Commercial Advertiser*'s editor had printed everything discovered about

Hamilton in his news-breaking story on June 19—"He is said to be a native of Virginia"—and that was nothing more than a second-hand snippet from the talk doing the rounds of the Port-au-Prince counting houses. In the newspaper frenzy, of course, rumor rapidly became fact. The *American Mercury,* summarizing and glossing the coverage from other newspapers, stated authoritatively that Hamilton "was a mullatto man from Virginia, who was employed as the tool of New York sharpers," and other editors did much the same.[6]

Months later, well after the furor about the Haitian expedition had died down, someone managed finally to put some flesh on the bare bones of Hamilton's story. In November 1828, Russwurm reprinted in *Freedom's Journal* another anonymous letter from Port-au-Prince, one that a correspondent in Baltimore had passed on to the African American editor. This time the evidence was more compelling, the informant claiming to have spoken to a Virginian gentleman "who says he knew this fellow from his boyhood" and could confirm that Hamilton was a "native of Richmond" and had been raised to the barbering trade. Residents there had known him not as Jeremiah but as Jerry, and he "was noted as a great rogue when a boy, having been guilty of many low tricks and but little thought [of] by the respectable people of colour."[7] Hardly charitable, but how often does local knowledge of the newly notorious turn out to be generous? And then, forty-seven years later, the writer of a brief obituary in a New York newspaper detailed very specifically that he "was born in Richmond, Va, in the old brick house on Marshall street, corner of Fourth, long ago used as a Methodist church, of free parents."[8]

Eight years after he first gained notice in New York, in very early 1836, Hamilton's origins became an issue in legal skirmishing around a dispute over $15,000, or slightly in excess of $3 million in today's dollars. His white adversaries—Jonathan Leech and William B. Johnson—asserted that Hamilton "is a native of one of the West India islands and is not a native of the United States," a fact they insisted made the black businessman what we would now term a flight risk. Indeed, they were certain "that he has recently declared his intention of settling his affairs and leaving the United States early in the ensuing spring." Hamilton flatly rejected these charges. In a sworn statement he "denie[d] that he is a native of one of the West India Islands, and he says he is a native citizen of the United States of America and was born at Richmond in the State of Virginia." Contrary to the gossip apparently circulating in the city, he had never announced any intention of settling his affairs, or of leaving New York, although "he has said he might take a mercantile Voyage to Calcutta in the spring." A few months later, the editor of the *New York Herald,* commenting on the grand jury's dismissal of a related perjury charge, conceded with uncharacteristic generosity—for James Gordon Bennett was a fearsome denigrator of anything involving blacks in general and disliked this particular black man intensely—that "Hamilton, otherwise called Jerry Hamilton, is a very favorable specimen of the African race" and added that he "was born in Richmond, where his father was a good barber."[9] In much the same fashion, some seven years later, in August 1843, the black businessman, now charged with conspiracy, signed a sworn statement under the watchful eye of Justice George Matsell stating, "I am 33 years old [and] was born in Richmond Virginia." Newspaper commentary on this and subsequent court appearances often included detail such as the *Daily Plebeian*'s "this Hamilton is a very genteel looking mulatto, aged about 30 years, [and] was born in Richmond, Va."[10]

If Jeremiah Hamilton did indeed come from Virginia, he would not have stood out on that count in the New York of the 1820s and 1830s. Probably a majority of its African American inhabitants had been born elsewhere, and the city appeared to be awash with runaway slaves from the South. As the free black population increased, New York became more and more attractive to fugitives. For some, the city itself was the destination, a large, anonymous place where they could start over as free men and women; for others, it was a way station to somewhere else, in many cases Canada. Occasionally the arrival of fugitive slaves was spectacular enough to warrant notice in the newspapers. The *Daily Advertiser* reported that at daybreak on July 23, 1829, a thirty-foot pilot boat nudged up to the wharf at the end of Dover Street. As soon as the boat docked, six black men and one woman jumped ashore and disappeared into the city with "light hearts and nimble heels." Rumor had it that this group of slaves had stolen the boat while escaping from the Eastern Shore of Virginia and was now hidden, "secure from the search of the most vigilant." More typically, fugitives slipped quietly into New York in ones and twos by land or sea. Whites complained vociferously that "the increase of Negroes in this place is a subject of alarming observation"; indeed, New York had become "the point of refuge to all the runaways in the Union."[11]

Nor was it only slaves departing from the South. In the course of her trial for theft in March 1833, Ann Beckett, a black woman, told the court that she had been born free in Accomac County, Virginia, and that about four months earlier she had left, with "a cargo of other negroes, who, born free, like herself, were expatriated for the sin of being born free, and for fear of the contagion of their opinions and examples being communicated to the slaves." In the wake of the Nat Turner slave revolt in 1831, whites had subjected free blacks in Virginia to much closer control, a circumstance that, the *Courier and Enquirer* suggested, could "explain the reason why so many free blacks from the south, are roaming our streets."[12]

The best known of these African American migrants to New York was Thomas Downing. Born free in Accomac County, Virginia, in 1791, Downing arrived in New York about 1819 and in the mid-1820s opened an oyster house at 5 Broad Street, premises that he expanded over the ensuing decades by taking over the adjoining buildings.[13] While the décor of his cellar was barely more prepossessing than that of any other dive in town, Downing's culinary skill, the freshness and quality of his fare, and his establishment's location attracted a rather different custom, mostly Wall Street bankers, merchants, politicians and the like, an elite clientele often prepared to while away an hour or two over a drink and a dozen oysters. This was a place where you met people and did business. Downing himself was rumored to have considerable influence in the nearby Custom House, Post Office and City Hall, and other movers and shakers often supped there.[14] Everyone knew Downing, and yet whites liked to tell one another that no matter how successful he became, this was a black man aware of his place: in 1855, the editor of the *New York Evening Post* averred that Downing never had shucked off "the humility and modesty which is one of his most noticeable characteristics."[15] For at least a century, Downing's family members and others savored stories about how, when the newspaper proprietor James Gordon Bennett faced ruin in the 1830s and was lamenting his fate in the oyster cellar, the black man quietly slipped out, returning a short while later with several thousand dollars that saved the fledgling *New York Herald* from closing down.[16] There was probably at least an element of truth to this tale—it certainly helps explain the surprisingly gentle treatment that Bennett, no friend of the Negro, meted out to Downing in his paper.

Downing was an intriguingly complicated man, more so than is suggested by the way various whites depicted him in the nineteenth century. Although on the one hand he refused to serve blacks in his establishment, on the other he fought segregation and liberally donated money to causes for the benefit of the race. Downing had an austere, verging on the biblical, presence and a clear sense of his own rights, one that often clashed with the views of his fellow New Yorkers. He had not become one of the richest black men in antebellum New York—in 1845 he was reputed to be paying taxes on $90,000 worth of real estate—by allowing anyone, white or black, to walk over him.[17] More than that, there was an aggressive edge to his behavior most plainly evidenced in business matters. In early 1850, Downing catered a 250-guest ball for the benefit of an alderman from the Seventh Ward. Underpaid for the event by some $140, the black man not only sued the entire Committee of Arrangements, including a number of powerful politicians, but doggedly pursued the case through appeals and a new trial over nearly four years. Undoubtedly, his legal costs exceeded the shortfall.[18] Thomas Downing was a formidable and prickly personage.

For most of the fifteen years after Jeremiah Hamilton burst onto the New York scene in 1828, the consensus among those interested was that Hamilton, as with so many other African Americans in the city, had migrated, or fled, from the South. Although this story had at the very least the tacit agreement of the man himself—after all, he twice signed legal documents in which he admitted to being born in Richmond—there was always some uncertainty as to its correctness. Of course, a studied vagueness about how and why they had ended up in New York was common enough among the city's black population, a good proportion of whom had compelling reasons for concealing their pasts. Like so many of his fellow black migrants, Hamilton deliberately left murky the details of who his parents were and where he had come from. More than this, as the only black businessman operating on Wall Street, he habitually kept his cards very close to his chest, for in the lily-white world of finance his ancestry, whatever it may have been, was always going to be an exotic aberration. His past was malleable, something to be used as he saw fit and, most of all, deployed to his advantage.

From the mid-1830s onward, rumors that Hamilton was not born in the United States and in fact came from the Caribbean gained more traction. Leech and Johnson had honed in on this in 1836 when they questioned, without success, the received wisdom in their legal action. A few months later, in July 1836, the editor of the *Herald* published an article fairly dripping with vitriol in which he sneered: "Some years ago, when Hayti was in her glory, and darkies were cheap, one of the dingy subjects of the island of St. Domingo grew weary of being confined to such a small compass for action, and took passage for this port, and by the grace of God arrived in safety." Although Bennett did not mention Hamilton by name, no one had any doubt about his target. More convincingly, a few weeks later, in August 1836, Benjamin Day, founding editor of the *New York Sun,* penned a sympathetic story in which he explained that Hamilton was "a West Indian, who came to this city a few years since with a handsome cash capital."[19] This is intriguing. Only just acquainted, Day and Hamilton were beginning to cement a close and long-lasting friendship. His new confidant—and Hamilton was always very conscious that Day was a newspaperman—reported in the *Sun* what the black man was now telling of his past, but, of course, it was not necessarily true. Hamilton, for instance, most certainly did not arrive in the city "with a handsome cash capital." From this time on, he would still on occasion—as in his court appearance in 1843—insist on his Richmond origins, but increasingly Hamilton intimated to anyone interested that he was born in the Caribbean.

This change in his story coincided with his marriage to Eliza Jane Morris, followed soon after by the birth of their first child; significantly, most evidence of Hamilton owning to a West Indian past comes not from public commentary in the press, but more from sources touching, albeit frustratingly lightly, on his family's private life. When the federal census-taker came knocking on his door in both 1850 and 1870, Jeremiah Hamilton answered the standard question "Where were you born?" with the "West Indies."[20] Nowadays personal data contained in the enumerations of the U.S. population taken every ten years, as demanded by the Constitution, may well be the standard coin of historians, biographers and genealogists, but at the time Hamilton's admission was, for all intents and purposes, confidential. Furthermore, the paper trail left in the wake of Hamilton's death on May 19, 1875, confirmed that, as far as his family was concerned, their father and husband had come from the Caribbean. Eliza Hamilton supplied her husband's physician with the details required by law to fill out the necessary paperwork: the death certificate recorded that he had been born in the West Indies and listed Port-au-Prince as the birthplace of both his mother and his father. As well, the form his widow lodged when Hamilton was buried in the family plot at Green-Wood Cemetery detailed that his birthplace was the West Indies.[21]

By the time of his death there was no talk at all of a Virginian past, and it was generally accepted that Jeremiah Hamilton had arrived in New York from the Caribbean, although where precisely was another matter. A flurry of brief newspaper obituaries reported that he "had formerly been a slave in the West Indies." Another obituarist sniped that "he did his best to pass off for a Spaniard, but did not succeed," a vague-enough charge, but one suggesting Hamilton claimed a lineage from somewhere in the Spanish Caribbean.[22] The most detailed notice of his death—in the *New York Tribune*—stated authoritatively that Hamilton "was born in 1810 in Porto Rico," adding for good measure that "his parents were in comfortable circumstances and gave him a good education." One newspaper, the *Albany Evening Journal,* managed to run different obituaries within days of one another, seemingly unaware or unconcerned that their varying versions of his origins did not mesh together that well.[23]

Jeremiah Hamilton's family's memory of him hardly clarifies matters. At the first federal enumeration after his death, in 1880, four of his adult children—Miranda, Evelina, Josephine and

Theodore—all then living with their mother in the family house at 122 East Twenty-Ninth Street, told the census-taker that their father had been born in Cuba.[24] No census schedules from 1890 survive, but, muddying the waters further, Evelina Hamilton twice applied for a passport in the 1890s. The first time in 1895 she claimed that her father had been a native citizen of the United States; the second time, in 1898, she filled out on the form that he had been "a naturalized citizen of the United States."[25] In the 1900 census, three of Hamilton's adult children, still living with their mother, detailed again that their father had been born in Cuba. By the time of the next census, in 1910, Eliza Hamilton had died, but Josephine and Evelina, both unmarried, lived together in Orangetown, Rockland County, on the west bank of the Hudson River, some fifteen miles from Manhattan. After they had spoken to the official who came to their home, he summarized tersely what they had told him of their father's birthplace as "Porto Rico—Spanish." A decade later, by which time both sisters were more than seventy years old, the census-taker simply marked down on his sheet that "Porto Rico" had been their father's place of origin.[26]

If Hamilton did indeed come from the Caribbean he would have had compatriots in the New York of the 1820s and 1830s. While not nearly as numerous as migrants from the South, blacks from Haiti and elsewhere in the Caribbean were still found easily enough about the city. Some had come as slaves, brought in the 1790s and early 1800s by their owners fleeing the Haitian Revolution. Others had been caught up during the 1820s in the black to-ing and fro-ing between Haiti and New York, as well as Philadelphia and other cities, which occurred as the Haitian government subsidized migration to the island. Following the abolition of slavery, production in the Haitian countryside, particularly on the large sugar estates, had collapsed, and these migrants were given tracts of land all over the island in order to try to reestablish a different mode of agriculture. One African American participant in this scheme commented publicly that conditions in rural Haiti were so dire "that much the greater part of the colored people who went from the U.S. to Hayti, became early dissatisfied, and that all who have been able have contrived to return." In fact, probably about one in three of the state-sponsored migrants gave up and left the island.[27]

The best-known black migrant to New York from Haiti—in fact, still called Saint-Domingue when he left—was Pierre Toussaint. Born a slave in 1766, Toussaint accompanied his owners to New York in 1787 ahead of the conflagration in Saint-Domingue. One of the reasons Toussaint appealed so much to white opinion was the way he worked as a hairdresser in order to support his widowed owner "in the comfort to which she had been accustomed." Some even believed, incorrectly, that he had rescued her from the "revolt and massacre" on Saint-Domingue by getting her onboard a New York–bound vessel. For many whites, Toussaint epitomized the ideal of the complaisant and grateful slave. In return for his loyal service, Toussaint's owner freed him just before her death in July 1807. For the following four decades he ran a flourishing and profitable business catering to a clientele of upper-class women—one historian has labeled him as the Vidal Sassoon of his time. According to Hannah Lee Sawyer, who published *Memoir of Pierre Toussaint, Born a Slave in Saint Domingo* (1854) in the year following his death, "as a hairdresser for ladies he was unrivalled"; indeed, "he was the fashionable coiffeur of the day." Another contemporary remembered that he was "the negro most respected in New York," certainly "an exception" to the rest of the city's blacks, in short, "a pure and noble soul under a sable skin." A devout Catholic, attending mass every morning at six o'clock, Toussaint was charitable and apolitical. In 1997 the Holy See decided that he was "Venerable," an initial step in the convoluted process of having Toussaint declared a saint.[28] It is difficult to imagine anyone further removed from Pierre Toussaint in either style or demeanor than Jeremiah Hamilton.

Both stories of Hamilton's origins—from either Richmond, Virginia, or the West Indies—are at the very least plausible. Here, I have to admit to having changed my mind well over a dozen times about what is the more likely account. At various points over the last few years, depending on which aspect of Hamilton's life I have been investigating or writing about, I have found one or the other more convincing. And I remain uncertain, although more inclined toward a story of Caribbean origins.[29]

In such circumstances, what contemporaries on the scene concluded takes on particular force. When interested parties were trying
to find out anything about Hamilton in the months after the Haitian
authorities stumbled across his counterfeiting expedition, they uncovered only the story of his Richmond birth. Tellingly, inquiring
merchants turned up evidence to support this story not from their
own bailiwick in Port-au-Prince, or even in Haiti, but from Virginia,
and in the convincing form of testimony given by a gentleman claiming to have known Hamilton from boyhood. Even the added detail
about Hamilton and his father both being barbers—although we
should remember that this came from others, not from Hamilton
himself—is persuasive. Barbering was one of few skilled occupations
into which southern free blacks made heavy inroads; for much of the
half-century or so before the Civil War, perhaps half of those following the trade in Richmond were black.[30] Of course, the other half
were white—and, more likely than not, Hamilton's father was white.
It all fits neatly enough. Last, naïve as it may seem—and after having
spent much of the last few years writing about con men and crooks
of various sorts for whom misleading others was a way of life, I
should know better—ferreting out, and holding in my hands, legal
documents with Jeremiah Hamilton's elaborate signature affixed in
which he swears that he was born in Richmond, Virginia, still car-
ries considerable weight for me and in fact is what stops me from
plumping more solidly behind the idea that he had a Caribbean past.

The story of West Indian origins was a later creation but still
has much to recommend it. If Hamilton had Haitian parents and
was born in either Haiti or Cuba, it would help to explain a number of things, ranging from his fluency in French—not too common
an accomplishment among African Americans in the 1820s—to the
expectation that, if the conspirators had been successful in shoving their counterfeit coin in Port-au-Prince, he would have been able
easily to sail the brig *Ann Eliza Jane* under the Haitian flag. There
is also the tantalizing hint of a possible explanation for Hamilton's
somewhat unusual first name. One hundred and twenty miles from
Port-au-Prince, in the Grand'Anse, a district on the peninsula that
extends to the south and west of the capital, is the port town of Jérémie, named after Jeremiah, the prophet of Lamentations. When the

French traveler Louis Moreau de Saint-Méry visited in 1788, there were some 180 quite pretty houses. One author has recently labeled Jérémie "the unofficial mulatto capital of the Western world"; its most famous son, born in 1762 of a French father and a slave mother, was Thomas Alexandre Dumas, who became a general in the army of the French Revolution and father of Alexandre Dumas, author of *The Count of Monte Cristo* and *The Three Musketeers*.[31] Perhaps Hamilton's parents gave him the name Jeremiah, or he might even have taken it himself, as some sort of marker of Haitian mulatto origins. But this is only speculation.

The chaos and bloodshed of the Haitian Revolution, invasion, war and the founding of the Haitian Republic caused a tumultuous decade and a half, with large numbers of whites and blacks becoming refugees as they tried to avoid a turmoil that descended all too frequently into notably pitiless violence. Blacks and free coloreds fleeing the war in the very early 1800s ended up all over the Caribbean. Cuba, in spite of its determined support of slavery (ironically, the institution had been, and would continue to be, strengthened by the collapse of Haitian sugar production), remained an attractive destination, and, interestingly, many made the short trip from Jérémie to Santiago de Cuba in the nearby Spanish colony.[32] It is perfectly conceivable, then, that Hamilton's parents lived in Port-au-Prince but fled, and that not long after, in 1807, their son, Jeremiah Hamilton, was born somewhere in Cuba, or even in Puerto Rico. From 1836 on, Hamilton and his family owned to some version or other of this story of Caribbean origins. This is also a story associated with racial passing, not so much of Hamilton—too many newspaper stories had stamped him forever as being colored—but of his children. I will return to the issue of passing, but here it is pertinent to note that at least one of his children was quite dark-skinned. Although the census-takers always marked down Evelina as being white, in the 1890s, different notaries, filling out their section of her passport applications, thought Hamilton's daughter "very dark." As well, an obituarist, in an oft-reprinted notice, could not resist recounting that Hamilton "at one time offered a large sum of money to any white man who would marry one" of his daughters.[33] In the last decades of the nineteenth century and the beginning of the twentieth, an era when racial distinctions were policed as zealously as at any time in American history, Spanish ancestry helped account for a "white person" having a dark complexion.

The fact that Hamilton arrived in New York City in February 1833 on the brig *Prince Edward* sailing from Matanzas fits in neatly with this story. Throughout his business life Hamilton maintained very strong links with Cuba, and the Caribbean more generally, and conceivably he may also have had family, perhaps parents, living on the Spanish island. Hamilton used various stories about his past as it suited him or his family. In the end, though, and as was commonly true of other migrants, it did not matter greatly where he came from—he reinvented himself and became a New Yorker.

Establishing when Jeremiah Hamilton arrived in New York is difficult, but so is piecing together his early years in the city from the surviving fragmentary evidence. In Hamilton's obituary in the *New York Tribune*, the writer claimed that subsequent to his arrival in 1833, he "owned a number of vessels which were engaged between this and West Indian ports." Another obituarist wrote that after he came to New York, Hamilton "engaged in the coasting commercial business, his vessels running from New York to Savannah, Charleston, and to Havana and other West India ports."[34]

This all sounds grand enough, and may well even have been correct by about the mid 1830s, but, as mentioned earlier, Hamilton seems to have done it tough earlier in the decade. Cases that bilked creditors had brought against him dotted the New York court calendars. He had borrowed $100 from Silvester Judson, a chandler, on June 13, 1829, promising to pay back the money in two years. By the time the suit, instigated by Judson's widow, reached the New York Supreme Court in late 1834, Hamilton, with extensions, further loans and interest, owed $784.86. He put his name to notes for shorter and shorter periods of time—never a promising sign. On December 6, 1832, he agreed to pay back Camman, Hosack & Bohlen $202 in six months. Shortly after, Hamilton took out four-month and ninety-day promissory notes with Eugene Grosset, ending up owing him some $750 by March 1833.[35] He also borrowed money from Arthur Tappan, who, along with his brother Lewis, had moved to New York from Maine and founded a silk-importing business in

1826 and the *Journal of Commerce* in 1827. The pair of business-men combined entrepreneurship with evangelism, and both were well-known abolitionists. As a consequence of his views on the slav-ery issue, Arthur Tappan found the idea of a black man of business something to be encouraged. He was known to have aided consider-ably a black man who opened a dry goods store in Hudson Street. However, when Hamilton did not deliver the promised $553.56 on time, the prominent reformer sued him vigorously, taking the case as far as the Chancery Court.[36]

There was a frenetic, almost desperate quality to the way Ham-ilton borrowed money in these years. He postponed repaying debts as long as he possibly could, usually way past the due date, and, in what was a sign of things to come, never panicked or worried when he was hauled before a judge. All the time, he kept on sweet-talking new prospects—and Hamilton could always talk the talk—looking for the next person whom he could touch for a loan. I have managed to uncover in New York's legal records some ten cases of people suing Hamilton between 1830 and 1835; doubtless, there were others, pos-sibly quite a few others, who I missed or who had not yet commenced legal action. Hamilton resembled nothing so much as a hustler work-ing at an upturned wooden crate on the sidewalk, moving around his shells and never letting the mark know under which one he has secreted the money. Several of his creditors certainly thought that something akin to a shell game was going on. At least twice the sheriff tried to enforce judgments against Hamilton and came back empty-handed. The sheriff may have been satisfied Hamilton had no prop-erty, but the creditors were not. Theophilus Peck's lawyer claimed in December 1833 "that the said Jeremiah Hamilton keeps some of his business secret for the purpose of preventing his property from being discovered and applied to the payment of his debts." Six months later the sheriff went out again on behalf of Thomas Woodward in search of $286.50 but concluded "there were no goods, chattels, lands or tenements" that he could seize. Woodward's lawyer demurred, insist-ing there was a deposit of at least $500 in the Bank of New York, "more than sufficient to pay off and satisfy the said judgment."

In much the same fashion as a talented three-card-monte player, Hamilton kept his nerve, ignored every distraction, focused on the mark and eventually came out a winner. It is hard to pin down exactly when the shift in the tenor of his life occurred, but sometime toward the end of 1834 or the beginning of 1835, the black businessman seemed to find himself on a much sounder financial footing. No longer was Hamilton always a defendant; instead, he was suing white businessmen, and the sums of money bandied around alongside his name were now in the thousands of dollars. Some of the deals he was always trying to make paid off; to coin a phrase, his boat had come in.

Central to any understanding of the rise of Jeremiah Hamilton to this more secure position was his fraught relationship with New York insurance companies. In 1827, the combined capital of the insurance companies doing business in New York State, mostly in Gotham itself, was $16 million. By 1860, that figure had mushroomed to $75 million, marginally more than the capitalization of all the banks in New York City at that time.[37] Intriguingly, the success of what would become the insurance industry signaled capital's own apprehension at the instability of the market at capitalism's core. Insurance socialized capital by distributing risk across a group of investors, but the tension between the difficult job of managing risk and the "existential thrill of taking a risk" was, as one historian has argued, "at the very operational and moral heart of both capitalism and a rising liberal order."[38] Underwriting offered a way of pursuing a more stable world, or at least one in which the wilder swings of fortune were moderated: in the boom/bust economy of antebellum America, little wonder that increasing numbers wanted to take out insurance policies of all sorts.

Of the four main types of insurance—accident, fire, life and marine—the last was initially the most developed in the United States. While there had been individual brokers in the port cities of British mainland North America, the vast bulk of colonial shipping and trade had been insured in London, the center of underwriting. After the American Revolution and War of 1812, American firms underwrote more and more of this business, particularly in the new and lucrative China trade, as well as the ever-increasing traffic across the Atlantic. The industry itself marks January 18, 1820, as the beginning of a "true market" of American insurance of American hulls, cargoes and freights. On that date the board of the New York Insurance Company resolved to form an association of all the city's marine insurance companies. In 1832, nine insurance companies founded a successor organization, the Board of Underwriters of New York, an institution that played the determining role in setting premiums and regulating the business as a whole.[39]

There was always a gamble, or at least a large speculative element, to marine insurance: underwriters rarely even sighted the ship or cargo for which they, for a price, accepted partial responsibility. And when any disaster did occur, litigation was often required to arbitrate the rights and wrongs of what had happened. Most infamously, in 1781, Captain Luke Collingwood of the *Zong* informed the crew of his slaver that "if the slaves died a natural death, it would be the loss of the owners of the ship; *but if they were thrown alive into the sea, it would be the loss of the underwriters.*" After tying together the hands of 122 sickly slaves, the crew dumped them overboard. Ten more Africans, horrified by the gruesome spectacle, jumped into the sea, drowning themselves. When the insurer refused to pay damages for the dead slaves, the owners sued.[40] Cases were usually more routine than this, but, to a considerable extent, sorting out insurance claims depended on the word of any witnesses who, almost invariably, were themselves interested parties. And there, of course, was the rub, for not all involved in the commercial movement of goods were honorable men. Nineteenth-century court records and newspapers are littered with cases of insurance companies defending themselves against everything from sharp practice to outright fraud.

From Jeremiah Hamilton's first known visit to New York in January 1828, he gravitated to the underbelly of American business life, associating with, and undoubtedly learning from, some of the rather shady characters preying on the edges of the economy. The prime example here is Paul R. Jehovitch, the man from whom Hamilton had leased the brig *Ann Eliza Jane* for his counterfeiting expedition. Later that year, Jehovitch would be charged by the District Attorney with conspiring to scuttle another of his vessels, the *General Vittoria*, in order to defraud the insurance company. At the ship owner's trial in June 1828, Daniel Hazard testified at length about his recruitment to the position of captain of the *Vittoria*, explaining how Jehovitch proposed to pay him the very large sum of $5,000 "if he would run the vessel ashore." Having broached the subject of wrecking the *Vittoria,* Jehovitch had hastened to reassure him that "he would not wrong any individual, but did not think there was any impropriety in cheating the Insurance Offices."[41] Even the ethics of antebellum business were not quite that elastic: no matter what was said, both men were well aware that they were planning to break the law. Padding a claim was one thing—the principals of insurance companies themselves were hardly paragons of virtue, and, then as now, no one mourned if someone extracted a few extra dollars from one of these unloved institutions—but overvaluing a ship and cargo and deliberately sending them to the bottom of the Gulf of Mexico was entirely another matter.

Spectators at Jehovitch's trial, as well as readers of the next day's press coverage, were treated to a primer in the illicit arts of modern business. Correcting someone else's misapprehensions about smuggling, Captain Hazard, who had sailed to the Gulf at least nine times, offered his professional opinion that "smuggling is generally performed in the bay of Mexico by bribing the Custom House officers." Most of all, though, everyone's attention was riveted by the testimony about how to scuttle a vessel. In one of the more memorable moments of the trial, Hazard disclosed that one of Jehovitch's confederates had warned him about the disastrous consequences of failing to sink the *Vittoria* on the shoal near Tampico. If that happened, "he ought to have a good auger on board to bore a hole in the bottom [of the vessel]" in order to founder it, or else "he would ruin Jehovitch." Perhaps the talk of an auger, a tool for boring a hole in wood, was more metaphor than practical advice—sinking a brig by drilling a hole below the waterline might take some time—but it did set the tone of the conspiratorial conversations. When cross-examined, the witness added the nugget that Jehovitch had advised him "after he had run the vessel ashore to give her a good thump, in order that nothing might be saved." The *Commercial Advertiser*'s court reporter observed that Hazard "made no objection to [that] proposition": in fact, when the captain told Jehovitch he would make the voyage, the owner was "under the impression that he [Hazard] would destroy the vessel."[42]

Testimony at Jehovitch's trial also revealed, for anyone interested, how surprisingly vulnerable the insurance industry was to fraud. Perhaps Jehovitch and his vessels were merely unlucky, but underwriters had settled claims with him a disconcerting number of times. He had only been able to buy the *General Vittoria* because of an enormous payout of $17,000, or well in excess of $4 million in today's currency, "from Insurance offices." As well, Thomas Merry, assistant president of Neptune Insurance Co. and one of the key witnesses for the District Attorney, testified that his firm "had met many losses of his." Merry had known Jehovitch for years, acknowledged he had a terrible reputation, and admitted "we did not like to write for him," but until very recently they had continued to insure his business ventures. Questioned directly by the court about Jehovitch's integrity and honesty, the Neptune senior executive answered "he did not think well of him" and that now "they would not underwrite for him." Neptune's persistence for so long in insuring Jehovitch's vessels gave a better indication of the industry's preparedness to deal with fraud than did the recent decision finally to turn away his business. Similarly, although the trial did reveal clearly that New York insurance companies in the 1820s were beginning to collaborate, it was only in strangely ineffectual ways. When the Neptune assistant president heard that Hazard had been hired specifically to scuttle his vessel, he straightaway "cautioned the Ocean, the Union and other insurance offices, and begged them not to write the Vittoria"—and yet Jehovitch still managed to insure his voyage.[43] For the unscrupulous, New York marine insurance companies remained an invitingly ripe target.

Jeremiah Hamilton could not resist the temptation. In the earliest New York court case involving the black businessman that I have managed to find, filed by the Chancery Court on June 8, 1830, he sued the American Insurance Co. in order to compel them to pay a sum of money not specified in the surviving documents. Three years later, Theophilus Peck's lawyers, trying to cajole the sheriff into enforcing a monetary judgment against Hamilton, argued that he had concealed assets, including a claim against Jackson Marine Insurance Company and another against Neptune Marine Insurance. In late 1834, Arthur Tappan's legal representative knew that "a verdict for about three thousand dollars was rendered in the Superior Court for the city of New York at the last term to wit the October term of said Court in favor of the said Jeremiah G. Hamilton against the said Jackson Insurance Company," but worried, as he informed the judge, that the defendant would use the money for purposes other than repaying the debt he owed his client.[44]

Admittedly this is all circumstantial evidence, but at the very least, in the first half of the 1830s Jeremiah Hamilton had claims against three of the nine founding firms of the Board of Underwriters of New York. Probably there were more. Although I have been unable to uncover any further detail about these cases, the chances are that he was scamming the insurance companies—his victims certainly thought that was the case. Hamilton, it seems, was an apt pupil and had managed to turn himself into just as much of a Jonah as had Jehovitch and others of his ilk. Being able to identify and exclude such unlucky souls from taking out policies was one of the factors impelling underwriters to band together. In the early 1830s, the Board of Underwriters, attempting to prevent losses and particularly to reduce large payouts, took a very active role in the industry, suspending captains who had lost vessels and not hesitating to tell even large shipping concerns whom they might employ as captains, and tried to stamp out criminal wrecking and fraudulent claims. By late 1835, and possibly earlier, New York insurance companies had combined to impose a ban on Hamilton: as a writer in the *Spectator* reported, "the offices in this city have resolved among themselves not to insure" any of his business ventures.[45]

As so often happened in antebellum New York, a court case laid bare details of the chicanery that was a not always acknowledged, but perhaps inevitable, accompaniment to the city's much-vaunted business life. In November 1835, the brig *Meridian* left New York and set sail for Charleston, South Carolina. Arriving off the bar on November 26, one of the crew signaled for a pilot, but none came. The weather was tempestuous, and a looming gale threatened to make it even worse, leaving the captain the options of trying to reach the safety of the port or of putting out to sea. He chose the former, but in the pitch black at about midnight his brig struck the South Breakers. Although the captain and crew escaped unharmed, the *Meridian* was a total wreck. Or that at least was the story told the Sea Insurance Company, which had underwritten the vessel for $12,000, and the New York Superior Court, which had to adjudge the case when the insurance company refused to pay the policy. The Sea Insurance Company's justification for turning down the claim rested on two arguments. First, although the plaintiffs—Joseph Tinkham and Simeon Hart—had taken out the insurance, "the vessel, in point of fact, belonged to Jeremiah G. Hamilton." This was crucial, as "the Company had made a rule, not in any case whatever, to insure for him [Hamilton], and the plaintiffs had therefore committed a fraud on the defendants." Second, "there was no Pilot on board when the vessel went aground, and [it was clear] that she had been designedly sunk." Tinkham and Hart's lawyer, F. B. Cutting, who coincidentally often worked for Hamilton, tore the defense to pieces. At the time Tinkham and Hart took out the policy, they had had a lien, or a claim, on the *Meridian* for the $2,000 spent recently on repairs and thus "were virtually part owners, and had a right to get her insured in their own names." As it happened, almost immediately after the policy was agreed to, someone—and although no one could prove anything, everyone knew it was Hamilton—had "liquidated," or paid off, the lien, meaning that he was once again the sole owner of the *Meridian,* but now, contrary to the wishes of the New York insurance companies, the vessel was underwritten for its impending voyage, on which, unluckily, it happened to sink. Even putting aside all of the legal fancy footwork over the standing of the plaintiffs, there was no testimony to show that Tinkham and Hart had done anything wrong or "knew of the resolution of the insurance offices not to insure for Hamilton, as it was not told them at that or any prior time." As to the other accusation, there was "no evidence of any intentional wrecking of the brig," and such a serious charge could not be countenanced unless "supported by indubitable proof." The judge charged in favor of the plaintiffs, agreeing with Cutting that the insurance policy was valid and legal; the jury, "after a few moments deliberation," awarded Tinkham and Hart the $12,000, as well as $620 interest and costs.[46]

There is no doubt that by the time this verdict was handed down Jeremiah G. Hamilton had arrived in New York City. The

maneuverings he employed to insure the *Meridian* were impressively
creative, devastatingly effective, and, according to a Superior Court
judge, perfectly legal. Hamilton was establishing a name for himself
in New York as a man who got things done and made money. True,
there often would be a taint to his methods, but until the authorities caught him breaking the law, there was no particular reason
why this black man should be held to a higher standard of behavior
than any of his contemporaries in and around Wall Street. What is
most intriguing about the fleeting mentions of Hamilton's doings in
the records of the first half of the 1830s is that they seldom, if ever,
mention the fact that he was black. It is as if Hamilton was just another businessman. But he was not. That he was one of the first, if
not the very first, broker to have the New York insurance companies
place, to coin another phrase, a black ban on him can hardly be coincidence. Not for one moment did anyone dealing with Hamilton
forget his color. Most telling of all, it was in these early years in New
York that Wall Street bequeathed him his anything but affectionate,
and certainly not race-neutral, nickname—Jeremiah Hamilton had
become the Prince of Darkness.

THREE

THE GREAT
FIRE, 1835

The evening of Wednesday, December 16, 1835, in New York City was bitterly cold, with the temperature reaching as low as seventeen degrees below zero. A fierce, gusty northwester pounded Manhattan. Conditions were even worse than on the previous day, when firefighters had been up until all hours struggling to control two persistent blazes. About nine o'clock a fire started in Comstock and Andrew's five-story warehouse on Merchant Street. Within ten minutes five or six buildings were burning, and half an hour later New York south of Wall Street was little short of an inferno. Not only were all the wells and the East River iced over, but also any water residents did manage to find simply froze solid in the hoses. Already-exhausted firemen basically had no working equipment, no water and no chance. One justifiably awestruck reporter later wrote of the flames: "The raging element was unavoidably permitted to roll on unobstructed until it had gained such tenacious power that resistance, for the time being, became entirely useless."[1]

At least for a few hours, all anyone could do was help shift whatever was moveable from the fire's path. The Great Fire, as it was very quickly called, was the single most important event of the decade in New York City and would play a significant role in burnishing further the Prince of Darkness's growing notoriety.

Time and again on that grim night the fire's grasp and speed outstripped everyone's expectations, reducing supposed havens to ashes. Volunteers using barrows, carts and their bare hands filled the open space of Hanover Square with enormous heaps of saved "goods promiscuously piled together," much of it "of the most valuable kind" from nearby fancy dry goods stores, but the fire roared through Pearl Street so quickly that almost everything that had been rescued was destroyed in minutes. The low point of the night, though, occurred in the early hours of Thursday morning at the Merchant's Exchange. This building—described by the diarist Philip Hone as a "splendid edifice" and "one of the ornaments of the city"—was only a few years old, built of marble, and presumed to be fireproof. As the *Commercial Advertiser*'s man put it, the "exemption" of this structure from the blaze "had been so strongly confided in, that a vast amount of goods was deposited there for safety." But once the roof caught alight the building was destroyed with such speed that almost none of the salvaged property or that of its numerous tenants could be snatched from the flames. "When the dome of this edifice fell in," Hone wrote in his diary, "the sight was awfully grand." Only the "magnificent marble columns fronting on Wall Street" remained standing.[2]

Eventually, on Thursday, firefighters, by a combination of using gunpowder to blow up buildings in order to create firebreaks (which may or may not have helped), slightly improving conditions, and luck, managed to control the fire. Although bales of cotton in the warehouses along South Street, a cargo of indigo near Franklin Market, and other scattered debris would continue to blaze for days, the threat was over. New Yorkers immediately began assessing the damage. Some twenty-four hours after the fire started Philip Hone summed up the outcome: "Nearly one half of the first ward is in ashes; 500 to 700 stores, which with their contents are valued at $20,000,000 to $40,000,000, are now lying in an indistinguishable mass of ruins." This was more than three times the amount of money it had cost to build the Erie Canal, finished almost a decade prior. A day or two later the *Courier and Enquirer* published its count, revealing that 674 buildings were "now levelled with the ground."[3]

No one present on the night of December 16 had experienced anything quite like it. Newspaper writers immediately labeled it "the most destructive conflagration which ever took place in this city, or on the American Continent." The press's superlatives were justified—in terms of physical damage to New York, it would not be until terrorists crashed two planes into the World Trade Center that there was any comparable disaster. Contemporary commentators, groping to convey the spectacle and destructive power of the fire, fell back on classical allusions, most often referring to Pompeii or Carthage, comparisons that resonated all the more as the stark silhouette of the Exchange's remaining pillars resembled nothing so much as the ruins of an ancient temple.[4] Commonly, writers lamented the inability of mere words to suggest what they had seen and been through. When Hone finally had found time to sit down and open his diary on that Thursday night, he did not know how "to describe the most awful calamity which has ever visited these United States." Indeed, he was "fatigued in body, disturbed in mind, and my fancy filled with images of horror which my pen is inadequate to describe." Many of those covering the story for the newspapers that still managed to print had much the same reaction. The *Journal of Commerce*'s reporter witnessed the collapse of the Merchant's Exchange: "a grand and terrific scene, but we are unable to describe it." Similarly, a *Commercial Advertiser* writer, recalling the night, could "neither describe the grandeur of the spectacle, nor its terrors, nor the desolation brought more distinctly to view by morning light."[5]

As it happens, these writers underestimated their collective abilities. Even today, 180 years after the event, anyone reading the extensive press coverage of the fire and its aftermath cannot help but be impressed by the accounts of the fire's ferocity. Often it is the meticulously reported minor details that are suggestive of the inferno's intensity at its zenith. Perhaps most remarkably, an item in the *New York Spectator,* only one sentence long, reported that the light from the fire was seen one hundred miles away in Philadelphia, "and that so distinctly that many firemen turned out, believing that it arose from a conflagration in the immediate neighborhood of that city." A few months later, in May 1836, the *New York Herald* printed a couple of sentences under the caption "STILL BURNING," detailing that half a year had "elapsed since the great conflagration took place" but "the fire is not extinguished yet." Apparently, a lot immediately to the rear of the construction occurring at 35 Water Street "continues burning."[6]

If nothing else, fire was a great leveler. This was particularly so at a time when any decent-sized catastrophe bankrupted most of the still-fledgling insurance industry (following this disaster, twenty-three of the city's twenty-six fire insurance companies collapsed). A *Commercial Advertiser* reporter noted piquantly that "many of our fellow citizens who rested to their pillows in affluence, were bankrupts on awaking." The Great Fire, which devastated the city's business interests, demonstrated that the old "walking city," with mixed neighborhoods and the rich and poor living cheek by jowl, had gone the way of the dodo. Increasingly, the city's inhabitants stratified precincts by class and purpose. There was almost no residential housing left in the vast commercial swath south of Wall Street and east of Broad Street, and that was at least part of the explanation for the death toll of only two, which, given the size and intensity of the fire, was, on the face of it, quite surprising. Reporters on the scene acknowledged that almost all of the damage had been to commercial interests. After mapping out the destroyed portion of downtown street by street, one reporter commented that "those acquainted with our city will at once perceive that nearly the entire seat of its greatest Commercial transactions has been destroyed." Another added that "the sufferers by this terrible calamity, were the bone and sinew of our great Commercial Emporium."[7]

Other observers were also well aware of the changes being wrought to their city and the rather more evident class and ethnic tensions. Philip Hone was "alarmed by some of the signs of the times which this calamity has brought forth." A few of the "miserable wretches who prowled about the ruins, and became beastly drunk on the champagne and other wines and liquors" they had found "seemed to exult in the misfortune." There were indeed New

Yorkers who may not have lit the fire but were hardly upset by the result. A horrified Hone wrote down that "such expressions were heard as 'Ah! They'll make no more five per cent dividends!' and 'This will make the aristocracy haul in their horns!'" As well, there were all sorts of stories circulating about New York cartmen, often Irishmen, charging extortionate rates for moving goods away from the flames on that appalling night.[8]

Most of all, though, there was looting, not only on the Wednesday evening of the fire but also in the following days and weeks. According to a writer in the *Commercial Advertiser,* "the most revolting circumstance attending this calamity was the infamous extent of plunder." The amount of pillaging, and the New York establishment's shocked reaction to it, revealed a serious rent in the city's fabric. Hone's unease at the "signs of the times" was prescient. Almost from the moment the fire started, the police were "constantly occupied in arresting persons making their way from the conflagration laden with booty, recovering plunder from depositories in every section of the city." According to the *New York Spectator,* "several hundred vagrants of all colors, sexes and ages, have been brought up, and dispossessed of their booty, amounting to many thousand dollars."[9] The *Commercial Advertiser* reporter chimed in: "The army of plunderers was so numerous, and they displayed so much boldness and dexterity, that a large amount of property was carried off." From my reading of the city's surviving court records there was some exaggeration here as to numbers, but, more interestingly, such comments suggested a shocked sense of a world losing its bearings. For Hone at least, not all pillaging involved actual theft. When "low Irishmen" started a run on the Bank for Savings immediately after the disaster, the diarist was scathing. In fact, these poor immigrants were desperately concerned about their life savings, but as far as Hone was concerned, "these men, rejoicing in the calamity which has ruined so many institutions and individuals, thought it a fine opportunity to use the power which their dirty money gave them."[10] Apparently, the money accumulated by Hone and others of his ilk was cleaner.

Although this was an exceptionally large and destructive example, fires had long been part of the warp and woof of a still-combustible city's fabric. According to Moses Beach, the second publisher of the *Sun*, writing a couple of years after the Great Fire, "New York may be appropriately termed, *par excellence*, the 'City of Fires!'" "No other metropolis can exhibit so imposing an array of conflagrations," he continued, "nor can any compete with it, in the rapidity with which they are extinguished." The sights and sounds of fire are "incorporated with my earliest recollection." Slowly the drama would build up: in the beginning, "the watchman strikes the sidewalk with his well seasoned club, the echo of which reverberates with fearful distinctness," followed soon after by "the slow measured chimes of the great bell on City Hall coming booming over the roofs of the houses, insinuating themselves into your ear in the dead watches of the night." For all Beach's familiarity with such events, "yet even in me the occurrence of an imposing fire at night creates no little excitement and interest."[11] He was not alone. "'When the fire breaks out tonight,' Carl said to me one night, 'we'll go out and take a look at it,'" the Swedish émigré Gustav Unonius recalled of his time in New York in 1841. "It was like deciding to go to the theater to see a play that had been announced and that could be counted on with certainty to come off. And sure enough, we did not have long to wait for the spectacle."[12]

Large numbers of New Yorkers flocked to watch the flames, particularly of any decent-sized conflagration. In his famous diary detailing almost four decades of everyday life, George Templeton Strong captured well many New Yorkers' ambivalence about fire, the way in which young men in particular were mesmerized by the spectacle, simultaneously exhilarated by the drama of the event itself and horrified by its effects. Writing on December 16, 1836, the then-sixteen-year-old recorded: "This is the anniversary of the Great Fire—what a terrible night that was!—and yet the excitement of it seems almost pleasing in retrospect." Dropping everything at any news of a blaze to race across town to the site, the young Strong became a connoisseur of conflagration, "disdaining mean and uninteresting fires and taking a great interest in the really spectacular ones of which he wrote as careful a review as he would of a stage performance." As his twentieth-century editor added drily, this New Yorker "was usually on the side of the fire." January 27, 1840 "has been an igneous evening": Strong "didn't stay to see the end of the combustion" on Water near Broad Street, "for there were so many 'soap locks' and 'round rimmers,'" or young white gang members identified by their hairstyles and hats, who were "hustling and swearing and rowdying" that he left. Minutes later, another fire "in South Street was making quite a show and the temptation was irresistible," so he "made for the scene of action." Nearly three years later, after leaving a performance of "Christmas Bells" at about eleven o'clock at night, Strong observed that "there was a great fire burning downtown, and never was anything more splendid than the effect it produced." Indeed, "the whole sky was lit up with a bright soft crimson glow," and "the snow reflected it back," creating "a most magnificent and unearthly appearance." It was a bad fire, and "four or five large stores came thundering down with a prolonged roar that seemed to shake the ground," a display that "was very fine."[13]

In mid-March 1836, the proprietors of the New Grand Moving Diorama advertised the fresh attraction they were adding to their usual fare of alpine scenery and shipwrecks. Just three months after the Great Fire, New Yorkers could view a simulacrum of "one of the most awfully grand and alarming sights ever presented" at the diorama, with the undoubted highlight being a reenactment of the burning of the Exchange building. At the show, residents were seen scurrying away from the fire, "carrying goods, furniture, books, papers, and whatever they have been able to rescue from the grasp of the devouring element." The "Closing Scene" revealed "the ruins of the Exchange" as it appeared the next morning, "still throwing out smoke and flame." The combination of exciting new technology with the opportunity to relive the horror that so many of the customers had experienced proved to be a winning one. A few months later, a reviewer for the *New York Mirror* recommended that "one of the most delightful ways of spending an hour or two in the evening, is to step into the City Saloon and see Mr Harrington's display of the wonders of mechanical ingenuity." According to this spectator, "the scene of the great fire in December brings back that awful night which laid waste so fair a portion of the metropolis." As he pointed out, "the best proof of the interest excited by these exhibitions is afforded by the numbers who attend them."[14]

Although only a minority of Americans had the chance to watch the re-creation of a conflagration in a diorama, everyone living in any of the country's countless towns and cities in the first half of the nineteenth century had a shared experience of fire. In a world still heavily reliant on wood for building, it was simply a fact of life. When Thomas Jefferson, mulling over the slavery crisis in the months leading up to the Missouri Compromise, wrote to John Holmes in April 1820, he drew on powerful imagery instantly familiar to his fellow citizens: "But this momentous question, like a firebell in the night, awakened and filled me with terror." Aside from being a wonderfully vivid sentence endlessly quoted ever since, in it Jefferson, one of the country's most skilled ever wordsmiths, deliberately associated slavery and white guilt about the peculiar institution with fire. The link between slavery and fire was an old one, but ever since the Haitian Revolution, the flames of Cap Français had tormented white Americans, especially southern slave owners such as Jefferson. There was a constant nagging fear of the fire next time. In antebellum America, even in a northern city, African Americans should be an essential part of any history of fire. Key events of New York City's history look different, even if sometimes only slightly, once it is realized that African Americans took an active role in the way things played out. As it happens, there was something totally novel about the involvement of African Americans in the Great Fire of 1835, but in order to appreciate what that was, we first have to consider the history of blacks and fire in New York.

In his 1793 tract against capital punishment, William Bradford, formerly Pennsylvania's Attorney General, classified arson as the "crime of slaves and children." Almost invariably, according to Bradford, the motive for incendiarism was revenge, and "to a free mind the pleasure of revenge is lost when its object is ignorant of the hand that inflicts the blow."[15] Periodically in the last decades of the eighteenth century, recalcitrant New York slaves had indulged themselves in such anonymous pleasures, burning down the odd haystack or barn in the countryside, but in the 1790s there was a more serious turn of events, as blacks made several attempts to fire the principally wooden and immensely flammable buildings of the state's major cities.

Regardless of what Bradford may have argued, in the late eighteenth and early nineteenth centuries, nervous whites worried that arson signaled the beginning of a slave revolt. The specter of the conflagration in Saint-Domingue, reported extensively in American newspapers and magazines, haunted the Atlantic seaboard. Events at Cap Français, in particular, played on white imaginations. On June 20, 1793, and in the days following, most of Le Cap had burned to the ground and, in the fighting, somewhere between 3,000 and 10,000 people were killed. Samuel Perkins, an American merchant, later recalled "the sight of a great city in flames . . . is sublime, and we sat watching the flames until daylight," but it was more than just an awe-inspiring spectacle. "The destruction of Le Cap," one historian has recently written, "proved to be a turning point in the struggle for freedom in Saint-Domingue."[16] This connection between fire and the pursuit of freedom had particular resonance in New York, where black arsonists immediately brought to mind stories of the 1741 conspiracy. In March and April of that terrible year, ten fires, at least some of which were set deliberately, spurred panicked whites into discovering a planned slave uprising: after a trial before Judge Daniel Horsmanden, which may have taken place in the colony's Supreme Court but resembled nothing so much as the frenzy of the Salem witchcraft trials, thirteen black men were burned at the stake, and seventeen black and four white men were hanged.[17]

A few months after Cap Français's immolation, in November 1793, two young black girls, Bet and Dean, incited by a third slave, Pomp, were prevented from reducing the state capital of Albany to ashes only by a heavy fall of sleet. As it was, twenty-six houses were destroyed and an estimated £100,000 worth of damage inflicted. A rash of copycat fires were swiftly extinguished but still disconcerted white residents and kept everyone on edge. All three slaves were tried speedily and, in the terminology of the time, a period (or full stop) put to their existence at the gallows on Pinkster Hill, subsequently Capitol Hill.[18]

Three years later, in November 1796, there was an outbreak of arson by blacks in New York City. Some unknown African Americans tossed burning coals wrapped in oiled paper into open cellars, starting several fires and prompting newspapers to print lurid stories of a "combination of incendiaries" intending to burn New York to the ground. Quite a few Saint-Dominguans had fled to the Middle Atlantic states, bringing some of their slaves with them, and a number of rumors linked these blacks to the New York fires. In a conversation between two French and three American blacks, rather improbably overheard on a street in New York, one of the French blacks muttered: "Ah, you Americans are animals; you do not know how to set fire—we at the Cape know better." Ominously, all those present agreed to try again when the wind was high. As well, L. F. Sonthonax, a French commissioner sent to Saint-Domingue in 1793, supposedly had rewarded a number of blacks who had traveled to the United States in order to fire the cities.[19]

Notwithstanding the strengthening of New York City's watch and a spate of newspaper articles that not only implicated the "French Negroes" but also warned citizens to keep their eyes open, there were at least half a dozen more attempts in December 1796. William Bradford's suggestion that arson be removed from the list of capital crimes doubtless received short shrift in such a tense atmosphere. Lewis Morris, aristocratic grandee and signer of the Declaration of Independence, lamented in a letter to his son that New York had experienced "a most terrible time lately" because of the fires. Much property had been damaged, and "all exclaim loudly now against the freedom of Negroes it has been a fatal stab to that Business." He also told of New York gentlemen serving on the watch every night, evidently with some success: they had secured a few blacks while others had been "shot down owing to their not answering quick." Morris was writing from his estate at Morrisania, nowadays the South Bronx, and the contents of his letter are almost certainly more useful as an indicator of white concern and of the rumors that were circulating than of the situation in the city itself. What is significant about the letter, however, is the connection he drew immediately between arson and the protracted debate over ending slavery in New York, a connection that was inevitable in the shadow of Saint-Domingue.[20]

As it happened, the Founding Father's pessimistic death notice for the business of antislavery was premature, but Morris himself did not live to see the enactment of the gradual law he had advocated for so long. Within three years, in 1799, the New York Assembly legislated to end slavery, although the measure was a compromise demonstrating both the continuing power of the slaveholding inter-ests and the respect accorded property rights, even if the property was human beings. The bill freed only those slaves not yet born, and they had to serve a lengthy apprenticeship. Those who were still slaves on July 4, 1799, were abandoned to their fate; not until 1817 would the legislature agree finally to liberate such persons—and even then, they would not be free actually for another decade, until July 4, 1827. The legislature had ensured abolition would occur at a glacial pace. Many slaves took things into their own hands, ne-gotiated some sort of a deal with their masters, and obtained early release from bondage. To a large extent, then, the details of slavery's demise in New York City were worked out on an individual basis. By their own initiative and hard work, most slaves managed to achieve freedom well ahead of the lackadaisical timetable set in place by the legislature.[21]

As a result, there was always something capricious and piece-meal to the way slavery ended in New York. Accidents of ownership (some owners refused to negotiate with their slaves, while others readily made a deal) and accidents of birth (a slave born in Janu-ary 1799 was going to remain in that condition for life—or until the 1817 legislation freed him or her in 1827—whereas one born in December 1799 would be held in some form of indentured servitude or apprenticeship until age twenty-five if female or twenty-eight if male) made an enormous difference to the lives of slaves. Holdings of only one or two slaves—typically, in the city, husband and wife had different owners—meant that it was not at all unusual for one or more family members to remain enslaved for some time after their kin had achieved freedom. As the slave system unraveled, and clearly by the early nineteenth century the institution's New York days were numbered, there were, nevertheless, many unhappy African Ameri-cans who found themselves still trapped as slaves or indentured ser-vants with little prospect of any improvement in their lot for years. Furthermore, in these transitional decades between slavery and free-dom, African Americans, both slave and free, exhibited a heightened sensitivity to the way that they were treated. There was a new uncer-tainty about who was entitled to do what to whom: most noticeably,

African Americans were no longer prepared to tolerate the use of the whip, that hated symbol of their enslavement.[22] For both blacks and whites, a momentous and very unsettling change in the way things were done was taking place; that occasional violent acts resulted was probably inevitable.

What is most striking about the court records from these years is the involvement of very young African American females in violence against their owners. Freedom may have been in the air, but the legislature had left both slave and indentured girls and young women—often the least likely to be able to negotiate a deal—in the thrall of their owners for decades to come, and some black youths, seemingly almost unaware of the consequences of their actions, lashed out at those who tried to control them. Perhaps understandably given their ages, few appear to have given much thought to whether or not they would be caught when they turned on their owners.[23] In June 1810, Jemima, a twelve-year-old slave in the household of the butcher William Wright, took a shovelful of embers from the kitchen fire and tried to burn down the house. She had done so at the prompting of Louisa Davis, a slave in the same house, who told Jemima that she "did not like Mr Wright or any of his family except James Wright one of her Master's little sons." Jemima was convicted of arson. In another case, a master whipped Charlotte, a very young indentured black girl, "because I did something naughty"; she had "pulled up my petticoats before a little white boy which my Mistress had before forbidden me to do." Later that day Charlotte took a lighted candle into the cellar and set fire to some paper adjacent to several large casks of beeswax. The fire, however, was quickly put out. In a similar instance in December 1811, an eight-year-old black servant girl, having been whipped by her mistress, used a burning log from the kitchen fire to try and incinerate her owner's stables.[24]

Such troubling incidents emphasized just how vulnerable the servant-employing classes were to fire. Expressing a general fear, one New York judge pointed out that arson was "among the most atrocious of human offences"; "in the hour of repose," he continued, "what guard can shield us against the wicked purposes of those in whom we are obliged to place confidence?" The best-known arson case from these years involved Rose Butler, not a child but still young. Born "free" in Mt. Pleasant, Westchester County, in November 1799, only months after the passage of the gradual emancipation law, she owed twenty-five years of service to the Straing family. Twice Butler's indenture was sold, and she ended up in the household of William Morris in New York City. Continually clashing with her mistress, who "was always finding fault with my work, and scolding me," she later admitted: "I never did like her." Finally, in March 1818, Rose Butler decided to torch the Morrises' house. She failed in the attempt: no one was injured, and onlookers extinguished the fire with little damage other than a set of stairs burning down. During and after her trial, Butler's demeanor was anything but contrite; she was "rude and offensive" to all, particularly to the clergy who insistently visited her in prison. Such behavior, however, was immaterial. Given the state of public opinion and the trepidation arson induced, her fate was all but sealed. While the governor was considering whether to commute her sentence to a prison term, the *Evening Post* editorialized on the "salutary effect" the execution of a black man found guilty of the same crime three years prior had had on the number of house burnings. On July 9, 1819, the nineteen-year-old Butler was marched up to the Potters Field, hanged in front of several thousand spectators, and buried a few yards from the scaffold. An eight-year-old Thomas F. De Voe was part of the onlooking crowd and never forgot the experience. More than forty years later, the butcher and chronicler of the city's markets recalled wistfully that "the witnessing of this execution still remains in my memory, as being one of the most prominent transactions of my boyhood."[25]

Although slavery would last to the bitter end in the New York countryside as owners dragged things out until the legislature forced their hand in 1827, most city blacks managed to achieve their freedom much earlier. It would still take decades for the effects of the institution to begin to wane, but by the 1820s fires associated with blacks had become almost entirely accidental and not deliberate. In January 1823, an African American inadvertently started a fire in Frankfort Street. The "black fellow," whom the *Spectator* did not deign to name, had arrived only recently from Delaware and was earning a living by walking the streets selling oysters. He and his family slept in a shack at the back of a house in Spruce Street, where he also cooked his oysters in a large tin boiler with a receptacle at the bottom for the blazing coals that provided the heat. After "he had taken out as many oysters as he calculated to sell during the afternoon," the black man "heedlessly" returned his cooking apparatus to the floor, and, somehow, a little while later, the coals sparked a fire. The unfortunate street hustler "was promptly arrested" and "ordered to leave the city in two days, or take a tour of duty on the treading mill." As the *Spectator*'s man noted, "it is not difficult to conjecture what was his election." He concluded sententiously: "The exposure of such a city to fire by carelessness should . . . be deemed a matter worthy of the judge, and it is gratifying to see an example made."[26]

More often than not blacks were now the victims of fire, as the squalid tinderboxes that poverty and the city's perennial housing shortage forced them to cram into went up in flames. On a Saturday afternoon in April 1835, a fire broke out in a collection of derelict wooden buildings, just south of the corner of Essex and Delancey streets, owned by a well-known slum landlord named William Slam. The timely arrival of the firemen prevented the blaze from spreading, but these tenements were "occupied by poor hard working colored people, nearly all of whom have lost the whole of their clothing and furniture." Later on the same day a house on the corner of Houston and Elizabeth streets accidentally went up in flames in what the *Transcript* called "another still more distressing fire." The owner had just fitted out the building, "into which four or five colored families had moved the day before," all of whom lost most of what little they possessed in this world.[27]

Increasingly, newspaper writers emphasized that drink played havoc with black life, although in reality alcohol abuse was more likely a symptom of the appalling conditions in the city's slums than a cause of it. Accounts of the demise of individual black men and women were commonplace. Early on a Saturday night in May 1832 a colored woman named Patterson and four or five friends "were in a state of intoxication" at a house on the corner of Hamersly and Varick streets. The others went out and left her alone sitting near the fire. Apparently she fell asleep, her clothes caught alight and she burned to death, or so the coroner reasonably concluded.[28]

He certainly had a depressingly large amount of experience at making such determinations in these years. Reporters considered African Americans vital contributors to the tone of life in the neighborhood of the Five Points, "the great sink of iniquity into which all the sewers of immorality in New York pour whatever is loathsome and vile." In a series of articles about an 1845 fire, a *True Sun* writer thought that "the pen of Eugene Sue, or that of Charles Dickens, could but feebly represent" what had occurred. Within fifty yards of the threatening inferno—and it was a big fire—"a crowd of men and women, almost in a state of nudity, and one negro girl actually without a rag to cover her, were seen dancing in a cellar to the music of a drunken fiddler, all of them being more or less intoxicated." As he continued, disdainfully, "bedlam never contained maniacs who raved more blasphemously than these drunken debauchees."[29]

For most whites, the sudden eruption of a city fire, or any other crisis, come to that, revealed once more the shortcomings and inadequacies of free blacks. Often it was believed that they had caused the fire and that they certainly could not be expected to do anything about putting it out. In such a telling, the very real danger posed by the flames merely magnified and highlighted the foibles of the well-established caricature of African Americans personified most commonly in the stereotypical dandies and dandizettes supposedly seen every day promenading down Broadway. After a fire in September 1839, a *New York Herald* writer went to town in a piece titled "Incidents at the Late Fire." According to him, pouring out of "negro houses of assignation," or brothels, on Church Street were "frail ladies of color by dozens, their dresses and ornaments of the toilet table, rouge, hair powder, pomatum, curling tongs, small tooth combs, nail brushes, pots, tooth brushes, perfume, cologne, berganot, and sweet oil, were thrown out of the windows before they waddled out of the doors." Over on Leonard Street "the negro church on fire struck terror into the hearts of the sable souls that worshipped there, and some of them almost turned pale with fright"; black spectators "looked all ways and all colors, and made all sorts of hieroglyphical motions with their mouths"—indeed, "some laughed, some cried, some sung 'Hallelujah! O be joyful!' some shouted."[30] Such descriptions, freighted in language and racial assumptions that were increasingly becoming identified as American, could have been filched from the stage directions for a minstrel show or its blackface antecedents.

It was this suffocating belief that African Americans were either vicious arsonists or suffering victims that made what happened in New York's Great Fire of 1835 all the more novel and startling. For the first time, the city's crucible of fire produced both a black hero and also a new type of black villain. Improbable as it may seem, the pair of African Americans taking on these rather different roles would become the two richest black men in antebellum New York City.

Thomas Downing, oyster-seller extraordinaire, featured as the hero. On the night of the fire, Downing and his customers, drawn outside by the pandemonium, spilled onto Broad Street, where he and all the other spectators could see the rapidly approaching inferno. With the water pipes frozen, Downing and a man named N. M. Brown hastened to the rear of the *Journal of Commerce*'s lot, where there were half a dozen hogsheads of vinegar, which they "broached by the head, and their contents, together with a few pails of water which happened to be in the printing offices, were applied so successfully to the exposed part of the office and another building similarly situated, that both were preserved." Ignoring the intense heat and the threat of the nearby blazing church at any moment collapsing on top of them, Brown and Downing, armed only with pails, dippers and vinegar, prevented the fire from progressing any farther west and then stayed on watch throughout the rest of the frigid night, for which, according to the *Journal of Commerce*, they "deserve especial commendation." A few days later a citizen wrote to the newspaper lauding the notice the press had given the pair's achievements, which "was gratifying particularly to those whose property was saved through their efficiency," and adding that Downing's efforts were also of great utility over on Exchange Place.[31] There may have been a self-serving element to Downing's actions—after all, his oyster cellar lay in the path of the fire—but he was still a hero and acknowledged as such by New Yorkers. In an almost-contemporary and well-known image of the fire, with a key underneath naming the depicted individuals, Thomas Downing was one of only fourteen men identified. Five years later, the still-grateful editor of the

Journal of Commerce recalled that "these exertions of Downing and a few others prevented the conflagration from extending through to Broad street," and "a million dollars at least was thus saved from destruction."[32]

Jeremiah G. Hamilton played the villain. Unlike his slave predecessors, in order to do so he did not have to light any fire; more in keeping with the spirit of his own times, the black man exploited the fine print in financial contracts to take advantage of, and profit heavily from, one of New York's largest-ever disasters. Although rumors and gossip of Hamilton's maneuverings undoubtedly circulated earlier, no details made the papers until seven months after the event. In July 1836, James Gordon Bennett, editor of the *New York Herald,* published an article—tucked away on his paper's usually not very interesting front page—extraordinary for its vitriol even by his own pioneering standards. "Have you heard of the Prince of Darkness? No! Well then, you shall know." The piece bristled with snide asides, many of which played on the black man's appearance. When Hamilton had arrived in New York, "his first move was to shave off his ha–, wool I mean, and procure a wig of fine flowing black hair." Every weekday, the article reported, he finished his business on Wall Street by lunchtime and in the afternoon rode out to his house at Bloomingdale, today the Upper West Side near Columbia University, in order "to be charmed by the smiles of an Houri, whom he has ensconced—not a black one, that would not do, but as fair and as frail a woman as ever trod apart from the right path." Hamilton was "one of the most fortunate men that ever commenced business of any kind." True, "he cannot be admitted into the society of any respectable ladies—but what is that, so long as he can cheat the men." Indeed, Hamilton's "good fortune has even followed him through the disastrous fire of December 1835."

The core of the piece was a parable of New York business. Sometime in the second half of 1835 several Pearl Street merchants visited the now much-in-demand Hamilton at his "snug office in Wall street" and invested $25,000 with the black broker. This was a very large sum of money, the equivalent of more than $5 million in today's dollars. "Out of this amount he calculated to realize something immense," and "the gentlemen for whom he was acting would pay him well." But before any profits could be reaped the fire intervened. At first light on December 17, 1835, the Pearl Street merchants discovered that their premises were destroyed and they were "utterly ruined." The *Herald* had little difficulty reconstructing their reaction:

> "At all events," thought they, "there are $25,000 which the Prince has—we can start on that again."
>
> "Yes, but you know our books and papers are entirely destroyed, we have no vouchers for the amount. Will he give it up?"
>
> "How can you wrong him by such a suspicion? Come, let us go and see him at once."

On entering Hamilton's office, untouched by the conflagration, they found the man that Bennett insinuated was little better than a profiteer, "rolling in money," with "plenty to lend at 2, 3 or 5 per cent per month." These were usurious rates of interest. The Pearl Street merchants explained to the black broker that they had lost everything and had "no other voucher for the money than your honesty." Word for word they recounted Hamilton's chilling reply:

> "Gentlemen," said Darkee rising gracefully. "I have not the most instant recollection of any such sum having ever been in my possession—but now I am very busy, if you can call tomorrow or next week, I will look over *my* books and see if there is any mention of such an account."

The denouement was inevitable. With no written record or any other proof, legal redress had to fail, and Hamilton kept the money. "This Prince of Darkness," the *Herald* scathingly pointed out, "may be safely said to *live on the interest of the money he owes*." Furthermore, "he is probably the only person out of the whole number of our population, who have been benefitted by that most untoward event." Indeed, the Prince of Darkness—and here Bennett's anger boiled over, as he mangled together two classical allusions into one heartfelt condemnation—"arose like a Phoenix from the ruins and carried aloft with him *twenty five thousand dollars* in his Icarian flight."[33]

A few days later Bennett published in the *Herald* a short, sharp letter in which the correspondent reaffirmed that the Prince of Darkness was "perhaps the most finished villain the city ever harbored." Referring to Hamilton's counterfeiting venture, he wrote: "The President of Hayti, his own black blood, offered a reward of $10,000 for his head before it was shaved of its wool"; referring to Hamilton's unlucky maritime history, he suggested: "Ask the merchants and underwriters what they knew of him." This, though, was only the beginning of Hamilton's wrongdoing: "Of his frauds in London, Cuba, St. Domingo and in our own city enough is known to fill a volume." He ended, "You can do much good by exposing this infamous vagrant," signing the letter, A NEW YORKER.[34]

As he had done before in 1828 when the press had traduced him (by his lights at least), Hamilton immediately took up his pen.[35] Rather than responding to the savage attack on him in the *Herald*, the details of which he ignored completely, the black businessman retaliated by excoriating Bennett. Having lived in the expectation that "your wretched little paper [would] sink into merited oblivion; and being painfully disappointed in that hope," he wrote to complain, "your Herald is sent forth daily with a new cargo of infamous and most injurious lies." Hamilton implored the editor to "make your paper a decent one—change it to a vehicle of truth, and support none but virtuous principles," and thus "regain your lost character." Fascinatingly, even in a moment of crisis, Hamilton evinced more interest in the mechanics of the way the press worked than in his own position. He remained confident that Bennett would "dare not publish" this letter, as "it contains too much truth, and truth is a thing you are at such enmity with, that you will never let it appear in your columns." The editor did print it, however, and, inevitably, he also chimed in with the last word. "I know the writer of the above," and he is "an infamous rascal in Wall street, who has cheated enough to send him to the State Prison for 15 years." According to Bennett, never afraid of penning an advertisement for himself, he had upset Hamilton because his own writing in the *Herald* had "told too much truth and fact."[36] And there the matter rested.

Although no one who lived through New York's Great Fire of 1835 ever forgot the night's events, it barely caused a hiccup in the city's growth. The fire had reduced dozens of acres of the commercial heart of the city to charred rubble and caused more than $20 million (or $4.5 billion in today's dollars) worth of damage, but business hardly missed a beat. Within four days the stock exchange had reopened, and other businesses were just as quick in setting up shop in temporary quarters. Rebuilding started almost immediately. Streets lined with Greek Revival granite warehouses, several stories tall, transformed the area and imbued it with a novel grandeur: locals certainly thought New York came back both bigger and better. On the first anniversary of the "desolating calamity," Philip Hone jotted down in his diary that businessmen already had erected 500 stores on the site of the fire, at an average cost of $10,000, and to such effect that "the whole is rebuilt with more splendor than before." Twenty-two months after the fire, a *Herald* reporter began his piece on "The Burnt District" by asking: "Where is it?" According to this New York booster, "the edifices that have sprung up from the ruins of the great fire of 1835 are not more remarkable for their beauty than their convenience." No other metropolis compared. London might have had some architectural merit here and there, but the city "taken as a whole, is dark, narrow and dirty," forcing visitors to "leave with a heartache if they are given to reflection, and a headache if not." On his ramble through rebuilt New York, retreading the fire's rapacious route, the reporter repeatedly had to resort to words such as "remarkable," "magnificent," "elegance," "great beauty" and the like in order to describe what he saw. And there was a larger meaning to events too: What other city could have achieved all this while the economy stuttered and stalled through the panic of 1837? "It seems perfectly talismanic," he opined, "when we reflect that not two years since this superb portion of the town was a confused heap of black smoking ruins."[37]

Life went on too for both the black hero and the black villain. Although Downing did not trade on the fact, for the rest of his life he would be associated with that night's events. After his death, stories about him were handed down among African Americans, eventually making their way into the black press. In 1922, a *Chicago Defender* writer honored Downing as the "first capitalist of our race," the man who had "saved" New York by directing the firefighters to use the "huge supply of cider and vinegar" he had stockpiled in his own cellar that enabled them to conquer the fire.[38] Ironically, Downing's real role had been considerably more active and significant than the one assigned him in the myth. And Jeremiah Hamilton? After the events of December 1835, his notoriety had increased considerably; of more moment for him, though, the black broker now had an extra $25,000 of his own to play with on whichever investment market he fancied.

FOUR

BUSINESS

J eremiah Hamilton was a hard and ruthless businessman. The only black principal in New York's financial district, he had little choice about how he behaved if he wanted to succeed in beating the rather steep odds confronting him. These circumstances forced Hamilton to be at least as cavalier about such niceties as keeping within the law as any of his white contemporaries. Wall Street has never been a place for the faint of heart, but in the antebellum era, with remarkably few rules of any sort yet established, New York businessmen played hardball, and, at least initially sensing an easy mark, they lined up to play with Hamilton. The black broker, though, always returned what he had received—and with interest. Unfortunately, if not surprisingly, no one ever thought to preserve any of Hamilton's ledgers or commercial records from these years: there are no surviving account books in which Hamilton, or a clerk, has scratched in with a quill pen his humdrum debits and credits, material that an historian could exploit to reveal the everyday existence of this uncommon black broker. Instead, in this chapter I want to use the newspapers and court records to unravel one complicated and fraught series of transactions that, although perhaps not typical, still might enable me to suggest something of the way Jeremiah

Hamilton and many of his white peers conducted business in the Gotham of the 1830s.

Later on, James Gordon Bennett would state in the *New York Herald* that "this case is one of the most singular in commercial morals which has come up for many years," but its beginnings were simple enough.[1] Jonathan Leech and William B. Johnson were partners who owned the *Sandusky,* a steamboat they claimed was a "good and valuable vessel worth about the sum of fifteen thousand dollars," or slightly more than $3 million in today's currency. The pair had to liquidate what was their major asset, preferably for a profit: having heard that there were good prospects in Cuba for doing just that, they approached Benjamin Basden, a partner in Hernandez and Basden, merchants based in Matanzas, who was residing temporarily in New York. He was well-connected, his firm "one of the first mercantile houses in Cuba," and, based on his local knowledge, he "thought favourably of the proposition." Basden advanced the businessmen $1,000 so that they could afford to patch up the *Sandusky* and steam her down to New York from Salem. Potentially, if Leech and Johnson could sell her in the Caribbean, everyone concerned would make a killing—there was even fanciful talk of a price of between $40,000 and $50,000—but it was also obvious that before that could happen they had to spend a lot of money. Although the language of a later legal affidavit is clumsy, the message is clear enough: "Repairs were necessary to be made on the said steamboat Sandusky and upon her tackle furniture and machinery as well in order to fit her for her voyage to Cuba as to adapt her more completely to the uses for which she would be needed in the said Island of Cuba and to the peculiar Navigation trade and necessities of the said island." These modifications and improvements were going to cost at least a further $6,000.[2]

At this point Hamilton entered the picture. Although Basden, already $1,000 out of pocket, was unable or unwilling to lend Leech and Johnson any more money, he introduced them to "his intimate friend" Jeremiah Hamilton, who decided to finance the deal. After the *Sandusky* was rendered seaworthy, the pair would sail her to Matanzas, where Hernandez and Basden would arrange the sale. The Cuban firm would then invest the proceeds in coffee and sugar and

consign the goods back to Hamilton in New York for him to sell. All of the "commissions accruing from the operation were to be equally divided between Hamilton and his friends of the Cuba house."[3]

Hamilton agreed to hand over four drafts totaling $6,000 and maturing at different dates. After he had made the initial payment of $2,500, the black broker began to hear stories about the character of his business partners—"that Leech was an Atheist," that the title to the *Sandusky* was not clear of debt—and tried to walk away from the deal. Although Leech and Johnson and, more importantly, his friend Basden talked him into staying the course, things were never quite the same again. Tension was further exacerbated by the spiraling costs of repairing the steamboat, and, increasingly, suspicion corroded relations between Hamilton and his New York partners. But the prospective profits were certainly attractive enough, and Hamilton carried on lending money. In November 1835, Leech and Johnson had a bill for $2,500 due at the West Point foundry. Hamilton agreed to pay it if Leech and Johnson would repay him $3,000 in six months' time and then negotiated a discount with the foundry so he only paid them $2,350, potentially earning a 27 percent return on his six-month investment. Leech and Johnson paid a high price, though, for increasing and extending their line of credit—not only were they forced to agree to steep interest rates, but also an increasingly circumspect Hamilton demanded more and more security before advancing additional monies.[4]

The complicating factor here was the Great Fire on December 16, 1835, that burned down Leech and Johnson's store at 53 Front Street, incinerating all their documentation of what had become a complicated series of transactions. Although they insisted Hamilton had copies of various agreements, he never directly answered anyone's queries on that point—another instance in which the black broker benefited from the Great Fire. By early 1836, Hamilton had advanced Leech and Johnson some $15,000, or in excess of $3 million in today's currency. On the other side of the ledger, Hamilton was in possession of a bill of sale for the *Sandusky;* a carriage worth $250, an oil painting of Diana with bathing nymphs valued at $100, an oil painting of the Holy Family valued at $500 and a French clock supposedly worth $400, all of which a Mr. Harwood had left with

Johnson to sell on commission and now wanted returned; and deeds for a mansion house and fifteen-acre farm in Stonington, Connecticut, a property that was mortgaged and whose ownership was contested by several people.

As if this was not already a complex-enough mess, an accident had befallen the *Sandusky*. Well, it seems to have been an accident, but one never quite knows with Hamilton's unlucky run of maritime mishaps—a cautious person would have thought long and hard before accompanying the black broker on the Brooklyn ferry. Repairs to the *Sandusky* had been finished finally, and on December 14, 1835, the steamboat set off for Matanzas. The following night "she was run into or came in contact with a vessel or brig called the 'Tom Cringle,' by which casualty the said steamboat Sandusky was so seriously injured and disabled, that she was forced to put back for New York to repair and refit." At this point, Hamilton, the only person with any claim to title supported by paperwork, assumed control of the steamship, settled with the Sea Insurance Company for $1,500 compensation for the damages caused by the collision (money that he promptly pocketed himself), and, as Leech and Johnson soon after discovered, was now suing the owners of the *Tom Cringle* for further recompense as well.[5]

After the collision with the *Tom Cringle,* no New York insurance company would underwrite the *Sandusky*'s voyage to Matanzas. Hamilton claimed he could insure the vessel in Philadelphia, and on better terms, but the truth of the matter was that the black man's welcome with underwriters had well and truly worn out, and that a Cuban sale of the steamboat, at least while he was associated with her, was unlikely. Hamilton had to acknowledge this fact, and indeed, the fresh modifications he had ordered made to the vessel rendered her unfit for use in Cuba, further irritating Leech and Johnson. When Hamilton tried to auction the *Sandusky* locally in February 1836, Leech and Johnson took out an injunction and halted the sale. After a struggle Hamilton succeeded in having the injunction lifted, and finally, in May 1836, a John Delafield bought the steamboat for $20,000.[6]

What is particularly fascinating about the unraveling of the agreement to sell the *Sandusky* is observing the way participants relied on the legal system to sort out their differences. Not that many antebellum businessmen were naïve enough to conceive of the courts as an impartial arbiter—the law was more a tool to be used, with litigants applying pressure, leverage and money to influence the decision. As the economy grew in size and sophistication, as it seemed to be doing at an exponential rate in the early 1830s, there was a concomitant explosion in the amount of all types of commercial litigation. Complex transactions moving goods over large distances and transferring money from one financial center to another, often over a period of months, so easily fell apart—occasionally this was the result of problems that no one reasonably could have anticipated, but mostly it was caused by fault or a too-careless discounting of the risks involved. Any businessman engaged in New York's dynamically mushrooming mercantile and financial sector could expect at regular intervals to have his day in court, a fact that applied with at least equal force to the few African Americans managing to make their way in the city. Even though Thomas Downing was only a restaurateur—admittedly one with significant property holdings—I have managed to come across, in the newspapers and legal archives, some fifteen instances between about 1830 and 1860 in which he either sued someone or was himself sued. Every New York businessman needed a lawyer on retainer—and preferably a good one.

When it came to the law, though, Jeremiah Hamilton was in a class of his own. The lawsuit became his chosen weapon; Hamilton has left a lasting impression on the historical record as a serial litigant. I have uncovered well in excess of fifty cases involving the black businessman suing or being sued. Over his near four decades of working in New York City, there were very few periods when Hamilton was not party to at least one suit meandering through the courts. Sometimes he won, sometimes he lost, but as a biographer of the similarly litigious Cornelius Vanderbilt observed of the Commodore, "even when the courts did not give satisfaction, legal action gave him leverage in negotiations."[7] Hamilton creatively imagined the legal system as simply another feature of the financial terrain, an institution little different from banks or insurance companies and there, above all, to be exploited. If a deal disintegrated and the matter ended up in front of a judge, so be it: far from panicking,

Hamilton pursued the case vigorously, hiring the best legal talent—and he usually had a string of top lawyers available. This was how Hamilton and the new breed on Wall Street conducted business.

By the second half of 1836 the situation between Hamilton and his erstwhile partners was at a stalemate. They had been in and out of court several times without resolving anything, and Leech and Johnson, with financial ruin pressing, appeared to have been outmaneuvered by the black broker. Something had to give, and Leech and Johnson decided to make a preemptive strike. On August 4, 1836, they had Hamilton charged with perjury, alleging that the black man had sworn to owning the steamboat *Sandusky* back in January 1836 although he knew this to be incorrect.[8] Perjury was not a common charge in the business world—when deals turned sour most litigants preferred to use the more direct approach and rely on straightforward offenses such as larceny and conspiracy—but seemingly, at one time or another, every African American who managed to achieve a measure of success downtown had to defend himself against the accusation that he had perjured himself. William Thompson, a black man who for most of the 1830s owned three blocks of land worth some $10,000, and who will feature in Chapter Six, suffered this indignity in 1841. A decade later, James McCune Smith, ruminating about "This Wealth Problem" among African Americans, noticed that when Thomas Downing had successfully sued a businessman, "the latter in revenge swore a complaint of perjury against him." As the black intellectual commented, "this very case adds force to my sermon above," in which he had argued that the pursuit of wealth without first seeking liberty was futile.[9] Aggrieved whites—for more than a modicum of spite was involved as well—were using the accusation of perjury to remind prominent blacks of their status in New York.

If the charge of perjury was unusual the details of Hamilton's arrest were even more so. "Messrs Homan and Merritt," police officers, were "engaged," as a writer in the *New York Times* put it, to secure the businessman very late at night. Likely, this arrangement involved a backhander, or favors of some sort or other. At this time the black broker was living outside of the city in Bloomingdale (in today's terms, above Central Park near Columbia University). The

police arrested Hamilton at almost midnight and brought him downtown, refusing to allow him to communicate with anyone en route,
although, as the *Times* pointed out, "he could readily have obtained
[bail] from various quarters" even at that hour of the night. Homan
and Merritt conveyed him directly to the watch house and locked
him up in one of the cells. Leech and Johnson intended to ensure
Hamilton had an unpleasant night and to humiliate the black man in
as public a fashion as possible. To this end, the vengeful pair had also
contrived one more surprise for Hamilton. As a writer for the *Times*
explained a couple of days later, "some person"—and little imagination was required to work out who was responsible—"procured a
paragraph to be put in two of the morning papers, blazoning what
had been done to and with him in bold relief, and much to his prejudice."[10] As soon as the bailed Hamilton walked free, early the next
morning, he discovered that what had occurred only hours before
had already made the papers. The piece in the *Morning Courier and
New-York Enquirer* recounted the arrest of "a notorious character,
named Jeremiah G. Hamilton, commonly called the Prince of Darkness," who was "well known in Wall street, where he has made several victims."[11] It was a cunning ambush.

What happened in the press in 1836 mattered in New York in a
way it would not have even a mere five years earlier. Few New Yorkers as of yet were wholly aware of the changes being wrought in the
wake of the invention of the penny press in 1833, but newspapers
themselves now were playing more of a role in the life of the city
than they ever had before in its history. On this development, James
Gordon Bennett was prescient. Commenting specifically on the imbroglio started by Leech and Johnson's charge of perjury, and writing with an almost biblical cadence, the *Herald*'s editor spelled out
some of the implications of this transformation in two remarkable
sentences: "There is no law—no justice—no truth—no honor—no
integrity, but what is in the newspapers. We are the bar, the pulpit
and the bench united."[12] Exaggerated perhaps—the courts were not
totally under the sway of the press—but Bennett did recognize how
the ground on which public life was played out had shifted decisively.

It had all started with Benjamin Day. Born in 1810 in West
Springfield, Massachusetts, the young man arrived in New York in

1830 and drifted from job to job, mostly as a compositor, working "at the case" setting type at the *Journal of Commerce,* the *New York Evening Post,* and the *Commercial Advertiser.* Such prints were known as the sixpenny papers, their almost-universal price, although a stranger in town would have needed to make an effort to buy a copy for six cents, as usually only the printer sold individual issues—almost all sales occurred through annual subscriptions, each costing $10. In modern parlance, these newspapers were not reader friendly: they consisted of four pages (one huge sheet folded in half) and were quite a bit larger than today's *New York Times,* with nine or even ten columns of tiny, often-smudged print on each page. They are a handful to read—the only time I ever bother to wear my prescription glasses is in the New-York Historical Society or the Library of Congress, hunched over the cumbersome bound volumes of New York sixpenny newspapers. Moreover, their content did not have a universal appeal. Most of the space in the dozen or so major New York newspapers was filled with advertisements, shipping news, financial news, international news and politics, and the anticipated readers were merchants, businessmen, politicians and officials. Consequently, the best-selling newspaper in 1833 was the *Courier,* with a circulation of 4,500; the *Journal of Commerce* sold about 2,300 copies and the *Evening Post* near 3,000, paltry figures in a city of almost a quarter of a million people.[13] In retrospect, it is difficult not to see the brittleness of the newspaper world of 1833—it was an antiquated system, ripe for challenge.

On the face of it, though, Benjamin Day, an intriguing and neglected figure in New York's history, was far from being the most likely candidate to mount such a challenge. Good with his hands and practical (he delighted in fixing things and making ingenious mechanical toys for his children and grandchildren with the tools he kept in his upstairs retreat), Day, unusually for an editor and proprietor, was someone who did not try to dominate the conversation, a man sparing with the spoken word. One of his grandsons remembered affectionately the twinkle in his eye as he watched and listened to people, and that "even with his old friends grandpa did little talking," but he "was interested, sardonically, in hearing what other men thought." His obituarist in the *New York Times* claimed that he "concealed a very warm heart behind a brusque address."[14] For all of his terse, even diffident, manner, this New Yorker, as we shall see later, was not afraid of going out on the town with his friends and having a good time.

The story of the founding of the *New York Sun* has remained framed by Day's telling of it, and his version of the paper's genesis convincingly emphasizes the role of happenstance and serendipity rather than any grand ambition on his part. In the early months of 1833, Benjamin Day set up shop as a jobbing printer, renting a twelve-by-sixteen-foot room at 222 William Street. Business was terrible partly because the lingering effects of the previous year's cholera epidemic had depressed demand but mostly because there were too many printers all undercutting one another as they tried to secure custom. In what he later characterized as a "sink-or-swim venture," Day conceived of the idea of a handbill containing the news of the day selling for one cent that would display the excellence of his printing. According to Day, it was always more of a publicity stunt advertising his print shop than an attempt to found a permanent newspaper. On Tuesday, September 3, 1833, with "not a dollar of capital" and after an all-night effort, the twenty-three-year-old launched the cobbled-together first issue of the *Sun*. He had "borrowed" advertisements from some of the sixpenny papers to give his enterprise the veneer of a going concern and purloined a poem, long enough to fill nearly a whole column, from some out-of-town newspaper. Early on that Tuesday morning he went out, bought a copy of the *Courier and Enquirer* and rewrote, slightly, the stories it contained about Monday's doings in the police courts. Almost single-handedly he then used his rather aged press to print 1,000 copies of the paper, a job that took the exhausted editor some four hours. It was one of the heroic days in the history of American journalism.[15]

The *Sun* was an instant runaway success: within four months Day had achieved a circulation of 5,000, and within a year he was selling 10,000 copies six days a week. Why was the *Sun* so successful? Most important were Day's marketing decisions, for it was here that he displayed flashes of genius. The obvious innovation was in the paper's appearance—early issues were eleven and a quarter by eight inches in size, barely bigger than a sheet of letter paper. Success and the consequent need to accommodate advertisers' demand for space soon forced Day to use larger paper stock, but in the early months, as the tyro editor was trying to attract readers who rarely had bothered to purchase a paper before, the *Sun* was much less daunting than, say, the *Journal of Commerce,* which resembled nothing so much as a small blanket. The crucial decision, though, was to sell the *Sun* for a penny and not for six cents. At this price, hordes of clerks, artisans, tradesmen and even ordinary laborers could afford to buy their own copy of the paper. Day, too, was concerned particularly to promote the everyday purchase of individual newspapers. To this end, he advertised in the second issue of the *Sun* for unemployed men to vend his paper—Day would sell them one hundred papers for sixty-seven cents cash, or seventy-five cents on credit, and they then would resell them at the full face value of one cent and pocket the profit. Thus was born the newsboy: the first was Bernard Flaherty, a ten-year-old who had come from Cork and later in life became a famous comedian.[16] The well-known black hollers of New York such as "he-e-e-e-e-er's your fine Rocka-a-way clams" and, most famously, in the autumn months, the ubiquitous "h-a-u-t corn," "h-a-urt ca-irr-ne," were, from 1833 on, joined by the querulous cries of white children hawking newspapers. According to the author of a celebratory history of the *Sun,* the invention of the newsboy was "the greatest change in journalism that ever had been made, for they brought the paper to the people."[17]

Inevitably, Day's strategy for selling the *Sun* affected the content of the newspaper, although, particularly early on, the changes were more of degree than of kind and were perhaps not quite as dramatic as some have intimated. Occasionally, historians have seemed to suggest that Day, by employing a police roundsman to report court proceedings, created the newspaper true crime genre, but the fact that the young editor plagiarized the *Courier*'s Police Office items for the inaugural issue of the *Sun* undermines such a claim. As early as 1820, in one of the first issues of the daily version of *The American,* the editor explained that "we have made arrangements which will enable us to give a daily summary, and sometimes a detailed account of the trials," as this material, "always entertaining, frequently interesting, and sometimes instructive, will be gratifying to the generality of our patrons." Court reporting had become a staple of the New York press well before the advent of the *Sun*. And it should be added here that, contrary to the way some have chosen to depict the sixpennies of the 1820s and early 1830s, by no means were all of them staid and dowdy—papers such as the *National Advocate*, the various incarnations of the *Courier and Enquirer*, and even on occasion the *Journal of Commerce* could be quite lively, often printing prose displaying the dexterousness and mordant wit of a Mordecai Noah or some other editor. Nevertheless, there still were significant changes in the approach and subject matter of the *Sun*: most particularly, there was more of an emphasis on New York City news than had been the case in the sixpennies. As well, Day eschewed party politics but not politics as such, for his democratic leanings were often visible in the stances his paper took; he omitted almost entirely business and mercantile news, leaving the field to the *Journal of Commerce*; and George Wisner, hired for $4 a week to get up and attend the police court at four a.m. and then to craft into pungent prose the often-inebriated mumblings of arrested New Yorkers, if not quite the Balzac that one earlier historian of the *Sun* suggested, was still a talented reporter who did make a difference.[18] Day made some modifications, emphasizing this feature less and that one more, usually ad hoc responses to circumstances and perceived demand, an approach according with his claimed lack of overarching strategy for his newspaper. For all of that, there was something engagingly fresh about the *Sun* and little doubt that in the wake of its success the newspaper world was going to have to adapt.

Indeed, wittingly or not, Benjamin Day had let slip the forces of the free market into what had been a sheltered oligopoly of sorts. The other daily papers' fragility and their editors' unconcern about how many copies they sold derived from the facts that most of their readers were yearly subscribers and that they relied on advertising revenue to pay the bills. Day, by selling his paper for a mere penny and beginning to uncouple sales from subscriptions, made every literate New Yorker a potential purchaser of the *Sun*. He introduced a new imperative into newspaper publishing, compelling editors to realize they were running businesses in the marketplace and had to notice circulation figures. The trick was not just to attract readers, but also to retain them, to get them to buy the paper tomorrow and the following day as well. There was continual pressure to provide customers with excitement, to give them something in return for their daily penny, and failure to do so was readily apparent, measured simply by bundles of unsold newspapers. In only the *Sun*'s third issue, Day confessed: "We newspaper people thrive best on the calamities of others."[19] Newsboys certainly loved nothing more than having a macabre murder to shout about, as it allowed them to move more product and make more money, but sensation of any sort sold papers.

The most telling example of the brave new world Benjamin Day was bringing into being occurred in late August 1835, about the same time that Benjamin Basden introduced Leech and Johnson to his intimate friend Jeremiah Hamilton. It began with a teaser on August 21, a small notice that "Sir John Herschel, at the Cape of Good Hope, has made some astronomical discoveries of the wonderful description, by means of an immense telescope of an entirely new principle."[20] Four days later the *Sun* began running articles thousands of words long explaining in detail the workings of the telescope and then revealing, day by day, what Herschel had observed on the moon, including a delightful valley "abounding with lovely islands and water-birds of numerous kinds"; a lake 266 miles long and 193 wide dotted with volcanic islands; a beaver that walked on two feet, lived in impressively large huts "and from the appearance of smoke in nearly all of them there is no doubt of its being acquainted with the use of fire"; culminating in the discovery of human-like creatures who could fly. Most of New York was agog at the revelations. The *Daily Advertiser* opined that Sir John "has added a stock of knowledge . . . that will immortalize his name and place it high on the page of science"; the *Times* thought the stories had an "air of intense verisimilitude"; and the *Mercantile Advertiser* began reprinting the articles for its own readers. The hoax was exposed only when Richard Locke, its author, tipped off a fellow journalist at the *Journal of Commerce*. In the middle of the furor, on August 28, 1835, the *Sun* sold 19,360 copies, some 14 percent more than the London *Times*' circulation of 17,000. A few days shy of the second anniversary of the *Sun*'s founding, it was the best-selling daily newspaper in the world.[21]

Inevitably, the *Sun* had its imitators. Some, such as the *Transcript,* came and went, but the most important was the *New York Herald.* If Benjamin Day seemingly lucked into proprietorship of the country's most successful newspaper, the driven James Gordon Bennett early on set his sights on conquering the world. It just took a while for him to get started. Born in Scotland in 1795, he emigrated when he was twenty-five and spent a decade and a half working around the traps as a reporter for various papers, including both the *Enquirer* and the *Courier,* and even started his own short-lived publication titled the *Globe.* At forty Bennett was running out of time when, spurred on by Day's success, he scraped together $500 and started publishing the *Herald* in May 1835. He too initially sold his new paper for a penny and deliberately targeted "the great masses of the community—the merchant, mechanic, working people—the private family as well as the public hotel—the journeyman and his employer—the clerk and his principal."[22] The newspaperman harbored grand ambitions for his tabloid, admitting that "Shakespeare is the great genius of the drama, Scott of the novel, Milton and Byron of the poem—and I mean to be the genius of the newspaper press."[23] More mundanely, with his considerable experience reporting financial matters, Bennett refused to abandon Wall Street to the *Journal of Commerce.* In his second issue he ran the first money-market report, and a few days later he began listing stock exchange sales. For the first three years of the *Herald*'s existence, Bennett visited Wall Street every day and wrote his "Money Matters" column. A gaunt, arrogant and often-unpleasant individual, Bennett was probably the most-hated American newspaperman of the nineteenth century. Philip Hone, the diarist and former mayor of the city, dismissed Bennett as "an ill-looking squinting man" and was one among numerous members of New York's establishment who loathed both him and his newspaper.[24] Regardless of their opinion, Bennett was a great editor and the *Herald* an immediate success, selling some 7,000 copies within two months of its founding.

For all the undoubted vibrancy of New York newspapers in the mid-1830s—and I have often thoroughly enjoyed myself reading long runs of these prints—there was also something far too self-referential about what could be a closed, if not suffocating, world.

Competition among all the New York editors was cutthroat. They differed on politics, economics, for the most part simply did not like one another, and constantly feuded with, and sniped at, competitors. As their premises were all located in a dozen or so blocks, not far from Wall Street, they also often ran into one another on the street or at eating establishments such as Downing's. Public thrashings and brawls were a commonplace, and on at least one occasion a pair of rival editors ventured across the Hudson and fought a duel in Hoboken. Verbal stoushes between proprietors were an everyday occurrence. On one occasion, Day memorably wrote of his antagonist at the *Herald:* "Bennett, whose only chance of dying an upright man will be that of hanging perpendicularly upon a rope, falsely charges the proprietor of this paper with being an infidel, the natural effect of which calumny will be every reader will believe him to be a good Christian."[25] Insults, often as sharply crafted as this one, were traded all the time. Anyone who has read extensively in the dozens of newspapers printed daily and weekly in the New York City of the 1830s and 1840s could be forgiven for concluding that the offense of libel had been created solely to enable newspaper editors to settle their innumerable squabbles. They constantly sued one another and then gave extensive coverage to the legal proceedings in their publications. At frequent intervals, most members of the press convulsed into a frenzy over some event or other, some imagined or real slur, in what was the 1830s equivalent of "going viral." It was a claustrophobic milieu that clever men manipulated to their own advantage.

Although Leech and Johnson's ambush had taken Jeremiah Hamilton by surprise, the black businessman brushed aside the rude interruption to his sleep and subsequent night in a cell as little more than an opening skirmish. The bail hearing early the following morning was quick—several of Hamilton's friends were in court to offer security "in any amount, $5,000, $50,000 or $100,000, should it be required." A judge fixed the sum at $5,000, and Tinkham and Hart, the firm that had taken out the insurance policy on the brig *Meridian* that had sunk so unfortunately off the Charleston bar, entered into the required bond. Once released from custody, Hamilton, along with his confederates, began organizing their counter-offensive. This was less a legal matter—in this case, at least,

Hamilton left the law up to his lawyers—and more an issue of how to deal with the newspapers, what nowadays we call "spin." Someone went and had a chat with the editor of the *Morning Courier and New-York Enquirer,* and by the time his next edition came off the press the following morning he had begun to backpedal, acknowledging meekly of Hamilton that "it is said he is prepared with a sufficient defence—a circumstance we were not aware of when pronouncing so harshly on his conduct in yesterday's paper."[26]

Much more importantly, Benjamin Day, making an unusual foray into Wall Street matters, took a decisive stand on the merits of Leech and Johnson's actions, as became very clear the next afternoon when newsboys with the first copies of the *Sun* hit the streets. Quite likely Day was one of Hamilton's friends who had rushed to the Police Court and advised him on how to proceed, but even if he was not present, this story was already gloriously suited to his own anti-establishment predilections. He began his brief for the defense in slashing fashion with "*The Shylocks of Wall street,* on repairing to their respective plundering dens yesterday . . ." and continued on from there, flaying both the *Courier* and the city's financial sector for a thousand words, a very long piece by *Sun* standards. He depicted Hamilton as the brilliant outsider pitted against an incompetent if still-vindictive establishment, a tale with which the editor himself readily identified. The black man's "business abilities are of the brightest order," Day emphasized, although his very success had "rendered him the envy and fear of a horde of small fry vampires of Wall street, who, at first fastening upon him under the supposition that he was green and could be made an easily plucked pigeon, have found to their cost that he was not only able to cope with them in their 'tricks of trade,' but to turn their artifices upon themselves and to his own advantage."

Benjamin Day discerned a pattern to recent events in Hamilton's life, one that suggested a sinister conspiracy against the black broker. Resentful men "of similar moral and business characters with his present prosecutors" on several occasions recently had initiated proceedings against Hamilton, but the charges had all been tossed out of court by grand juries that had been so unimpressed with the accusations they had not even required the black man to explain himself. An attack "which a few weeks since appeared in a certain loathsome publication"—this referred to Bennett's revelations about the Prince of Darkness in the *Herald* almost a month previously— had only been printed in the *Herald* because of a $100 bribe paid "by those very bloodsuckers whom he [Hamilton] had foiled with their own weapons." However, "like all their efforts to crush their superior in every respect, their own characters alone suffered by the mendacious publications put forth by their purchased tool."

Most particularly, Day detected a conspiracy animating Leech and Johnson's reprehensible behavior: the style of Hamilton's arrest "speaks volumes as to the *spirit* of the prosecution." Indeed, "such an arrest, at midnight, of a man whose stability is double that of all his prosecutors combined" was "without precedent in this country." On the morning after Hamilton's arrest a "whole levy of persons belonging to the insurance offices, and of Wall street 'victims,' appeared at the police office" expecting to witness the black broker's further humiliation. When Hamilton easily made bail, "the disappointed group of 'victims' left the office with their nether lips between their teeth."[27]

That weekend, Benjamin Day did not rest on the Sabbath. Monday's *Sun* featured a 1,552-word article making even more explicit his contempt for the forces arrayed against Jeremiah Hamilton. Much of the piece rehearsed the salient features of the case, for the first time revealing publicly details of the aborted deal. The peroration, though, was vintage Benjamin Day. Leech and Johnson, according to the editor, had prosecuted Hamilton "with all the acrimony and malice of defeated cupidity and thirsty vengeance." But the wrongdoing was hardly confined to this pair: "Subscriptions have been entered into, in which persons connected with certain insurance companies, and other individuals, have joined with the prosecutors in raising a fund for the purpose of crushing, if possible, the object of this malevolent prosecution." This anti-Hamilton cabal was driven by the need "to gratify a revenge generated in thwarted chicanery and nurtured by malice *openly avowed and boasted of!*" The outraged editor concluded furiously: "We hazard nothing in saying, that for barefaced imposition, not only upon private but public rights, and downright prostitution of the laws and institutions of our state, this prosecution, so founded and so supported, is without a parallel in disgrace in the criminal records of the country."[28]

On Wednesday the Court of Sessions considered the case. If the grand jury had been sequestered in a locked room somewhere in New Jersey perhaps its members might have remained unaware of Day's unusually ferocious attack on the prosecution's legitimacy. They had merely spent the night in their Manhattan houses, however—and threw the case out of court unanimously and straightaway. Hamilton's lawyers immediately gave notice that their client intended to sue for malicious prosecution.[29] The editor of the *Courier*, doubtless also leery of an impending lawsuit, was still backpedaling: in a brief notice the next day, he claimed now that he had not even seen the initial story that his paper had run, and he confessed the article was one that "we have reason to believe did great injustice to the character of Mr Hamilton." Indeed, "we hope therefore that this explanation will remove any impressions injurious to Mr Hamilton, which our former report may have given rise to." In victory, Benjamin Day, having demonstrated comprehensively the power of the press, especially that of the *Sun*, stilled his pen—well, almost: he could not resist quoting one member of the grand jury, who "stated in our presence" that the charge was "one of the most infamous attempts at persecution which any of them had ever known."[30]

After the perjury charge was dismissed, Bennett, who had been very quiet about the whole affair, commented in the *Herald* that "the papers have been engaged a few days past in discussing certain private business transactions." Although he could not stop himself from trying to goad Hamilton by calling him "Jerry," he had to admit that "in the present case, however, Jerry has completely out-generaled the Yankees." Bennett, of all people, then went on to recommend that both sides "should bear and forbear with each other—to settle their differences in a legal, quiet way, and to keep out of the newspapers." He wound up his short piece by stating: "Jerry Hamilton is one of the most remarkable men of his race, and we shall give a historical sketch of his life and adventures one of these days." No matter how condescendingly, Bennett, for all his race-baiting proclivities, was honest enough to concede that the black broker had handled himself with aplomb in the bear pit that was Wall Street, an arena in which the *Herald* editor was an astute judge.[31]

Neither Hamilton nor Leech and Johnson were much interested in heeding Bennett's sensible advice to keep out of the newspapers. Remarkably, both sides sought publicity and commenced buying space in the press in order to continue what had become a very public feud. The following day, August 11, 1836, the *Sun* printed an unusual letter addressed to the editors. According to the writer, "the crime of perjury too often escapes its just punishment," and in the Hamilton case many "respectable counsellors" thought it "a clear case of perjury," all of which went to show that there had been "nothing very malicious about" proceeding with the charge. Furthermore, Hamilton "has been arrested several times," which should have made it clear "that his character is not so spotless as he would have the public believe." Day appended a note to the letter explaining why he was printing a paragraph so out of kilter with the rest of the *Sun*'s coverage of the case: "We give place to the foregoing as a matter of business solely"—or, in other words, it was a paid advertisement. The editor dismissed the content of the notice as unworthy of comment: "It furnishes, in its own weaknesses, an ample security of harmlessness to every body." Nevertheless, "its authors had a right to demand of us on complying with our advertising terms," and, even if Day's commentary had undercut completely his customers' purpose, they now had had their chance of "saying their say."[32]

The litigants in the case of the *Sandusky* resembled nothing so much as a pair of dogs unable to stop worrying a juicy bone. Almost immediately, Hamilton bought space in the *New York Evening Post* so he could respond with what he called "A CARD," published on August 15, 1836. In a three-paragraph notice, Hamilton claimed Leech and Johnson had "lately made a false, wicked, infamous, and malicious accusation of perjury against me, which charge was *immediately dismissed by the grand jury,* and . . . still are industriously, and *falsely* circulating a report that I have been and am now attempting to swindle them out of property on which I advanced them money." In order to quiet their slurs, he now had two offers for them. Hamilton would return all their property on being paid the $14,266.04 they had acknowledged owing him. Alternatively, he would give them the property he had received as payment for the *Sandusky* provided they paid all they owed him and an adjustment was made for the difference in value between the steamboat and the property. His italicized exasperation rubbed salt in his opponents' wounds: "*I would willingly give* $1000 to have them accept either of these offers, as I would thereby lose less than I am likely to lose now, as the balance due me is large and they are *insolvent*." He would not "comment upon the conduct of these men, nor their aiders and abettors," but stoically would "endeavor to bear the injuries they have done me." The card was signed JEREMIAH G. HAMILTON.[33]

Three days later Leech and Johnson responded in kind in the *Evening Post,* disputing the correctness of Hamilton's account. They made a counter-offer, to let the matter be arbitrated by "three respectable persons." Furthermore, they wanted "no gratuity" from Hamilton; indeed, they would "make him a liberal discount" to encourage him to put up security guaranteeing everyone would abide by the arbitrators' decision. Clearly stung by Day's articles in the *Sun*—and who would not be—Leech and Johnson ended by jibing that "nor shall we pay editors to pour forth their vituperations in Mr H's condemnation, nor yet in our own justification." The following day, and for the final time, Hamilton purchased more space in the *Evening Post* to argue the point all over again. This extraordinary public dispute between Hamilton and his two white former business associates concluded with the black man issuing what could only be described as a barefaced threat. The last sentence of his notice read: "I now take leave of these gentlemen, not however, without assuring them that *matters of more importance to them, will engage their attention on the meeting of the next grand jury.*"[34]

A few days after Hamilton's threat, and now almost three weeks since Leech and Johnson had ambushed the broker and had him taken into custody, the denouement to the perjury accusation played out. Very early on the morning of August 23, officers Welch and Brink arrested Leech and Johnson at their homes on charges of fraud and perjury arising out of the Great Fire that had taken place eight months earlier. The pair had insured the contents of their store at 53 Front Street for $5,000 with the Eagle Insurance Company. As with almost every other insurance company in the city, the fire had bankrupted Eagle, and they had paid off their obligations at the rate of only thirty-four cents to the dollar. Leech and Johnson had sworn to the correctness of their claim, detailing a loss of $5,600, and eventually received a settlement of nearly $1,700. Now, unnamed witnesses had come forward alleging that at the time of the fire, and for some months previous, Leech and Johnson's inventory had not been worth $500, let alone more than ten times that amount. The judge set bail for the duo at $10,000, a sum that, if they were as strapped financially as had been intimated, must have been a struggle to find. And, tit for tat, after their release from custody, they could hardly have avoided reading Day's mauling of them in the *Sun* underneath the caption *"Audacious and Heartless Villainy."* He excoriated them for being a pair of "as precocious scoundrels as ever preyed on the confidence of any community," who had tried to evade repaying a $15,000 debt to Hamilton "by crushing him beneath a criminal conviction and incarceration." Now they had been caught perjuring themselves and attempting to swindle $5,000 from a bankrupt insurance company, thus depriving "scores of widows and orphans" of what was rightfully theirs. Invoking "widows and orphans" in such a fashion may appear hackneyed to our world-weary eyes, but in 1836 it was fresh, a lovely, deft touch. Day concluded that this was the "character of the men who would use our public courts, and the public press, to crush our merchants of responsibility and unimpeachable integrity."[35]

A Mr. Glover, secretary of the Eagle Insurance Company, may have preferred the charges against Leech and Johnson, but now that his firm was defunct he was little more than a cipher. The editor of the *New York Spectator* stated unambiguously that these were accusations "which Jeremiah G. Hamilton has been endeavouring to procure against them."[36] Everyone understood that this was revenge and very personal: indeed, had not Hamilton, only a few days previously, even forecast in the *New York Evening Post* that something such as this was going to occur? Three weeks after Leech and Johnson were arrested, the grand jury unanimously threw out this indictment as well. Not that it mattered much by then—the black broker had made his point. You crossed Jeremiah Hamilton at your own risk.

Puzzlingly, the *Sandusky* imbroglio fizzled out in anticlimax. For six weeks in August and September 1836 the sound and fury of the clashing rival parties had filled the law courts and newspapers, but there followed months of total silence. And then, in June 1837, the cryptic result of *Jonathan Leech & William B. Johnson v. Jeremiah G. Hamilton* was filed in New York's Superior Court. The sole document in the file is a printed form, a record of judgment directing Hamilton to pay $20,000 to the plaintiffs. This is a curious decision that flies in the face of what had happened—or, more accurately, of what I understand to have happened. Presumably Leech and Johnson still had to reimburse Hamilton the money they had borrowed, but there is no detailing of this, or indeed of anything else, in the archive. Similarly, if there was some mention, let alone explication, of the result of the case in the press, I have failed to find it. After the verbosity of the struggle itself all that remains of its conclusion is the bald statement of the result in the court records. Historians are at the mercy of their sources, and sometimes they simply dry up.

Notwithstanding the decision, it was still a remarkable case. For the most part, African Americans took a fearful pummeling in antebellum newspapers as writers depicted them in almost nothing but a viciously caricatured fashion. Hamilton's exploits, though, forced the newspapers to allow that a colored man could be not only smart but also smarter than whites. Portraying a successful black man besting whites, and in a field of endeavor unthinkingly assumed to be the preserve of whites, was simply unprecedented. New York's two most important newspapers—the *Sun* and the *Herald*—freely trumpeted Hamilton as someone whose "business abilities are of the brightest order," a man who had established himself to the point at which his "stability is double that of all his prosecutors combined." James Gordon Bennett concluded that the black broker had "completely out-generaled" Leech and Johnson. And they were right to do so: Hamilton's skill at business intrigue and his awareness of the coming importance of the press and how to manipulate it were exceptional.

The case as a whole reveals a glimpse of Hamilton and Day, two clever young men in their twenties, as they were making names for themselves, one black, the other white, taking on all and sundry as they carved up everyone in their path. And yet no matter how effective the pair may have seemed at the time (and, to this historian at least, still seem), the court found against Hamilton. Perhaps Benjamin Day's hints at the existence of a conspiracy were less rhetorical flourishes and more a perceptive summation of the way things were in antebellum New York. To be sure, Hamilton was cocksure, aggressive and undoubtedly broke the law, but then this could equally describe any number of his white contemporaries. What was different was Hamilton's color—not many appreciated having a vociferous black man upsetting the business world's genteel equilibrium. The crude violence of ejecting a black from a railroad car or of enforcing the new racial etiquette that accompanied African American freedom could be left to the denizens of New York's streets; even though they were increasingly beleaguered by economic change, the gentlemen still running Wall Street could afford to be more subtle. All that was needed was a nod here and a word there, and the pioneering black man would be undone. Day had pointed to a conspiracy keen to avenge past wrongs, and the perplexing conclusion to the case meant that these shadowy figures achieved, at least partially, their aim. This would not be the last time that Jeremiah Hamilton's way of doing things would needle members of the establishment into trying to silence him.

FIVE

JIM CROW NEW YORK

July 5, 1827, was a signal day in the history of New York City. Ten years earlier the state legislature, prompted by New York governor Daniel D. Tompkins, and with none-too-subtle symbolism, had picked July 4, 1827, as the date on which the last New York slaves would, finally, be set free. Tompkins's choice of the Fourth of July posed some awkward questions for African Americans. Should they accept the all-too-easy assertion of a link between the founding principles of the Republic and their freedom, particularly given the persistence, indeed expansion, of the hated institution of slavery in the South? More practically, how could they celebrate safely when much of the state's white population, hardly friendly to blacks at the best of times, was intoxicated and in a mood to be rowdy or worse? African New Yorkers were divided about how to respond to this challenge. A public meeting in Albany resolved: "Whereas the 4th day of July is the day that the National Independence is recognized by the white citizens of this country, we deem it proper to celebrate the 5th." This resolution, slyly subversive of so many white expectations, prefigured Frederick Douglass's blunter question delivered famously to a Rochester audience on July 5, a quarter of a century later: "What, to the American slave, is your 4th of July?" In 1827, another group of more conservative blacks, anxious to avoid airing dissent, planned to mark the original date of the Fourth of July in order "to express our gratitude for the benefits conferred on us by the honorable Legislature" and do so demurely—to avoid "disorder" they would "abstain from all processions in the public streets on that day."[1] At issue in the dispute were such questions as: What did emancipation mean, and how had African New Yorkers achieved it? Was freedom something given to them by benevolent whites? And, now that they were free, should they just do as they were told and fade decorously into the background?

In New York City, in spite of scads of advice from newspaper editors and various "friends," African Americans failed to agree on what to do. As a result, there were two celebrations of slavery's demise. On July 4, 1827, a "large and respectable" gathering of blacks attended the Zion Church and listened to an oration by the black clergyman William Hamilton. The hall was decked out with banners from several of New York's black societies and portraits of white benefactors, including John Jay and Matthew Clarkson. And then on July 5, between 3,000 and 4,000 African Americans, by the *New York Daily Advertiser*'s count, marched through "the principal streets, under their respective banners, with music and directed by a marshal on horseback," and assembled at the Zion Church, where they too listened to a speech. The parade was such a triumph that it settled the issue of how to memorialize the end of slavery. Next year, on July 5, 1828, blacks assembled by nine a.m. for a march that would traverse much of New York City—the marchers were not due at the church until two-thirty p.m.—and the parade in all its boisterousness, rather than the more subdued service, was clearly the centerpiece of the day's proceedings. Not that success silenced the critics. John Russwurm, editor of *Freedom's Journal,* remained a bitter opponent of ostentatious behavior of any sort, haranguing his fellow African New Yorkers "that nothing is more disgusting to the eyes of a reflecting man of colour than *one of these grand processions,* followed by the lower orders of society."[2]

Yet the last word on the parade should not be left to naysayers such as Russwurm, or even the flat descriptions of white journalists filing their terse copy for the daily newspapers. July 5, 1827, *was* a signal day in the city's history, the march an acknowledgment of the role of ordinary African Americans in achieving their freedom. It is difficult to convey the inspirational effect, on participants and on-lookers alike, of the shocking sight of a large body of blacks taking possession, if only for a short time, of the city streets. Some of the exuberance of these liberating times is captured in the black intellec-tual James McCune Smith's recollection, from the vantage point of the 1860s, of that first parade to celebrate slavery's abolition in New York, a description whose exhilarating language reverberates down to us through the history of the civil rights movement: "That was a celebration!" Smith wrote. "A real, full-souled, full-voiced shouting for joy, and marching through the crowded streets, with feet jubilant to songs of freedom!"

> It was a proud day in the city of New York for our people, that 5th day of July, 1827. It was a proud day for Samuel Hardenburg Grand Marshal, splendidly mounted, as he passed through the west gate of the Park, saluted the Mayor on the City Hall steps, and then took his way down Broadway to the Battery &c. It was a proud day for his Aids, in their dress and trappings; it was a proud day for the Societies and their officers; it was a proud day, never to be forgotten by young lads, who, like Henry Garnet, first felt themselves impelled along that grand procession of liberty; which through perils oft, and dangers oft, through the gloom of mid-night, dark and seemingly hopeless, dark and seemingly rayless, but now, through God's blessing, opening up to the joyful light of day, is still *"marching on."*[3]

To be sure, in New York City itself very few slaves were freed on July 4, 1827—almost all had negotiated an early release from their owner years before—but it was still a glorious occasion. Held annually un-til 1834, the freedom parades were attempts to foster unity among an increasingly disparate African American population; they pro-claimed to a skeptical and often-hostile white audience that blacks were no longer slaves and that as American citizens they, too, had a right to the streets.

The chances are that Jeremiah Hamilton was in New York City for that first emancipation parade—if not, he arrived soon after, in the celebration's wake. He was definitely there for the second parade on July 5, 1828, as he was then caught up in the imbroglio over the Haitian counterfeiting expedition. Whether or not he participated in any of the celebrations was altogether another matter. More than likely, he avoided them. During all the years he lived in New York, he had nothing to do with other African Americans. That was his choice. What he had no choice about at all was how other New Yorkers categorized him. American ideas of race had little room for the subtleties of color gradations common in the Caribbean or South America—in New York you were either black or white. No matter how much Hamilton tried to distance himself from other African Americans, to anyone who saw him on the street he was just one more Negro. No matter how little he liked it, the changes in the way African New Yorkers were treated in the 1820s, 1830s and 1840s impacted every day of Jeremiah Hamilton's life. The struggle to establish what emancipation meant had consequences for not just those who saw themselves as Negro or colored but ev-eryone white New Yorkers deemed to be not white. Regardless of Hamilton's wishes, his story was a part, even if an atypical one, of a much larger process—the transformation from slavery to freedom in New York City.

Under the impetus of slavery's demise, African American life in New York displayed an edgy vitality in these transitional years, a mood expressed in everything from clothing styles to dance, music and street parades. On the streets and in the cellars, where so many were forced to dwell, ordinary African Americans forged a vibrant culture, one that not only reflected their new and exhilarating sta-tus as free people, but also fascinated and not infrequently horrified white onlookers. The resulting conjunction between black creative activity and white voyeurism was unprecedented and would not re-cur until the Harlem Renaissance of the 1920s.[4]

It did not take long for infuriated whites to detect that blacks were treating them in new ways, ranging from insouciance to contempt and outright aggression. The struggle over how African Americans should be treated took place in the workplace, in the courts, and, most obviously of all, in the city streets. The demeanor of free blacks—the way they dressed, talked, or walked down Broadway—offended a substantial number of white New Yorkers, not least because such behavior betrayed a lack of gratitude for what whites saw as their generous act in emancipating the slaves in the first place. Mordecai Noah, then editor of the *New-York Enquirer*, expressed himself on this subject with particular asperity, but the tenor of his remarks was in step with white public opinion. In August 1827, a month after slavery's end in New York, Noah wrote that blacks generally were "an evil and a blotch upon the face of American society," and that New York's free blacks were "a nuisance incomparably greater than would be a million slaves." Everything about African New Yorker behavior on the city streets, from the "boisterousness of their manners" to the "disgusting indecency of their language," offended him. Most of all, though, he was irritated by blacks' ingratitude: "Instead of thankfulness for their redemption, they have become impudent and offensive beyond all precedent."[5]

In the years before emancipation began in earnest, New York slaves had been an accepted part of city life, attracting for the most part surprisingly little comment. Once freed, however, and with numbers swollen by fugitives and migrants, the city's blacks were marked off as a separate group and increasingly demonized. This process was often expressed in terms of the body—blacks were an affront not merely to whites' eyes, but to almost the full range of their senses. If the look of "dandified" African Americans strolling on the Battery caused offense, so too did the touch of the black body that shouldered whites from the sidewalk, the "savage" sounds of black street cries or loud conversation, and, somewhat less frequently, the smell that black bodies were believed to emit. More and more, whites recoiled in horror at the thought of physical contact with African New Yorkers. In June 1823 one letter writer, protesting bitterly to the *National Advocate* about black behavior on the streets, concluded by explaining that "they are so rude, and talk so loud, and smell so bad, what are we to do—to whom shall we apply, Mr Editor, to keep them more orderly?"[6] In large part such unhappiness was caused by the deliberate actions of African Americans who declined any longer to remain quiet and unobtrusive. In reaction, whites developed new ways of perceiving and treating the city's black inhabitants.

Increasingly, whites insisted on a physical separation from African New Yorkers in public, at first merely in fact, but later in rules and regulations; the earliest attempts at what was called Jim Crow segregation, named after the theatrical blackface figure made famous by T. D. (Daddy) Rice in the 1830s, are to be found in the North rather than below the Mason-Dixon line. The new insistence on keeping blacks at a distance had its teething problems: the results, to our eyes anyway, were often absurd. The Lafayette Guards, so named after the regiment had been assigned to escort the Marquis on his triumphal visit to New York in 1824, had a band made up entirely of African Americans. In the fall of 1835, at a grand parade of several regiments on Twenty-First Street, what the *New York Herald*'s James Gordon Bennett termed a "*fracas*" occurred. On the order to "strike up" nary "a drum was heard, and the trombones and fifes of the different bands refused their office." Taken aback, officers hastily sought the reason, only to discover that the problem was the presence of African American musicians at the parade. The other bands "would not disgrace themselves by playing in such company." Embarrassed and furious officers "remonstrated, entreated and threatened," but to no avail. Only after the humiliated black band was marched off the parade ground would the other musicians deign to take up their instruments. Bennett learned "that it is the determination of the white bands to carry on unceasing and uncompromising warfare with the black sons of harmony, and that they will never play when they are present." For the editor, sympathetic to the white musicians' cause, the lesson was clear enough: "Put down this as another instance of the effects of the Abolition movement."[7]

New York blacks bore the brunt of an increasingly virulent racism, the vituperativeness of which simply amazed many travelers. In 1829, a visitor from Montreal remarked that in New York all blacks "indiscriminately are looked upon with aversion by the white population." African Americans may have been free, but neither the legislature nor anyone else knew "how to talk or to act towards them." If "these 'Niggers' are on board a steam boat they dine together after the other passengers." If they attend church "they are crammed into some corner like a proscribed body." They were unable to join the army because whites did "not choose to stand shoulder to shoulder with a 'Nigger.'" In 1817, the English traveler Henry Fearon could scarcely conceal his bewilderment at the fact that a black hairdresser who wished to retain his white clientele could also not service a perfectly respectable-looking black man. A few years later, J. S. Buckingham, another traveler, commented that, whereas in the South slaves would shake the hand of whites when they met, "at the North I do not remember to have witnessed this once." Not in "Boston, New York, or Philadelphia would white persons generally like to be seen shaking hands and talking familiarly with blacks in the streets."[8]

Ironically, exclusion gave added impetus to the development of separate black institutions, but, in a cruel twist, their very success attracted harassment from surly and resentful whites. Any organized black activity received a churlish response. Black churches bore the brunt of these attacks. White children and young men repeatedly threw stones at black churches, trying to annoy worshippers inside, and hung around their doors on Sundays attempting to provoke scuffles. Some, usually under the influence of liquor, inveigled themselves into churches only to disrupt services by "stamping, clapping and swearing aloud." One frigid February morning in 1842, John J. Manus knocked on the door of the African Church at the corner of Leonard and Church streets and warned the occupants of a fire. He then inserted a hose from a hydrant into the church and "completely deluged the congregation with water, covering the floor, wetting all in its range, and compelling them to mount on the pews to avoid the watery charge."[9] Undoubtedly, these hooligans thought that such "pranks" or spoofing blacks worshipping, as they often thought they were doing, were hilarious—African Americans demurred stoically.

Travelers were frequently baffled by the unbending barriers whites erected to fend off blacks—seemingly, New Yorkers paid no attention to class, respectability or any other factor when it came to distancing themselves from African Americans. Regardless of how much property Jeremiah Hamilton owned, in public he was just another black man and not supposed to associate with white men, let alone white women. An English traveler, ruminating on what he found a strange practice, related the story of the son of a Haitian general who visited New York in the early 1830s. This man, an educated mulatto, had "high anticipations of the pleasure that awaited him in a city so opulent and enlightened." On landing he directed his baggage to be taken to the best hotel but "was rudely refused admittance." Indeed, after numerous humiliating rebuffs, he could secure a bed only "in a miserable lodging-house kept by a Negro woman." Locals scorned the young Haitian as "a degraded being, with whom the meanest white man would hold it disgraceful to associate." That evening, dressed to the nines, for he was something of a dandy, he attended the theater but, trying to buy a ticket, had his money "tossed back to him, with a disdainful intimation, that the place for persons of his colour was the upper gallery." This was the last straw—the young man "returned to his native island by the first conveyance, to visit the United States no more." As the Englishman commented, he "should have gone to Europe." If a young Haitian with money in his pocket visited England, there was no hotel "from Land's End to John O'Groat's house, where he will not meet a very cordial reception." Indeed, "churches, theatres, operas, concerts, coaches, chariots, cabs, vans, waggons, steam-boats, railway carriages and air balloons, will all be open to him as the daylight." As long as he carried "golden ballast about with him, all will go well." Mind you, as soon as he ran out of money, "God help him."[10] English racial equality had its limitations too.

Occasionally, northern newspapers agreed with foreign opinion and editorialized about the idiocy of the situation. In January 1843, a writer in the *New York Daily Express* admitted that northerners had "the most absurd prejudices about color," views that were "difficult to account for." Not only were "people of color driven into the dark corners of our churches," he continued, "but they are excluded, even when reputable, and genteel . . . from the public tables of our hotels and steamboats." Indeed, the whole white world was guilty of "crying out in holy horror of a black man, as if a black man were a veritable demon!"[11]

More commonly, though, white New Yorkers, far from being embarrassed by their backwardness, reveled in telling stories about uppity African Americans falling foul of an increasingly rigid racial etiquette. In early September 1846, a respectable-looking black man "walked into the Court of Common Pleas, and stood gazing around the room." An attendant scurried over, ordered "the African to take a seat, and at the same time pointed him to the seats appropriated for persons of color." The black man objected and "refused to take a seat among 'common niggers.'" Informed that he had no choice and that if he did not comply with the rules he would be ejected, the black man stalked out of the courtroom "meditating upon revenge." The decidedly unsympathetic *New York Courier* reporter had not the slightest intention of questioning segregation. When the *New York Morning Express* reprinted the piece, the editor was of the same mind, captioning the item "IMPUDENCE."[12]

A typically forthright James Gordon Bennett of the *New York Herald* made no apology for his belief in the rightness of separating blacks from whites. In the summer of 1843, an American booked passage from Liverpool to New York on the steamer *Great Western*. When he arrived at the dock, he discovered that the Reverend James W. C. Pennington, an escaped Maryland slave and now a prominent abolitionist, was, as Bennett put it, "his *compagnon du voyage!*" The use of both French and an exclamation mark underscored how ridiculous it was to expect a white man to share sleeping quarters with a black man. On complaining to the agent, the unhappy white man was informed, with "characteristic *nonchalance*," that nothing could be done and he "advise[d] him to keep clear of Africa in future." For the voyage's duration, the disgruntled American, refusing to sleep in the same cabin as the black preacher, had to make do on the less-than-comfortable sofa in their sitting room. Hearing of this, an outraged Bennett damned the Liverpool agent's action as "indefensible." American prejudice may have been brushed aside as absurd in Europe, but that was never enough to mute the powerful editor's views. He thundered ominously that such behavior "will not be tolerated here." As well, the editor consistently publicized any laxness in New Yorkers' enforcement of segregation. A few years earlier, in February 1839, he had editorialized about slipshod seating

arrangements in a courtroom where the presiding officer was an abolitionist. He acknowledged reasonably that this man had a right to
be an abolitionist if he so desired, "but he has not right to introduce
amalgamating practices in his court, by allowing negroes to sit side
by side with respectable white people." This practice, he made very
clear, "must be remedied."[13]

As the city grew and the public transport system took on increasing importance, the indignities of segregation became more irritatingly obvious, particularly to respectable and successful African
New Yorkers, such as Jeremiah G. Hamilton, whose exclusion from
almost everything so puzzled visitors. New York's population, some
200,000 in 1830, increased to over 300,000 by 1840 and exploded
to half a million people by the middle of the century.[14] The expanding
cityscape filled in block after block of Manhattan's famous grid—
New York was now anything but a walking city, no longer a place
where anyone could get around easily on foot. In 1832, the New
York and Harlem Rail Road began constructing a line from City
Hall to Harlem, mostly along Fourth Avenue, but it took five years
to complete. Finally, in 1838, a New Yorker could travel almost the
length of Manhattan Island for a quarter, although city regulations
required that south of Twenty-Seventh Street, horses and not engines
pull the rail cars along the tracks. Even with the inconvenience of
having to break longer journeys to hitch and unhitch horses, the new
line was an enormous success. According to the railroad company's
figures, in the month of August 1840, it carried a staggering 138,032
passengers. This number was spectacular enough for the *New York
Daily Express* to wax grandiloquent, asking: "Is there any rail road
in any part of the World known to have received fare from this number of persons in a single month?" In the 1840s and 1850s other
railroad companies would try to elbow in on this lucrative business.
Still, in the 1830s and into the 1840s, New York remained, as one
newspaper announced, "the City of Omnibuses." In 1837, there were
108 of these horse-drawn vehicles servicing the transport needs of
New Yorkers—or, more precisely, the needs of white New Yorkers.[15]

A regular procession of humiliations visited on African New
Yorkers trying to travel on public transport revealed both white an-
tipathy and extensive belief in a carefully circumscribed idea of the

meaning of black freedom. Early in the summer of 1837, a black man on Broadway hailed a passing omnibus. According to the *New York Times* writer, when the driver realized "the color of his new passenger, [he] jumped up, in great fury, and flourished his whip high in the air, threatening the negro with a sound flogging." Although the determined African American did his best to board the vehicle, a flick of the whip close to his ear convinced him otherwise, and he retreated, muttering something about a lawsuit. The *Times* man found it all rather droll. "Coachee shook his whip in defiance—the negro shook his head, and the bystanders shook their sides with laughter." Almost everything about this incident and its reporting appalled the editor of the *Colored American:* if it would not be "casting pearls before swine, we would rebuke, severely, the whole posse of the above, the editor, the driver and the merrymaking bystanders." The black newspaperman added: "We hope the insulted colored man will seek legal redress."[16]

Although New York blacks bitterly resented Jim Crow, no one followed the *Colored American*'s editor's advice and turned to the courts at every provocation. Indeed, some care appears to have been taken in choosing when and where to make a stand. Whether this was by plan or simply happenstance is not clear. What is striking, though, is that African New Yorkers, in their challenge to segregation, ended up being as shrewd, if not as successful, as, more than a century later, the civil rights movement would be in focusing on Rosa Parks. As with the Montgomery buses, several incidents in New York caused barely a ripple. In November 1840, a black woman "applied for a passage from Harlem to this city in the rail road train and was refused." She then tried various stages running on the same route, but all of them turned her away. In the end, "she was compelled to walk the whole distance." A FRIEND OF HUMANITY, careful to emphasize that he was no "Abolition fanatic," still considered such treatment "an instance of flagrant injustice" deserving of "public censure." Not only was she "to all outward appearance as decent a female as any, of whatever color, in our city," but she was also "the wife of a respectable *citizen*, who is the possessor of real and personal estate." Yet, other than publication of A FRIEND OF HUMANITY's letter in the sympathetic *Journal of Commerce*, no one took any notice. About the same time, a well-dressed black man, an elder in the Presbyterian Church, and his equally respectable wife were "turned out," peaceably, of one of the cars on the Harlem Railroad. This incident attracted even less attention.[17]

And then, on the second to last day of 1840, the perfect litigant presented himself. The oyster restaurateur, Thomas Downing, only months shy of turning fifty, had been uptown on some business for St. Philip's, the Episcopal church where many of the city's finest black families worshipped.[18] Downing boarded the New York and Harlem Railroad's city-bound car No. 7 near Fourteenth Street and took an inside seat at the opposite end of the carriage to two white women. As everyone knew, this was forbidden—under no circumstances were colored passengers allowed inside the carriages. African Americans either had to ride on top of the car or, if downstairs, stay outside on the platform. Agent William Skirving ordered Downing out, yelling: "No nigger should be in the car." Downing identified himself to the official and told him that he was in a hurry to get back downtown—seldom winning tactics in such a situation. By this time the driver and a couple of others had joined them, and they told Downing "they did not care who he was, that he must get out." He refused and, again more than a century ahead of his time, the black man wedged himself in, bracing against the seat: with considerable difficulty, the officials loosened his hold, then beat him up badly and tossed him off the car. A shopkeeper on the corner of Thirteenth Street and the Bowery clearly heard a vengeful Downing yell back at his assaulters that "he would make them pay for it."[19]

Although the New York and Harlem Railroad employees may have had no idea of who Downing was, other New Yorkers only had to glance at a newspaper over the following day or two to be better informed. Under the caption "OUTRAGE IN A CAR" the *New York Daily Express* labeled him "a highly respectable colored man"; the *Commercial Advertiser* identified him as the "proprietor of the celebrated oyster house." For the *Journal of Commerce,* he was "an intelligent, respectable citizen, possessing considerable property and universally esteemed by those who have been accustomed to visit his refectory." This editor also reminded readers that Downing was the hero of the Great Fire whose efforts had saved at least a million dollars' worth of property from destruction, including the *Journal*'s own building. "But," as he added scathingly, "Downing is a *colored man*, and therefore may be kicked out of a Rail Road car and wantonly beaten at pleasure." Perhaps most revealing of all was Bennett's reaction, caught between his fondness for Downing—whose money probably had saved the *New York Herald* from folding—and his support for segregation. The day after the incident, he ran a puff piece proclaiming that the black man's establishment in Broad Street was "one of the most remarkable places in New York. Downing himself is a remarkable man—and Mrs Downing the most remarkable of all."[20] And then there was silence—the *Herald* simply ignored the story. Not only was Thomas Downing precisely the sort of successful African American who had haunted travelers' commentary about race relations in the North, he was also so respectable that such a violent assault on him began to prize open tiny cracks in segregation's gleaming new edifice.

The remarkable furor over Downing's bashing was one more sign of the way in which the penny press had changed the city's public life. Unlike the *Herald,* the New York and Harlem Railroad Company, a listed company whose shares were traded on Wall Street, could ignore neither the story nor public clamor. A couple of days later, a lengthy affidavit from Lucius Delliber, the driver of car No. 7, was released, ostensibly by Delliber himself, to the *New York Daily Express.* He claimed it was "an unvarnished statement" of events; more likely the lawyers had glossed his testimony with several coats of shellac. In Delliber's recollection, far from barking out, "No nigger should be in the car," his fellow employee had "informed the said Downing that it was the order of the company (meaning the Harlem Railroad company) to permit no colored person, on any occasion, to ride inside of the car, and that he must go out of said car." The driver himself had only joined in the struggle on the back platform of the car "as he imagined in performance of his duty, and without any passion, aided, and with no more force than was necessary to put the said Downing" off the vehicle. Summing up, he "thought the said agent acted with much forbearance, and the said Downing with much determined obstinacy after being made acquainted with the orders of said Company at the time deponent heard agent repeat them as aforesaid."[21]

Downing's stature and connections altered substantially the way events panned out. Thanks to his involvement, this was never an incident that would just go away as so many had before. Within hours of the assault Downing had preferred charges against both Delliber and Skirving, warrants had been issued, and the pair had been arrested and each held for $200 bail. After the beating Downing had gone to the depot in order to identify his assailants. An almost-obsequious Samuel R. Brooks, president of the New York and Harlem Railroad Company, came over and demanded of his own employees "how they came to beat Mr Downing in so outrageous manner." Unsatisfied with their answers, Brooks fired both the agent and the driver. As came out at the trial, Brooks "had known Mr Downing several years" and considered the black restaurateur "a civil, peaceable man." When the railroad officials had roughed up Downing, they had also destroyed his hat. On learning this, Brooks immediately told Downing "to get another and he would pay for it."[22] This was an unusual moment in the history of race relations in New York.

Much of the trial, which took place in the second week of February 1841, less than six weeks after the assault had occurred, concerned the operation of segregation on the railroad. On the one hand, there had been "a standing order since 1834 against permitting colored persons inside of the cars." In his testimony, the president of the railroad was keen to emphasize that this regulation was not the result of malice but had been adopted "from a regard to the tone of public feeling and the interests of the stockholders." And, of course, it was such sentiment that Downing himself paid attention to when he refused African Americans entry to his own Broad Street oyster house—a telling point the defense lawyer relished making. Public opinion supported the separation of the races, and at least one railroad agent had been discharged for not enforcing the rule. On the other hand, almost everyone acknowledged it was an everyday occurrence to see "colored people riding in the cars." Downing himself testified that he had often done so and certainly no one had objected to his taking a seat inside earlier that morning when he had ridden uptown. Clearly, enforcement was, at best, sporadic—the railroad's president admitted offhandedly "that 40 or 50 ladies had complained of colored people riding inside and no notice had been taken of it," and, it turned out, for the previous two years the company had no longer bothered to display any notice of the company's African American policy.

Legally, the railroad was entitled to exclude whomever they wanted from their conveyance provided the regulation was made public and well known. Even though there had been laxness in posting signs, Downing knew he was ignoring the rules. The result of the case would hinge on the reasonableness of the violence—if indeed there had been any—used to remove Downing. Put on the witness stand, the New York and Harlem Railroad management squirmed. Although the superintendent of the railroad cars claimed "no violence was ever allowed to be used," he also had to admit that "there were no directions as to the manner in which colored people should be ejected from cars." Most revealing, though, was Brooks's reaction to the enforcement of his own company's policy. The railroad president may well have supported segregation in principle, but the details of this case made him very uncomfortable. He recoiled from the violence his former employees had meted out to his black acquaintance. But popular sentiment was nowhere near as squeamish—whatever force was needed to put uppity Negroes back in their place was justified. The agent, Skirving, untroubled by what had occurred, informed the court: "He would not allow colored people to ride in the cars: he would do to-morrow as he had done that day, if it should cost him his life." To this white working-class man, Downing's respectability made not a whit of difference—he was still simply a black man, not entitled to the respect accorded a white man. Delliber, the driver, agreed. And so too did the jury. At the end of the judge's directions to the twelve white men they retired for barely a couple of minutes. On their return, the foreman announced "Not Guilty" to the crowded room, and spectators "broke out into a tumultuous applause, which the Court found difficulty in restraining."[23]

An optimist might have seen the seeds of a later shift in public opinion in some newspaper editors' and railroad management's pained reaction to Downing's treatment. In the meantime the courtroom cheers of the spectators held sway in New York. African Americans would continue to be discriminated against on public transport and, if they ignored the rules, face the possibility of vicious attacks that were now sanctioned by the courts. Furthermore, whenever the give and take of everyday life did begin to loosen things up, there was always the vigilant James Gordon Bennett to remind everyone of proper standards of racial etiquette. In September 1845, he complained in the *Herald* that "in the Harlem cars ladies are often subjected to the necessity of being seated by the side of monstrous specimens of the negro race." This, he knew, "must be particularly annoying to ladies" and "not in a practical point of view particularly pleasant." He admonished the railroad, whose "stock sells at a good price in the market," to fix up its shabby, dirty cars and, in words all understood, "to have everything of an offensive nature excluded."[24]

On a Thursday evening in June 1847, it was pouring with rain. A well-dressed, if wet, African American hailed the Broadway omnibus near Eighth Street, boarded and sat down near the door. Politely, he expressed the hope that, because of the horrible weather, he might be allowed to stay inside. Immediately, two young white men, "by no means so decent in their appearance as the new comer," jumped off the car without paying—they were not going to "ride with darkies." The black man offered to reimburse the driver for the lost revenue, indeed to pay the fare "of any other person who might leave on his account." One passenger spoke up for the bedraggled interloper. It made no difference—the driver peremptorily ordered the black man back out into the rain. In contrast to the standard practice of Bennett at the *Herald*, Horace Greeley, editor of the *New York Tribune*, did not run the story to revel in the discomfiture of this black man. Indeed, just the opposite. He wanted "to hold up to notice and to the increasing contempt of the reflecting, the absurd prejudice against color." Greeley remained adamant "that the prejudice is decreasing: the time will come when good sense will dictate a more intelligent as well as more humane course of conduct."[25] To which impatient African New Yorkers could only ask: "When were the 'reflecting' going to start doing something?"

Jeremiah Hamilton lived an absurd existence. In business, he was a Master of the Universe, but the moment he stepped out of his office he was, by the lights of most New Yorkers, an inferior being. All those English travelers visiting the city who were so perplexed by the shabby treatment of respectable black men could have been writing specifically about Hamilton. And there was the continual threat that shabbiness would slip into angry confrontation and then violence. Even walking from work at 137 Front Street to home at 68 Greenwich Street involved an element of risk.[26] If anything, success, discernible in everything from his manner to the cut of his jib, made him more of a target. Only one thing could have made life on New York streets more dangerous for Jeremiah Hamilton—to marry a white girl.

It is uncertain how Jeremiah Hamilton and Eliza Jane Morris met or when their relationship started. She was born into a Philadel-phia family in October 1822. By the mid-1830s, Eliza Jane Morris was living in New York with her widowed mother, Margaret Morris, who ran a boardinghouse. In 1837, Hamilton, who had been born on May 27, 1807, was twice as old as the fifteen-year-old Eliza Jane. There is also doubt as to when Miranda, their first child, was born. According to the 1850 federal census schedule, their eldest daughter was thirteen years old that year, which would make her date of birth 1837 or 1838. The state census-taker in 1855 recorded Miranda's age as seventeen, making her born in 1838 or 1839. Unfortunately, details often are not consistent from one census to another. In the 1870 census Miranda owned to an age of twenty-nine, making her born in 1841; and in 1880 she told the census-taker she was thirty-seven, making her born in 1843. As a rule of thumb in such circum-stances, my preference is to give the most credence to the earliest census entry, the one closest to her birth. In my view Miranda was born in 1837 or maybe 1838—if that is correct, Eliza Jane Morris was fourteen or fifteen years old when she became pregnant.[27]

To be sure, in antebellum America it was not that unusual for women to get married at a young age to rather older men. Even so, for Jeremiah Hamilton, a black man, to father a child with a white girl barely half of his age must have caused tongues to wag. Not that we know from any of the surviving sources. The only reference in these early years to any partner of Jeremiah Hamilton that I have found is in a savage attack published in the *New York Herald* on

July 14, 1836, lacerating the black broker for ruining several white merchants in the aftermath of the Great Fire. According to Bennett, after Hamilton had finished for the day in Wall Street he rode out to his "snug little box near Bloomingdale to be charmed by the smiles of an Houri, whom he has ensconced—not a black one, that would not do, but as fair and as frail a woman as ever trod apart from the right path. There are his evening's passed."[28] "Houri" is a term of Arabic origins and refers to a beautiful, voluptuous young woman. The word "ensconced" means established or set up, although it hints at an element of secrecy as well. Possibly Bennett was referring to another woman and not to Eliza Jane Morris. But if he was speaking of Morris, he was describing the situation in 1835, and for most of that year the young girl was only twelve years old.

To us, at this distance, Eliza Jane Hamilton tantalizes—she remains a will-o'-the-wisp, present for the next four decades of Hamilton's life although always just out of our reach. Surviving sources tell us almost nothing. The temptation to conjecture is irresistible. Time and again I have been puzzled by the fact that the name of the brig Hamilton chartered for the counterfeiting expedition in 1828 was the *Ann Eliza Jane*. It must be coincidence—after all, back then Eliza Jane Morris was five years old and still living in Philadelphia. What possible link could there be? But I bridle at the idea of coincidence, am unable to accept there is not at least a faint connection. Perhaps when they were introduced, Hamilton had attracted her attention with tales of his counterfeiting and derring-do in a vessel with a strikingly similar name to hers, seducing her with his worldliness and wealth. What could be more exciting for a barely pubescent girl? Who now can know?

What can be known with certainty is that, in the volatile mix that was antebellum New York, amalgamated couples, to use the then-current expression, had a difficult time of it. The word "miscegenation," with its overtones of science and racial inferiority, would not be coined until 1863. Its predecessor "amalgamation" was a broader term, meaning the promiscuous blending of cultures, and could apply to anything from dancing to a gang of con men that included whites as well as African Americans. But in the 1830s the word increasingly was used to refer to interracial sexual relationships.

Interracial sex was hardly unusual in antebellum New York. The practice was associated most obviously with the Five Points, rapidly becoming a byword for urban poverty and squalor. Black and white prostitutes plied their trade, indifferent to the color of their clientele's skin. The area was notorious for its dance cellars, venues that hosted an underground dance culture that was both amalgamated and almost as lively in reality as it was in the febrile imaginings of those who never set foot near the place. Late one evening in March 1842, Charles Dickens slipped the tedium of his official engagements and visited Pete Williams's dance cellar in the Points. A *Herald* journalist reported: "Most of the places they entered were the resort of blacks and whites, mulattoes and mustees, mixed together like whortleberries and cream."[29] Dickens's Place, as Williams's establishment was known from then on, became notorious: prototypical slummers, often accompanied by an officer of some sort, as Dickens himself had been, visited to experience it for themselves. Even white southerners, hardly deprived of the opportunity to witness African American culture back home, thought this one of the things to do while in town on business.[30] Such genteel voyeuristic interest may have been new, but, to a greater or lesser extent, what these visitors observed—racial mixing among ordinary men and women—had occurred in the port city since the days of the Dutch.

What was novel in the 1830s and 1840s was the idea of a respectable white woman—or perhaps, more accurately, a formerly respectable white woman—consorting with a black man. For many white New Yorkers such an unnatural coupling encapsulated the inevitable and terrible consequence of freeing the slaves. With the advent of the abolitionists in the 1830s and their radical demand for an immediate, not gradual, end to slavery, the threat loomed large. "Amalgamationist" became a term of abuse hurled at abolitionists at every opportunity. Any instance of an interracial relationship—and commonly such liaisons were uncovered in the Police Office or courts—was seized on by the newspapers. The image of a lady in the arms of a black man gnawed at white imaginations—and I use "image" advisedly. To a quite remarkable extent, the artist Edward Clay, with his widely disseminated caricatures, sliced open the flesh to expose the raw nerve of this issue for so many white men and women.

In particular, his Amalgamation series of 1839, including *Practical Amalgamation (Musical Soiree), An Amalgamation Waltz, Practical Amalgamation (The Wedding)* and *The Fruits of Amalgamation,* depicted grossly caricatured black men usurping the role of white men in polite society. Editors employed "Practical Amalgamation" as shorthand to caption stories their reporters had trawled in the courts and police offices.

In the 1830s, the best-known—perhaps by this time "notorious" is a better word—black man in New York to have a white wife was the actor James Hewlett. And he had more than one. Although Hewlett had been the mainstay of the black theater troupe playing at the African Grove theater in the early 1820s and then for years had performed his own one-man show, the blackface acts of George Washington Dixon and T. D. Rice in the 1830s put him out of business. He was no longer in vogue; theater-going New Yorkers eschewed a black man imitating famous actors in favor of watching white men, faces daubed with burnt cork, imitating blacks as they turned about and jumped Jim Crow. Undoubtedly, the irony of it all was lost on the black performer.[31]

In 1836, Hewlett, by then at least in his mid-forties, set up house with an attractive twenty-one-year-old white girl from Staten Island—they may not have married, but she took the name Hewlett. When Elizabeth Hewlett was convicted of theft in 1837, most of the opprobrium for the relationship she was in fell on the young woman's shoulders. Not that her link to the actor was of particular relevance to the charge at hand, but the Recorder, a municipal officer of New York City, sentencing her to one month of hard labor, felt impelled to remark "with much severity on her disgraceful and unnatural connection with a man of color." Well aware that the court reporters were scribbling down everything he said, the Recorder added, for good measure, "that nothing but a grossly depraved mind could induce a white woman to cohabit with one of the negro race."[32]

Although Hewlett in his glory days had been a talented and popular performer, the last New York years of his life were tawdry, a soap opera acted out in the city's courts. But then, until very recently, stories of black artists in New York seldom had happy endings. Unable to get work on the stage, Hewlett turned to petty crime and was in and out of the penitentiary, grist for the mills of newspaper editors. Even on his way down, the thwarted tragedian enlivened court proceedings by quoting, among other texts, *The Merchant of Venice* and *Henry IV, Part I,* amusing even the judge and delighting the reporters who were present. The black actor always made good copy.[33] In June 1839, his personal life made the papers yet again. For this story, the *New York Herald* used the caption "A Practical Amalgamationist" and the *Morning Courier and New-York Enquirer* "Practical Amalgamation," while the *Journal of Commerce* went with "An Amalgamationist in Trouble," and the *New York Sun* was unable to resist "Othello and Desdemona." During his last stint digging rocks on Blackwell's Island, Hewlett had met Ann S. Haskins. She was English, "very pretty," about twenty-eight, and in the penitentiary for some minor offense committed while intoxicated. As the *Journal of Commerce*'s reporter cynically put it, as soon as Hewlett discovered "she had an annuity of $170 per annum, he fell desperately in love with her and persuaded her to marry him." Apparently Elizabeth Hewlett was no longer around, for, on their release, Hewlett promptly married Haskins. Jacob Matthews, a colored minister, officiated at the ceremony. Hewlett's new wife was fond of a drink and, one night in June 1839, became "uproariously drunk, and riotous and disorderly," ending her evening languishing in a cell.[34] Trying to secure her release, Hewlett went before Justice Taylor, who was more interested in questioning the actor closely about "how he came to marry a white woman." Hewlett's answer, rendered here in the *Morning Courier* reporter's strange attempt at black dialect, was a masterpiece in reversal: "Whoy, yer worship, I thought she was as good as I was, and so why not." The sharp jab was probably wasted on this particular judicial mind. At any rate, Ann Hewlett's income prevented the judge from convicting her of the usual charge of vagrancy, and she was set free "to the great joy of her sable companion."[35]

To an extent, the press and the courts played James Hewlett's familiar and increasingly buffoonish figure for laughs. Yet the jokes only barely masked a very intrusive questioning of his sexual relationships and a complete bewilderment at what could induce respectable white women to want to marry the black actor. Other African

Americans with white wives were seen to be rather more threatening than Hewlett. Certainly, as was demonstrated regularly, violence was never far from the surface.

For African New Yorkers in the 1830s and 1840s, summer was camp meeting time. In the first week of August, the city streets emptied of black faces as thousands of African American men and women headed, often for several days, to meeting grounds at Flushing on Long Island, Yonkers, a site near Sing Sing up the Hudson River, and a number of places in New Jersey. Much more than just religious gatherings, these were also social and cultural events of enormous significance in African American life. On the evening of Sunday, August 11, 1839, a number of black men and women returning from a camp meeting at Monmouth, New Jersey, were running late, forcing Oliver Vanderbilt, captain of the steamboat *Wave,* to delay his departure for Manhattan. Made to wait, the on-time passengers were unimpressed. Several became irascible when they noticed that one of the latecomers, Caleb Alexander, "a grey headed negro," had not just a white wife, but a very young white wife. As the *Wave*'s deckhands cast off, "some rowdies on board, envying the old man the smiles of a fair young creature of some 17 years old, who was leaning on his arm," started playing what the *Daily Express*'s court reporter termed "tricks" on the African American. These included "pouring cold water upon him, smacking his face and other little disagreeable attentions." They tormented Alexander for the duration of the trip and then, after the steamer had docked, knocked him to the deck and committed "a most violent outrage upon the old man"—details of the outrage were never printed in the press, but apparently the marks were still evident at the trial eleven months later.

Eight or nine young white men committed the assault on Alexander, although two "particularly distinguished themselves" in directing proceedings. But as soon as the *Wave* was tied up, all scattered into the maw of the city, and the authorities were unable to locate any of them. Probably they did not look too hard. Stymied by the disappearance of his assailants, Alexander resorted to a creative charge of assault and battery against the captain, Oliver Vanderbilt, a cousin of the much-better-known Cornelius Vanderbilt. The grounds were not that Vanderbilt had participated in the violence, but, first, that by surreptitious winks and similar signs to the thugs he had facilitated their hooliganism, and second, that, as the *Wave*'s owner, it had been his duty to have stopped rather than encouraged the violence.

One of the striking features of black life in New York, and elsewhere, throughout this period was a remarkable faith in the efficacy of the legal system. Perhaps there was no other forum in which to seek justice. Regardless, this case offered a crystal-clear illustration of how and why that faith was so often misplaced. At every turn, the prosecution ran into a brick wall of discrimination. Race was not just an undercurrent of this trial but manifestly throughout proceedings the key issue. The prosecution hammered away about racial prejudice to such an extent that the judge opened his charge to the jury by observing: "The plaintiff being a colored man, or having a white wife should make no difference." Simply by uttering this, of course, the judge conceded the prosecution's claims.

The crucial moment of the trial occurred when two of the black passengers testified that they had observed Vanderbilt standing by as the assailants slapped Alexander around; they also told the court of the broad winks of support the captain had given to the young toughs. Unfortunately for the prosecution, though, one of these African Americans had "exhibited strong feelings when giving his testimony," enough of a show of emotion for the *Journal of Commerce* court reporter to conclude that the witness had not "convince[d] the auditors of the truth of his statement." Apparently a black witness not only had to be courageous enough to take the stand in open court and testify against a white man, but also had to give his evidence in a calm, modulated voice—or be disbelieved. Not that it mattered in this case. By the time the white pilot and a couple of white passengers had sworn that Vanderbilt "did all he could to suppress the rioters," the result of the suit was a foregone conclusion. Probably it had been futile from the start, but once respectable white men had contradicted the African American testimony there was never a chance of the jury convicting Vanderbilt.

Perhaps the most revealing feature of the trial was the various comments made by the supposedly impartial judge. Caleb

Alexander's lawyer had emphasized white prejudice to such an extent that, in his address to the jury, the judge felt obliged to meet this issue—head on. "Counsel for the plaintiff has spoke of an improper feeling existing in the minds of white men against the colored race," he elaborated. The judge was even prepared to acknowledge that "to a certain extent such a feeling does exist." What followed in his directions to the jury was more surprising. "If an improper feeling exists among one part of the community," he continued, "an equal if more improper and irrational feeling exists towards them in another part of the community." From this dubious proposition, and in a breathtakingly confused piece of thinking, he managed to conclude: "There is therefore a fanaticism on both sides, and perhaps the fanaticism in their favor is stronger than that against them." The scales in New York, apparently, now had tilted in favor of African Americans.

The jury certainly knew how to take a hint. More likely than not, guidance from the judge was unnecessary anyway. They dismissed the case out of hand without bothering to leave their seats in the courtroom in order to confer. That was rubbing salt in a raw wound. Not even the segregated South at its zenith would come up with such a contemptuous public gesture of dismissal. An elderly black man being beaten up on a boat for having married a seventeen-year-old white woman may have been someone's problem, but it definitely was not the responsibility of Captain Vanderbilt of the *Wave*.[36]

Neither Jeremiah Hamilton nor Eliza Jane Hamilton would have to spend long reading the New York press before they came across dire warnings of what could very easily happen to them if they walked arm in arm down the street. The newspapers are full of accounts of confrontations, usually signaled by the provocative caption "AMALGAMATION." On August 3, 1838, the *Journal of Commerce* reported that two days previously there had been "quite a rumpus" in the upper reaches of Broadway. It had been caused "by the promenading of a colored man and a white lady, arm in arm," along the city's major thoroughfare. Young boys set up the cry: "'White woman and nigger!' 'White woman and nigger!!' 'White woman and nigger!!!'" with the escalating number of exclamation marks signaling the gathering feeding frenzy. Bystanders raced over and began following the pair, but "the procession soon became quite too long and noisy for the comfort of the promenaders." The pair separated, with the white lady darting into a grocery store while the black man carried on walking down Broadway. He did not get very far before several men grabbed hold of him and dragged him back to the store, where a crowd was now gathered. Inside, the visibly agitated woman was telling anyone who would listen "that she was an English woman, and not aware of the state of public feeling here on the subject of color." She claimed "the negro with her was in the employ of her brother, and that she had taken him with her only as a protector." Luckily for the couple, two officers arrived on the scene and "took both man and woman to the watch-house for safe-keeping, until the embryo mob should be dispersed." Later on the reporter found out, secondhand from the captain of the watch, that the pair was in fact man and wife.[37] The practiced ease with which she came up with a plausible-enough explanation to make the hostile crowd hesitate suggests this was not the first time her choice of a husband had caused strife.

This incident occurred on August 1, the anniversary of the abolition of slavery in the British West Indies. Conceivably, the earlier procession and display of black solidarity may have already ruffled a few feathers among white New Yorkers, making them particularly sensitive to perceived slights to their beliefs. Everyone always seemed so touchy on any day blacks wanted to celebrate anything. The reality was, though, that many white New Yorkers considered a black man and a white woman walking together on any street at any time a provocation. A few months later, in the summer of 1839, and this time down at the other end of Broadway on the Battery, the southern tip of the island, "a huge negro" promenaded "with two well dressed white women, one on each arm." As the *Herald*'s editor snorted approvingly: "The mob got up an excitement, and the delicate females were obliged to cut and run."[38]

The 1830s and 1840s—years in which Jeremiah Hamilton made and lost his first fortune—saw African New Yorkers take advantage of their freedom to create a distinctively urban black culture. Not that there was much chance of catching Hamilton anywhere near a Five Points dance cellar or a black church, let alone a camp meeting.

But that mattered little. "Nigger Hamilton" was well known, and, inevitably, his everyday comings and goings in New York involved him in the ugly white reaction to African American freedom. The black broker's wealth, while he had it, made almost no difference; the fact that he had married Eliza Jane Hamilton, a young white woman, did not just exacerbate matters but introduced a real element of danger. The Prince of Darkness's very existence taunted many fellow New Yorkers—Jeremiah Hamilton was a racist's nightmare come to life.

SIX

REAL ESTATE

After the Great Fire of December 16 and 17, 1835, a cashed-up Jeremiah Hamilton cast about for investment opportunities. At this time he was still party to the rapidly disintegrating deal with Jonathan Leech and William B. Johnson to refurbish the *Sandusky* for sale in Cuba, and doubtless there were other broking opportunities of various sorts that also turned up in the normal run of his business, but in early 1836, Hamilton changed tack and plunged heavily into the real estate market. Unusually for him, in making this move, Hamilton merely followed the herd—and it turned out to be the worst business decision of his long career.

Talk of the enormous profits to be made buying and selling land was everywhere in the mid-1830s as a speculative real estate boom of epic proportions gripped the United States. Americans had been acquiring an average of 1.5 million acres of government land every year between 1828 and 1833, but in the twelve months ending in July 1835 they bought 4.7 million acres, with that figure soaring to 12.6 million acres in the ensuing year and the rate of purchase continuing to climb every month. Trying to envisage the size of this land grab is difficult: another way of looking at it is that in the twenty-four months between January 1835 and December 1836, settlers and speculators bought from the government some 50,000 square miles of land, or an area roughly the size of England. As one taken-aback correspondent from Ohio commented: "The mania for obtaining land . . . is astonishing." Although most of the real estate sold by the government was located in the South and the West, the East Coast, including New York City, was anything but immune from the contagion.[1] In the older, already-settled areas such as Manhattan Island the seemingly insatiable demand for land was met, at least partially, by the breaking up of some of the large family estates into town lots.

There was something reassuringly tangible about investing in land. As far as most Jacksonian Americans were concerned, real estate was safe, a secure form in which to leave money, ranking almost as highly as gold and silver and some distance above paper currency, stocks, securities and the like. Specie, so the thinking went, was an intrinsically valuable commodity, but a bank note or share certificate literally was only a piece of paper whose value depended on trust that it could be exchanged for specie or goods and services. There was a widespread chariness—and for very good reason—of any form of currency that was neither gold nor silver.

In order to comprehend economic behavior in the decades before the Civil War, it is important to realize that Americans every day had to negotiate their way through a bewildering snowstorm of paper that was either money or something masquerading as money. Although everyone came in contact with bank notes and they were essential to the functioning of the economy, sensible persons avoided scrutinizing too closely the monetary system's basis. And periodically, as in the panic of 1837, the entire edifice collapsed into chaos. By our lights, many of the advantages of paper currency—for example, certainty and reliability throughout the entire country—were simply absent. The most obvious difference from today was the sheer variety of notes in circulation. In 1859, *Hodges Genuine Bank Notes of America* detailed 9,916 different notes issued by some 1,365 banks, and that listing was hardly complete.[2] Moreover, the value of individual notes varied as well. Not only were bills discounted in everyday use, usually roughly according to distance from their place of issue, so that a Maine bank note was worth closer to its par value of, say, $1 in Portland than it would be in New York, but also, as everyone knew, banks failed regularly. Even if not bankrupt, on occasion these institutions suspended specie payments for their notes. Although disasters such as these rendered the paper money of those banks virtually worthless, the notes could not be instantly withdrawn, and they continued to be used, often unwittingly and sometimes fraudulently, for months and occasionally years. On top of this, as we saw earlier, forgeries were an enormous problem. Overall, in some way or other, as many as one in four bank notes in circulation were spurious.

Antebellum American bank notes, anything but standardized and interchangeable as they are today, were variegated, distinctive, even memorable. Individuals commonly could detail not just how much money they had in their pocketbook, but the denominations of the notes and which banks had issued them.[3] As a numismatic historian summed up: "There was no single, universal value for any given note, from any given bank."[4] It was a perversely unwieldy basis for the country's economic life, one that forced businessmen to learn to cope with the lack of certainty about the value of the medium they used for all their transactions. With good reason, the economist John Kenneth Galbraith pronounced antebellum America's monetary system as "without rival, the most confusing in the long history of commerce and associated cupidity."[5]

In sharp contrast to the quicksand of paper currency and securities, land ownership retained a lingering aura of solidity and respectability. Partly this was inherited from England, but it was also caused by the fact that land was an obviously palpable commodity. In the early decades of the nineteenth century, those who made money on the stock exchange were not considered to have come into proper wealth until their paper assets were converted into real property or land and buildings. Writing in the *Herald* in 1835, James Gordon Bennett, who understood Wall Street better than most, poked fun at such old-fashioned ideas that he for one did not subscribe to, with his sardonic throwaway line that "lots," or plots of city land, "are supposed to be the solid article after all—stocks—fancy stocks—are mere air bubbles" (fancy stocks were particularly speculative ones).[6] Regardless of what Bennett thought, the older ideas of where real value in society lay remained tenacious.

And yet, no matter how much anyone may have wanted to maintain English ideas about land as a marker of class status and military power, they had a limited relevance in the New World. There was simply too much land in the United States, and, relatively speaking, it was so much less expensive than on the other side of the Atlantic, for English practices such as primogeniture and entail to gain traction. In the first half-century of the new nation, judges and legislators had simplified American property law and shucked off much of its English past to the point at which, as one legal historian has put it, "land had become to a great extent, just another commodity to be bought and sold." The intention—to remove unnecessary impediments to the development of real estate and the nation—was realized: as the lawyer Henry Dwight Sedgwick remarked, "lands in this country are nearly as much the subject of traffic, as the public stocks."[7]

Sedgwick published this comment in 1824; within a decade no attentive onlooker could have been so timid as to qualify his or her observation with that "nearly." The boom in New York City real estate took away contemporaries' breath as the value of land in Manhattan, worth some $87.6 million in 1830, rose sharply to $143 million by 1835. Over the next year this figure soared to $233 million, a staggering 63 percent increase. All manner of New Yorkers were using their own money or mortgage-backed loans to speculate in land, some of them making huge profits.[8] In late April 1835, Philip Hone, former mayor of New York and indefatigable diarist, noted that "real estate is high beyond all the calculation of the most sanguine speculators," but, for all the typically measured caution of his outlook, even he had to acknowledge that "immense fortunes have been made and realized within the last three months."[9] Legions of his fellow citizens, less circumspect, caught the speculative fever, driving the market to dizzying heights.

The city's public prints of 1835 and 1836 overflowed with advertisements for land and puff pieces playing up the boom. Some newspapers became little more than shills for real estate interests, and often it is difficult to tell the difference between articles and advertisements. A piece in the *New York Daily Advertiser* in late August 1835 conveys something of the buoyant outlook of the times.

"Never within our recollection," the writer began breathlessly, "have the prospects for sales of Real Estate been more flattering than they are at present." Indeed, all the economic indicators were bullish: "The vast increase of our population extending our census beyond 270,000 (possibly to 330,000) with an actual scarcity of houses, the price of labor steady and encouraging to the industrious mechanic— produce of every kind abundant in supply and yet saleable at fair prices.—Money not scarce, nor likely to become so." In short, "our city [is] blessed with health almost unprecedented, and the whole aspect of affairs [is as] smiling and prosperous as the most sanguine can desire." The writer then directed readers to the *Advertiser*'s notices detailing the breaking up of the Arden estate and the imminent auction of lots on Eighth Avenue at Thirty-First, Thirty-Second and Thirty-Third streets.[10]

In the wake of the Great Fire and its devastating impact on the financial heart of the city, many anticipated that New York's real estate boom would fizzle out, but the opposite occurred. Three months later, in March 1836, Bennett commented in the *Herald*: "The extraordinary rise of real estate on this island and the vicinity has astonished everybody." After the conflagration, many businesses had to scramble for temporary premises, and Broad Street, near its intersection with Wall Street, became "the great emporium for sales of real estate." With increasing regularity the financial pages highlighted that "nothing remarkable took place in Wall street yesterday, but wonders were seen in Broad street." One day in early March, 600 Brooklyn town lots were sold for about $75,000; uptown Manhattan land also achieved high prices, realizing some $30,000; and a single block on downtown Pearl Street fetched $42,000. According to the *Herald*, "many of those capitalists who formerly dealt in stocks are withdrawing from that business, and turning their attention to lots and real estate." Three months later, in June 1836, the boom had only intensified. Bennett estimated that "a capital of $100,000,000 is at this moment employed in the United States in forcing up the price of real estate." In New York, "the stockbrokers have little to do now a days but stand in the streets with their hands in their empty pockets." Broad Street had muscled its way to the very center of the city's financial activity: "All the haste, life, society, impulse, activity, force, steam power, and devil, are now with the real estate operators."[11]

What did the real estate bubble of the 1830s mean for African Americans? If not quite an irrelevance, it was something that operated at a tangent to the lives of ordinary blacks. Most African Americans' earnings were barely enough to subsist on, and as land in and around New York became more expensive, seemingly at an exponential rate, the idea of owning property was reduced to a pipe dream for all but a very few. Cruelly, at the same time that the prospect for blacks of buying a house receded even further into the distance, their exercising of the right to vote was made conditional on meeting a stiff property requirement, one not asked of whites. When members of the New York State Constitutional Convention had met in Albany in 1821, they may have enshrined universal white male suffrage, but they had also insisted that free blacks—and, not coincidentally, their numbers were increasing as July 4, 1827, the date on which slavery would end in the state, approached—meet stringent conditions before they were enfranchised.[12] In order to vote, a black man had to own a $250 freehold over and above debts and to pay taxes on the property.

In New York City very few African Americans were property owners. Of 12,499 blacks in New York County in 1826, sixty were taxed on their real estate, but only sixteen were taxed and owned enough to qualify for the vote. In 1835, there were 152 blacks paying taxes, but only 68 owned in excess of $250 worth of property and were eligible to vote; and a decade later, 346 were taxed, but only 91 could vote.[13]

Although the New York State Constitutional Convention had insisted on property ownership for blacks as a sign of their independence, respectability, and whether or not individuals deserved to vote, the reality of life in antebellum New York was that most whites had some difficulty conceiving of black property owners. Indeed, for a substantial rump of white New Yorkers still yearning for the way things once were, the very idea of a free Negro remained an absurd anomaly.[14] Pandering to such views, newspaper editors delighted in publishing odd little articles about black property owners. According to a writer in the *Journal of Commerce* in 1847, "an old blind negro man" had been sitting on the sidewalk near the old Brick Church, on the northeast corner of Beekman and Nassau streets in the heart of the financial district, with a hat on his lap into which passersby dropped coins. Bizarrely, this apparent beggar had "a large landed estate for a colored man to possess in this country" and was "the patroon owner of the 'negro colony' at Flatbush L.I." The reporter questioned the blind African American about the ethics of what he was doing. "'I do not beg,' said the old man, 'I only sit down here to rest me.'" Unsatisfied with the answer, the *Journal*'s man wrote his story as a parable of the consequences of "careless giving." Already, parents drove small children out of doors on frigid nights in order to panhandle; if "the stream of charity to street beggars" was not stemmed New York would soon follow the example of "some countries" where the people blinded or otherwise maimed their young in order "to move the sympathy of passers by and get their money." All that "careless givers" to poor blacks on the city streets were achieving was "patronizing this cruelty."[15] At its core, this confused jeremiad on the perils of charity hinted at a deep-seated unease at what the world was becoming now that slavery had ended.

It was easy enough to dismiss the blind beggar as an oddity; perhaps more troubling was a black man such as Thomas Downing. In October 1859 the *Richmond Whig* published a letter from a New York correspondent that was then reprinted widely in other newspapers. "I oystered up a few days ago at the justly celebrated 'oyster establishment' of Thomas Downing, on Broad street," the correspondent began. Back in the day, in Downing's youth in Accomac County, Virginia, he had befriended a white boy named Henry A. Wise, now governor of Virginia and a fringe candidate for the presidency. Downing "believes in Wise, and he prays night and morning that he may have a chance to vote in this State for Wise's Presidential electors." Here the letter writer underscored that "Tom *can* vote, for he is worth over $100,000, and he says he should now be worth $200,000 had it not been for those infernal wretches, Abolitionists and Black Republicans." The correspondent then tried to reassure everyone: "It is a singular fact, that *nearly all the colored portion of our city population,* especially those who, like Downing, own property, *are intensely opposed to Abolitionism or Black*

Republicanism." The editor reprinting these comments queried anxiously: "Will the *Anglo-African* [a New York black newspaper] tell us, through its columns, how much truth there is in this statement?"[16]

He was right to be skeptical, for it was never that simple. Even in the letter from the New York correspondent there was a hint of Downing's cantankerous independence. More often than not the black oysterman proved a handful. Downing had informed his customer, the letter writer, that it was only the fact that the city of Charleston would "jug a free colored man when he comes there" that prevented him from leading one hundred colored men to the Democratic Convention and then banging on the door "until they stopped 'dat knocking at the door,' by nominating his Virginia friend."[17] For many white New Yorkers, independent property-owning blacks remained a disturbing inversion of the natural order.

Of course, neither the blind beggar nor Thomas Downing was typical. Most African New Yorkers who owned property were trying, rather more prosaically, to establish a home and often a business in the thriving city, thereby incidentally securing their right to vote. Nevertheless, in the mid-1830s at least, they could hardly avoid being aware of the way real estate prices were increasing. Interestingly, a very few New York blacks had the resources and the audacity to join in the speculative mania simply to speculate. All the talk in the newspapers, on the streets and in the taverns emphasized that buying and selling town lots was where the financial action was, and the members of this intrepid band of black pioneers—for although they have never been recognized as such, this is precisely what they were—wanted to make money at least as much as anyone else in New York. They were confronted with one large problem, though. As with every boom the world over, the expectation of continued easy and large profits drew in new investors who were inexperienced, often touchingly naïve, and ill prepared to lose their painstakingly accumulated savings. Manhattan's real estate market in the boom of 1835 and 1836, regulated by remarkably few restrictions of any sort, created the perfect environment for swindlers of every stripe. It was the Wild West. Con men and fraudsters swarmed all over the island, and seemingly every African American trying to invest in land found himself taken in by grifters of one sort or another.

William Thompson was one of these black pioneers, although no one will ever build a monument in his honor. He was an unsavory character (admittedly not necessarily a bar to memorialization). Contemporaries were often put off by his appearance, with court reporters variously describing him as "a huge black fellow," "a mammoth sized colored man," and "a negro of the dimensions of Sir John Falstaff."[18] In the early 1830s, Thompson owned a junk shop in Greene Street, but by the end of the decade, and probably a good deal earlier than that, he was making his money from prostitution. He ran at least two brothels, one in Broome Street and the other in Chambers Street. Even by the unprepossessing standards of New York whorehouses, Thompson's establishments did not have much of a reputation and were known to be places "where frequent robberies were committed." As with most in his line of business, the black brothel owner was familiar with the inside of the Police Office and New York courtrooms. In May 1839, Thompson would forfeit the bail he had put up for Eliza Adams, who had been charged with stealing a watch and $20 from a customer's pantaloons, when the black woman disappeared quietly, probably back to Baltimore for a while, rather than await her inevitable conviction.[19] Thompson was a hard taskmaster, running his brothels in a methodical fashion: he visited "every day to see how much money they had made for him, and found fault when they had not made enough money." Unsurprisingly, his prostitutes bristled at such close scrutiny, and, after Thompson "quarreled with the three white girls because they did not make money enough for him," he laid them off "and got three colored girls there to live."[20] Searching for a more malleable workforce and larger profits, Thompson simply replaced his white prostitutes with black ones.

Very early on, the black junk shop operator and brothel owner shrewdly realized that he could increase his return by leveraging business earnings into real estate investment. Possible models that Thompson was emulating were not hard to find. John R. Livingston, brother of Chancellor Robert R. Livingston, one of the nation's Founding Fathers, was listed in the tax assessment records between 1820 and 1850 as the owner or occupant of at least thirty houses of prostitution. As one of the leading historians of New York's

nineteenth century has made clear, many of New York's prominent families profited from the sex trade.[21] In much the same way
as whites, Thompson invested money from his licit and illicit enterprises in property.

In February 1836, Epsom Hamilton, or Major Hamilton, as he
liked to be known (and who was white and no relation to Jeremiah
G. Hamilton), Benjamin Foreman and Asa Holden put out the word
that they had land for sale in the upper part of the city. William
Thompson purchased from them six lots on Seventh Avenue near
Ninety-Seventh Street for $265 in cash, a $200 promissory note, and
a horse and harness valued at $125. Just prior to the settlement in
the downtown premises of the lawyer James McKeon Esq., the black
man remarked "that he had had the titles searched and was satisfied as to them," which either was untrue or the person he employed
was incompetent: within twenty-four hours, Thompson discovered
that, for all their apparent respectability, the white businessmen had
swindled him and that the title "was not worth one farthing." As it
turned out, Thompson was hardly the only sheep waiting around to
be shorn. During the course of the legal proceedings, it unfolded that
the con men had also sold the same blocks of land to no fewer than
six other would-be investors, pocketing at least another $1,500 for
their efforts.[22]

What intrigues here is Thompson's desire to participate in the
real estate boom, and it begs the question as to whether this was a
more widespread urge among African New Yorkers. One place to
start considering this issue is Seneca Village, located on a few blocks
roughly between Seventh and Eighth avenues and Eighty-Third and
Eighty-Eighth streets (and only some ten blocks south of the land
that Thompson had attempted to buy in 1836). This settlement had
its beginnings around 1825 when a twenty-five-year-old African
American bootblack bought three lots of land, which grew to be
home to at least 264 people on the day in 1855 that the census-taker
came by, and was resumed and flattened by the city authorities in
1857 to make way for Central Park. Often disparaged by contemporary white observers as little more than a collection of shanties,
Seneca Village disappeared from visibility for well over a century
until its rediscovery by Roy Rosenzweig and Elizabeth Blackmar as

they researched their *The Park and the People: A History of Central Park* (1992). Accounts since then, both academic and popular, have played up the idea of Seneca Village as an oasis, a haven in a heartless world, almost seeming to portray the "community" as a black peasant village.[23]

By the standards of antebellum America, there was indeed an unusual stability to black settlement in Seneca Village: three-quarters of the households there in 1840 still were present in 1855. Within only a couple of decades of its founding many inhabitants had established deep roots. Nevertheless, there is another side to the coin. What has disappeared from more recent depictions of Seneca Village is a sense of the extent to which it was part of the city itself. As Rosenzweig and Blackmar were careful to make clear, at the time of the 1855 census not only blacks lived there, but at least 30 percent of the population was Irish. And what is particularly intriguing is the number of African Americans owning multiple parcels of land. Epiphany Davis owned seventeen plots of land, George Root nine. Joseph Marshall, a house painter, had purchased five lots in Seneca Village but lived miles away in his house on Centre Street near City Hall, and he was not the only absentee landowner.[24] Seneca Village flourished in the larger context of the city's uninhibited expansion, for these were the decades in which much of the remaining undeveloped land on Manhattan itself was snapped up by settlers, speculators and charlatans alike. That African Americans involved in Seneca Village, and other real estate ventures such as those of William Thompson, also exhibited a variety of motives should come as no particular surprise.

Indeed, for all the undoubted importance of the site in the city's history, the meaning of Seneca Village is not necessarily self-evident. Researchers have assiduously mined the city's records for traces of the settlement and have found them in census schedules, maps and fleeting mentions in newspaper stories. There is a nice particularity to this evidence, but it is very spare. This lack of explanatory detail, most obviously from African Americans themselves, has resulted in huge gaps in the record. In these circumstances, any new evidence that occasionally turns up is potentially revealing. By combing the city's newspapers and court records I have managed to uncover some

as-yet unpublished detail, material suggesting that the thrall of the
market reached into the heart of Seneca Village.

James Hunt was "a respectable colored man," unable either to
read or to write, who owned two lots of land and a "wooden tene-
ment" on the corner of Eighty-Fourth Street and Seventh Avenue. In
early 1835, Robert Ritter, a twenty-three-year-old black New Yorker
who followed "shoemaking & mending" and lived "near the 8th
Avenue and Bloomingdale Road" (in the vicinity of modern-day Co-
lumbus Circle, at the southwest corner of Central Park) approached
Hunt in order to try and buy his property. Eventually Ritter and Hunt
came to terms, settling on a price of $1,500. Ritter had to pay off
Hunt's $400 mortgage with a Dr. Wagstaff and take out a new one
with Hunt for the balance. Ritter hired an attorney named Harned
from downtown Fulton Street to draw up a mortgage agreement for
$1,100, payable in forty years' time at no interest, and convinced
Hunt to sign his name (which was about the limit of his literacy). In
a linked transaction, witnessed by a black man named Henry Davis,
Ritter handed over to Hunt two wads of $50 and $100 bills of the
Marble Manufacturing Company of the City of New York with a
face value of some $5,850. They agreed that Hunt would go down-
town and exchange the notes for silver, deduct the "consideration
money" (presumably the $400 needed to wind up Wagstaff's mort-
gage) and take the balance "to use & lay out in the purchase of property." Ritter evinced a keenness to draw on Hunt's local real estate
knowledge and let him know that he was well aware that the Seneca
Village resident had "acted as agent or had caused persons to buy
property in that neighbourhood." Within a day or two, albeit some
time after his skeptical and not very happy wife, Hunt realized that
the rather-too-glib Ritter had defrauded him. The proffered cash
was in broken bank notes, not forgeries as such, but bills issued by a
now-bankrupt entity, unredeemable for specie and hence worthless,
as Hunt soon found out when a downtown exchange office would
not touch them. Ritter, in fact, had bought notes to the face value of
nearly $10,000 for all of ten genuine dollars from, as he told the legal
authorities, a "Mr Jas Whiting a Speculator as I think" living near
the end of Sixth Avenue. No matter how often Hunt remonstrated
with him, Ritter pointblank refused to return the property deeds,

insisting that he and Hunt still had a deal and that he would soon raise the money. Hunt pressed charges, and a few months later Ritter was convicted of "False Pretence."[25]

The case is extremely messy. Buried in the District Attorney's file is the receipt for the Marble Manufacturing Company currency that Hunt was supposed to change into specie, signed by him in a hesitant hand. Elsewhere in the paperwork the total of the money is given as either $5,850 or "six thousand dollars one hundred & fifty more or less," although the receipt states in words that it was $9,500 but in figures, quite clearly, that it was $90,500. Legal documents and illiteracy mix awkwardly. More than this, a mortgage for $1,100 not payable until 1875 and with no interest was almost a nonsense, not quite as worthless as a Marble Manufacturing Company $100 bill, but certainly neither James Hunt nor his wife would have seen any of the money from the sale of their house and land.[26]

Perhaps that very messiness hints at the main lesson to be drawn from the case. In antebellum New York City, ordinary black men were using agents and downtown lawyers, employing as a matter of course sophisticated financial instruments such as mortgages and bonds, bargaining sums in the thousands of dollars, and buying and selling land—all within slavery's shadow, for the State of New York finally had ended the institution only a few years before. That African Americans occasionally hit a discordant note, or at times misunderstood what was going on, or even that white and black sharks continually circled searching for blood, hardly matters. Indeed, the presence of so many con men is probably as good a measure as any of capitalism's allure for blacks in these years. African New Yorkers were *learning* the new ways of a burgeoning economy in the early stages of its dramatic expansion.

It is difficult to gauge whether Jeremiah Hamilton would have found it more galling to be grouped with other African Americans or to be labeled as someone learning the ways of the economy. Be that as it may, too eager to share in the spoils of the real estate boom, Hamilton, similar to other black would-be investors, allowed himself to be outmaneuvered by one James B. Taylor, who conducted business in a fashion that was somewhere between sharp practice and fraudulent. Interestingly, Hamilton chose to make his forays into real estate not on Manhattan itself but in the peripheral if still very active markets in the orbit of the metropolis. In 1836, barely a couple thousand people lived in Williamsburgh, a town located in Kings County on the western end of Long Island, although within two decades the City of Williamsburg would be incorporated into the City of Brooklyn. By January 1836, it appears that Hamilton had already purchased some land there around North Seventh and North Sixth streets, property that was traversed by a creek and consequently not laid out in the usual orderly rectangular lots. Soon after, Taylor approached Hamilton and offered to sell him parcels of land to the north and east of the black man's holding that would enable the speculator "to make full lots of such as were now only parts of lots." The pair agreed quickly on a deal whereby Taylor would sell the equivalent of some fifty-one lots of land to Hamilton in return for two notes drawn on Calders, Russel and Co., endorsed by Hamilton and due six months later at the end of September 1836, for $637.25 and $650.25.

According to Hamilton, there was a rider to the deal—the black man's "professional advisor," one William S. McCann Esq., had to "certify as to the goodness of the title to all and every of the said lots and parts of lots." A few days later, Taylor called on Hamilton to inform him that McCann had stated "that the said deed was perfect and the title good," and consequently Hamilton handed over the two promissory notes. Subsequently, Hamilton discovered that McCann had not spoken to Taylor about the deed and that in fact "he was in no way satisfied with it," at least in part because there was an outstanding mortgage on the land. Irritated, Hamilton confronted Taylor, gave him back the deeds to the land and demanded the return of his money. Far from complying, Taylor promptly discounted the two notes, or, in other words, sold them to someone else, in order that Hamilton "might have more difficulty in tracing them." In the ensuing court case, Taylor denied that the deal depended on McCann's opinion of the title and claimed that not only was Hamilton aware of the mortgage on the land but also that this knowledge had not deterred him in the slightest from wanting to purchase the land. The judge found against Hamilton and made him pay the defendant's costs of $82.11.[27] As with so many of the court cases about real estate, it is difficult to work out what was going on from the bare details left in the legal file: in this instance, my guess is that both Taylor and Hamilton were trying to out-shyster one another and were about equally duplicitous, but that the black man, outfoxed, came off second-best.

Neither Jeremiah Hamilton nor the brothel owner William Thompson allowed setbacks to deter them. Unsurprisingly, the real estate market was not a level playing field, and there were extra penalties imposed for being black, but, in spite of discrimination, at least a few blacks persisted in their attempts to participate in this booming sector of the economy. Judging by the apparent ease with which he had been conned, Thompson may appear to have been little more than a neophyte in his real estate dealings, perhaps understandably stumbling as he entered what was for him new territory, but one small detail in the coverage of his fraud case suggests that this is not quite correct. The *New York Herald*'s reporter began his account of the trial in the General Sessions by noting that Thompson had already "made sufficient money to purchase considerable quantities of real estate."[28] Perhaps the swindle worked less because of Thompson's gullibility and more because the con men were very good. Details of Thompson's property dealings eventually turned up buried in the file of a long and complicated perjury case brought by the District Attorney in 1841.

Earlier, in 1833, Thompson had bought several adjoining lots of land with frontages of fifty feet on Seventh Avenue, fifty feet on the Bloomingdale Road (or Broadway) and 112 feet on Forty-Second Street. Over the next three years the black entrepreneur employed Lewis Berry, a white carpenter, to build three speculative houses on his land. Eventually, Berry took possession of one of the dwellings as payment for his work. Later on in 1840 Thompson deposed that he had received three cash offers of $10,000 for his Forty-Second Street holdings.

Thompson was as careless about the law as any of the white businessmen then laying the foundations of their financial empires as the American economy began to take off, for all of its occasional stops and starts, on its seemingly inexorable rise. Although the details of Thompson's complicated maneuverings are now hard to follow the result is clear enough: by the time he sold his property in 1839, admittedly after two hard years of recession and falling prices, he had mortgaged the land and buildings to several different people for rather more than it was worth.

Yet for all the similarities between Thompson and an assortment of businessmen and other investors riding the speculative wave there was one fundamental difference—William Thompson was black. In 1840, when he became guarantor for the bail of an African American named John Johnson charged with stealing $30 in notes and a pocketbook valued at twenty-five cents, Thompson claimed to own "at least the sum of twelve thousand dollars over and above all demands against him." A little over six months later, the District Attorney charged Thompson with perjury, arguing that he was worth nothing like that amount of money. As we have seen, perjury was an unusual charge, although other prominent black businessmen were forced to defend themselves against this accusation as well. The black entrepreneur, daring to compete in a white world, was a marked man and fair game for the DA, who pursued him vigorously for running a brothel and secured a conviction that sent him to the penitentiary: Thompson slipped from view, consigned to the dustbin of history, totally forgotten for 175 years.[29]

At this point I should explain for those probably very few readers who have not already figured it out that the lots of land William Thompson owned for some six years during the 1830s were located on Forty-Second Street at the southern end of what would later become Times Square. Today most Americans would undoubtedly find it inconceivable that, less than a decade after the end of slavery in New York, a black man not only owned part of what is now one of the city's emblematic landmarks, a piece of real estate more valuable than most in the country, but also erected some of the first buildings on the site. Given the current antiseptic and anodyne state of the area, even a modest plaque acknowledging his pioneering role would be wholly out of place, although for much of Times Square's vibrant existence, the brothel-keeper, penitentiary bird, and failed businessman would have fitted in nicely.

Jeremiah Hamilton too kept on trying to participate in the real estate market. Continuing his strategy of buying large quantities of town lots in Manhattan's orbit but not on the island itself, in May 1836, Hamilton purchased, successfully this time, forty-seven blocks of land in Hallet's Cove, situated in Newtown, Queens County. The sale was the result of William Price and his wife breaking up and selling what locals still called the McDonough Farm. Today the area is part of Astoria, and within a handful of years of Hamilton's investment developers would transform Hallet's Cove into a recreational destination for Manhattan's wealthy.[30]

Hamilton's other and more significant real estate plunge took place in Poughkeepsie, a community of some 7,000 souls in 1836, located on the east bank of the Hudson River midway between Albany and New York City (and within a five or six hours' sail of each, even less by steamboat). It is not clear why Hamilton chose Poughkeepsie, but as with his other property investments his decision displayed a shrewd appreciation of value and potential. Poughkeepsie was changing rapidly in the 1830s. As an enthusiastic editor of the *Poughkeepsie Journal* rhapsodized in 1836, earlier in the decade the settlement had been little more than "a country village, beautifully situated, it is true," but "now, it is rapidly becoming a great manufacturing and commercial town, with the enlarged projects of business, the extended enterprises, the energy, activity and bustle, and with the spacious and costly public edifices and elegant private residences, of a large and wealthy city."[31] What was known as the "Improvement Party" had driven much of this transformation, funneling public money into clearing land, surveying, laying out new streets and welcoming any new industrial enterprise. Unsurprisingly, the Improvement Party functioned mostly as a lobby group for real estate developers. Important figures associated with it included locals such as George P. Oakley, who had started off in the 1820s as the town's lottery agent, sold his lucrative business and moved into real estate, and John Delafield of New York City, and these were the people Hamilton dealt with in Poughkeepsie. By the mid-1830s, the town was seized by a real estate mania as intense as anywhere else in the United States. The *Journal* and the *Poughkeepsie Telegraph* were awash with stories of improvement, progress and the sales of town lots for unheard-of prices.[32]

In 1836, Hamilton bought from George P. Oakley a half-acre of land on the north side of Union Street, down near the Union

Landing. He also purchased the actual Union Landing, a 400-foot-long dock, including the three large storehouses on it, as well as a nearby five acres of land, the dwelling formerly occupied by Joseph Harris and the barn and house that Jeremiah Platt had lived in. And there was the possibility for further development, for, as Hamilton was well aware, this property included an elevated site suitable for the construction of a new house, "commanding a most extensive view of the beautiful scenery of the Hudson River." These substantial investments in Poughkeepsie, combined with his purchases in Hallet's Cove, cost him some $27,000, more than $6 million in today's dollars.[33] Furthermore, on May 23, 1836, Hamilton purchased from John Delafield several lots with frontages of sixty feet and depths of 190 feet on the northeast corner of Poughkeepsie's Mansion Square. As well, he bought the "splendid dwelling" known as the Mansion House and various outbuildings. This was a very large structure, "well calculated and arranged for a Hotel, or extensive Family Boarding House." Indeed, "for architectural beauty, delightful location, and arrangements" it was, he later claimed as he tried to sell it, unsurpassed. Although in the middle of town today, in the late 1830s this locale was a new development: two years later, the local authority still was assessing owners for the grading, graveling and curbing of the roads. Hamilton did not pay cash for this portion of his investment but took out a mortgage with Delafield for $20,000 at 7 percent per annum, with the interest to be paid every six months and the loan to be discharged in two years on May 23, 1838.[34]

It appears Jeremiah Hamilton had every intention of moving to Poughkeepsie and setting himself up as one of the developers improving and modernizing the Hudson River town. In January 1837, he let it be known that he was in the market to buy two steamboats of about 175 tons each, "calculated for the Freighting and Towing business on the North River." At the same time he advertised that he wanted to employ someone to run the Union Landing. This person had to "possess an extensive acquaintance in Dutchess county, and a knowledge of the Freighting business as conducted on the North River."[35] Hamilton was abandoning New York and going to become a very prominent man in Poughkeepsie.

Although Hamilton may well have been mortified at being categorized with other African Americans desirous of investing in land, he could have taken solace from the one crucial difference—the sheer size of the position he ended up staking out dwarfed that of every other black man, and that of all but a very few whites as well. Jeremiah Hamilton, never one to do things by halves, was betting on the property market continuing to boom and betting big, to the tune of well in excess of $10 million of today's dollars.

In July 1837, Benjamin Day published a short piece about Poughkeepsie in his newspaper, the *New York Sun*. This "delightful and thickly populated village" exhibited "a degree of real stamina," illustrated by "her large proprietors, settled population, and her business to be found only in a city which has grown up upon its own inherent advantages." As Day intimated in his story, he was ruminating on what he had observed on a recent trip: "We were surprised, on visiting Poughkeepsie, a few days since. . . ." Perhaps he was merely using the editorial "we," but I like to think he had accompanied his now seemingly inseparable friend Jeremiah Hamilton on a tour of the black man's new domain. Indeed, the newspaperman's concluding reference to the "public spirited, persevering, and indefatigable capitalists who have invested an enormous interest in the improvement of that highly favored village" was a barely veiled paean to his black companion.[36] And yet, for all the achievement of Jeremiah Hamilton and other blacks who had brushed aside incredulity, prejudice and fraud and pegged out their claim to a share of the profits of what had seemed to be the most dynamic sector of the burgeoning economy, it was all to no avail. The black real estate investor had been under increasing financial pressure for a while and had to abandon any idea of moving up the Hudson River. Since April, Hamilton had been advertising to rent, or to sell for some $45,000, his Poughkeepsie holdings.[37] Not for the last time in African American history, black pioneers had forced open the door and gained admittance only to have the building collapse around them.

By the time Hamilton's friend had penned his piece in July 1837, the economic indicators were looking grim. Canny man that he was, Day, unlike Hamilton, had hedged his bet, writing of Poughkeepsie: "Whether prosperity smiles, or adversity shall long continue to frown," this "peculiarly favored spot *must,* in either event, inevitably and permanently flourish."[38] But what was occurring in the financial markets in the second quarter of 1837 was more than a mere correction. Although some did not comprehend it yet, there were signs everywhere that America's first great depression had well and truly started. A month or two earlier, in late April, Philip Hone recorded in his diary that lots up near Bloomingdale around One Hundredth Street that investors had bought for $480 the previous September were being sold for $50. "The immense fortunes which we heard so much about in the days of speculation, have melted away like the snows before an April sun"[39] Investors disappeared—by July, even finding a buyer scavenging for bargains in foreclosure sales was difficult. Although Hamilton still maintained a front, he had already been told that, as someone had very elegantly put it to him, Tinkham and Hart, a firm he often dealt with, had "yielded to the pressure of the times." It would drag out over years, but Hamilton was going down for the count. As with the rest of the country, the black broker and real estate speculator would have to adapt and learn to cope with adversity's frown for some time.

For just a moment and against all the odds, Hamilton had grasped the prize, only to have it slip through his fingers. No other African American had even thought of daring to breathe Wall Street's rarified air, let alone made it as far as had Jeremiah Hamilton. Ironically, Benjamin Day was quite right about the long-term prospects of Poughkeepsie. Indeed, in the long run Hamilton's investments in Hallet's Cove and Poughkeepsie, and Thompson's speculative houses built on Forty-Second Street as well, would all have been fine. It was not as though these men had bought Florida swampland. But mere astuteness was insufficient when an economic maelstrom overwhelmed the country. Although Thomas Downing sat it out, no African American on the make could afford to wait for the long run. Large mortgages and plunging property prices were a lethal combination. The unforgiving market, with its excesses and manipulations, always devours its young and could not care less about either race or history.

SEVEN

BANKRUPTCY

As early as the summer of 1836, a few financiers in New York, New Orleans and London started harboring reservations about the sustainability of the flows of capital then buoying transatlantic financial markets to new highs. Jeremiah Hamilton was not conflicted by any such doubts—that same summer he had wagered heavily that the good times were going to last at least long enough for him to make a tidy profit. Although a first-time investor had only a slim chance of being able to discern threatening economic developments, it is clear, with the benefit of hindsight, that he managed to buy his real estate near the market's peak, just before the bubble burst. And he was hardly alone in his bullish optimism. Unfortunately for these speculators, faceless men in distant London boardrooms were rather less sanguine about America's immediate prospects. Even though the United States had been independent for more than a half-century, its economy still was yoked firmly to that of Great Britain. British demand had driven up cotton prices through the mid-1830s, and British investment had fueled the American boom. Attracted by much higher returns than they could find locally, British financiers invested enormous amounts of capital in state bonds, canals, railroads and land in the United States. But, as the preeminent historians of New York City Edwin G. Burrows and Mike Wallace observed dryly, "what the English had given, the English decided to take away." The Bank of England—an institution that Philip Hone noted grimly was "arbiter of the fate of the American merchant"—jacked up its discount rate and staunched the flow of money to the United States. Falling cotton prices and an insistence, with credit now dried up, that American debts be paid in gold resulted in a flow of the precious metal back across the Atlantic. The monetary conditions that had promoted the boom were now reversed, causing an acute shortage of specie and ready currency in the United States that started to strangle the economy—it was just a question of how long it would take.[1]

Even as early as November 1836, the consequences of the new policies were becoming apparent. Stock prices had fallen, interest rates had risen sharply and, according to Hone, "real estate is a drug." By March 1837, the squeeze's full impact was felt in the city and all manner of businesses began to fail, inevitably dragging down even more firms in their wake. They went over like dominos, inducing what has been known ever since as the panic of 1837. A shaken Hone recorded in his diary in the first week of May that "the number of failures is so great daily that I do not keep a record of them, even in my mind."[2] Within days the besieged banks had no choice but to take the drastic step of suspending specie payments, or, in other words, no longer honoring their promise to buy back their bank notes with gold or silver. It was little short of an economic cataclysm.

In New York the dire effects percolated quickly throughout the entire city. The construction industry was devastated. During 1836 New Yorkers had built 1,826 new structures, including some 868 houses and 805 stores. In 1837 only 840 buildings, less than half of the previous year's total, were completed, of which 117 were stores and 549 were houses. The plunge in commercial construction, often larger jobs, was especially dramatic. A reporter for the *Daily Express* summed up: "By this falling off in building alone from 1836 to 1837, over 15,000 workingmen have been turned out of employ in this city."[3] Large numbers of New Yorkers were unable to find work of any kind. In August a visiting Philadelphian was shocked by what he found. While it was true that there was at least "an appearance of life . . . visible in the chief thoroughfares," if one entered "the counting rooms and workshops" and asked about "the state of affairs," then "the true condition of business may be ascertained." He could only conclude that, in New York, "the condition of things is truly lamentable."[4] This was America's first great depression, and it would be more than five years before the city managed to drag itself fully out of the doldrums.

If, by the beginning of 1837, Jeremiah Hamilton noticed any of the signs of economic contraction, he ignored them. What may have blinkered his view of the looming financial meltdown was that, unlike the majority of his compatriots, Hamilton's business interests were oriented southward and not across the Atlantic. Although his focus on the Caribbean was mostly a result of connections and local knowledge, factors determining where he was likely to see the chance of making a profitable deal of one sort or another, the more ready acceptance in the racially diverse Caribbean of a merchant with Hamilton's skin color also must have been a consideration. Such an orientation also inevitably meant that Hamilton's hands were tainted by slavery. The institution, and more particularly the insatiable European demand for sugar that bolstered slavery was the heart of the entire region's economy. Although a few individuals publicized the link between human bondage and sweetened tea, Hamilton and almost every other businessman in the Atlantic world focused on the potential returns on capital to be made by trading in sugar.

Still bullish about the New York markets, in February 1837 he ordered 500 boxes of sugar from Joseph Vargas, a Havana merchant. The rectangular wooden boxes that Havana and Matanzas commercial houses used to pack the clayed sugar they produced each weighed about 450 pounds, and the total cost of the shipment was some $12,800 (or $2.47 million in today's dollars).[5] Even if he was paying scant attention to news from London, Hamilton's sugar purchase still involved an element of burying his head in the sand, as by this time New York markets themselves were in turmoil. Mind you, hindsight in such matters is all too easy. Regardless, by February 1837, Jeremiah Hamilton, leveraging his own and borrowed money, had taken a position in real estate and sugar that represented an investment of in excess of $15 million in today's currency. If the markets had carried on behaving as they had a year previously, he would have made a killing.

In order to pay Vargas in Spanish currency for the sugar, Hamilton followed normal business practice and arranged an accommodation with a firm that had credit in Havana. He often dealt with Tinkham and Hart, and they had an extensive network of business contacts in New Orleans, Mobile, and throughout the Caribbean; indeed, they had had previous transactions with Vargas. According to Hamilton's sworn account, he deposited American dollars for the sugar with Tinkham and Hart and then sent drafts, drawn on them, to Vargas in Havana. But the firm failed in mid-April 1837, so that by the time the drafts reached Vargas and he presented them for acceptance they were dishonored. In August 1837, Joseph Vargas, attempting to recover payment, sued Hamilton at common law in the Circuit Court of the United States for the Southern District of New York.[6]

Events were starting to close in around the black broker. By the end of May 1837, he had failed to make the interest payment on the $20,000 mortgage he had negotiated with John Delafield in order to pay for the parcels of land on Mansion Square in Poughkeepsie. He had been so confident of himself when he took out the mortgage a year previously that he had agreed that if he failed to meet his obligations he would be liable to "the Penal sum of forty thousand dollars lawful money." Delafield had run out of patience: he had "frequently and in a friendly manner applied to the said Jeremiah G. Hamilton and Eliza Jane his wife aforesaid," but they had ignored his chidings and "no part of the said principal has ever been paid." In August he sued, requesting the Chancery Court to insist on payment of what was owed, plus interest, "by a short day to be appointed by the order of this honorable court," and that failing, to move for foreclosure. Things moved quickly, and by September 1837 Hamilton had lost the lots in Poughkeepsie.[7]

As far as the matter of the sugar was concerned, a vexed Jeremiah Hamilton claimed vehemently that he had paid the money and that Vargas and his lawyers were railroading him. Repeatedly he informed anyone who would listen that "he always considered the claim an unjust one & which might by possibility for want of proof on his part or from technicalities of the law pass against him." Hamilton even admitted "he has frequently expressed himself in angry terms in relation thereto." Nicholas Vargas, the agent of his brother Joseph in the prosecution of the suit, remembered things slightly differently, particularly in the early stages of the legal proceedings. Between September and the first week of December 1837, he had between half a dozen and a dozen conversations with Hamilton, and they "were always of a friendly character." Yet, no matter how genteel a tone there was to these negotiations, both sides displayed a steely resolve not to be bested. At one point Hamilton proposed a compromise, the terms of which Vargas "considered so absurd that he would not listen to them." Nicholas Vargas's strongest memory of these conversations was Hamilton's repeated insistence that "he knew as much law as any lawyer, that he never lost a law suit and that there were many ways of evading payment and he should make use of all of them."[8] Although his bluster was palpably untrue—he had lost plenty of lawsuits in his time, and his lawyers would certainly have argued the point about his legal knowledge—that was irrelevant. Hamilton's conduct was not calculated—undoubtedly his battery of legal advice prayed fervently for him simply to shut up—but his mixture of honeyed words with an aggressively arrogant swagger was perfectly of a piece with the times. Any number of self-made men of business behaved in a similar fashion—but, of course, they were white. That a black man, a Wall Street pioneer, conducted himself in such a fashion was truly remarkable, for, in antebellum New York, hubris was only allowed to whites. If Hamilton had tried it on any other street in New York, violence would have ensued.

As the economy spluttered almost to a halt, Hamilton, similarly to most other denizens of the financial district, grew increasingly idle. Other than avoiding or placating creditors there was little to be done in such circumstances. Throughout 1837, as his financial affairs worsened, Jeremiah Hamilton spent more and more time in the *Sun*'s offices on the corner of Nassau and Spruce streets. Most days he dropped by to chat with Benjamin Day and Horatio S. Bartlett, the police reporter, and whiled away many an hour lounging on what everyone regarded as his sofa in the editorial room. Newspapers and newspapermen intrigued Hamilton, and probably even at this stage he had started writing occasionally for the *Sun*. It was a commonplace to see Hamilton, Day and Bartlett strolling arm in arm to the nearby Second Ward Hotel. Although New York's population had reached nearly 300,000 people by the late 1830s, the score and more blocks of the financial district centering on Wall Street still retained a few small-town features. Someone was always watching. Besides, as the three knew, a notorious black man cavorting down the middle of Nassau Street with a pair of equally well-known white men was an unusual sight. People noticed them, talked about their amiable sociability, and remembered what they had seen. Not that the friends gave a damn.[9]

James Gordon Bennett, editor and proprietor of the *New York Herald*, certainly noticed Jeremiah Hamilton's close association with the *Sun*. Whenever the opportunity arose he and Benjamin Day still sniped at one another in their papers, but early in 1838 Bennett began remarking on the *Sun*'s ownership. He vilified the "small decrepit, dying, penny paper, owned and controlled by a set of woolly headed and thick lipped negroes about town" before claiming, disingenuously, that he had "no wish to disturb a set of negroes in their new vocation of conducting a penny paper."[10] No one ever accused Bennett of reticence. A few days later he used his cherished literary facility to write a 600-word piece, replete with black dialect, on the "Philosophy of Boot Blacking," a title telegraphing its belittling humor. The conceit of the heavy-handed article involved a bootblack, anxious about a new business rival, calling on Bennett to try to ensure his continued custom. Perplexed, Bennett asked him to explain whom he was talking about. The bootblack replied:

> "To de new boot brack, what him sot up at de corner ob Spruce street."
>
> "What! the negro rascals who conduct the SUN newspaper?"

Bennett reassured the minion of his status as "the Napoleon of boot blacks," telling him, "You will yet be the editor and proprietor of all the penny papers in New York, if you go on as you do." Nothing could have horrified the black man more.

"No want fur to be dat. De dam bobalition niggers may do dat—
dose dat cut him wool off, and wear de wig. I want for to polish de
boot—de werry *nonderstandings* of dis dislightened age—ha! ha!
ha!—yah! yah! yah!"[11]

"Bobalition" was an early-nineteenth-century neologism created by
white Bostonians to denigrate the city's black freedom parades but
that soon spread to other northeastern cities. It was a verbal play
on the supposed inability of African Americans clearly and properly
to enunciate "abolition": like children, they had inserted an extra
syllable and mangled the word, demonstrating once more that they
were incapable of emulating their white betters. By the time Bennett used "bobalition," it had become a catch-all derogatory term
that embodied a churlish and spiteful response to the new status of
free blacks.[12] The word suited perfectly the *Herald* editor's purposes.
Mention of shaving off hair and wearing a wig referred pointedly
to Jeremiah Hamilton. From the time he had moved to New York,
whites had commented ceaselessly on Hamilton's distinctive wig and
were fascinated by his hair, or lack thereof.

A fortnight later, the *Herald* editor, unusually, backpedaled, acknowledging that "we have seen an affidavit stating that the Wall
street broker, ship-owner &c., has not—nor ever had any interest
in that concern." Several days later he explained: "We have frequently alluded to an individual as 'a commission merchant, ship-
owner, broker, &c.' and stated that he was the owner of a certain
penny paper called the Sun." Someone had misinformed Bennett
that Hamilton "had purchased that paper," and "we supposed him
to have prompted certain articles which appeared in it, in deroga-
tion of us; and it was under that impression that we wrote several
articles of him."[13] The editor admitted that his sources had led him
astray. Bennett may have got his facts wrong, but he was hardly one
to let that force him to retire a catchy phrase: from this time on,
Bennett commonly traduced his rival as the "nigger penny paper"
or the "nigger Sun."[14]

That James Gordon Bennett mistakenly thought for some time
that Hamilton had bought the newspaper suggests how closely the
black man was linked to the *Sun*. What the misconception also

reveals is that Bennett, a knowing judge of the financial world, still considered Hamilton as having the wherewithal to be able to buy the tabloid. Hamilton maintained an office on Front Street, a residence on Varick Street, and, in spite of his business difficulties, put on a convincing front to the rest of the world.[15] But this could not last.

By early 1838, Hamilton owed money all over the place to all manner of people, ranging from lawyers to various businessmen. He could not convert any of his assets into ready money. Those who owed him were just as strapped for cash as he was, and in the unlikely event that he could find a buyer for his remaining real estate investments, the price would have been only a fraction of what he had paid. The most pressing problem, though, was the Vargas suit. Hamilton employed the same strategy as he had used earlier in the 1830s when creditors were pursuing him, albeit for rather smaller sums of money—avoid paying any debts, delay any legal proceedings for as long as possible, and hope things turn around.

At the end of September 1837, the court had published notice that the matter of *Vargas v. Hamilton* would go to trial during the October term. One week later, Simeon Hart took passage for the West Indies, sneaking out of New York under an assumed name. All of Hamilton's dealings with Tinkham and Hart had been with this partner. The much-older Joseph Tinkham had almost nothing to do with the day-to-day running of the firm, and indeed had not even been in New York State for the three months previous to its failure. According to Vargas's lawyer, Hamilton and Hart "were well acquainted together and had transactions together of considerable extent." Hamilton's lawyers insisted that Hart's testimony was crucial to his case and secured a postponement of the trial so he could be deposed in Havana. However, the commission supposed to conduct this examination had not turned up in the Cuban capital by April 1838, which did not surprise Vargas's lawyer, who "always considered that the motion was made with no other object than of gaining time." Hamilton responded indignantly that he had made inquiries "but found that the said Hart was not stationary, at any particular place but was travelling to and fro, among the Bahama & West India Islands." He was, however, informed, and believed, that Hart would return to New York in May 1838.[16]

The continual focus on Hamilton's dealings with Hart remains perplexing. Seemingly, the black broker managed to exploit his absence to delay proceedings, but in reality anything Hart might have had to say should not have been relevant to the matter at hand, which was whether or not Hamilton had paid the money to Vargas. My own suspicion, possibly shared by Vargas's lawyer, given his insinuations about the close business relationship between the now-absent Hart and the black broker, is that Hamilton protested too much and that, in fact, back in April 1837, realizing the way things were going for himself, and also for Tinkham and Hart, he had never handed over the money. Vargas's lawyer certainly did not trust Hamilton. In April 1838, he informed the court that "a source entitled to credit" had let him know "that this said *defendant is selling off his property & making arrangements to leave this city & deponent* is informed he intends to *leave for Europe very shortly.*"[17] Vargas wanted justice meted out quickly.

The informant was correct about Hamilton selling some of his property, but then so too were a large number of other desperate businessmen. May Day 1838 in New York City was even more frenetic than usual. Although most New Yorkers were none too fond of the custom, the first of May was moving day and had been so for longer than anyone could remember. Leases expired on May 1, and, thanks to an oddity of city law, tenants were required to vacate rented premises by nine o'clock in the morning. The result was a bonanza for cartmen and chaos for everybody else. In 1835, one resident complained: "May Day is a day of horror." If locals thought the custom irritatingly inconvenient, visitors just were baffled by it. A taken-aback Frances Trollope, perhaps the most notorious nineteenth-century English traveler to the United States thanks to her caustic views of American life, commented: "Rich furniture and ragged furniture, carts, wagons, and drays, ropes, canvas, and straw, packers, porters, and draymen, white, yellow, and black, occupy the streets from east to west, from north to south, on this day." To the underwhelmed Englishwoman, the shambles resembled nothing so much as "a population flying from the plague."[18] But the economy, not biology, had caused the scenes Trollope witnessed: thanks to the peculiarities of New York leases, moving day was the city's real estate market made manifest in a highly concentrated form. For those who knew how to read it, May Day was a barometer of the city's financial well-being.

May 1, 1838, was the first moving day since New York had felt the full brunt of the economic slump. A writer in the *Daily Express* had never experienced anything like it: "There has been more moving . . . than we have ever known." The spectacle prompted him to reflect that "many persons, who, a year ago, felt themselves not only in comfortable circumstances, but rich . . . have been ruined." Further, "hundreds who enjoyed in comfort the earnings of former years, and who were enabled to live, if not in affluence, yet with every convenience about them, have had to leave . . . their neat dwellings for very humble abodes." As straitened circumstances forced ruined men to sell up, fire sales of furniture and household items glutted the market.[19]

Jeremiah Hamilton was all too familiar with the dismal scenes of financial failure and humiliation that the *Daily Express* reporter recorded. Although until May 1, 1838, he had "kept house" at 69 Varick Street, Hamilton had no choice but to let go of these premises and, as well, "advertised my furniture for sale, and sold the same at public auction." He then rented furnished rooms at 68 Greenwich Street, an establishment that was somewhere between a boardinghouse and a hotel and was run by Margaret Morris, his mother-in-law. It was this last fact that a year later aroused the suspicion of David Codwise, a master of the Court of Chancery who was inquiring into Hamilton's finances relative to the proceedings in the Vargas case. He questioned the black man closely. Apparently, when Hamilton moved in, Morris had only recently set up business at 68 Greenwich Street. To Codwise's question: "Did you advance or contribute any money towards the purchase of the furniture in the house occupied by Mrs Morris in Greenwich Street where you boarded?" Hamilton answered: "I did—but have been repaid what I advanced." Unconvinced, the master of the Court hammered away at the point, and Hamilton conceded that when he disposed of his furniture at public auction "some articles of furniture which I then had, I sold to Mrs Morris at private sale." Codwise still was not satisfied:

Question—What was the value of the furniture so sold to Mrs
   Morris
Answer—I can not recollect
Question—Was it one thousand dollars
Answer—I cannot say.

The master then elicited from Hamilton that, even earlier, he had advanced Morris money to buy furniture for her other establishment in Liberty Street. On being asked how much, the black man answered: "I can not recollect it is so long since. . . ." Shortly after this unpersuasive answer, a somewhat-ruffled Hamilton told his inquisitor, "I do not keep house, & I have no furniture, and do not think [it] proper to state where I board, considering the inquiry is not pertinent"—and then clammed up.[20]

To be sure, many people, perhaps most, on the verge of financial ruin try to bend the law a little and squirrel away whatever goods and money they can with friends and relatives. Although clearly Codwise could not prove anything, he seemed to be suggesting that Hamilton was engaging in something more serious. The sum of $1,000 that he deliberately raised as the possible value of items sold off on the quiet to Hamilton's mother-in-law was a very large sum of money for furniture, several times an ordinary worker's annual income. Certainly, a plethora of television dramas and legal thrillers makes us today skeptical of the veracity of answers such as "I can not recollect" and "I cannot say," responses Hamilton doubtless gave under instruction from his counselor. It is unlikely that the master of the Court of Chancery found such statements any more satisfactory, particularly in the light of Hamilton's often and loudly proclaimed intention not to pay Vargas one cent.

Hamilton was one of thousands forced to sell his goods and chattels in what was just another grim sign of the times. In the first half of 1838, every surviving New York business, other perhaps than debt collectors, struggled. This included even the *Sun,* then the most successful newspaper in the world. Benjamin Day would later depose in a legal matter that in 1837, newsboys were selling 30,000 copies of his newspaper daily. He had cleared as much as $20,000 in a single year from the *Sun,* although usually the profit was about half that figure.[21] Now, as city and nation stagnated economically, the *Sun*'s operating expenses were some $300 a week more than revenue from newspaper sales. Advertising receipts, down drastically due to the dullness of business, were almost enough to make up the shortfall. The *Sun* was barely breaking even.

On top of this, Day lost a libel suit, and the damages awarded against him were, for once, not a nominal sum. Back in May 1837, the *Sun*'s court reporter mentioned in a story that a lawyer named Andrew S. Garr had been indicted previously for conspiracy to defraud but omitted the crucial detail that the jury had acquitted him. Garr sued. Almost immediately Benjamin Day removed his own name from the *Sun*'s masthead and replaced it with "Published daily by the proprietor," a maneuver he later on admitted "was merely in consequence of some libel suits." Whatever legal difference such a change might have made, it was too late to affect this case. In February 1838, the court awarded Garr $3,000 in damages, a sum that a pained Day acknowledged would "be extracted from the right-hand breeches-pocket of the defendant." Although they had finalized the deal many months earlier, on June 27, 1838, Day announced that he had sold the *Sun* to Moses Yale Beach. The price was $40,000. Half a century after the founding of the *Sun,* in 1883, Benjamin Day ruefully conceded to an interviewer that "the silliest thing I ever did in my life was to sell that paper."[22]

Moses Beach, born in Wallingford, Connecticut, in 1800, was ten years older than Day. He married Day's elder sister, Nancy, in 1819 and for some time in the early 1830s ran a paper mill. As Day told his interviewer, Beach "supplied me with white paper. Finally, he failed up in Saugerties and came into the office as a clerk." Day's somewhat-dismissive tone was influenced by later events. Beach kept the books and supervised the press itself, but he was never a great newspaperman in the vein of a Benjamin Day or a James Gordon Bennett.[23] Once he took over the *Sun* things were bound to change.

Joseph Vargas continued to try and drag a reluctant Hamilton into a courtroom. Eventually he succeeded, and on November 21 and 22, 1838, the case was tried and the court awarded the Havana merchant a verdict, including damages and costs, for $13,425.58.

Unfortunately for Vargas, there was a minor error in the paperwork and his lawyer had to apply to the court to have the verdict amended. As it happened, and in yet another sign of the smallness of New York's financial district, Vargas and Hamilton bumped into one another on the street during this delay, and the latter informed Vargas, in no uncertain terms, that if he "should obtain judgment upon his verdict, he would never get a cent of the money." He also let him know "that there were many ways to avoid the payment of a debt in this country" and that "he should assign his property, to prevent the collection of the claim." The court finalized the judgment on December 14, and a day or two later Hamilton saw Vargas's lawyer in Nassau Street near the Second Ward Hotel, went up to him and repeated what he had told Vargas—and by now a modicum of anger did infuse his words.

On December 14 one of the judges had stayed proceedings for ten days to allow Hamilton the opportunity to prepare a case for a new trial. That delay was later extended for six more days, and then, on December 29 Hamilton's lawyers pleaded for yet another stay. At this point, Vargas's lawyer insisted that before they would acquiesce, Hamilton had to put up enough security in order to pay the judgment in the event that the court denied the application for a new trial. In a brief note to the plaintiff, Hamilton indicated that he would deliver the required money by the two o'clock deadline on December 31. On that day, Vargas and his lawyer were waiting around the clerk's office when they discovered that they had been ambushed. Earlier, Hamilton and one of his lawyers, Elisha Morrill, had registered an assignment of the black broker's property. Assignment was a way for a debtor to attempt to control the selling off of his assets. Rather than the deeds to the property simply being handed over to Vargas, a party rather more friendly to Hamilton, namely, his lawyer Elisha Morrill, was charged, theoretically at least, with selling his assets in the most efficacious manner and disbursing the proceeds among *all* of Hamilton's creditors. In the first indenture of assignment, Morrill gave consideration of $1 in return for all of Hamilton's remaining Poughkeepsie property. In the second, also for $1 consideration, Hamilton conveyed to Morrill his forty-seven lots of land in Hallet's Cove.

Hamilton later justified what he had done by arguing that the peremptory requirement that he find security caught him unawares and was the final straw that had made him change tactics. He was "utterly unable in so short a time to be able to procure security for so large a sum & plaintiff's attorney threatening to enter judgment the same day" meant that he was forced to abandon all of his prepared arguments for a new trial and had no choice but to assign his property "as he was advised he has a right by law to do for the purpose of rendering equal justice to all his creditors." Vargas, still smarting from being taken for a fool yet again, viewed things differently: as far as he was concerned, the documents must have been prepared days before the ambush, and the assignment was only another delaying tactic, one that Hamilton had had the nerve to state publicly weeks before that he would employ.

A chagrined Vargas claimed that Hamilton had "executed or pretended to execute" the assignment of his real estate, which was "of great value and worth much more than the amount of the said judgment and consists of various lands, houses, wharfs and stores at Hallets Cove, Poughkeepsie and other places in the State of New York," and that this was done solely "to hinder, delay and defraud . . . [Vargas] . . . of the recovery of his demands: and is fraudulent and void." Early in the new year, at the plaintiff's behest, the court issued a writ of execution against Hamilton to the marshal of the Southern District of New York for $13,425.58. The marshal returned it to the court, unvacated, a day or two later on January 8, 1839: according to him, he had investigated and, other than the assigned real estate, "the said Hamilton has no goods, chattels, lands or tenements in his district, whereof he could make this amount of the said judgment or any part thereof."[24] Hamilton was certainly making a good fist of denying Vargas even one cent of the money he was owed.

Only the sketchiest traces of Hamilton's life over the next couple of years are present in the surviving sources. The black broker continued to delay whenever and however he could proceedings in the Vargas matter. For most of 1839 and 1840, a master of the Court of Chancery, in effect a receiver, inquired into his finances, but Hamilton did not bother even to attend some hearings and, when present, was deliberately unhelpful. Although he answered "questions generally that were put to him," he refused "to answer any that did not strictly bear upon the subject." The master had to resort to obtaining a court order to guarantee some semblance of cooperation from Hamilton. In December 1840, the vice chancellor heard "an application from a receiver appointed by the Court, to compel him to answer certain delicate questions." Not all of them were especially delicate. For example, he refused to answer one inquiry—"Did you receive certain sugars?"—fundamental to the whole transaction. Hamilton, who the *Herald*'s court reporter reminded its readers was "a 'highly respectable' colored gentleman, of some celebrity in Wall street," was in no hurry to reach any sort of resolution of matters. The vice chancellor ordered the master to issue a fresh summons for Hamilton to appear before him and instructed the recalcitrant broker that, when he did so, he was "bound to answer all proper questions touching his possession or control of any property."[25] But that hearing would not be scheduled until 1841.

Vargas's dogged pursuit of Hamilton in 1840 did yield one success, of sorts. On August 8, Anthony Bleeker, marshal for the Southern District of New York, auctioned off Hamilton's forty-seven lots of land at Hallet's Cove, Long Island, at the nearby Steam Boat Hotel. Apparently, Elisha Morrill, who still retained tight control of the assigned Poughkeepsie properties, relinquished the less valuable of his two holdings as a sop to the authorities. Hamilton had bought this land in 1836 for $4,700; at auction in 1840 the forty-seven lots went under the hammer for a total of $400.[26] Real estate remained a drug on the market. Interestingly, George Bowman, Vargas's lawyer, purchased the land: perhaps he simply recognized a bargain when he saw one, or possibly something more underhanded was occurring— at this distance, who can tell?

During these years Hamilton remained a regular visitor at the offices of the *Sun,* continuing to see his friend Horatio Bartlett, still the paper's court reporter. There is even a suggestion that on occasion and for short periods Hamilton was on the *Sun*'s payroll: he certainly wrote at least occasional pieces. In July 1839, a writer in the *Colored American,* the city's new black newspaper, inveighed against an account, published in the *Sun,* of emancipation in the West Indies and the United States, an article detailing "that the two races could not live together in freedom and the enjoyment of rights, but must of necessity, be subjected the one to the other or be separated." The indignant black correspondent demanded to know "if the Editor, the Sun, and Jerry Hamilton could be enfranchised in the same country?"[27] Although the question itself remains almost totally opaque, this was one of the few times any of the black newspapers mentioned Hamilton's name: if nothing else, the obscure reference suggests he was still linked in the public mind to the successful penny newspaper.

From the beginning of Beach's ownership of the *Sun,* Hamilton's relationship with him had been fraught. Moses Beach, never as affable as Benjamin Day, disliked Hamilton, and, judging by later events, the color of his skin was probably a factor in this. Everyone knew Hamilton remained a close friend of Beach's brother-in-law, the founder and impresario of the *Sun*'s glory days. While Beach needed to maintain continuity with the paper's past, he also was trying to remake it as his own, and, just to stir the already-volatile mix, his marriage to Nancy Day, Benjamin's older sister, was exhibiting signs of strain that would soon become public.

In spite of these tensions in the *Sun*'s office, Hamilton still dropped by most days and conversed with the new proprietor about the share market, bought and sold shares for him, allowed him to borrow some of his paintings, and even purchased silver from Beach and lent him money in a crunch. Beach's son, also named Moses, testified later that in the period from when Day left at the end of June 1838 until Bartlett quit the *Sun* in March 1843, Hamilton visited the office "very often." Asked to elaborate about how frequently he had seen Hamilton in his father's office, the son replied: "As many times as there were days in the year." Compared to the halcyon era of Day's ownership, though, there was now something forced and artificial about the atmosphere at the *Sun*. One former editor at the paper remembered that although Beach was invariably "courteous" to the black man, he "always seemed to be dissatisfied at Mr Hamilton's coming to his office." Beach's son concurred, recollecting that his father "did not relish his conversations" with Hamilton.

Unspoken resentments bubbled to the surface in a remarkable incident involving the editorial room's sofa and chairs, an arrangement of furniture that everyone treated as Hamilton's nook. Sometime after Day's departure, Beach reorganized the layout of the *Sun*'s workspace, selling the sofa and moving the chairs into his own office. He made these changes for one reason and only one reason. Moses Beach Jr., who had carried out "his father's order" to get rid of the furniture, remembered vividly that "the reason he gave for it [was] to prevent Hamilton's coming there." Undoubtedly, the black man knew what was going on, although, perhaps inured to the sting of such slights, he chose to ignore this particular indignity. The remodeling certainly did not affect the regularity of his visits to the *Sun* building. According to Beach's son, Beach and Hamilton "frequently after the removal conversed about stocks," but, he added, his father "always treated Hamilton coolly." Another court reporter scribbled down the younger Beach's words slightly differently, rendering them as "his father treated him coldly."[28]

In February 1840, one of the ubiquitous political squabbles broke out between the *Albany Evening Journal* and the *Sun*. The editor of the former concluded his attack by claiming: "It is understood that one of its principal proprietors is a negro!" This revisiting of James Gordon Bennett's earlier accusations in the *Herald* that Hamilton was an owner of the *Sun* touched one of Moses Beach's exposed nerves. He was very touchy about his relationships with Benjamin Day and Jeremiah Hamilton. Beach responded furiously, claiming the charge to be "filthy billingsgate" and "a wholesale falsehood." He continued in a deliberately insensitive outburst: "It is from beginning to end a lie blacker than any negro's skin, as black as the *Journal*'s malignity—it could not well be blacker." The *New York Sun* was "owned, and solely owned, by one man, whose name it bears as proprietor."[29] Moses Beach's pent-up feelings, frustrations and increasing dislike of Benjamin Day and his African American friend were becoming more and more obvious. An eruption of some sort seemed inevitable.

In all likelihood, Hamilton's life would have limped on in this fashion for some time, with the wily debtor fending off insolvency and, all the while, trying to carve out an alternative existence away from Wall Street in the offices of the *Sun*. Perhaps Vargas might even have come around to admitting that the black broker was right, that

Hamilton did know the law and that he was not going to be reimbursed one red cent. The leniency accorded those who had failed financially continually nonplussed travelers to America in the 1830s. Alexis de Tocqueville noticed the "strange indulgence that is shown to bankrupts." He concluded that "in this respect the Americans differ, not only from the nations of Europe, but from all the commercial nations of our time."[30] In spite of the supposed lack of resolve behind the law, Hamilton still had to live a constrained existence, with creditors waiting to pounce on any assets he accumulated. Debtors in Hamilton's position often slipped away quietly and began a new life somewhere else or traded surreptitiously under an assumed name; already, there had been rumors of the former, and the latter was a strategy he had definitely pursued. Although Hamilton may have been down, he had lost not one whit of his ambition: this black man had not migrated to New York merely to eke out an existence. Ironically, for antebellum America was a time and place that epitomized an all-but-unbridled free market, it was the federal government that threw a lifeline to Jeremiah Hamilton, and tens of thousands like him floundering in the aftermath of the financial panics of 1837 and 1839.

In 1841, the Whig-dominated 27th Congress created a federal bankruptcy system. Something had to be done about the number of failed financiers, merchants, small storekeepers and artisans obviously languishing in every one of the nation's cities and towns, and this was a way of trying to garner their political support. The Bankruptcy Act offered the down and out a chance to discharge their bankruptcy, to free themselves of their debts and start again, and allowed debtors, not just creditors, to initiate these proceedings. Its provisions were based on the generous assumptions that business failures were often caused by events beyond the individual's control and that American lives deserved a second act; as well, the legislation as a whole displayed a democratic impulse, making bankruptcy an option not just for the elite, but for everyone. The Bankruptcy Act was a noble experiment that cut across the grain of the Old World shibboleths of Alexis de Tocqueville and almost every other European traveler sojourning in the United States. Indeed, the measure was so liberal to debtors that squeals of complaint from creditors and those worried about centralized power forced Congress to repeal it on March 3, 1843. Nevertheless, in the thirteen months of the act's operation, some 33,000 individuals took advantage of the legislation, received a certificate discharging all their debts, and restarted their lives with a clean slate.[31]

On the morning of February 2, 1842, William W. Campbell, appointed commissioner under the Bankruptcy Act by Judge Samuel Rossiter Betts of the U.S. Court for the Southern District of New York, opened an office at 12 John Street not far from Wall Street. A writer in the *Sun* labeled the day the "Jubilee of the Bankrupts."[32] From the start Campbell was busy. On the fourth day of operation, a Saturday, Jeremiah Hamilton filed his petition for bankruptcy. Following the procedure, Hamilton published notices in the *New York Standard,* the *New York Evening Post* and the *Morning Courier and New-York Enquirer* daily for nearly a month. In April 1842 he was instructed that "notice [must] be given to all creditors who have proved their debts" to appear in court on June 29, 1842, an order that he fulfilled by publishing details in the *Morning Courier and New-York Enquirer* for seventy days. On that date, at ten o'clock in the morning in the District Court, in City Hall, Jeremiah Hamilton was discharged and handed his certificate as a bankrupt. Later in October 1842, Hamilton's assets—mostly debts owed him by other bankrupts such as Tinkham and Hart but also including "his residuary interest in an assignment made 31st Dec. 1838 to Elisha Morrill Esq. of certain real estate," or, in other words, his Poughkeepsie investments—were auctioned off at a general assignee's sale at 47 Liberty Street, only a few houses up from where he was now living with his mother-in-law.[33]

In common with thousands of newly discharged American bankrupts, Hamilton, now unencumbered with debt, was free to begin afresh. Unlike most of the others, though, Hamilton did not wait for the declaration of his bankruptcy to do so; he had already started buying and selling shares under an assumed name and probably transacting business in his wife's name. Hamilton had a very elastic view of the letter of the law as it applied to him, and I will pursue the details of some of his subterfuges later on. Perhaps surprisingly, making money off the books was far from being the most remarkable thing that Hamilton dabbled in from February to June 1842 while his bankruptcy petition was running its course—that distinction goes to an activity that did not break any law and involved Moses Beach.

In April 1842, Beach used the imprint of the Sun Office to publish *Wealth and Wealthy Citizens of New York City*. Almost the entirety of this eight-page pamphlet consisted of an alphabetical list of New Yorkers worth $100,000 or more. Next to each name was an estimate of the individual's wealth: supposedly Philip Hone was valued at $100,000; Cornelius Vanderbilt at $200,000; Moses Beach himself at $150,000; and, richest of all, John Jacob Astor at $10 million. In spite of its crudeness and obvious shortcomings, *Wealth and Wealthy Citizens* sold surprisingly well, and over the next six weeks three more editions rolled off Beach's press. The newspaperman ended up publishing twelve editions of the book, the last in 1855. Inevitably, success spawned imitators, and within a few years similar publications were on sale in Philadelphia, Boston and even Brooklyn. Mind you, it is not at all obvious who bought these compendiums of a city's well-to-do or why. Clearly, the round figures printed by Beach were only rough approximations, little more than guesses at a person's wealth: disconcertingly, the valuations of numerous individuals varied widely between successive editions of *Wealth and Wealthy Citizens* even when they were published within weeks of one another. These were hardly numbers on which merchants and banks could rely as a proxy for a credit rating or indeed for any business purpose. And yet these pamphlets sold.[34] Beach had initiated a curious genre that, if nothing else, memorialized an exuberant American ability to reduce everything and anyone, whether accurately or not, to a dollar value.

Beach's pamphlets had a second life of sorts in the first three quarters of the twentieth century as a variety of historians, no matter how hesitantly, used them as a source to reveal patterns of wealth distribution among antebellum New Yorkers. All this ceased in 1971 when the historian Edward Pessen confirmed some of those earlier scholars' misgivings by laying bare the many shortcomings of using these publications for such a purpose. Since then fashions of historical inquiry have moved on from the social to the cultural, and, for some decades now, no one has exhibited much interest in what is too often dismissed as dour economic history.

There is, however, one never-before-revealed twist to the story of these pamphlets that concerns the authorship of the first edition of *Wealth and Wealthy Citizens*. At the time, Moses Beach himself was frustratingly vague about how the pamphlet was compiled. Before publication he advertised in the *Sun* that persons "thoroughly acquainted with the business and businessmen of our great metropolis" had prepared the pamphlet. Much later, in the tenth and twelfth editions, he suggested that in the early 1840s businessmen pooling their information had come up with their own list that they asked the editor of the *Sun* to print for their convenience. This last scenario is unlikely—not only was there still a disreputable air to the *Sun* but its editor did not associate, or feel comfortable, with New York's financial establishment.[35] Beach's comments about the pamphlet's origins, perhaps deliberately, simply muddied the waters.

James M. Smith, a very impressive lawyer who will feature in my story later, first aired the suggestion that Jeremiah Hamilton was the person most responsible for compiling the first edition of *Wealth and Wealthy Citizens* in a libel case some twenty months after the pamphlet's publication. According to the *Herald*'s version of what happened at the trial, Smith, while cross-examining Lucius Robinson, a former editor of the *Sun,* stated: "Mr Hamilton prepared the manuscript for the pamphlet relative to the wealth of citizens of New York." The *True Sun*'s court reporter rendered Smith's words differently: "Do you know about the writing of the pamphlet in relation to wealthy citizens, and that the first difficulty was in relation to Hamilton's claiming the manuscript of that book?" Robinson brushed aside the question, claiming that he did "not know that I ever saw that manuscript." Undoubtedly, Smith's preparatory conversations with Hamilton before the trial informed his line of questioning, but what was likely the black man's version of events is, at the very least, credible. Hamilton, familiar with Wall Street and the business world, probably played a prominent role in compiling the first edition of *Wealth and Wealthy Citizens*. Argument over credit, and recompense too, for the black broker was bankrupt and short of cash, likely led to a further souring of the already-cool relations between Hamilton and Beach. After Bartlett left the newspaper in March 1843, Hamilton ceased visiting the *Sun* office.[36]

If Hamilton did indeed contribute substantially to the compilation of the material in *Wealth and Wealthy Citizens,* then the ironies are almost too exquisite to contemplate—a black man responsible for drawing up a list of white New York's elite, an insolvent debtor waiting for his bankruptcy to discharge compiling a directory of the city's wealthiest men. Even more striking, on the last two pages of the pamphlet were compendiums of useful information, including a list of the city's thirty-four insurance companies and their capitalizations.[37] Asking the Prince of Darkness, who had been blackballed and deemed uninsurable by these very firms, to put this information together was akin to asking a wolf to count the sheep in a farmer's pen. Even as Jeremiah Hamilton undertook the steps that allowed him to purge his financial failure, he did so with a grand style that marked him off from every other bankrupt in the city.

EIGHT

STARTING OVER

James Gordon Bennett of the *New York Herald* was a razor-sharp hack, but also capable of using his considerable intelligence to write strikingly original articles unlike anything any of his contemporaries was publishing. A few of his pieces still astonish well over a century and a half later. In December 1842, under the caption "Bankruptcies as Illustrative of the Social Condition," he mused on the Bankruptcy Act, which had then been in operation some eleven months. For Bennett the federal legislation was less a measure to ameliorate economic ruin, although this was undoubtedly Congress's intent, than a source of compelling material for examining the human condition. The 10,000 schedules spelling out the affairs of the nearly 2,000 New York City applicants for relief under the law "form a library of the most remarkable and instructive character," Bennett wrote. Indeed, "no collection of tomes in the known world, from that in the Vatican to the Bodleian Library, could compete with this extraordinary assemblage of manuscripts." They revealed "a perfect picture—drawn with all the stern fidelity of legal accuracy and precision—of the actual condition of society, the errors, follies, vices, and indiscretions of men—the course and progress of finance, morals and religion." Individual records, "these most curious of all auto-biographies," laid bare "the whole history of a man's career, with all its bounding hopes, its disappointments [and] its hypocrisies." Centuries ago, "they had their illuminated manuscripts, and with wonderfully graphic power did the artist often unfold and illustrate the story; but the plain, familiar, and unpicturesque numerals which occupy such conspicuous place in the bankrupt's schedule, have more significant expression than all the cunningly devised works of monkish illuminators." Each volume in this "extraordinary library" contained a text "written with admirable simplicity," one that we can comprehend immediately, for "it is the story of a life."[1] Bennett's eloquent advocacy of the power of these documents was at once refreshingly inclusive in its implications and startlingly prescient.

The prosaically labeled Schedule A, debts, and Schedule B, property, of Jeremiah Hamilton's bankruptcy file, as Bennett intimated would be the case, capture the black broker's life in early 1842. Most of his debts resulted from judgments against him handed down in a range of courts: as well as the $13,827.81 owed to Joseph Vargas, there is an April 1839 Superior Court judgment to Horace Larned of Providence for $6,867.53; a September 1839 judgment to Wainwright, Shiels and Higgins for $3,025.40; a June 1840 judgment to Rawson and McMurray for $1,112.52; another June 1840 judgment to the Bank of New York Dry Dock Company for $927.09; an April 1840 judgment to the same for $1801.21; and a May 1841 judgment to John Wood for $1,555.93. Lacking ready cash and with credit nonexistent thanks to the depression, Hamilton's affairs teetered on the brink of being out of control, their downward spiral marked by frequent appearances in front of a judge. As well, there were debts "claimed but not admitted" by Hamilton to three firms of brokers—$7,500 to John Ward and Co., $6,000 to Brown and Son, and $3,500 to Vaux and King—which doubtless in due course would have resulted in more judgments.

What these pages of figures reveal with remarkable clarity is the extent to which Hamilton used the legal system as a routine part of business. Forever hustling, disputing debts in order to postpone their payment, Hamilton looked on lawyers as a necessary, albeit expensive, tool. According to the schedule, by 1842 he owed Elisha

Morrill $150; John Anthon, counselor at law, $250 "for law services in 1839 & 1840"; Tillou and Cutting, attorneys and counselors at law, $600 "for law services in 1838, 1839, and 1840"; and McCann and West, attorneys at law, $125 "for law services in 1839 & 1840." He had employed other lawyers as well, though, perhaps needing to keep them on side, he paid their fees more promptly.

Hamilton's assets were also a litany of lawsuits, as well as transactions destined for adjudication in court, the only place anyone was likely to be able to sort them out. The broker claimed that Tinkham and Hart owed him "about $24,000" for "advances on mercantile operations in 1834, 35, 36, & 37," suggesting that the firm's failure cost him an extra $10,000 on top of his loss in the Vargas sugar deal. John J. Crary owed "about $10,500" for Poughkeepsie real estate and stock in the Silk Company of Poughkeepsie sold him by Hamilton in January 1837. Hamilton had advanced Stephen Hendrickson $35,000 in August 1835 and had only been repaid some $25,000, so was owed a further $10,000. He also claimed that J. L. and S. J. Joseph, one of the earlier and most spectacular bankruptcies of the 1837 panic, were in debt to him for $15,000. His most valuable asset, at least nominally, remained the Poughkeepsie real estate that Hamilton had assigned to Elisha Morrill on December 31, 1838, an investment that had cost him $27,000.[2]

In any totting up of the balance sheet, Hamilton came out comfortably in the black. His debts totaled $55,807.49, or slightly more than $13 million in current dollars, and his assets, including the assigned real estate, added up to $97,359.89, or more than $22 million in today's dollars. Of course, the problem was that all these figures, no matter which side of the ledger they were on, were fictitious, a listing of how much things had cost before the 1837 panic. The business failures of that year, followed by five years of depressed conditions, rendered much of the paper written during the boom—be it property deeds, stocks, bills of exchange or even bank notes—worth only cents on the dollar, if that, by 1842. Although Hamilton had invested $27,000 in his Poughkeepsie property, in 1842 it was worth only a fraction of that inflated price; similarly, several of the debts owed to him by other bankrupts were almost worthless. For Jeremiah Hamilton and thousands of others, the Bankruptcy Act was a godsend, offering the opportunity to be forgiven for, and to forget, mistakes they had made in the madness of the boom, allowing them not to bother trying to reclaim money owed from other debtors, to write off their own debts, and to start over with a clean slate.

Although Jeremiah Hamilton was very keen to forgo his debts, he was more reluctant to part with his assets. Here, once again, Hamilton demonstrated a remarkable knowledge of the way things worked. Between the spring of 1842 and December 1844 American towns and cities took on the appearance of a gigantic fire sale as the authorities disposed of the remaining assets of thousands of bankrupts. The *Morning Courier and New-York Enquirer* earned $20,000 in fees advertising such auctions on its back page. Furniture, paintings, jewelry and the like were sold off, as were the stock of failed stores, livestock, real estate, mortgages, a remarkable variety of book debts, and, in the South, slaves. For most of this period the economy continued to wallow in the doldrums, and prices stayed at rock-bottom levels. Anyone who was cashed up—for auctioneers usually insisted on cash on the barrelhead—could choose from an astounding variety of items at ludicrously cheap prices.

Successful scavenging at bankruptcy auctions depended on intelligence, on knowing which assets had a potential resale value and which were worthless. According to the leading historian of the 1841 federal Bankruptcy Act, in New York there were about twenty individuals who bought most of the items sold at bankruptcy sales. What remains completely opaque is how these men and any other interested parties arranged matters at the auctions to ensure that they did not bid against one another and drive up prices. The record of sales certainly suggests they were successful.[3]

On October 6, 1842, Jeremiah Hamilton strolled up his street to attend the general assignees' sale at 47 Liberty Street. Lot 81 consisted of eight debts to Hamilton totaling $68,359.37 and his residuary interest in the assignment of real estate to Elisha Morrill. No value was included with the last, but in boom times it had cost Hamilton some $27,000. It is unknown if there were any other bids, but Hamilton paid $20 cash for debts and real estate that back in 1836 had been worth some $95,000. While he was at the auction, he also bought two other lots, twenty shares in a railroad company for $12.50 and a small debt for $25. The main thing, though, was that he was now free of any debt and had retained ownership of his Poughkeepsie real estate—and all for the outlay of $20.[4]

For critics of the Bankruptcy Act—and they became more numerous and vociferous as the months went by—the legislation brushed aside the rights of creditors and granted debtors far too painless an absolution for their sins. In January 1843, a writer for the *New York Sun* went so far as to label it an "obnoxious law," one "so full of festered, putrifying sores that it has become offensive to all honest men." Creditors, he lamented further, "have nothing to do but watch the desolation and havoc it made with their credits and hopes."[5] Those who had lost large amounts of their capital were galled even more by the knowledge that at least some debtors were exploiting the law to its fullest, declaring bankruptcy only in order to renege on the whole gamut of their debts—and to do so without any legal penalty.

From the moment on only the fourth day of the law's operation when Hamilton filed his petition for bankruptcy, the black man exuded the air of someone manipulating, if not breaking, the law for his own advantage. Mind you, this was an accusation that could have been leveled at many white New Yorkers. It was certainly the case that during the five years following the 1837 panic, and most particularly in the latter stages of this period, Hamilton, for all of his supposedly straitened financial circumstances, did not live an abstemious life. His debts included livery stable charges, extensive medical bills, and even a $1,200 charge to a real estate agent for guaranteeing the rent of Margaret Morris, his mother-in-law. As well, these were the years in which Hamilton haunted the offices of the *New York Sun* and he and his friends, Day and Bartlett, gadded about town frequently, loudly and obviously. There was also an entry on the schedule of debts for "about $3500" owed to Benjamin Day "for money lent by him to me in various sums in 1840 and 1841." The wording here makes it unlikely that these loans related to business; more probably, his friend advanced Hamilton money to meet his not inconsiderable living expenses.

For critics of the legislation, a supposedly bankrupt petitioner living large would have been offensive enough, but other actions of

Hamilton went well beyond the pale and could only have confirmed their belief that federal government intercession in the market did little more than encourage criminal behavior. A fortnight before Hamilton received his discharge and certificate of bankruptcy, on June 29, 1842, a Daniel Robinson sued Jacob Carpenter, a partner in the Wall Street brokerage firm of Rowlands, Graham and Carpenter, for the return of $250, a deposit for a sixty-day option on the purchase of one hundred shares of Long Island Railroad Company stock. Curiously, not once during the case did Robinson cross the threshold of Judge Oakley's courtroom. Instead, as the *Herald*'s reporter recorded, "the plaintiff was represented by the renowned 'colored' broker—(beg his pardon)—Mr Jeremiah G. Hamilton." By "represented" the writer did not mean that Hamilton was Robinson's lawyer, but simply that the black man stood in for the plaintiff during the proceedings. Although Carpenter's counsel made a particular point of informing everyone present that Hamilton "was the only Daniel Robinson that existed, or rather that no such man as Daniel Robinson existed at all," the court remained uninterested in this strange fact. Indeed, counsel and press seem to have treated Hamilton's replacement of Robinson with a certain amount of levity. Conceivably, no one present realized Hamilton was days from being discharged as a bankrupt.[6] Regardless, clearly the black broker was trading in the market under a false name—and likely this had occurred more often than this one time that came to light. Not only was Hamilton breaking the law, but the transaction underlying the option—the purchase of one hundred shares of Long Island Railroad Company stock—involved a considerable sum somewhere in the high four figures. Once again, Hamilton had ridden roughshod over everyone else, treating legal requirements with all the disdain of a Cornelius Vanderbilt or any other white tycoon in the making.

By the middle of 1842, Hamilton was a man in a hurry, desperate to reestablish himself as a financial player in the city and to make up for five lost years. No longer burdened by debt, but needing to make money quickly, Hamilton turned to a familiar cash cow, one he had milked ruthlessly in his early years in New York—the marine insurance industry. It was an obvious choice for him, and, after all, he had only just re-familiarized himself with the business as he compiled the list of thirty-four insurance companies and their capitalizations for the endpapers of *Wealth and Wealthy Citizens of New York City* (1842). The lurid details of what would occur over the ensuing year were disputed at the time and, even though extensively raked over by the press and courts, never resolved properly.

The story began a decade earlier. On November 5, 1832, the *India,* captained by Hatherly Barstow, sailed from New York for Peru. In Callao, the port for Lima, the captain picked up a cargo of bullion bound for Cadiz. Peter Harmony and Co. had arranged insurance with the Atlantic Insurance Company for six boxes of specie valued at $17,250 and fives boxes containing 1,229 silver marks worth $29,150. The *India* then traveled some 700 miles southward to Guayaquil, Ecuador, where dockworkers carried onboard a box containing 973 gold castellanos, insured for their value of $2,375. For a premium of 1.25 percent (about $610), Atlantic had underwritten $48,775 worth of bullion, belonging to a Jose Maria Lunar, for the trip to Cadiz.[7] On May 2, 1833, the *India* set sail, but on September 3, 1833, near the end of her long voyage across the Atlantic, the ship was "by the perils and dangers of the seas and stormy and tempestuous weather and by the force and violence of the winds and waves, wrecked, foundered and sunk, whereby the said silver, specie and bullion were wholly lost to the said Joseph Maria Lunar."

Surviving the wreck of the *India,* Captain Barstow arrived in New York on November 6, 1833. Soon after, the captain, claiming to be Lunar's agent, demanded Atlantic pay out the policy, but the company refused on the ground of alleged fraud. Although Barstow sued, the Superior Court stayed proceedings, insisting that he produce authority from the plaintiff named in the suit. In December 1834, Barstow told his wife Cornelia that he had "to proceed to South America to find Mr Lunar and bring him here, or procure further documentary evidence of his ownership of said property." He left New York on Christmas Day 1834, and although months later she heard of sightings of Barstow in Vera Cruz and Guatemala, Cornelia Barstow never saw her husband again.

Six years later, a William Thompson, purporting to be a Wall Street insurance broker, visited Cornelia Barstow and insisted "that he could recover for her the money that her husband had in litigation with the Atlantic Insurance Company." He cajoled her into taking out letters of administration and recommencing the suit. She placed the matter in the hands of Tillou and Cutting. Later on she remembered that twelve to eighteen months after Thompson's visit "she was called upon by a Colored man, said to be named Hamilton." He told her that not only had Lunar arrived in New York, but also "Lunar was there at his Hamilton's house, and also . . . that he could produce Mr Lunar at any moment in Court." Armed with Lunar's power of attorney, Hamilton requested that Barstow hand over voluntarily the documentation of the case against Atlantic Insurance, explaining that if she did not he would be compelled to resort to the force of the law. Recounting the detail of this conversation, the *Herald* reporter could not resist italicizing and marking with an exclamation Hamilton's proffered reasoning—"*but he was reluctant to enter on such a course as she was a female!*" This was less commentary on Hamilton's patter to the widow and more broadcasting a black man's effrontery in talking to a white woman in such a fashion. Nevertheless, Hamilton's veiled threat was persuasive. Barstow instructed Tillou and Cutting to deliver the papers to Hamilton's lawyer, John Anthon, and that, as she later related, was the last that the widow heard of the case.

Fifty thousand dollars was a small fortune—more than $11 million in today's currency. In all likelihood stories about the *India*'s cargo of insured bullion had animated the tavern and eating-house talk of the coterie of brokers and merchants involved in the Caribbean and Latin American trade for years. Two men clearly had heard about the shipwreck: one was Jeremiah Hamilton, and the other James Bergen. Bergen, born in New Haven, Connecticut, about 1810, made his livelihood as an insurance broker and notary public. In December 1835, only days after the Great Fire, he advertised in the *Journal of Commerce,* offering his services as a broker to anyone needing to insure their property with Boston underwriters now that almost every New York insurance firm had failed. Occasionally, he also picked up work as an arbitrator, adjudicating disputed claims against insurance companies in a process that, if both parties agreed, could be a quicker and much cheaper alternative than a full-dress trial in court. Although he had a good reputation and was clever, as with so many other New York brokers, the 1837 panic and its aftermath laid waste to Bergen's business. In 1842 he petitioned for bankruptcy, and in April 1842, a couple of months before Hamilton, he received his discharge and certificate.[8] The pair, hungry to make money, knew the insurance industry inside out. Unfortunately, it is impossible to know who approached whom with a proposal to scam Atlantic Insurance. Both Hamilton and Bergen refused to answer all questions about the claim, and no court or district attorney ever enticed, or trapped, either of them into changing this sensible stance. Most of the public knowledge of what supposedly happened in the early stages of the conspiracy came from a third person, Richard Sutton, who, once arrested—and in marked contrast to the others—found it difficult to stop talking.

Richard Sutton, sometimes Sutter, a shipmaster, had three children and a wife living with one of his sons in Buenos Aires. Spanish-speaking, he mostly worked on Caribbean and Latin American routes and had first become acquainted with Bergen in New York about 1840 as a result of the latter's underwriting of several of his voyages. In October 1842, Sutton visited Bergen's office several times, and on two or three of those occasions the insurance broker dropped into the conversation that he was attempting to recover "a large amount of money" from an underwriter for a lost cargo of bullion. On November 16, 1842, Bergen took Sutton out to lunch at George Brown's establishment on Water Street.[9] They whiled away a couple of hours there drinking brandy diluted with a splash of water and then a considerable quantity of wine with their meal—the *New York Tribune*'s later gloss was that by the time Sutton left Brown's, he "was pretty thoroughly fuddled, and his moral senses completely blunted." After the pair returned to the office, Bergen explained that the case he had spoken about was "nothing more or less than *an intended fraud upon the Atlantic Insurance Company*" and that he needed someone to swear they knew Lunar and had seen him sign an affidavit. Sutton, still "pretty much excited by liquor," agreed, "having been promised that he should receive some thousands of dollars for such service."[10]

Straightaway, an obviously prepared Bergen produced a drawn-up affidavit and escorted Sutton to the office of William Austin, a commissioner of deeds, at 14 Wall Street. There Sutton signed the document, attesting that he had met Lunar in Cadiz twenty-two years previously and that he had witnessed him signing a particular affidavit. Bergen then walked the still-somewhat-the-worse-for-wear shipmaster to another commissioner of deeds in a nearby office in the *Courier and Enquirer* building. Here Bergen brought out a second prepared affidavit, one in which this time Sutton swore that he was in fact Jose Maria Lunar, the owner of the bullion that sank to the bottom of the Atlantic with the *India*. As Sutton would explain later, he was "perfectly ignorant" of the contents of the second document and did not have a clue what he was swearing to.

At this point, Sutton had met Hamilton on a couple of occasions in Bergen's office but without speaking more than a word or two to him. Next time Sutton came by, Bergen confided to the shipmaster that Hamilton too was involved in the conspiracy, and "this produced a confidence between all parties," prompting several conversations "upon the business and its prospect of success." Subsequently, Sutton had three meetings with Hamilton at the black broker's house at 124 Greenwich Street, the last time without Bergen being present. On these occasions "Hamilton and he consulted about how their future movements were to be regulated, and the plans for carrying out the fraud were more fully matured." Very quickly, Sutton concluded that Hamilton was the "chief mover" in this illegal enterprise.

Unsurprisingly, the principals of Atlantic Insurance were suspicious of the resuscitated claim against them for $50,000. Early in January 1843, Atlantic's counsel asked the Superior Court to make Lunar "show where he resided at the time of the shipment, and his history since." On January 19, Bergen called on Sutton and told him they needed him to sign another affidavit. Picking up Hamilton at his house, all three proceeded to Isaac Labagh's office on the corner of Centre and Chambers streets, where Sutton again impersonated Jose Maria Lunar. This time, though, the affidavit added the details that Lunar was born in Madrid, was unmarried, had no fixed place of residence, and when he insured the specie back in 1833 was temporarily living in Callao making a livelihood as "a general trader along the west coast of South America." Although on this occasion "he was sober," Sutton confessed some months later that yet again he "did not know a single word" of the document to which he had affixed Lunar's name. In all likelihood Sutton, who spoke Spanish whenever he dealt with Bergen, could not read English. On March 6, 1843, the court, unsatisfied by the laconic deposition, stayed proceedings until "more information has been obtained relative to the plaintiff's residence in South America, at the asserted time of shipping the specie."[11]

Hamilton and Bergen were well aware that when they crossed Atlantic Insurance, they were taking on a powerful entity. According to *Wealth and Wealthy Citizens of New York City* (1842), Atlantic was capitalized at $350,000—outstripped by only six of the thirty-four New York insurance companies. Over the previous dozen years it had been immensely profitable. In June 1843, the directors declared a dividend of 35 percent, a phenomenal return by anyone's standard. Since June 1830, Atlantic stockholders had received dividends totaling more than four times their original investment in the company.[12] Needless to say, the directors of Atlantic were not going to lie down and pay out $50,000, or near 15 percent of the company's capitalization, without a fight.

Atlantic Insurance had refused adamantly to pay the claim for reimbursement of the lost bullion on the *India* since 1834. The initial ground used to deny Barstow the money was "alleged fraud." Right from the start there was a taint to the case: likely, talk that someone had made a switch and the specie had not been onboard when the ship went down had helped keep the story alive. Certainly Sutton had heard such rumors. In one of his statements, he revealed that "a Gentleman who was on the West Coast of South America" had informed him long ago "that it was all a humbug about the money that was said to have been shipped." As far as Atlantic was concerned, the original attempted fraud from 1833 was now being complicated in 1843 by different perpetrators trying on a con. It was a case encapsulating the perennial problems of switched cargoes and suspect identities that bedeviled marine insurance. And right at the center of the whole affair was their bête noire, a man whose reputation with them was so bad that, some seven years previously, the entire New York marine insurance industry had combined to impose a ban on underwriting any venture associated with Jeremiah Hamilton.

Atlantic Insurance placed the case in the hands of the New York police in January 1843 and immediately brought pressure to bear on the authorities, resulting in an unprecedented deployment of scant resources on the investigation. According to the *Herald,* two police officers, one clerk in the Police Department, and a special justice named George Matsell "traced the steps of the parties through seven dreary months to establish the case beyond the possibility of controversy," moving "with great care, circumspection, and secrecy."[13] Needless to say, this was many times the manpower ever used in searching for the murderer of an African American in the Five Points.

On August 4, 1843, a pair of policemen took Bergen and Hamilton into custody. The arrest was a sensation, an event the *Herald* marked the next day with one of its longer and more lurid captions atop a story that ran to nearly 3,000 words:

Extraordinary Charge of Conspiracy to Defraud the Atlantic Insurance Company—Arrest of "Nigger" Hamilton, and James Bergen, a Notary Public—Wall street in an Uproar—Committal for Trial—Letter from Bergen to the Editor of the Herald—Impudent Letter of "Nigger" Hamilton to the Editor of the Herald—Attempt to Suppress the Publication of the Proceedings by Bribery and Threats.

According to the *Herald,* considerable excitement "existed in Wall street, and round the Tombs, in consequence of the arrest of James Bergen, a Notary Public, and Jeremiah G. Hamilton, better known as the 'Nigger proprietor of the *Sun*,' on a charge of attempting an enormous fraud on the Atlantic Insurance Company." Although at this time James Gordon Bennett was absent on a four-month tour of England and France, his reporters understood well enough to work "Nigger" twice into the caption and the now-familiar intended slur about Hamilton owning the *Sun* into the first sentence of the article. Having impugned the black man, the *Herald* reassured its readers that everything was legitimate and that there had been a lengthy investigation into the conspiracy, although the case "was not 'ripe' until some few days ago."[14]

After their arrest, Justice Matsell set bail, as the *Herald* reporter put it, for "Nigger Hamilton in the sum of $8000, and to justify in $22,000" and for "Mr Bergen in $8000, and $10,000 to justify in." Although a short while later Hamilton's friend Benjamin Day entered the necessary bonds for Hamilton, Bergen was forced to linger for several days in custody. According to the *Herald* reporter, once bailed, Hamilton approached him in the Tombs "and begged us to withhold the publication for one day, and that he would pay any amount we would require." When his request was turned down, Hamilton "added something about suits for damage, or former liberality," but the *Herald* man was "too busily engaged to suffer anything which such a character could say or offer."[15]

At the end of the piece, the *Herald* printed two short letters. The first, from James Bergen, registered his surprise at his arrest that morning and suggested that "by attacking the Company, in due season" he would convince everyone "I have never yet committed an act for which I should hide my head with shame." The second, from Hamilton, attracted an irritated editorial comment: "We also received at a late hour last night the following impudent letter from 'Nigger' Hamilton, which speaks for itself." Hamilton also dismissed the accusation of conspiracy, which "will prove to be infamously false and wickedly malicious and corrupt," but clearly what rankled the *Herald* writer was the missive's last sentence. Hamilton concluded: "I hereby notify you that I shall hold you legally responsible for the publication of any ex parte statement relative thereto in your paper."[16] "Impudent" was a word to slap down a black man who did not jump out of the way quick enough on the sidewalk or fail to show suitable deference to his white better. An African American man insisting that he was going to hold a white institution legally responsible for its actions was unprecedented and caught everyone by surprise. Hamilton's refusal to satisfy expectations of the way he should behave riled influential whites.

Other newspapers gave the story extensive coverage as well. The *Daily Plebeian* editorialized that "the public are deeply indebted to the extraordinary discretion, perseverance, and tack of Justice Matsell, Mr Osborne, Clerk of the Police, for ferreting out and establishing upon the celebrated Jeremiah G. Hamilton, alias 'the Prince of

Darkness,' (a well known mulatto merchant of Wall street,)" and
Bergen the charge of conspiring to defraud Atlantic "out of about
$50,000." Most of the attention focused on Hamilton, who contin-
ued to fascinate the press, and it did not take long before assumptions that were likely influenced by race worked their way to the
surface. "As has been remarked by a magistrate," the *Plebeian* reporter surmised, Hamilton "was doubtless the master mind of the
whole plot, and had duped Bergen." An out-of-town commentator,
presumably drawing simply on the coverage in New York papers,
quickly managed to discern that Bergen had an "excellent character for truth and honor" and that "many think Bergen innocent,"
but could only conclude "Hamilton is known to be a consummate
scoundrel." Although there was the occasional hint of caution—the
Commercial Advertiser reporter reminded his readers that they only
had "one side of the story" and that more information "may give a
very different aspect to the whole affair"—for most whites there was
little, if any, doubt that the black man was guilty as charged.[17]

Indeed, every now and then, there was a hint of admiration at
Hamilton's nerve. According to the *Plebeian*, "so successful was this
whole scheme of Hamilton's managed, that the Insurance Company
sometime since offered to settle the matter by paying half of the
amount claimed." The reporter could "not recollect to have ever
heard of a more stupendous attempt at fraud in this country." Similarly, the *New York Evening Post*'s brief account of the arrest ran under the caption "Daring Attempt to Defraud an Insurance Office."[18]

That sentence in the *Plebeian* was the only suggestion in any of
the commentary on, or documentation of, the case that Atlantic was
remotely interested in a compromise. More noticeable in the days
after Hamilton's and Bergen's arrests was the insurance company's
presence everywhere. On Monday, August 7, there was a hearing on
a writ of habeas corpus issued by Bergen in an effort to get out of
prison. The district attorney himself appeared for the people, accompanied, as the *Herald*'s man observed, by "several legal gentlemen
of this city, who were understood to be counsel for the Insurance
Company." Also present in the chambers were "the President of the
Atlantic Insurance Company, several directors and stockholders,
and the Inspector of the Company."[19]

In his letter published in several New York newspapers on August 5, Bergen had lambasted his opponent, referring to "the infamous management of the officers of the Atlantic Insurance Company, who have been my personal enemies for years, and who would crush any man who dared to oppose their interests as fearlessly as I have done."[20] As far as its critics were concerned, some suggestion of how far Atlantic was willing to go to crush its opponents surfaced in a bizarre incident that occurred on the following Tuesday night.

The *Sun* was first with the story although spare with any detail of what had happened. According to the paper's reporter, Jeremiah Hamilton had "had a respectable citizen brought before the Police yesterday upon a charge of being hired by the Atlantic Insurance Company to drown him—the negro!" The writer reported that the magistrate "very properly dismissed the charge at once," but after that he ran out of news and puffed out his article with invective. As was intended, what followed cut to the quick. Hamilton, according to the *Sun,* was "a walking forgery, having shaved his wool close, and wearing a wig of straight hair, which, however, cannot conceal his flat nose and thick lips." For years he had been a friend of Moses Beach and reporters on the *Sun*'s staff, an intimacy that made such a personal attack all the more vicious a betrayal. The writer brought up Hamilton's past—"queer stories are told of his adventures in Hayti, where 'tis said his colored brethren owe him no good will"— and added, for good measure, that it was "commonly reported that he had been black-balled in every Insurance Office in Wall street." He concluded his hatchet job sententiously: "It is a pity the world could not have his full history."[21]

In contrast, the *Herald* covered the story in greater detail and also treated the black man with at least some respect. Although Bergen still languished in the city prison, Hamilton was out on bail and "so extensively notorious, he had been selected as the victim or participator in a counterplot, the effect of which must have been experienced to be fully felt." On Tuesday morning Hamilton had received an anonymous note from a man who, although he had speculated away most of his wealth, had a proposal to put to him, a scheme that would require little money but needed the presence of someone in South America on short notice. The message hinted that the plan was of doubtful legality and requested a meeting at the end of Pier No. 1 on the North River at nine o'clock that night. At the nominated time, Hamilton, followed by two friends, walked to the end of the wharf and "there found an athletic man very genteelly dressed." Hamilton accosted him, demanding to know what he wanted, but the man, seeing the broker's bodyguards lurking in the shadows, refused to explain himself. A jittery Hamilton, concluding that his life was in danger, called his friends over, and they compelled "the gentleman in black" to accompany them to the watch house. Once there they established that the "mysterious stranger," "instead of being a genius of darkness ascended from below to aid Hamilton in his present insurance difficulties," as the *Herald* reporter sarcastically put it, turned out to be "the somewhat notorious Seth Driggs now an applicant to John Tyler for a consulship to some South American port, and who, we believe, formerly represented this country in that capacity." The following morning, before Justice Merritt, Hamilton confronted Driggs, who admitted that he had indeed written the anonymous letter "but gave no explanation as to the cause for such singular conduct." As there was no legal ground to hold him, Driggs was released, "and this endeth this plot and counter plot against Jeremiah G. Hamilton."[22]

Although the mainstream newspapers—and by now the *Sun* and the *Herald* deserved that label—spilled considerable ink on the alleged conspiracy, there was a sameness to the stories they printed. The coverage, characterized by all-too-easy racist assumptions about Hamilton, certainly looks from this distance as if it was fueled by adroit leaks to journalists from the district attorney or Atlantic Insurance. That changed when Mike Walsh, editor of the *Subterranean,* started to develop an interest in the story. Almost singlehandedly, he changed the way everyone regarded the case.

Mike Walsh had been born in County Cork in Ireland in 1810 and migrated to the United States as a young boy. A lithographer and journalist by trade, he was a vocal advocate for the rights of workers and harbored, as Sean Wilentz, the major historian of the American working class in this period, has put it, an "increasingly vitriolic anticapitalism." He also had an enviable way with words—his electioneering speeches mauling the city's elite were often very funny and the

Subterranean, with the motto "Independent in everything—Neutral in nothing" emblazoned across its masthead, one of the era's livelier newspapers, its writers regularly hauled into court on charges of libel and obscenity.[23]

Walsh's first discussion of the conspiracy charges, published on Saturday, August 12, began quietly, noting that the name of Jeremiah G. Hamilton "has been the unceasing topic of abuse during this past week." He then proceeded to turn that "abuse" on its head. All he had to go on was the published accounts in the other newspapers, but to him it appeared that Hamilton "has had the cunning and address to circumvent and outwit a band of swindling depredators, in the shape of an Insurance Company." While it was true enough that "robbing even them" was against the law and should not go unpunished, "the idea of getting up sympathy for such wholesale plunderers is absurd in the extreme, as well as insulting to real misfortune." Walsh found it "amusing" to watch "the capering of rotten magistrates and pettifogging litterateurs," all supposedly motivated only by "moral devotion."

Walsh's radical iconoclasm afforded him a perspective unlike that of any other commentator, and this particular case also allowed him scope to settle a few scores on the side. He, for one, had little trouble accounting for "the painful clamor of the Herald curs, and the bed bug perseverance and malignity of Beach." The first had been stymied "in an attempt to collect black mail—always a legitimate groundwork for their attacks." Beach, on the other hand, still "smarted under a lively recollection of the kicks and cuffs frequently bestowed on him by Hamilton during their early intimacy." Elaborating on this, Walsh sneered at Beach's "impudent and stupid presumption in attempting on several occasions to overreach and out financier one who was so much his master." For Walsh, these personal grudges explained the current clamor. He had almost no knowledge of Hamilton beyond the public record, but "it requires very little discernment to see that he is far ahead, both in talent and *character* to the miserable wretches of the Sun and the Herald."[24]

Although commentary died down for a while as the city's legal machinery commenced processing the conspiracy charges, the matter erupted a fortnight later in the aftermath of another article Walsh

published in the *Subterranean,* a piece that could be fairly charac-
terized as investigative journalism. Its headline read, in part: "VILE
CONSPIRACY TO DEFEAT A CIVIL SUIT" and "WHOLESALE BRIBERY
BY AN INSURANCE COMPANY IN WALL STREET." The intrepid journalist had uncovered a "nefarious and high-handed plot or conspiracy"
to indict Hamilton and Bergen for "an alleged attempt" to defraud
Atlantic Insurance. It turned out that, earlier in the year, William
H. Thompson (indeed the same man who had claimed to be a Wall
Street broker and pressured Cornelia Barstow into recommencing
her suit against Atlantic) was in prison awaiting determination of
the six indictments for grand larceny against him. Sometime in May
1843, Special Justice George Matsell, who was pursuing the investigation into the claim against the insurance company, spoke to the
then-acting district attorney and arranged to have a verdict of *nolle
prosequi* entered on the indictments against Thompson (in other
words, the charges would not be prosecuted). Walsh's researches in
the records of the Court of Sessions failed to uncover any trace of
these indictments, a development he considered "somewhat strange."

On Thompson's release from jail, Stokely, one of the police officers on the task force investigating the conspiracy, accompanied him
to Port Richmond on Staten Island, where he took lodgings in the
same house in which Richard Sutton was boarding. There, Thompson fulfilled handsomely his side of the deal he had struck with
Matsell. Over a number of weeks he befriended Sutton—generously
dispensing to him both liquor and money, as well as making further
"large promises of cash and advancement," or "tampering" with the
witness, as Walsh characterized his actions—and then convinced
him to agree to swear to a false statement concocted by Thompson
himself. Having achieved this, Thompson "got Sutton peculiarly intoxicated by drugs and liquors for the occasion" and accompanied
him on the ferry across the river to the city, where he took him before
Justice Matsell and the clerk of police. This pair "enlarged the said
statement, and put it in the form of an affidavit, which Sutton swore
to, whilst in a state of stupefaction." Matsell had Sutton confined
immediately in the Tombs and "sent for Walter R. Jones, President
of the Atlantic Insurance Company, in order that he might have an
interview with Sutton, and *come to a mutual understanding and*

agreement." Since then, the shipmaster had been kept under lock and key as a way of avoiding having anyone question his testimony. Apparently, the story Sutton was now telling was "so difficult for his memory that he requires a daily drill, Sunday not excepted." Walsh had also heard secondhand that, after using "Sutton for their vile purposes," Matsell and his confederates planned to cut loose their stool pigeon, convict him of perjury and send him to the state prison, obviating the need to deliver on any of their promises to him.

These sensational charges of corruption went to the heart of the administration of justice in New York. Walsh demanded "that the public should be informed of the nature of the agreement between the insurance company, the police magistrate, the police officers and the thief Thompson." He damned the lot of them as "thieves and vagabonds who are attempting by similar means to crush us!" and ended his peroration by asking, "How much will they rob us out of next week?"[25]

Other newspapers began to pick up the story. Horatio Bartlett's *Sunday Bulletin* chimed in that Sutton had been bought for $5,000 and "an opportunity to luxuriate unmolested on the banks of the Rio Grande," although, now that he had told his story, he had "a fair prospect of exchanging Rio Grande for Sing Sing for the ensuing ten years." A taken-aback writer in the *True Sun* simply added that "if one half of what the Subterranean puts forth on this matter is true, there will be some singular developments at the next term of the Court of Sessions."[26] Walsh reveled in the furor. In the next issue of the *Subterranean* he boasted that his article had "created quite a fluttering among all the rascals about the Tombs" and, as a bonus, had irritated both Matsell and Stokely by bringing to light their "infamous proceedings." Furthermore, Walsh had heard that "all the parties belonging to the Insurance Company *now* condemn" the conduct of those entrusted with law enforcement in the city. Walsh may have been unmoved by such a protestation, but for most this was a plausible denial, certainly one believable enough to allow the focus to shift away from Atlantic Insurance and any broader consideration of corporate behavior.

Just as he had seven years earlier when fighting Leech and Johnson, Jeremiah Hamilton worked the press—he sent them notes, visited editors and sent emissaries to chat with them. He sensed that the struggle with Atlantic Insurance was one in which the court of public opinion could be decisive, playing almost as large a role as the actual legal system. Within days of Hamilton and Bergen's arrests, the *Daily Plebeian* had printed an apology of sorts. "We are led to believe," the editor wrote, with the passive voice obscuring who had changed his mind, that the *Plebeian*'s story "did great injustice to both Mr Bergen and Mr Hamilton." Although the editor now claimed not to have read the original piece, he acknowledged that "it should have appeared in a form embodying the plain facts of the case without any irrelevant allusions."[27]

More significantly, in early September a statement about the "Alleged Conspiracy Case," issued under James Bergen's name (but it is difficult to believe Hamilton was not involved in its composition as well), was sent to the *New York Evening Post,* the *Morning Courier and New-York Enquirer,* and other papers. In it, Bergen attacked the confessed perjurer Richard Sutton's accusations, particularly the claim that Hamilton and Bergen had induced Sutton to impersonate Jose Maria Lunar. The police had since summoned two of the three commissioners of deeds to the city prison to look closely at Sutton, and these officials now swore that Sutton was not the man who had signed the documents they had witnessed more than six months previously. The third commissioner, already acquainted with Sutton for a couple of years, reconfirmed that it had not been Sutton who signed as Lunar in his office. Bergen ended by suggesting that "personal revenge" was at play in the fabrication of false charges against them, that enemies had used "the *name* of the *state* . . . not for the public good, but for private malice, and to serve unworthy purposes, in a civil suit."[28]

Most significant of all, the *Herald* commenced a campaign to find out more about the dealings of officials with William Thompson. The first article on this subject prompted a visit to the *Herald* office the next day from Thompson, demanding to know who had written the piece in question. Such threatening behavior only reinforced the determination of the paper's reporters to get to the bottom of the affair. For weeks, the *Herald* persisted in asking questions. "Why is it that 'one-eyed' Thompson is not re-arrested?" "Why is it that the entries of the *nolle prosequis* were kept so secret from the reporter of the Court of Sessions, contrary to all practice and precedent?" "What other important service did Thompson render the police, that he is now allowed to prowl through the streets of our city?" "Has it come to this that such a being can be used as a decoy duck to the police, on which to procure the arrest of citizens without strong conclusive and overwhelming confirmation?" None of these questions would ever be answered—the only response, as the *Herald* writer noted, was "a studied silence and secrecy."[29]

Over the next few months the case of *Atlantic Insurance v. Hamilton and Bergen* wended its way slowly to the inevitable anticlimax. The public had glimpsed the unsavory life wriggling under the rock, but no one really wanted to know any more about it—the rock was replaced quickly, and everyone pretended nothing had ever happened. In mid-September, counsel for Hamilton and Bergen argued the case in demurrer, a hearing questioning not so much the merits of the plaintiff's argument itself but more whether what was alleged, if proved, constituted a crime or not. The lawyer vigorously put it to the court "that the Grand Jury had not presented the accused as guilty of any crime whatsoever, and that the acts of the three parties were casual and not combined"—and that hence there was no conspiracy. Perhaps the bench, consisting of the recorder and two aldermen, decided the case solely on legal grounds and was able to disregard the extraordinary clamor in the press. Perhaps. A month later the recorder handed down a decision sustaining the demurrer. Early in 1844, lawyers for Atlantic, and not the district attorney this time, drew up a second indictment of Hamilton and Bergen but made such a mess of it that at another demurrer hearing in early February their distinguished counsel had to concede, embarrassingly, that the document was defective. The court quashed the indictment, and thus ended the case against Hamilton and Bergen. Richard Sutton, still being held in prison as the prosecution's main witness, was released finally. As well, the court discharged the recognizances for Hamilton's and Bergen's bail, and Benjamin Day's bond for $10,000 that had secured Hamilton's release from prison was returned to him.[30]

No one will ever know with any certainty whether Hamilton and Bergen were involved in a conspiracy against Atlantic Insurance.

The case was thrown out of court on narrow technical grounds before the lawyers examined forensically competing claims about what, if anything at all, had occurred. My own suspicion, based on Hamilton's history and Cornelia Barstow's testimony, is that he and Bergen intended to defraud Atlantic Insurance of $50,000. What happened with Sutton is much less clear—by the time Atlantic and alcohol had played their parts, it is difficult to place much credence in anything he said. It also seems apparent that the principals of Atlantic were determined not to lose $50,000, were very keen to crush Jeremiah Hamilton, and were not much troubled about how either of these goals would be achieved. Perhaps their cavalier disregard for the law did not quite extend to hiring the nineteenth-century equivalent of a hit man to drown Hamilton—though after reading the *Subterranean*'s coverage of Atlantic's shenanigans, I would not discount entirely Hamilton's jumpy conclusion about the denouement intended to occur at the end of Pier No. 1 on that dark night— but it demonstrably included suborning witnesses and bribing and developing cozy relationships with police and judges that in all likelihood could not have withstood any judicial scrutiny. In the end, an attempt at a huge fraud was foiled by the at least equally fraudulent actions of Atlantic Insurance and the legal authorities—the cavalier disregard for, and unimportance of, the truth throughout the whole affair was quite astonishing. For all that, from our perspective at least, there was still a refreshing ineptitude and clumsiness to the way Atlantic went about things—even their lawyers displayed incompetence. Over the ensuing decades, the corporate America that was just beginning to emerge in the 1840s would learn to tidy up its loose ends more effectively and discreetly.

What is striking about the whole affair is the remarkable adroitness with which Hamilton, a black man, negotiated his way through a complex, difficult and lily-white world of finance, lawyers and police without going to prison. At the end of it all, though, he was none the richer. Hamilton was still a man on the make, one with as questionable a set of ethics as anyone else on Wall Street. Mind you, as he well knew, there were plenty of sheep waiting to be shorn in the vicinity of the stock exchange. His time would come.

NINE

THE TRIAL

O stensibly, the article Moses Beach published in his *New York Sun* on August 7, 1843, was about the Atlantic Insurance conspiracy case, but its content and language were so over-wrought even the most casual of the paper's many readers had to have sensed that a personal grudge was being settled. Two days previously the paper's reporter had ended his account of the arrest of Hamilton and Bergen by promising "to ascertain who bailed the ne-gro, that the public may be advised"—the person in question, as he now knew, was Benjamin Day, founder of the *Sun* and Moses Beach's brother-in-law. Having reported this, the *Sun*'s man raised the then-vexing issue of "straw bail," or whether the guarantor indeed had the wherewithal to pay the sum set by the judge. After glancing through court records, he estimated that Day had committed him-self, in several different causes, to being liable for some $30,000 and "one thing is certain, if he should have the whole amount to pay, it might puzzle him a little to raise the ready cash, and would at all events, make something of a hole in his fortune." As if this stricture about the newspaper founder's promiscuous role as bail guarantor was not pointed enough, the writer offered Day very public advice about how he should behave.

The course lately pursued by Mr Day has given his friends no little pain. His intimacy and constant intercourse with this black fellow, and with a former police reporter by the name of Horatio S. Bartlett, the reciprocal sympathies and bosom friendship existing between the three, have caused deep regret on the part of the friends of Day. He has respectable connexions, and might by pursuing an elevated and honorable course of conduct, and being more careful about the company he keeps, maintain a respectable stand in society. But for some months past, Day, the negro, and Bartlett have been like the Siamese Twins, or perhaps we should say, like Siamese triplets. . . . Morning, noon, and night, have often found these loving friends together. The black fellow would call on his *chaste* friend Bartlett, and they both together would call on Day. Sometimes the order of calling would be reversed, and then again the three would be seen locked arm-in-arm and marching to and fro in the streets. Few hours ever passed over their heads without a meeting.

According to the article, Day's relatives were grieving over his conduct, fearing that his honor would be "blunted" and his habits "contaminated" if he did not "cut loose from such associates." Feigning concern, the reporter added: "We would in all kindness appeal to him as one not yet wholly lost, to have respect for the feelings of his friends and for himself." In one final revelation about the events of the previous Friday after Hamilton's arrest, he disclosed "Mr Day, the negro's bail, also became the negro's messenger," delivering very late on that night Hamilton's "impudent" letter to the *Sun* Beach had published on that Saturday. "Whether the 'black prince' made him trot round with similar messages to the other papers" the intrepid reporter had failed to find out, but "we hope not, for his own credit." Having depicted Hamilton as the *éminence grise,* who had Day firmly in his thrall, Beach concluded with some more "friendly advice" for his brother-in-law: "We entreat him again and again to mend his ways, and select his companions with better taste and more discrimination."[1]

The break between Moses Beach and Benjamin Day, a while coming, was now out in the open. As if to emphasize the split's finality, a couple of days later, Beach used the *Sun* to ridicule Day's close friend as "a walking forgery," denigrating both Hamilton's appearance and his history. Although press feuds were two a penny in antebellum New York and more often than not the vitriol became personal, even by contemporary standards, there was still something shocking about Beach's vindictiveness. Left with little choice, Benjamin Day sued Moses Beach for libel. The trial was set down for the week before Christmas 1843 and, of necessity, would be a very public scrutiny of the friendship between a black man and a white man. Not only was this a novel subject, certainly one never considered before by New Yorkers, but also Moses Beach, Benjamin Day and Jeremiah Hamilton were all well-known in the city—this trial would attract considerable attention.

1843 had been a tempestuous year for Moses Beach, one in which the proprietor of the *Sun* struggled strenuously to get out from under the shadow cast by Benjamin Day, who, a little embarrassingly, was a decade younger than him. At the *Sun*, things had come to a head early in the year. In March Horatio Bartlett, the veteran police reporter, had left and Jeremiah Hamilton stopped coming around, severing two of the last links with the Day years. At the same time Beach, even though by his own boasts the newspaper was making money, cut wages. Eight of the *Sun*'s compositors walked off the job and on March 20, 1843, commenced publishing the *True Sun*, a new morning newspaper. Their jointly signed prospectus, printed on the front page of the inaugural issue, recorded their resentment at the "indignity" with which Beach had treated them in his rush to trample over the rights of all working men. For the previous five years, Beach had used the *Sun* "merely as an instrument of puffing into notoriety the various speculations of its proprietor, and misleading its readers with false and interested statements, calculated to defraud the public, and fill Mr. Beach's pockets." Beach prided himself on his financial acumen—which was why Mike Walsh's belittling comparison of Beach's and Hamilton's abilities on Wall Street hit its mark—even if his former compositors saw only "his *cent-per cent* shaving operations in some 'Jacksonville Bank,' or 'Oil and Steamboat' speculation." The following day, the *True Sun*'s editor elaborated, explaining that Beach, dismissed as the "Usurer and

Speculator," not only was indifferent to the interests of the *Sun*'s mainly working-class readership, but also "shave[d] the hard earnings of the industrious mechanic, for whom he professes so much respect and sympathy." As the name, the *True Sun*, advertised, the compositors intended to run their paper more in accord with the promise of the early years of the *Sun*.[2] Beach may have shucked off, indeed repudiated, Benjamin Day's legacy at the *Sun,* but he was now confronted by an avatar of his brother-in-law in the guise of a rival newspaper whose principals were bitterly opposed to anything he did and would lose no opportunity to embarrass him.

The timing of Moses Beach's divorce of his wife, Nancy, Benjamin Day's sister, could scarcely have been worse. Although Beach had been a serial adulterer for years, after his wife had confronted him about his infidelities he had made her life unbearable, committing what later legal documents described blandly as "various acts of unkindness and cruel treatment." More sensationally, days after a hearing in the divorce case, an anonymous publication appeared entitled *The Awful Disclosures Developed in the Divorce Case of Moses Y. Beach, Publisher of the New York Sun, for Adultery with Eight Different Women.—Before the Vice Chancellor, New York, April 18th, 1843. For Sale by the News Boys.* Not only were newsboys, Day's invention, distributing the pamphlet all over New York, but also its supposed compilers were Horatio Bartlett, employed at the *Sun* until only a few weeks earlier, along with his partner at the fledgling *Sunday Bulletin,* Cyrus K. Thompson. In the scandalous publication, names were named and trysts catalogued. Libel writs flew everywhere—according to a report in the *Sun* on May 1, "some eight or ten libel suits have already been commenced," another fourteen were in train, and the courts had already set more than $20,000 worth of bail in these cases.[3]

This was a very public divorce that no one could hush up. Three weeks later, near the end of May 1843, at a Chancery Court hearing to assess Moses Beach's liability for Nancy Beach's legal and living expenses while the divorce case proceeded, the husband's counsel specified that the wife had fled from their house—"without provocation," according to him—leaving behind six children, and had "taken refuge with parties who are hostile to her husband in business and other relations." He was referring to Benjamin Day, for she was now being sheltered from her husband at her brother's house. Moses Beach's counsel at this hearing complained futilely about a "novel" circumstance of the case—"there are reporters here present from hostile and rival establishments, ready to spread any of the facts which may appear to make against my client before the greedy ears of the public." Not only was he right, but more than that, the pleasure taken in seeing the never very popular Beach's comeuppance was almost palpable—the editor of the *True Sun,* scarcely controlling his glee, published 1,268 verbatim words from the hearing in the next day's paper.[4] Moses Beach was discovering that if you live by the sword, then you should anticipate dying the same way.

To complicate further his already-turbulent life, throughout most of 1843 another particularly determined litigant was also pursuing Beach in a second libel case, a suit that soon developed into a running sore. Back in February, in what was just one more episode in the perpetual bickering between the *Sun* and the *Herald,* Beach ran a supposedly facetious piece insinuating that Bennett's not yet two-year-old son was illegitimate. Bennett sued, complaining that this "malicious and libellous paragraph is calculated and as deponent believes intended to destroy the domestic peace and happiness and to vilify and ruin the character and reputation of his wife." He was right about the intention. In June 1843, Bartlett, the author of the offending article and by then anything but beholden to Beach, explained at a hearing how the offending piece had come to be written, and of course the *True Sun* printed every word of his statement. Apparently, Beach had known exactly the effect he wanted to achieve and instructed Bartlett to draw on two disparate items from the *Herald* and link them in an attack on Bennett's wife. On "hearing said Beach's ideas on the subject," Bartlett remarked "that it would be very hard for Mrs Bennett thus to be shown up in a public print." Beach answered: "I know, but it's the only way to make the damned bugger feel." Rarely burdened by scruple, the editor added that he could not touch the *Herald* or Bennett himself, and the only way to get to him was through his family. After having read Bartlett's draft, Beach told his writer that the "article was not sufficiently pointed," that he "did not think it cutting enough." Bartlett, by his account, refused to change a word, forcing Beach to acquiesce and publish the piece as it was.[5] The final disposition of this libel case, in which Beach pleaded guilty, was scheduled to occur in the same week as the hearing of Benjamin Day's suit. Newspapers reveled in such messy incestuous dramas, and two libel prosecutions against Moses Beach in the same week added up to an early Christmas—there would be no shortage of reporters in the corridors of the Tombs in the waning days of 1843.

Supposedly, New York's Halls of Justice, built between 1835 and 1838 on Centre Street, was inspired by an image and description of an Egyptian mausoleum in a popular travel account. Almost immediately after its completion, New Yorkers started calling the odd-looking building the Tombs. For Charles Dickens it was a "dismal-fronted pile of bastard Egyptian, like an enchanter's palace in a melodrama," but a one-time inmate described the Tombs more bleakly as a "miserable architectural abortion." A good part of the city's legal apparatus was jammed into the structure, which contained 173 individual cells and two Police Court cells, as well as the Court of General Sessions, the First District Police Court and the offices of the district attorney, sheriff, and clerk.[6] Something of the chilling reputation of the building comes across in a minor incident that took place in 1849. The innocent injured party in a con, who had just had $50 snatched from his hand, ran away from a man whom he thought was a policeman rather than accompany him to the Tombs. Even nine weeks later at the trial of the men who had scammed him, the victim was still jumpy at the very mention of the notorious institution. "I never was afraid of any man that God ever made," he told the court, "but I did not want to go to the Tombs; I know every nook and corner of the place; I helped to build it; I worked nine months on the building; I know it well, it's a hard place."[7] It was indeed a very hard place.

In the week before Christmas 1843, "foggy, damp and disagreeable" weather shrouded the Tombs without softening its appearance; indeed, if anything, it made the setting even more depressing than usual. Because the hulking stone edifice was built on unstable landfill used to reclaim what had been the old Collect Pond, it began to subside within months of completion. After only five years there were four-inch cracks in the walls, and water and sewage regularly backed up in the lowest level. The previous year, an obliging jailer chatting to Dickens reassured him that only colored people were locked up in the "unwholesome" underground cells. In winter the damp gnawed at its occupants' very bones. On the day of Beach's trial, the gloom sapped everyone's energy, one reporter commenting: "The vital current seems to run sluggishly, the spirits flag, and we are not ourselves."[8]

The prosecution opened the trial by explaining that the complained-of piece in the *Sun* held Benjamin Day "up to public contempt and ridicule and was therefore calculated to create a breach of the peace." After the offending article was read to the jury, the defense outlined that they would show "the truth of the libel, and that it was published for good motives and justifiable ends." The trial began with a complicated discussion of "straw bail" in which it was established that Day was liable for nearly $40,000 worth of bail and damages, but all from the many libel suits arising out of Beach's divorce from his sister. Although it was confusing material, a juror's interjection did provide some light relief.

BY A JUROR.—Are these straw damages? (laughter)

The libel suits were against the *Bulletin,* co-edited by Day and Hamilton's friend Horatio Bartlett, but the court refused to allow James M. Smith, for the prosecution, to argue that "these very libel suits [were] for the purpose of annoying Mr Day." A paper merchant was called as a witness.

Q—Was Mr Bartlett at one time the publisher of a paper called "The Bulletin."
A—Mr Bartlett said he was. He purchased about $200 worth of paper of me about the second week it was started; he gave me two notes without any endorsement. Hamilton gave me an agreement as security for the payment of the first note.

As ever, Hamilton was fascinated by the press and had been only too keen to underwrite his friend's attempt at starting a newspaper.

The prosecution then spent some time questioning Lucius Robinson, an editor at the *Sun*. Although Smith attempted to examine the origin of the allegedly libelous article, the court hampered him by repeatedly overruling his questions. Eventually, Smith slipped in his point in argument and nicely punctured the idea of Beach as a newspaperman.

> SMITH.—Why everybody knows that Beach didn't write it—he never wrote an article of six lines in length—we wish to show that at the very time it was written, Beach expressed malice.

Several witnesses then testified about working conditions at the *Sun*, demonstrating that Hamilton visited the offices every day and establishing that Hamilton, Bartlett and Day were very frequently observed walking arm in arm down the street. At three o'clock in the afternoon the court took a half-hour recess for dinner.[9]

When the court reconvened for the evening session the counsel for the defense announced that now he was going "to prove the general bad character of Jeremiah G. Hamilton" in order to convince the jury that Day should not have associated with the black man, let alone put up his bail in the fraud case. After a desultory back and forth as to whether this argument was admissible or not, the court allowed that it was, "with the understanding that it was to be confined to the question of the general bad moral character of Hamilton." Even the judge's censorious wording intimated that Hamilton was in for an ordeal. All the spectators in court settled back and waited for the fireworks to begin, anticipating that counsel and witnesses would take apart the black man. As it turned out, the demolition of Jeremiah Hamilton was not the source of the fireworks.

First called to the stand was William Callender, one of the clerks in the lower police office.

> Q—What is the general moral character of Mr Jeremiah G. Hamilton?
> A—It is very bad.
> *Cross examined by* SMITH *for prosecution.*

Q—Are [you] not in the habit of reporting police matter for "The
    Sun" for which [you] receive a certain amount per week, paid
    by Mr Beach?

A—No, I am not; I have never made any arrangement or
    agreement with Mr Beach about reporting; I may have given
    his reporter some particulars relative to the former arrest of
    Hamilton, the same as I would other reporters; I have owed
    Mr Beach money, but have been paying it in instalments, the
    last of which will soon be paid in full.

Q—Who have you heard speak bad of Mr Hamilton?

A—I have heard many.

Q—Be as good as to name some one person or more.

A—I have heard Mr Barstow of Pine street, speak of his
    character as bad.

Q—When was that?

A—I cannot say exactly; it is some ten years since I spoke to Mr
    Barstow; and I cannot positively say whether it was him or
    others.

Q—Then you take back what you said before?

A—I cannot recollect positively who it was; I have heard many.

Q—Have you heard any one speak of his character as bad—any
    one single person whom you can name?

A—I do not know that I can recollect the name of any one, but
    when I was in business down town, I have often heard him
    spoken of.[10]

Although Day's counsel struggled valiantly to pin this witness down,
to force him to testify about specific individuals and incidents, it was
like trying to nail jelly to the wall. Testimony such as this probably
gives as good an indication as any of the incessant whispering and
racist assumptions against which Hamilton struggled during his entire business career in New York.

  Other witnesses damned Hamilton in similar tenor. William Applegate, a printer, when asked about Hamilton's character responded:
"Persons generally speak bad of him."[11] A good portion of this witness's printing business was with what was known as the flash press,
a group of weekly newspapers boasting titles such as the *Flash,* the

Whip and the *Rake,* which burst onto the New York scene and flourished between about 1841 and 1843. Brash, provocative, trenchant, and offering a titillating cocktail of gossip about prostitutes, theater, and the like, these ephemeral rags displayed their lack of legitimacy as a proud badge and provided a guide for sporting men to the pleasures of commercialized leisure in the city. They also pushed the boundaries of what a newspaper could publish—their editors were being hauled constantly into court on charges of libel or obscenity—and were notorious for blackmailing New Yorkers, threatening to publish sordid details unless a cash payment was forthcoming. It was all a winning and profitable combination: even today these newspapers dating back more than a century and a half remain a lively and enjoyable read.[12] Applegate's answer, when counsel insisted he name individuals who had denigrated Hamilton, probably surprised many in the courtroom:

> A—I have heard Day; he once came to me to get an article
> reflecting upon the character of Hamilton suppressed that
> was about to be published in a paper that was printed in
> my office, which article charged Hamilton with all sorts
> of offences and called him almost every name; Day said he
> knew Hamilton was a bad fellow, but he was doing some
> business for him, and he did not wish to have him showed up
> at that time.[13]

The *True Sun*'s correspondent took down a different wording of this testimony. He reported that when Day asked Applegate to suppress the article, "as he (Day) had done me many favors," the printer "concluded to oblige him" and that Day admitted: "He knew Hamilton deserved to be blown up."[14] The prosecution then cross-examined the witness.

> Q—What was the name of the paper in which this article was to
> be published?
> A—I believe it was in the "The Whip"—(laughter)—I am not
> certain whether it was in the "Flash" or "The Whip" but I
> think it was in the latter.

Q—Mr Woodbridge was a general publisher of these sheets,
   wasn't he?

A—Yes—he also published "The Libertine"—and it might
   have been in that—Hamilton came to my office the same
   evening—he gave me a good segar and I gave him one back.

SMITH—And you had a good cosy smoke together, didn't
   you?—(laughter)

A—O, yes.[15]

In fact, Applegate's memory had failed him, and he had named the
wrong newspaper. Two years earlier, on October 3, 1841, the *Sunday Flash* published what was, to its subject at least, a threatening sentence: "We're preparing a sketch of Jeremiah G. Hamilton
for the Gallery of Rascalities and Notorieties series."[16] This was at
the nadir of Hamilton's fortunes, a few months before he declared
bankruptcy and when he was trading on the stock exchange using
a false name—the *Flash*'s piece would have made fascinating, if not
necessarily reliable, reading. A fortnight later, the editor printed a
sketch of the businessmen Myer Levy, number 6 in the "Gallery of
Rascalities and Notorieties" series, that gave a scurrilous-enough account of its subject's sexual depredations to attract a criminal libel
prosecution.[17] There is a good chance this piece was a replacement
for the withdrawn Hamilton sketch. Until near the end of the twentieth century, even specialist scholars were oblivious of the existence
of the flash press, and today library holdings of these newspapers are
very far from complete. Ironically, individual issues of some of these
publications only exist because they were once evidence in obscenity
or libel prosecutions in the early 1840s. I have read the vast majority,
if not all, of the extant flash newspapers without finding any other
mention of Jeremiah Hamilton.[18] Apparently, Benjamin Day's intervention was not merely a temporary success: he forestalled for good
publication of the damaging information and prevented his friend's
name from being dragged through the mud yet again.

   Earlier in the evening session a police magistrate named Henry
W. Merritt had testified that Hamilton "is not spoken of well by a
good many—I should say by the majority; he is a broker in Wall
street, and they are none of them spoken of well." Now the defense

recalled him to the stand. What ensued, both in the Tombs courtroom and outside, was as extraordinary as anything I have come
across in more than a quarter of a century of reading New York
court cases. The first question counsel asked of Merritt—"Do you
know whether Jeremiah G. Hamilton is a negro?"—elicited an immediate objection, but the court allowed the witness to answer.

> A—I have an opinion on the subject founded on some facts.
> Q—What are those facts?
> A—I do not wish to make any statement. Mr Hamilton sits there
>   and the jury can judge as well as I can.
> Q—Yes, but we want your opinion based on facts.

At this point counsel argued further as to the propriety of this line of
questioning while everyone else in the courtroom gazed at the black
man sitting down at the front. Although the judge concluded that
Merritt's answer would be "a mere matter of opinion," he nevertheless allowed counsel to put the question.

> A—I do not believe he is a white man.
> Q—Why do you not?
> A—Because he does not wear his own hair—he wears a wig.
> Q—Have you ever seen him with his wig off?
> A—Yes—once.
> Q—Is the hair under it straight or curly?
> A—His hair was curly under it when I saw it.
> Q—Does his lips and nose exhibit the features of a negro?
> A—Why you can see them as well as me—they are something
>   like.

More than thirty years ago now the Harvard sociologist Orlando
Patterson, in his comparative study of the nature of slavery in sixty-
six societies, argued "it was not so much color differences as differences in hair type that become critical as a mark of servility in the
Americas." Color, he asserted, proved to be "a rather weak basis"
for differentiation in an interracial society. On the other hand, not
only were differences in hair type between blacks and whites sharper

than color dissimilarities, but the contrasts persisted much longer even as the races mixed. Patterson concluded that "hair type rapidly became the real symbolic badge of slavery, although like many powerful symbols it was disguised, in this case by the linguistic device of using the term 'black,' which nominally threw the emphasis to color."[19] Scholars may not have paid much attention to Patterson's argument, but Justice Merritt's testimony in this libel case provides striking evidence of the importance of hair in identifying race in antebellum New York.

Doubtless, well before the trial Day's counsel had explained to both Day and Hamilton what they could expect when they had their day in court, but no matter how prepared Hamilton was, this must have been an excruciating experience. And yet the defense counsel's and Justice Merritt's amateur ethnology meshed well with broader, often pseudo-scientific, currents in American society that, in the wake of the ending of slavery in the North, sought to delineate who was a Negro and to catalogue the characteristics of the race. Popular manifestations of this fascination with race could be found in commercial entertainment of all kinds. That very week, crowds were flocking to Peale's New York Museum, just a few blocks away on Broadway, opposite City Hall, and paying their shilling entry fee to gaze at the main attraction, a pair of "White Negroes" who were "perfectly white, with pink eyes, woolly hair, as white as snow, with the flat nose and thick lips of the African."[20] Best known of all, entertainers such as, most famously, T. D. Rice had been putting on blackface and performing songs and skits in New York for fifteen years, but earlier in 1843, and again only a few blocks away from the Tombs, in a hotel over on the Bowery, four white entertainers had formed the Virginia Minstrels and devised the first fully fledged minstrel show. With performers who blacked up their faces with burnt cork and ostensibly used authentic Negro dialects, songs, music, dance and jokes, minstrelsy became an immediate box-office sensation.[21] Although no one had to pay admission to be present in the Tombs courtroom, Jeremiah Hamilton's physical appearance was being put on public display and talked about just like the "White Negroes" and even blacked-up white performers.

When James Smith stood up to cross-examine Justice Merritt, he tried to undermine the witness's certainty in categorizing Hamilton as a Negro.

Q—Have you not seen West Indians as dark as Mr Hamilton?

A—Yes.

Q—Have you not seen Spaniards as dark?

A—Yes.

Q—Have you ever seen a negro with whiskers like Hamilton's?

A—I do not know exactly; people sometimes have their whiskers put on.

Q—Please look at his and see if they are put on; and then say whether you ever saw a negro with such whiskers—take a candle and look.

A—No, I thank you, I had rather not.

Q—But I wish you would.

A—I shall not, and I doubt whether you have power to compel it.

Q—Have you ever seen a negro's whiskers thick and curly—like yours for instance.

A—(Witness drawing his hand over his luxuriant crop which he takes much pride in cultivating)—No, I have never seen any negro's whiskers like mine exactly. (Great laughter).[22]

Smith could not shake the witness's testimony. Beach may have sneered that Hamilton was a "walking forgery" simply because he wore a wig of straight black hair, but white New Yorkers such as Merritt, experienced in dealing with free blacks on the city streets, remained confident of their ability to read the signs and not to allow what they viewed as the counterfeit to pass.[23] And yet, regardless of Merritt's certainty, this issue persisted in causing societal unease.

On redirect, Beach's counsel asked only one question of Merritt.

Q—Where did you first know Hamilton?

A—In my official capacity about ten years ago in the police office—it was there that I took his wig off.[24]

Having underscored his point, reminding everyone that when Merritt had been a police officer he had had dealings with Hamilton, Beach's counsel announced that here the defense would rest its case. Throughout Merritt's testimony a restive Hamilton had listened only with the greatest of difficulty, but now that his accuser had finished speaking he was no longer able to restrain himself. Abruptly, he stood up and loudly started addressing the courtroom. He asked the court to give him just two hours "to prove the falsity of the statement made by Justice Merritt relative to my being before the police at the time he alleges—as well as on the other points." If the spectators were surprised to see a black man hijacking a courtroom to argue with a white judge, then they were about to be truly shocked. Hamilton continued: "I can disprove all, and now wish to inform the Court that the reason why he has so testified relative to me is because I have refused to lend him money." Immediately, bedlam broke out. The *Herald*'s court reporter, with artful understatement, appended "(Great excitement)" to his transcription of this sensational claim. A heated and chaotic couple of minutes followed as the black man and the justice angrily confronted one another.

> Justice MERRITT. I pronounce this statement to be unqualifiedly
>> false. It is not true.
> HAMILTON—I can prove it.
> MERRITT—It is false—I pronounce it unqualifiedly false—I went
>> into Wall street sometime since to borrow some money, it is
>> true—and I met Hamilton, who asked me my business, and I
>> told him I wanted to borrow some money—he said he could
>> lend me, but I left him as I wished not to borrow of him.
> HAMILTON—That is false, and I can prove it.
> COURT—Order gentlemen.
> MERRITT—(Taking his seat and muttering)—That is utterly false,
>> and a lie without any foundation.[25]

After the judge managed to restore order, and it being nearly seven o'clock in the evening, he adjourned the court until eleven o'clock the next morning. As everyone filed out of the courtroom, through the vestibule and down the steps at the front of the Tombs, Merritt and Hamilton recommenced abusing one another and then jostling. Although accounts of what happened differ, it does seem clear that Merritt used violence first: he was, after all, a figure of authority in New York, and even the way he had spoken in court—for instance, employing the odd-sounding "I pronounce"—conveyed that he was someone not used to having his word questioned by anyone, let alone a Negro. According to one reporter, after Hamilton let loose a searing burst of invective, Merritt pushed away Hamilton, and then, as the black man continued to crowd him, "the Justice struck Hamilton with his cane."[26] Another thought that Merritt hit Hamilton twice with his cane. By now others were getting involved and the melée had spilled down the steps and into the street, where Hamilton seized a rung from a nearby cart and strode menacingly toward his opponent. A little boy named Sherlock, who was passing by, yelled out a warning, and the justice ducked out of the way "and thus saved himself from a blow that would have left its mark without any doubt." Summoned by noise of the disturbance, an officer named Walsh raced down the Tombs' steps, flung himself into the affray and seized hold of Hamilton, who was still clutching the cart rung. Although Benjamin Day and George Morris, Hamilton's brother-in-law, momentarily rescued Hamilton from the policeman, in the end the trio wound up being arrested. The judge, in the conveniently nearby police office, ordered that each of them come up with $1,000 bail, leading to some comical confusion that delayed their release. Finally, once someone bailed out Day, he then could act as security for Hamilton and Morris, and they all were free to go home. Given what had prompted the libel suit in the first place, the irony of the bail mix-up in the police office, with Day having to guarantee an extra $2,000 in bail, was not lost on anyone.[27]

Beach found the incident irresistible. "The closing scenes at the Court of Sessions last evening," he editorialized in the next day's *Sun,* should have made "Mr Benjamin H. Day regret that he had not followed our kind advice to keep better company, instead of suing us for giving it." According to Beach, as Merritt walked down the steps of the Tombs, "the negro renewed his insulting and scurrilous epithets" and then "the Justice wheeled, and exclaiming that he would not be insulted in that manner by a negro, rapped him soundly over the head with his cane." This sounds a likely account of the way the incident went down. Both Beach and Merritt expected African Americans to behave in a deferential fashion in the presence of their racial superiors, and, by their lights, the put-upon justice was not just entitled but duty-bound to remind Hamilton of his proper place with violence. Expressing faux concern—"it is with feelings of the most profound regret that we record the occurrence of such a scene at the very threshold of justice"—Beach remained unapologetic about what he had published. Indeed, summing up the day's testimony in the still-unfinished trial, Beach claimed that his counsel had made a "complete and thorough justification" of the original article printed in the *New York Sun* and asked, "Did we not speak truly and kindly when we advised Mr Day to seek better company?" If only Day had listened, he would not be involved "in this last shameful and disgraceful affair."[28]

Although the headline in the *Sun* had read "OUTRAGEOUS ASSAULT UPON A MAGISTRATE," in reality Merritt should have been arrested too—though no New York jury would have convicted him of assaulting a black man—and the outrageous assault that had been committed was by Moses Beach on the legal system. Counsel for the prosecution made precisely this argument before proceedings started the next morning. He pointed out that the article in that day's *Sun* already had "circulated pretty freely in this court," that Beach had committed "a high handed contempt," and demanded that the court issue an attachment against the paper's editor. "Here is a man on his trial circulating a paper in that very jury box," he argued. The prejudicial effect of the article was much the same "as if he had gone to them individually and told them such and such facts, are before you." He asked, "Is not *that* an attempt to frustrate the ends of justice?" Barely considering the complaint, the recorder brushed it aside as being improper but allowed that the issue could be raised again after the trial.[29]

It was time now for the final speeches to the jury. Clinton De Witt, for the defense, "spoke with great ability for more than two hours." Almost nothing of the content of De Witt's speech made the newspapers, other than one reporter's comment that he spoke learnedly and exhaustively on the subject of straw bail before "he got down to the phrenological developments of Day and Beach, their marriage connections, and the motives of Beach in publishing the article in question." Phrenology was the then very popular science, or pseudo-science, that involved examining, both by sight and by touch, a person's skull in order to determine his or her psychological attributes. Intriguing as De Witt's phrenological argument undoubtedly was, apparently no one recorded any details. James Smith's final address for the prosecution, however, received completely different treatment. He too spoke "with great energy, ability and eloquence," and also for about two hours, but his speech, even though well over 8,000 words in length, was reprinted in its entirety in the *True Sun*.[30] Partly, the editor devoted this much space to Smith's address because it was a very impressive piece of work, but mostly this was one more opportunity to slip a knife between the ribs of the paper's archenemy, Moses Y. Beach.

Shortly after four-thirty in the afternoon Smith stood up and began speaking to the jury, noting quietly that one of the pleasures of the legal life was that usually at the completion of a trial he was able to shake hands with his opponents "with the same kind feelings as when it commenced," before acknowledging that there were suits in which such gentlemanly courtesy was not possible. This was one of those unpleasant cases. The trial the jury had just witnessed was "calculated from its inception to its termination, to engender all the bitter feelings of our nature." He then discussed at length "straw bail" and Beach's malicious motivation, doing his best to make the jury aware that all the cases for which Day had put up bail were linked to Beach and his divorce from Day's sister, and that he had been limited severely by the judge's decision not to allow him to raise the issue directly during the trial. Counsel then moved on to consider Hamilton's role in the proceedings.

Why, Smith asked the jury, was Jeremiah Hamilton subpoenaed by Beach's counsel and made to attend the trial? Was it for anything other than "to gratify the fiend like malice of Beach"? He was summoned "with the full knowledge on their part that he was to be attacked in the tenderest point, to be maligned, to be ridiculed and to be disgraced." They "know well what effect it is to have on Day if they can effectually malign the character of Hamilton." Smith had come to the crux of the matter: "Now who is Jeremiah G. Hamilton, that it is such a gross offence in the eyes of Beach to be seen in his company"? The counsel himself claimed, perhaps for effect, never to have heard of Hamilton, but he then turned his attention to the witnesses called by the defense to denigrate Hamilton.[31]

Referring to the police clerk, Callender, Smith said, "You cannot but remember the kind of delight which he seemed to feel when he had it in his power to blast the reputation of that man." Indeed, "I hardly ever saw a man come on the stand with such a feeling of exultation." He reminded the jury of Callender's response to the question about Hamilton's character, how he responded "Oh—*bad, very bad,*" naming Barstow as someone who damned the black man but "when he finds out that Barstow is ready to come up and contradict him under oath, he backs off, and says that, upon recollection, Barstow did not say it, but he knew that some one had, but he forgot who it was." The counselor was almost as contemptuous of Justice Merritt's testimony: "This man, this Justice Merritt, had the audacity to tell you that, while Hamilton was in his charge, he took him into his private office, and for the gratification of his own malignant curiosity, he took off his wig to see if his hair was curly." Merritt assumed he "had the right to inflict this upon Hamilton simply because his skin was not quite so white as his own." Unable to conceal his distaste for the justice, Smith confided to the courtroom, "God forbid that such a man's testimony should ever be permitted to operate against me." For all the venom of what Merritt had said, the justice could neither name names of anyone badmouthing Hamilton, nor show that he had ever been convicted of anything.

At this point, Smith, drawing on his considerable histrionic skills, stood in front of the jury and puzzled out loud about what was missing from the case for the *New York Sun.* He thought it unusual, if Hamilton was so bad, "that the evidence thereof was not in Court—something beyond the mere cry of bad, bad—when by its production they might have succeeded in blasting the character of this man." The absence of any such proof was both striking and telling. Hamilton was not a party to this suit, "but I would ask; cannot a man be charged at the Police office with that of which he may be innocent without having the officers and the clerks of the Police to linger around the stain, and say that after ten years have elapsed the blot is there still"? Smith then gave a remarkably shrewd assessment of Hamilton's unusual position in the New York business community, one that is worth quoting at length:

> With such a man as Hamilton, it would be singular indeed, if some could not be found to talk against him. We see him in the company of gentlemen. We hear of his doing business in Wall street—of his associations with bankers and brokers, and it is I admit unusual here, to see a man of his color thus engaged, but in some countries it would not be deemed so—and it renders him the more liable to be talked against, especially by his enemies, and the very envy which such a man must excite, would be sure to beget slanders against him, and to create enmity. Yet with all these things against him, to combat, it is only the *Police* who are produced to blast him, and if they fail, I take it that he has been triumphantly sustained, because they have not adduced any proof wherewith to sully him. With such disadvantages where can you find a man who would have passed the ordeal without so much as the breath of slander having rested on him.

In short, the defense had failed manifestly to impugn the character of Day's friends, "for not a particle of testimony is adduced here to shew you that Hamilton is a bad man, or that Horatio S. Bartlett is not as pure a man as any in this community."[32]

Having canvassed the issue of "character," Smith moved on to consider "the other charge in the libel," that Hamilton was a Negro. "Well, to prove this charge he [Hamilton] was brought here and paraded before you, and where was the evidence?" he asked the courtroom. Here members of the jury had to make up their minds based on the testimony of only one witness, which Smith summarized for them as: "Why, Justice Merritt says he don't wear his own hair!" Continuing to savage the increasingly ridiculous-looking judge, Smith pointed out that Merritt "took the wig off to see, as he told you, not in the performance of his official duties, but merely to try the experiment and satisfy his heartless curiosity; and now, after a lapse of ten years, the Justice comes here to give you the result of his memory in the shape of a mere surmise." For Smith, the hair on Hamilton's head, or lack thereof, evidenced nothing.[33]

But this was not the end of Smith's consideration of Hamilton's hair, and here his address went off on a surprising tangent when he argued that Hamilton was not in fact a Negro. (To be fair, in retrospect, one can see intimations of this argument in Smith's cross-examination of Merritt.) At this point Day's counsel, following the lead of Merritt and De Witt earlier in the trial, assumed the mantle of the amateur ethnologist. "Let us look at his whiskers, and those we find as strait [sic] as any one among us, which never is the case in a negro." The only conclusion was "that the man is an East Indian," or someone born on the subcontinent of India. What buttressed this deduction was "the manifestations of his intellect"—or, in other words, Hamilton was far too clever to be a Negro. As had been shown earlier in the trial, Beach had been intimate with Hamilton and always treated him courteously, something that in and of itself suggested to Smith that the *Sun* owner did not consider him to be a Negro. "Now, I don't believe there is any man who would wish to have it said that his companions were negroes," the lawyer remarked. His opponents in this case "knew full well that he [Hamilton] was brought here merely for the purpose of wounding his feelings, smarting as he was under the outrage" of being labeled a Negro. Smith implied Beach was duplicitous as well as malicious.

Day's counsel openly admitted to believing in African American inferiority, "for the negro has not the same activity of mind, nor the same turn of thought, and differs in point of character mentally and corporeally." In this he was in agreement with the vast majority of white New Yorkers. Smith may even have convinced himself that Hamilton was East Indian—after all, racist assumptions about intelligence have played havoc with logical thought for centuries. Not that his beliefs were particularly relevant: Smith was Day's lawyer, not Hamilton's, and was duty-bound to try to win his client's case for him. If that involved putting doubt in the minds of the jury, or at least confusing them, by arguing that Hamilton was not a Negro and thus undermining any defense based on the truth of the alleged libel, then so be it. There is no record of what Hamilton made of the claim that he was East Indian. As to its truth, although there is plenty of evidence for a birthplace in Richmond or somewhere in the Caribbean, this unsubstantiated assertion is the only mention of a possible Indian origin that I have come across.[34]

Smith concluded by ridiculing the claim that the *Sun* article was intended to be helpful and not hurtful: "Is it no indication of malice to say that a man is the messenger of a negro, trotting about for him from place to place, and asking sneeringly, 'does the black Prince make him trot to all other publication offices as he did to ours?'" This was "concocted for the very purpose of outraging the feelings of Day." After Smith's address, the recorder charged the jury, and, eventually, late that night the jury retired in order to come to their decision: twenty minutes later, they returned and announced a verdict of guilty.[35]

Over the next few days there was considerable comment about the case. Jeremiah Hamilton, just as he had done in earlier crises of his life, penned a letter that several newspapers printed. According to Hamilton, accounts of the affray with Merritt "omitted to state that that gentleman assaulted and threatened to assault me in the Court Room of the General Sessions," and that out on the street he struck "me several times with a *large cane,* sufficient, in the hands of *a large athletic man, to inflict a blow that would produce death.*" Hamilton himself, while he did admit to having a cart rung in his hand, claimed that he was never close enough to have committed an assault. He added "that the assault and battery committed upon me by this *Special Justice for preserving the peace* were wholly unprovoked in my part, except that I replied to the insulting and abusive language with which I was first assailed by him." He ended that he was "indifferent as to the *malignant sneers and scurrilous abuse of the ignorant, worthless and vile;* next to the approval of God and my conscience, I am emulous of the esteem of the virtuous and wise."[36]

For James Gordon Bennett in the *Herald,* the case was "one of the drollest concerns we ever remember to have heard of or seen for many a day." Further, "its revelations in the mysteries of journalism and justice are equally droll—equally laughable—equally surprising." His use of "mysteries"—part of his article's headline also read "MYSTERIES OF NEW YORK"—referred to Eugene Sue's originally serialized novel *Mysteries of Paris,* then a runaway best-seller, with 15,000 copies sold in New York in little more than a month. The word, which quickly became a commonplace in newspapers, connoted a sordid exploration of a city's underworld, a meaning only reinforced by the publication of *Mysteries and Miseries of New York* in 1848. This was not Bennett's only literary allusion—"the proceedings inside of the Tombs, and the proceedings outside," he wrote, "are just as original and startling as the stories told . . . in the chapters of Boccacio's Decameron." And yet what is most revealing is that, for all the defense's attempts to demonstrate Hamilton's bad reputation and all the vague whispering of his "bad character" from various witnesses, the *Herald* editor remained unconvinced: "By all accounts Hamilton, who has long perambulated Wall street, has about as good an average character as can be found in that famous street." Disdainful of the street as a whole perhaps, but at least the editor put the black broker on an equal footing with his white peers. Bennett was most taken by the flagrantly evident corruption among officials working in the Halls of Justice: "Moses Y. Beach," he wrote, "seems to monopolize the banking business of the Tombs, and Hamilton appears to have got into trouble because he would not loan on the same security."[37]

Although Bennett may have suggested slyly that Hamilton had fallen foul of a corrupt officialdom by refusing to go along with the crowd, the more radical Mike Walsh in the *Subterranean* simply used the case to damn the administration of justice in New York, writing, "If all the sinks of loathsome depravity on earth were scraped there could not be such another lot found as those who appeared as witness for Beach during his late trial for a libel on Day." The one or two witnesses he did not know "were probably recruits from hell, or a part of the well disciplined corps connected with the tombs."[38] After the revelations arising from first the Atlantic conspiracy case and now this trial, it has to be said that there was merit in his position.

Further reinforcing Walsh's perception of the way New York worked, a day after the verdict, the recorder announced that the court considered Beach had committed "a mere *technical* libel" that only required nominal punishment. If not quite reversing, then at least neutering, the jury's decision, he stated that the truth of the article had "been fully proved on the part of the defence," and also that it had been established that Day "was in the habit of keeping company with Hamilton, who was a negro, and that Hamilton's character was bad." (No one, it seems, was convinced by Smith's argument that Hamilton was Indian.) Consequently, the court imposed a fine of only $50, a sum they seemed to think would cover the costs of the prosecution, and even this sentence was suspended until the next year.[39]

Hardly surprisingly, Beach regarded this decision as "a full justification" of his behavior. Indeed, he added, "we are at a loss to imagine what the fine was for . . . unless it was for giving Mr Day the good advice we did, and for advising him not to associate with negroes of bad character." Similarly, sentencing in Bennett's libel suit against Beach was postponed until the following year after the civil suit was resolved.[40] The editor of the *Sun* was insufferable. He referred his readers to the *Herald,* "in which notorious sheet James Gordon Bennett and Negro Hamilton, two well known characters in this community, come out with manifestoes in vindication of their characters." Beach then quoted from these documents:

Hamilton.—"I am emulous of the esteem of the virtuous and
    wise"—
Bennett.—"My wife and innocent child"—
Hamilton.—"Assault and battery"!—
Bennett.—"Our former lives"—
Hamilton.—While in possession of the rung"—

And so on, for twenty-six more lines. It was a strikingly effective and modern-looking way of ridiculing his enemies. Beach concluded his screed by asking: "What if Satan should seize his own, and foreclose the mortgage he holds on these beauties?"[41]

In the end, then, it was a Pyrrhic victory. Benjamin Day and Jeremiah Hamilton were held up to public ridicule, and Moses Beach got off almost scot-free. Day would pursue the *Sun* editor in other libel suits arising out of Beach's divorce from Nancy, his sister, winning $2,000 worth of damages in at least one of them, but those cases were not about interracial friendship.[42] This case had been fought about precisely that issue, and Day and his friend Jeremiah Hamilton, although victors, came out second best. Perhaps the most sobering realization to emerge from reading the transcripts and summaries of the trial printed in the newspapers is simply how difficult it was for a black man and a white man to be friends, let alone best friends. Clearly, Day, in parading down the street arm in arm with Hamilton, deeply shocked and upset his brother-in-law. This was not how a respectable white man behaved. Establishment New York, as represented by judges, reporters and lawyers, was little impressed as well. Even Day's own counsel assumed that no man "would wish to have it said that his companions were negroes," before coming up with an absurd argument about Hamilton not being a Negro, a contention that convinced nobody. As they walked away from the Tombs, after the recorder had sentenced Beach to a suspended $50 fine, Hamilton could well have uttered to his friend, "One more such victory would utterly undo us."

TEN

WALL STREET

The paragraph-long squib was droll enough for the editor of *The New World; A Weekly Family Journal of Popular Literature, Science, Art* to publish in August 1843 and others to reprint. Under the head "Literary," a writer announced that the following works "are said to be in press" and then listed four made-up titles. Most of the humor has long since evaporated. He included, for example, *The Confident Candidate, or Who's the Dupe,* purportedly a novel by John Tyler, the now-forgotten accidental president who had ascended to the office in 1841 when William Henry Harrison died a month after his inauguration. To get the jokes, of course, readers had to know something about the public lives of these individuals. Last of the fictitious forthcoming volumes was *Stocks, Their Rise and Fall,* by Jeremiah G. Hamilton.[1] For all his notoriety, Hamilton's inclusion on such a list still intrigues. The fact that Hamilton was so closely associated in the public mind with the rise and fall of stock prices says a lot about Hamilton himself; it also says something surprising about Wall Street.

By 1843 stocks and shares meant Wall Street, New York long since having outstripped Philadelphia as the nation's most important capital market. To be sure, the street was still more than a generation removed from becoming the financial behemoth with which we are all familiar. In the 1830s and 1840s most of the capital driving the expansion of the U.S. economy remained foreign—it came principally from England, but some originated in continental Europe. One historian has gone so far as to claim that "the New York market was still too small and clubby to provide more than a gambling arena for traders who had enough capital and leisure time to speculate on stocks."[2] Although there is certainly truth in such a characterization, too hasty a dismissal of the role of speculation in capital formation can lead to a mistaken discounting of the importance of the raw and energetic spirit that everywhere animated New York's burgeoning financial district. Wall Street was inchoate, frequently unruly and contradictory, but that was because it was also dynamic. The often-grubby realities of an almost-totally unregulated market juxtaposed oddly with the Greek Revival facades, replete with imposing classical columns, used to refashion the precinct after the Great Fire of 1835—and the area was rebuilt with remarkable speed. But the street's newfound grandeur testified to an almost-limitless ambition on the part of its bankers and brokers.

Today, what once took place on the floor of the New York Stock Exchange occurs in computers in buildings in New Jersey and Chicago, but thousands of finance workers still trek in to Wall Street every day. For all that, the street itself has the feel of a museum as tourists mill around. Although there were occasional tourists back in Jeremiah Hamilton's day too, they were interested in the present, not past, glories. Something exciting and new seemed to be taking place right in front of their eyes. The entire street from the East River up to Trinity Church on Broadway, or, as insiders point out wryly, from the river to the graveyard, was a market. After twenty years' experience working there, William Worthington Fowler could not "conceive of Wall Street values apart from the idea of their negotiability."[3] Everything, even the future, could be bought or sold, a fact immediately apparent to any visitor or commentator. Whether they appreciated what they saw or not, they were present at the creation, witness to the beginnings of modern American capitalism.

John Benwell came to New York from Bristol on board the *Cosmo* in the late 1840s. He arrived on a surprisingly warm October

day, and after weeks of being cooped up onboard—it had been a
long, dreary voyage—the English tourist accepted with alacrity the
offer of a lift in the captain's gig to a wharf at the foot of Wall Street,
if only to set his own feet down again, as he put it, on terra firma.
Benwell's first experience of the United States, then, was to walk,
albeit on wobbly legs, the length of Wall Street. His account of an
urban space bristling with human activity provides a counterpoint to
mid-nineteenth-century images of the financial center, almost devoid
of New Yorkers and dominated by the street's imposing architecture.
Crossing South Street, which ran along the waterfront, he noticed
immediately the "hundreds of rudely constructed drays" darting to
and fro, all heavily laden and drawn by mules and very light horses,
not English cart horses disliked for their ponderousness. It was the
bustle of the docks and streets that first impressed him: "The lower
part of Wall-street presented a busy mart-like appearance." Piles of
an immense variety of goods spilled out of warehouse doors onto the
street and were being sold off by auctioneers. Sales "were going on in
every direction, and the street rang with the stentorian voices of the
sellers." Most were genuine, although, as with many visitors to the
city even today, Benwell was more taken with the frauds.

Farther up Wall Street, between Hanover and Broad streets,
Benwell came to "that portion of it frequented by stock and real-es-
tate brokers." "Crowds of gentlemanly-looking men, dressed mostly
in black, and of busy mien . . . with scrip in hand" thronged the
cobblestones. Although much of the buying and selling of shares
occurred in the Merchant's Exchange building, there was also an
outside and less respectable curbstone market. Here on the street
stocks not listed inside were traded, and so too, particularly when
the market was running, were some more reputable shares. Most
days the *Herald*'s James Gordon Bennett, acting as his paper's financial roundsman, shouldered his way through the crowds of
"anxious looking men, whose whole talk is of dollars, land, stocks
or else elections." As far as he was concerned, "we never came
across a place so completely *sui generis* as Wall street." There was,
the worldly editor claimed, little resemblance to the way things were
done in the financial districts of either Paris or London. Certainly
bankers and brokers gathering in the street was an unusual sight

in those cities. In 1848, a "reformed stock gambler" informed his readers that commonly "more business is done in the open air" than inside. "In stirring times," he wrote, "large numbers of operators frequently congregate in this manner—one, two, or three hundred—and their movements very much resemble the whirling eddies of a strong current, as various prominent individuals offer to buy or sell." Such a system had its drawbacks. In early December 1835, for example, Bennett commented in the *Herald:* "The weather yesterday was so extremely cold that little business was done in the street"; indeed, the unfortunate stockbrokers sensibly had slunk away seeking shelter.[4] Yet New Yorkers, so often adroit at juggling tradition and innovation, persisted with their curb market until the twentieth century.

Adding further to what frequently appeared an urban scene chaotic enough for a Brueghel to relish painting, at any time between noon and three o'clock in the afternoon, this stretch of Wall Street was also the site of a dog market. A *True Sun* journalist sketched the scene of dogs "on foot and in arms, couchant and rampant, some with bushy curling tails, others with long straight ones." Potential pets "gaze wistfully at the bystanders and wayfarers, but, unlike them, have a sheep stealing, unprepossessing look, and these the salesmen occasionally kick to make them lively." Similarly, unlucky poodles had to put up with having their tails pinched when "any customer-like person approaches." Prices ranged from "$20 to a sum that brings the animal within the means of the sausage maker." The journalist couched the rest of his piece about the dogs as a market report taken from the *Evening Press*. He detailed: "Newfoundland pups much sought for, all in market held at $15, buyers refuse to operate except at a decline, to which holders refuse, the stock being all in one hand." Although poodles were a drug on the market, there was "a good inquiry for Spaniels and Greyhound pups, by elderly gentlemen for presents, but we could learn no sales, we give as the quotation $8 each or per lb for all Greyhound and $4 or $3 per lb for Spaniels, supply of all kinds equal to the demand."[5]

The writer's humor probably provoked the odd smile here and there, although nowadays the recognition of Wall Street for what it was—a market, pure and simple—seems more notable. As well, the sly acknowledgment of tricks of the trade used for primping the merchandise and deceiving customers had broader application. Antebellum Wall Street had a terrible reputation, and for more than just sharp practice. One journalist, trying with little success to explain stock "gambling" to his readers, warned that as soon as a respectable person "ventur[ed] into the vortex of speculation," he was already "a ruined man." The hapless victim might manage to "dance on the whirlpool for a season, one of the brightest bubbles on its surface, [but] he will eventually get within the spiral circles that lead into the abyss, and be 'sucked in,' as thousands have before him." There was widespread ignorance of Wall Street's deliberately mystified workings, and many disapproved of such an arcane world. Another journalist complained of "cabalistic expressions" assailing his ears out on the street. "I'll sell 500 Long Island 55 ½." "Say 55 ¼ ten days," to which some unfortunate who had bought a few days before at 63 and was potentially $1,000 out of pocket, shouted out, "D—n Long Island!" The reporter reproached: "These mountebanks are holding their puppet shows in little knots, all along Wall street, till the banks and their mouths simultaneously close at three o'clock."[6] Speculation itself was bad enough, but buying and selling shares meant dealing with people always trying to fleece the public. Locals were not the only ones expressing such sentiments. From the moment Benwell noticed the Wall Street denizens dispensing their "soft soap," he was "on guard" against "accomplished deceivers." For the rest of his stay in the city he remained wary of what he considered a loose, even careless, way of doing things. "The bustle and drive in the trading quarters of the city" did indeed impress the English traveler, but he was decidedly unimpressed by the accompanying "hurried manner of doing business, discernible in a moment to a stranger, which is much to be deprecated, and too often leads, as I afterwards found, to disastrous results."[7]

John Benwell could not help but notice one other difference from his native England. After rounding off his account of strolling up Wall Street with the dismissive aside that "it is well known that brokers and speculators on the American continent engage in the pursuit with the avidity of professed gamblers," he immediately commented on the number of African Americans he had seen: "Hundreds of

Negroes were hurrying to and fro through the streets, these were chiefly labourers, decently dressed, and employed either as draymen or porters." Benwell thought them happier than English laborers, recording further that as they toiled in the heat, "their faces shone almost like black satin or patent leather." As often was the case, a foreigner was more likely than a New Yorker to acknowledge the importance of African American sweat in making the city work. Generally, as Benwell noted, blacks were confined to laboring jobs. A year or two earlier, the editor of the *Journal of Commerce* complained that the floor of the Merchant's Exchange was "getting infested with small retailers." His querulous piece had been prompted in particular by the fact that "yesterday some negro merchants of door mats were present with their wares." Another journalist at the *Morning Express*, taken aback by his rival's unusual vehemence, chided that the editor was "not good natured this morning."[8] Whether this was so or not, what was clear was that, in and around Wall Street, blacks were expected to carry goods, not buy and sell them.

And there, of course, was the rub, the simple fact of New York life that made the career of Jeremiah G. Hamilton so remarkable. An incident related by Benwell suggests how out of place a black man doing anything other than physical labor was at this end of town. Attracted by a commotion outside the Astor Hotel, a few blocks up Broadway from Wall Street, the traveler crossed the road and discovered that Daniel Webster, the Massachusetts senator and the country's most renowned orator, had just arrived en route to Washington. Instantly recognized, the great man had been mobbed. "Glad to see you, citizens, glad to see you," he repeated as he shook every proffered hand—or almost every hand. When "a gentlemanly-dressed negro with a gold-headed cane pressed forward and held out his hand," the mood of the well-wishers changed abruptly. Benwell "heard several angry exclamations of disapprobation from the crowd, at the liberty he had taken, one individual in particular crying out, 'Kick that nigger off, what has he to do here.'" These threatening shouts cut like a knife through the hubbub. The African American "shrunk back in an instant, as if electrified."[9] For white New Yorkers this man was a black interloper, and the English traveler's description of his alarmed reaction hints at the psychological damage that status often must have caused anyone who, no matter how successful, was condemned always to be an outsider.

New York's financial precinct was as disdainful of those deemed not to belong as any other part of the city. Bankers and brokers may have been less likely than the inhabitants of the Five Points to resort to violence, but a refusal to shake a hand or the genteel turning of a back left their scars as well. Wall Street was its own small world run by its own strange rules; its denizens always were going to struggle to accept a black man as anything like an equal.

According to legend, organized stock trading in New York began with twenty-four men meeting under a buttonwood tree in Wall Street in the spring of 1792 and signing an agreement to give preference to one another in share transactions. More significant in the street's history, though, was the founding of the New York Stock and Exchange Board in 1817 and its reorganization in 1820. By 1845, the NYS&EB consisted of more than fifty brokers who had paid anywhere between $250 and $400 for their seat. Only members were allowed to trade, and all agreed to charge one another a minimum commission; nonmembers had to pay a higher rate. Quickly, the NYS&EB established itself as the most important market for securities, the place that set prices for brokers at the curb and in other cities: consequently, individual New Yorkers and nonmember brokers after the best price for shares often had to buy or sell them through a NYS&EB member and pay the higher commission.[10]

Although only a young institution, there was still much that was old-fashioned about the way the NYS&EB did things. An elaborate disciplinary system kept members in line: small fines were imposed frequently for this or that infraction of the rules, and more serious offenses could warrant expulsion from the organization. Every weekday all the members gathered from ten-thirty in the morning until noon—non-attendance merited a sixpenny penalty—in a large room in the Merchant's Exchange, rebuilt after the Great Fire with Doric columns and French floor-to-ceiling windows. Then the president, seated at a table on a dais, called the board, reading out a list of all the stocks and securities in the market. After each name was announced, the different brokers would shout their bids and offers and negotiate deals in that particular stock, and the secretary would record all bargains made. There was another shorter session in the afternoon. Above all else this was an institution whose members prided themselves on their code of honor and abhorred the idea of outside scrutiny, particularly from the legal system. Indeed, some forms of buying and selling, such as forward trading, in which the money for the shares was not delivered for, say, a month or two, were unenforceable by law, but, of course, gentlemen fulfill contracts. Not even a handshake was required to seal bargains made at the calling of the board.[11]

The governing body of the exchange was the board itself, or all its members, sitting in committee. It adjudicated in a careful and considered manner surprisingly infrequent disputes about share transactions. As well, the minutes of the board from 1833 to 1850 reveal a variety of other concerns, most of them not momentous. Every year when the lease on their rented premises came up for renewal members fretted out loud about what they thought of as the high rent they were paying and whether or not they should move. Occasionally, they managed to pass new regulations in an attempt to enforce their monopoly and protect their market advantage. In 1836, the board resolved to suspend any member buying or selling shares, directly or indirectly, out in the street. And yet, at a meeting a month or two earlier, the board had expended almost as much effort considering the trivial resolution "that a fine of not less than One Dollar be imposed upon any member who shall knock off the Hat of another." Although the stock exchange was transforming itself into a multimillion-dollar enterprise, some of its members insisted on continuing to behave in a fashion seemingly more suited to that of a modern-day fraternity than anything else.[12]

As with many exclusive clubs, the most important and time-consuming business was vetting prospective new members. Joining was difficult, with applicants first having to serve as a broker for one year or an apprenticeship to another broker for two years and then survive a ballot of existing members in which a mere three votes were all that was required to result in exclusion. Members of the board voted by placing in a container a white ball for yes and a black ball for no. This was the type of institution where, with a nudge here and a lifted eyebrow there, the necessary three votes to

veto could be mustered easily. In vote after vote, aspiring brokers
came forward offering themselves for consideration and were black-
balled—very few joined at their first attempt.

One story of rejection, hardly typical although still revealing,
stands out from the hundreds of pages of neatly handwritten minutes detailing the stock exchange's history in the 1830s and 1840s.
Myer Levy very much wanted a seat on the exchange. On May 8,
1837, Benjamin Nathan proposed him as a new member, and on
May 15 members voted, with the result being "15 white, 14 black."
Ten days later the count was "24 black, 16 white." These were humiliating margins. Time and again he was renominated, but a rump
of members ensured his rejection. By the end of August, after eight
losing votes and in a bid to end the awkwardness, the president of
the stock exchange entered the fray and endorsed Levy's candidacy,
but it made no difference. At last, on March 1, 1838, after a mortify-
ing fourteen attempts, the secretary was able to record in the minute
book that "unanimous consent was balloted for and elected 2 black
and 32 white balls." The wording here is opaque: it looks as though
some sort of deal had been brokered, but two members, ignoring
any arrangement, persisted in casting black balls. Regardless, Myer
Levy, by the smallest possible margin, was finally a member of the
NYS&EB. Although the minutes reveal only the bare details, it is
difficult not to conclude that the fact Levy was a well-known Jew
played the determining role in this extraordinary series of votes.[13]

The NYS&EB was a very profitable price-fixing cartel, and a
conservative one at that: inevitably, the excluded were resentful. In
the 1830s, some of those left out formed a "New Board," or rival
exchange. In spite of active opposition from the old board, the new
institution flourished initially, particularly in the boom years of 1835
and 1836. However, the panic of 1837 dealt the fledgling exchange a
mortal blow—some two-thirds of its members failed—and the new
board stumbled on for a few more years, never regaining anything
like its earlier standing. Over the ensuing decade many of its remaining members would be absorbed quietly into the old board.[14]

When Hamilton started trading with members of the old board
in the mid-1830s, the NYS&EB was not even two decades old, but
it often appeared archaic, something to poke fun at. An acerbic

James Gordon Bennett could reduce the institution to a laughing-stock whenever he wanted. The *Herald* editor published a piece in October 1837 in which he pulled aside the curtain on the closed proceedings of the NYS&EB and lampooned its members. He began by advising readers that if they assumed from the daily listings in the papers of stock prices and trades that the exchange was a place "where wisdom, order and decorum preside," then they were very much mistaken. "What will you think when you learn that no less a sum than $18,000 has been collected in fines, each not exceeding two shillings, for disorderly and riotous conduct in that should-be-sage and august assembly?" Bennett asked. He then devoted column inches of newsprint to skewering, with a coruscating wit and devastating precision, the calling of the board and the interplay between the president of the NYS&EB, or "P," and the brokers.

> P. "Fine those two brokers who are talking, a shilling each."
> "We weren't speaking, Mr. President."
> P. "Fine them both again."
> Six brokers rise. "Mr President they weren't speaking."
> P. "Fine the whole six." "Now, U.S. Bank."
> "I'll sell a hundred shares at 20 days at 117 ½."
> "I'll take—my hat, my hat."
> P. "Fine that man who pulled that broker's hat off."
> "It seems to be nobody."
> P. "Fine nobody."[15]

And this, almost a century before the heyday of the Marx Brothers.

In fact, the NYS&EB was in some disarray, a victim of its own success in attracting business. Ways of buying and selling shares were still based on a system of gentlemanly honor, but honor always sits uneasily alongside the imperatives of a free market. As turnover and the amount of money involved increased dramatically, tensions were inevitable and signs of impending change everywhere. In 1838, for instance, S & M Allen & Co. did not honor a future contract to buy fifty shares of Mohawk Rail Road from James W. Bleeker, who had to sell elsewhere at a 35 percent lower price and sued to recover his subsequent loss of $1,985.98. As a journalist at the *New York Sun* noted, the case "excited a great interest in the Wall street circles, in-asmuch as such purchases at the Board are deemed sacred contracts, in the performance of which the honor of the parties is supposed to be involved." The importance of holding the line was manifest. "Al-most all the enormous stock transactions of the city are conducted in the same way," the journalist wrote, "and if the precedent of a violation of them with impunity should be established, transactions to the amount of millions would be effected by it."[16]

Whether they liked it or not, all those millions of dollars were transforming older ways of conducting business. Not everyone wel-comed this. Writing in 1871, Abram C. Dayton made it clear that he did not think change was necessarily progress. In *Last Days of Knickerbocker Life in New York,* his elegy for a bygone era, Dayton contrasted the "small knot of bankers and brokers, who were the innocent forerunners of that busy, restless throng which now surges and seethes, as if the *'day of doom'* had come, and each one had *'to hand in his chips,'* when the new Trinity clock strikes three." Back in his youth in the 1830s, Wall Street had been transformed almost overnight: "From early morn till dark the street devoted to stock transactions was filled with an excited crowd of the new found worshippers of Mammon." He missed what he remembered rosily as "the peaceful Knickerbocker Wall Street, where hours of consul-tation and 'considering' were required before a share of stock was purchased."[17]

Dayton mourned the passing of an epoch, but many more wel-comed change and were decidedly less sympathetic toward the Knickerbocker gentlemen and the way they had run things. William Worthington Fowler, writing at almost the same time as Dayton, recalled things differently, characterizing a stock exchange old guard as being "remarkable for their conservative views in respect to mon-eyed operations." He elaborated vividly: "A few rich, grey-headed old fogies frowned down the more enterprising, but less wealthy 'Young America' element, which went in for bold, dashing moves, cliques, corners and the like."[18] Jeremiah Hamilton had arrived on Wall Street in the 1830s just in time to witness speculation, gam-bling and market manipulation on an unprecedented scale. The best-known broker from this decade, Jacob Little, was famous for his spectacular plunges and for fleecing investors. He was a notorious bear, that is, he gambled on the market going down and was not beyond ensuring that happened by spreading rumors about a company to drive down the price of shares. Thus he would sell shares he did not own and then, when it came time to deliver, buy them back at the cheaper market price. If the original sale had been on a delay of, say, sixty days and in that period the price had plummeted, his profits were substantial. Little made millions of dollars: honor—indeed, even bothering to keep his word after agreeing to a deal—had nothing to do with his success. Wall Street in the 1830s was no place for the timid.[19]

Jeremiah Hamilton certainly was not timid. To be sure, the stock exchange was a white world, but so was every other occupation in which New Yorkers accumulated large sums of money. He had no loyalty to the ways of a Wall Street determined to exclude him. As a black man, he was never going to become a member of an institution that used black balls to exclude prospective new members, that listed defaulting or bankrupt members in its "Black Book," and that trumpeted so loudly its reliance on a code of honor.[20] Not that he showed the slightest interest in challenging such gentlemanly forms of racism. There was no need to become a member in order to buy and sell shares. Rather than trying, futilely, to join the stock exchange, he was more interested in taking on its members. Brokers might have expected that their peers still would adjudicate any disputes, but Hamilton did not play by their rules. At every opportunity, he would force prominent individuals into court, challenge the way they had behaved and expose their practices to scrutiny. This did not make him popular.

Hamilton had recognized an institution in flux and, above all, had seen the potential of an increasingly important speculative market, a place in which clever and ruthless men were making fortunes. He was well aware of the challenges to the way the stock exchange was doing things. My suspicion is that Hamilton himself was the *Sun* reporter who filed the story detailing Bleeker's suing of S. & M. Allen & Co.—and if he did not write the piece, he certainly read it, for it was published during the time when the black man spent hours every day in the newspaper's office. Just as earlier he had used the press in his struggles and treated court appearances as an unavoidable consequence of business success, Hamilton positioned himself alongside those calling into question older ways of doing things. His motivation was less ideological and more the desire of a black man, with no investment in the establishment, to make money. Searching for any edge in the market, it was inevitable he would clash with Wall Street's brokers. When that happened he would sue them, and sue them again, until he ran them ragged.

Hamilton's first known row with a stockbroker began with a disputed transaction that occurred in August 1835. A John Wood had sold one hundred shares of the Jackson Marine Insurance Company and delivery was due, but he did not yet have possession of the stock that he had sold and would not for a further ten days or fortnight. His broker, Robert Atterbury of Booth and Atterbury, knew this and was also aware that Jeremiah Hamilton owned 200 shares of Jackson Marine. What happened next would be argued about in various courts for the next five years. According to Wood, Atterbury arranged a deal whereby Hamilton would lend him one hundred shares and in return would be paid $5,400, a sum that was $150 above the shares' current value. Almost immediately the share price plummeted, and when Wood tried to return the shares in September, Hamilton refused to accept them. Wood was left holding an asset rapidly diminishing in value that he unloaded in the market on December 4, 1835, selling the one hundred shares for $3,990. Wood sued Hamilton in an attempt to recover his loss of $1,410.

At the first trial on December 10, 1836, Jeremiah Hamilton gave a different account of the way things went down. Atterbury indeed had approached him about loaning the shares, but he had turned down the offer. The black broker did agree, however, to sell one hundred of his shares to Wood. As soon as their price dropped, Hamilton claimed Wood came up with some fanciful story about the completed transaction not being a sale, but rather a loan of $5,400, with the stock being held as security. What caught Hamilton completely by surprise at the trial was that not only did Atterbury appear on Wood's behalf—in fact, was his only witness—but also, as he saw it, the broker had lied through his teeth when he testified. Atterbury's claim of the existence of a loan ambushed Hamilton, his case collapsed and the verdict handed down was in Wood's favor, although it was understood that a higher court would review the rather unusual trial.

The further this case proceeded, the more it unraveled into a welter of accusation and counter-accusation. A now very angry Hamilton went gunning for Atterbury, whose turncoat testimony had been so devastating. He insisted that back in September 1835 the supposedly respectable broker had tried to blackmail him into accepting the loss on the shares. Hamilton explained, in a sworn statement in July 1837, that "there is an institution or association in the city of New York called the Board of Brokers having various rules . . . one of which is . . . that if any person with whom a Broker has made a stock jobbing contract for the delivery of stock on a particular day refuses to fulfill such contract, upon his being reported for such refusal to said Board, no broker belonging to said Board will afterwards be permitted to make any contracts for him or have any dealings with him at the said Board of Brokers." According to Hamilton, when he refused to accept the return of the stock, Atterbury threatened to report the black man to the board and "to bring him thereby under the operation of said rule." The consequences would be dire, for, as Atterbury lectured Hamilton, much as it caused him and his firm regret, "it would then be out of the power of any member of the Board to execute orders for him"—more bluntly, they would blackball him.

After this threat had failed, Booth and Atterbury conspired with John Wood to commence this suit against Hamilton. According to the black broker, Wood was merely a nominal litigant, a front for Atterbury. Wood's legal fees were being paid by Booth and Atterbury, and so far he had not bothered to appear in court even once in any of the proceedings. The only point of the vexatious suit was "to cast the loss on said stock on the shoulders of your orator [Hamilton]."[21]

When the case was about to be heard again in late June 1837, the New York chief justice declined to be involved in trying the cause. Here was Jeremiah Hamilton's opening. He promptly published an extremely partisan article in the *New York Sun* about the surprise decision, explaining that the justice "was too strongly prejudiced against the plaintiff's witness [Atterbury], by the 'manner' in which he testified on a former trial of the cause!" At the December 1836 hearing, Hamilton's counsel had cross-examined Atterbury with great finesse, eliciting "testimony which made it sufficiently evident to the whole court, that he was himself the actual plaintiff, and the real party interested in the suit." Indeed, the justice had become so convinced of this that he now had only "distrust and prejudice" toward Atterbury, "which induced him to decline hearing further testimony from him" and to step down from the case. The carefully crafted and anonymous piece mauled Atterbury without explaining anything about the larger circumstances and certainly never let on that its author was the suit's central figure. Hamilton emphasized that this was "a pretty severe expression of opinion on Mr Atterbury's veracity for a chief justice to pronounce." Not content with eviscerating Atterbury, he ended with a sarcastic broadside, suggesting that the chief justice's withering words "would touch the *fine sensibilities* of even a wall street broker."[22]

The case—or cases, for Atterbury instigated both civil and criminal proceedings against Hamilton for the libel on him caused by the "flagrant perversion of the language and meaning of the chief justice"—with appeals and a new trial stretched out for years. Finally, on May 8, 1841, a decision in favor of John Wood for $1,555.93 (the original $1,410 plus interest) was entered in the records of the Superior Court of the City of New York. Not that Wood, or Atterbury, come to that, ever saw a cent of this money. The debt was expunged when Hamilton went bankrupt in 1842. As to the rights and wrongs of the case: from this distance it is hard to judge, although once again Hamilton does appear to have been harshly treated. The last word, though, should be given to John Anthon, one of Hamilton's lawyers, an experienced man very familiar with the case's details. At a hearing in February 1838, he "contended that this whole case might come under the denomination of a regular Wall street stock jobbing shaving transaction; and that one side were as deep in the mud as the others were in the mire."[23]

For most of the lengthy duration of the Wood proceedings, Hamilton was fending off financial ruin. In late 1839 the Dry Dock Bank dragged a reluctant Hamilton, described by the *Herald* as "the well known Wall street stock jobber" and doing everything he could to delay the inevitable, into court for not honoring two notes totaling

$1,587. These notes had been payment for share transactions with Russell Stebbins, a member of the NYS&EB, who had discounted them to the Dry Dock Bank. Hamilton claimed that the notes originated from "illegal or fictitious sales of stocks" and had his counsel call Stebbins to the stand as a witness. The embarrassed broker could not answer a series of technical questions, but none of this made any difference, other than to Stebbins's dignity. Damages of $1,587 and costs were awarded against Hamilton and confirmed a few months later on appeal. This debt too was never paid, being wiped off the books by Hamilton's bankruptcy.[24]

Almost every day of these difficult financial years, from 1837 to 1842, Hamilton made his way to the *New York Sun* office. For all the diffidence, and later on coldness, with which Moses Beach treated him, the editor still knew that the ever-present Hamilton had his uses. On at least one occasion Hamilton bought silver off of Beach, probably also bought and sold shares for him as well, and, of course, would help in the compilation of *Wealth and Wealthy Citizens of New York City* (1842). Above all, though, the unlikely pair "conversed about stocks" or "used often to talk about the stocks."[25] Almost certainly Beach spoke to others as well, but his conversations about the share market with the knowledgeable Hamilton are of interest because under his editorship the *New York Sun* was paying more attention to what happened on Wall Street. No longer did the *Sun* abandon financial coverage to the *New York Herald* or the *Journal of Commerce.*

As well as the daily listing of the previous day's share transactions, the *Sun* now published occasional articles analyzing financial prospects in some detail. In late 1841, there was a sharp downturn in the market, and Beach tried to explain what was occurring to his readers: share prices were falling "as monstrous frauds and robberies incident to an inflated credit system are almost daily brought to light, timid men become alarmed, a kind of panic seizes them, and all confidence is for the moment apparently lost." But, the piece's author carefully pointed out, the stocks plunging, such as United States Bank, North American Trust, and Harlem, were "the products of speculation, destitute of any real value and undeserving of any confidence." If one looked at the "well managed insurance companies, the great majority of our New York banks, our rich and profitable lines of railroad," a different story presented itself, one of above-par prices and regular dividends. "There is no loss of confidence in them, and·they alone are fit to be denominated American stocks." He admitted to being gratified at seeing worthless shares "going down and sinking to their original nothingness" but thought it important to point out that "all sound financial and commercial operations" had nothing to worry about. A little over a week later, in late November 1841, Beach published an article on the panic that seemingly occurred at this time every year. The writer attributed this phenomenon to a number of factors, including the annual specie shipment to Europe, merchants from the west buying stock before the Erie Canal closed for winter inundating the city with "uncurrent money" that jobbers then sold for current money, causing a credit squeeze that was exacerbated by rumors about broken banks and the "apprehension of a general crash." On top of this, "a herd of animals called 'bears' in the stock market" resorted "to every profligate device" to depress prices. "A panic is a god-send, a harvest for them," the writer concluded.[26] To be sure these articles revealed a boosterish streak, but they were also acute analyses of both the stock market and the money supply, and were early examples of a newly sophisticated financial journalism. There is at least the chance that Jeremiah Hamilton's conversations with Beach had some influence on their content.

Two things were remarkable about the idea of contemporaries paying attention to Hamilton's views on the state of business. First, he was black, and second, he had long-overdue accounts all over town with stockbrokers who were never going to get a penny of their money. He owed Brown and Sons $6,000 from as far back as 1835, Vaux and King $3,500 for advances on stock purchased for him over several years, and John Ward and Co. about $7,500. Not that such a crushing amount of debt from previous losses inhibited Hamilton from further speculation. At some time in 1840 or 1841, he had bought 1,000 shares of the Long Island Railroad Company and paid the first installment of $5 per share. He had then transferred the shares to a Daniel Jackson as security for a loan of $2,500. Not only did the value of these shares drop sharply, but also Long Island made calls to the tune of $25 on each of their shares and sued Jackson for the owing $25,000. Although the court judged Jackson, as mort- gagee of the stock, not liable, Long Island still insisted that someone had to pay them their money.[27] Admittedly these were hard years for everyone, but whatever Hamilton touched was turning to ash.

He did have one small victory though. As mentioned in an ear- lier chapter, even as he was in the midst of declaring bankruptcy, Hamilton continued to trade shares under another name. He took out a sixty-day option on one hundred shares of Long Island Rail- road, agreeing to forfeit $250 in the case of his not buying them. The stock fell in price, so Hamilton did not exercise his option and lost his $250. Hamilton, or, in fact, David Robinson, the name he was using, sued Jacob Carpender of Rowland, Graham and Carpender, Wall Street brokers, for return of the $250 because he claimed that when the option was agreed to, the brokers did not own any Long Is- land Railroad shares (which was then a legal requirement for writing an option). A Mr. Ives, secretary of Long Island Railroad, gave evi- dence of registered shareholders contained in the company's books showing that on the day the option was written the stockbroking firm in fact owned no shares, although they did only a couple of days later. This rendered the transaction illegal, and the jury ordered the $250 penalty for noncompliance to be returned to the plaintiff.[28]

Two years later Hamilton was suing another brokerage firm and questioning another of the NYS&EB's venerable practices. Genin Lockwood and Co., composed of Sidney C. Genin and the improba- bly named Le Grand Lockwood, had opened for business on May 1, 1843, renting premises at 1 Hanover Street, only a door down from Wall Street. Sidney Genin became a member of the NYS&EB on No- vember 14, 1843, by a vote of forty-four white balls to two black.[29] In September 1844, Hamilton came to an arrangement with the still- fledgling firm whereby he would buy shares but Genin Lockwood would "carry the stock." In other words, the brokers would retain the purchased shares, charge Hamilton their usual commission, loan him the money for the cost of the shares and bill him for interest at 7 percent per annum, charging an additional fee of one-eighth of 1 percent on the par value of the stock. As well, Hamilton had to put up additional security in the form of either cash or other stock: if the shares he had bought declined in value, the brokers would require even more security.

In effect, then, Hamilton had agreed with Genin Lockwood that he would gamble on the stock market using their money—but at a price. Such arrangements work well in a bull market (when prices are rising). Everyone makes money—the broker earns commission and interest and the speculator, able to buy many more shares than would be possible if he used only his own money, consequently reaps a larger profit. Bear markets, though, are another matter entirely. As share prices tumble and the value of the speculation shrinks to less than the amount borrowed to buy it, the broker will insist on the very prompt delivery of more and more security to guarantee the loan. A sharply falling market quickly will wipe out someone gambling with borrowed money.

At the very end of September 1844, Hamilton began buying. On September 29 he bought one hundred shares of New York and Harlem Railroad Company, costing $3,675, and put up twenty-five shares of the Morris Canal and Banking Company as additional security. On October 3 he bought fifty shares of the New York Providence and Boston Rail Road Company for $2,543.75 and fifty shares of the Norwich and Worcester Rail Road Company for $3,825, handing over one hundred Vicksburgh Bank shares as more security. On October 10 he purchased 200 shares in the Long Island Railroad Company for $7,325 and gave Genin Lockwood another one hundred Vicksburgh Bank shares for security.

Even as Jeremiah Hamilton staked out a substantial position as a bull, the bottom fell out of the market—ironically, doing precisely what the *New York Sun* had explained that it always seemed to do at this time of the year. By the beginning of November, the Morris Canal shares Hamilton had employed as security were "worthless" and Hamilton replaced them with $292.19 in cash. But this was not enough to secure his position. As Genin later explained, the stock market "was very fluctuating and uncertain at about that time and generally falling or depreciating." Genin Lockwood required more security urgently and, when that was not forthcoming, began selling out Hamilton's holdings from underneath him at very substantial losses.

In mid-November, Hamilton sought an injunction in an attempt to stop Genin Lockwood from dumping any more of his shares into a falling market, and, most particularly, to prevent his shares that he had put up as security from being sold. He requested that the court appoint a receiver to sort out who owed what to whom. More insidiously, at least as far as the brokers were concerned, Hamilton's lawyer argued that his purchases of shares had been illegal and that the transactions should be voided. Not only would this necessitate the return of all the shares given as security, but it would also make Genin Lockwood liable for the now-considerable losses on Hamilton's purchases. The grounds for this were that the agreement between Genin Lockwood and Hamilton was "usorious and corrupt." Partly this was about the 7 percent interest the brokers charged, although they claimed reasonably that they had had to borrow the money themselves, but mostly it was directed at the way their commission was computed. At this time, as Genin Lockwood's lawyers explained, members of the old board charged their commission not on the market price of shares but on their par value. Thus, when Hamilton bought one hundred shares of Harlem at a cost of $3,675, the commissions were worked out not on that price but on $5,000 (or the par value of $50 a share). More equitably, members of the new board charged their clients commission on the actual cost of their transactions. Unfortunately, the court's decision in this case remains unknown. However, the surviving legal papers make it clear that the "usorious and corrupt" argument caused Genin Lockwood some unease, as they pleaded that if this reasoning was accepted, then rather than striking down the various transactions, the court should simply reduce the total amount of commission.[30] If nothing else, Jeremiah Hamilton had an unerring instinct for getting under the skin of other New York brokers.

Early in March 1845, Wall Street's regard for the black broker was revealed publicly in the most dramatic of fashions. Only the barest of details made it into the newspapers, but they were enough to spark a considerable amount of interest, and not just in New York. According to the *New York Herald*, a resolution was put before the new board, "the preamble of which set forth, that whereas J. G. Hamilton had grossly insulted a member of this board . . . that all members of this board are forbidden doing any business for him on penalty of expulsion." The story went on to claim that the resolution was opposed "and its ridiculous absurdity exposed, as the board had nothing to do with any personal matters." In a follow-up piece the next day the *Herald* journalist corrected the earlier story and confirmed that the resolution prohibiting members from dealing with the "well known operator in the street," or Hamilton, had indeed passed, but claimed that the matter would be sorted out properly at the board's next meeting. Apparently, members had overreacted to what was "merely a personal affair, and does not come within the jurisdiction of the board."[31]

The *New York Morning News* published the most convincing account of what had happened. A resolution had been "offered to prohibit the members from transacting business for a colored man, on the ground chiefly, of his being a defaulter to many of the members." It had passed "unanimously," but after further consideration what the reporter termed the "Hebrew party" reopened the matter. Consequently, "the transactions will be investigated" and the banning of Hamilton referred to a select committee. The writer added that it was important for brokers to protect themselves "against the contracts of desperate speculators." Members of the board were compelled to accept one another's contracts, rendering it imperative "to guard against the movements of those whose operations are 'heads I win, tails you lose.'"[32] Someone certainly had the measure of the way Hamilton preferred to conduct business.

Not only was the stock exchange's public blackballing of Hamilton extremely unusual, it was also newsworthy. Papers as far afield as the *Times-Picayune* in New Orleans and the *Baltimore Sun* reprinted the terse news items from the New York press. The details of the story were frustratingly vague—and, in spite of extensive digging in a variety of sources, remain so to this day. Editors, though, were able to add their own glosses to the few available facts. A writer in the *Charleston Courier* who identified Hamilton as being "known on Change in various speculations" without mentioning that he was black certainly was puzzled by the reports. "What the nature of his offence, or whether he has really committed any, did not transpire," the journalist noted, before dismissively concluding: "The Public

Stock Exchange, however, is a rather second rate affair, at best, and its quarrels scarcely worth attending to." For a writer in *The Farmer,* in a piece reprinted in the *Maine Cultivator and Hallowell Gazette,* the reason for the ban "appears to be, that said Hamilton is a colored man; and so, forsooth, his money is not be received in the same 'till' with theirs. Oh, 'the land of the free and the home of the brave.'"[33]

ELEVEN

LIVING WITH JIM CROW

A reporter once asked jazz great Duke Ellington how, as a touring musician, he adjusted to living under Jim Crow. With characteristic urbanity, Ellington replied: "You have to try not to think about it or you'll knock yourself out."[1] And this indeed was how, a century earlier, many African New Yorkers managed to get by most of the time. Nevertheless, the rising tide of segregation in the 1830s and 1840s provided more than ample reason for Jeremiah Hamilton to have second thoughts about the correctness of his decision to come to the city. Did he ever doubt his choice of New York as the place to make his mark on the world? What did he think of the way New Yorkers, both black and white, treated him? Here the sources, if not silent, are faint. Yet something of his views can be teased from a few surviving details of his life.

There were ways that allowed Hamilton, in Ellington's terms, to avoid thinking too much about the newly introduced segregation measures. Buried in the black broker's bankruptcy papers is a brief notation of an unpaid bill of $40 from 1840 for "horse keeping." Hamilton owed the money to Coddington and McMann, partners in a livery stable on Watts Street, near Canal Street. Using a horse, or a horse and carriage, at least some of the time, minimized the inevitable indignities a black man faced when using public transport. Even though in 1840 money had been in short supply for Hamilton as he kept at bay his creditors and financial ruin, he still ran up quite a bill at the stables. Later on, during the Civil War, when the U.S. government assessed and levied taxes to pay for the war effort, Hamilton was listed as owning a carriage.[2]

The black broker also put Jim Crow out of his mind as he invested on Wall Street. Much of the action on the New York stock exchanges in the late 1830s and 1840s occurred in the booming railroad sector. The New York and Harlem Railroad Company was an especially volatile stock with a high turnover (or a large number of shares bought and sold every day). As a reporter cautioned *New York Sun* readers in late 1843, "speculation in this stock has been the treacherous whirlpool in which millions have been lost."[3] An anonymous individual who described himself as a "reformed stock gambler" was similarly dismissive: "The history of this road since its commencement, and of the manoeuvres which have been executed with the Stock since it was first used as a foot-ball in Wall-street, would afford an abundance of *materiel* for a modern fashionable novel."[4] Write-ups such as this signaled the attraction of the stock for sharp traders, indeed, for anyone who thought they knew how Wall Street worked: if some investors were losing millions of dollars, the chances are that insiders, of one sort or another, were making a lot of money. During the early 1840s, Hamilton speculated heavily, to the tune of thousands of dollars, in the stock of New York and Harlem Railroad, Long Island Railroad, Boston Rail Road, and Norwich and Worcester Rail Road—all companies that discriminated against African Americans. Expecting the black broker to have boycotted buying and selling these shares is unreasonable— ideas of using economic leverage for the benefit of African Americans did not become commonplace until the "Don't Buy Where You Can't Work" struggles in Harlem ninety years later, and disinvestment would not become a serious issue for a further half-century, when the campaigns were launched against South African apartheid. Nevertheless, it is striking that within a couple of years of New York and Harlem Railroad employees throwing Thomas Downing from the car, sending him sprawling into the middle of the Bowery for the crime of being a black man in New York, Jeremiah Hamilton was plunging thousands of dollars into New York and Harlem stock. In effect, one of their shareholders could ride on the company's railroad only if the white agent—and of course they were all white—turned a blind eye.

Sooner rather than later, though, and as Duke Ellington well knew, an African American did have to knock him- or herself out. Inevitably, a black man or woman would cross the newly imagined color line, run afoul of some Jim Crow practice or another and be forced to deal with the discriminatory racial system. As it happens, there is one chance account of a minor incident that occurred in the wake of a "gentleman" referring to Jeremiah Hamilton as a "nigger." Hamilton's reaction was instructive. Anyone who spends any time at all reading the New York press of the 1830s and 1840s cannot fail to notice the frequency with which the word is used—not so much to shock, more as a matter of course. This was new. It was part and parcel of the racist response to the end of slavery in the state, an accompaniment to the invention of Jim Crow segregation. As with the seating regulations on the New York and Harlem Railroad cars or the New York omnibuses, demeaning African Americans as "niggers" cordoned off and demonized them. "Nigger Hamilton," as business peers often disparaged him, was certainly familiar with the word. James Gordon Bennett referred routinely to the "Nigger Sun" as a result of Hamilton's close association with the newspaper. Thus, in a piece in the *Herald* in December 1839, Bennett, boasting of his paper's coverage of a particular story, asked: "What did other newspaper establishments do?" It is not difficult to imagine the glint of malice in Bennett's eye as he answered his own question: "Our highly respectable nigger contemporary of the Sun, as all niggers do when they see a real Anglo-Saxon white man play trumps, tried to imitate us, and issued a bit of an Extra that made the news boys laugh."[5] No one deployed vitriol and racist stereotypes quite like Bennett.

Familiarity with the word meant neither that he was unscarred by the abuse nor that he would necessarily acquiesce when called "Nigger" Hamilton. The incident occurred probably in the 1840s, maybe in the 1850s, and was related by the antiquarian Charles Haswell, from his vantage point at century's end. He despised Hamilton and everything the bumptious broker represented, regaling his readers with a description of "the brazen manner in which he assumed the association of and the privileges of a white man." According to Haswell, the shameless charlatan "rode in street stages, ostentatiously exhibited himself at the lunch counter at Delmonico's in Broad Street, and addressed or referred to some acquaintances in a familiar manner." On the occasion in question, Hamilton, walking down the street, had accosted a "well-known gentleman of this city": "I hear you have said I was a nigger." The "gentleman" looked Hamilton "squarely in the face, and with his quiet manner, replied: 'Are you not?'" According to Haswell, who claimed improbably to have been watching from the other side of the street, "the manner of reply, added to its truth, was too much for Hamilton," who "stepped aside and proceeded on his way."[6] The cruel enjoyment that the old man took from retelling this story and damning Hamilton yet again is almost visceral.

For Haswell, this was a tale of gentlemanly sangfroid rendering speechless an inferior black man; he even indexed the story under "Hamilton, 'Nigger.'" There are other ways of cataloguing this incident. What is striking is not just Hamilton's refusal to submit to being called "nigger," but also that he sought out and confronted publicly the culprit about his use of the word. Even by the antiquarian's account the black man behaved "with an assumed attitude of defiance" when he "stepped in front of the gentleman." In fact, unwittingly, Haswell had depicted a black gentleman deliberately, almost flamboyantly, transgressing the new rules of Jim Crow. Hamilton rode streetcars, had integrated not some rough dive of an oyster house but Delmonico's, in the heart of the financial district, and treated whites no matter who they were as his equals. And he rebuked this "gentleman" for calling him "nigger." Haswell had no appreciation of how remarkable any of these actions were, although he did have enough sense to find Hamilton a disturbing figure. Possibly, the gentleman's "Are you not?" did nonplus the black man. Or perhaps it was Hamilton, and not Haswell's hero, who displayed the gentlemanly sangfroid. Conceivably, Hamilton's silence was disdainful rather than abject, indicating a refusal to accept the question, and the whole discourse of which it was part, as legitimate, as something he had to answer. It is easy to imagine Hamilton responding to the "gentleman" with a withering stare and then, having made his point, walking around him as if he was something distasteful on the sidewalk. In the end, we are left with an old man's story of a black broker declining to answer a gentleman's question. Whether the ensuing silence, or Hamilton's demeanor during the whole episode, reflects as badly on his character as the vindictive Haswell would have us believe is another matter entirely.

There is one other detail from Hamilton's life in the early 1840s that offers some clues about his state of mind. In 1842, as part of the process of bankruptcy, Hamilton, or his lawyers, had to file an inventory of his property. This accounting of the petitioner's life was a legal requirement: the document not only listed monies owed him and that he owed, but also included a careful reckoning of all his remaining possessions. We learn, for example, that at 76 Liberty Street he owned one writing desk, one bureau, and one table and that Eliza Jane Hamilton possessed a bed, wardrobe, two tables, six chairs and sundry other items settled on her before her marriage. As well, the list included:

> Books of the petitioner, in said dwelling house, to wit.
>> Works of Lord Bacon 2 Vols
>> " of Lord Bolingbroke 6 Vols
>> " of Aristotle 1 vol
> Two Maps—one of the city of NY
> —one of United States
> Milton's Paradise Lost 1 Vol
> Treasury of Knowledge 2 vols
> Ten Edinburgh reviews

An inventory from the nineteenth century of an African American's library is highly unusual—this is one of the earliest, if not the earliest, such document in existence.

To be sure, Hamilton did not own a large number of books, but the chances are that the twenty-two volumes he had left on his shelf were important to him. His collection contained nothing written by an African American. Not that this is surprising. Given Hamilton's vexed relations with his compatriots, the fact that he possessed no file of *Freedom's Journal* or the *Colored American* or even any former slave narrative is of a piece with everything else we know about him. Too often we expect blacks and whites to inhabit completely segregated worlds—but, no matter what the proponents of Jim Crow tried to achieve, this was never the way New Yorkers lived. While establishing African American literary traditions is an important endeavor, there is no need to neglect the way in which slaves, former slaves and free blacks read, when they could get their hands on it, the full panoply of the printed word. The best-known example of such a practice comes from the *Narrative of the Life of Frederick Douglass, An American Slave* (1845), one of the foundations of the American canon. As a twelve-year-old, Douglass, still enslaved, devoured the *Columbian Orator,* managing to draw meaning from the selections in a way the compiler of the volume had never intended. The young Douglass read "over and over again with unabated interest" Richard Sheridan's "mighty speeches on and in behalf of Catholic emancipation" and took inspiration from them. As Douglass recorded, "they gave tongue to interesting thoughts of my own soul, which had frequently flashed through my mind, and died for want of utterance."[7] What, then, could Jeremiah Hamilton have made of his singular collection of books?

First, a few educated guesses about precisely what was in Hamilton's library. Here it is necessary to remember that antebellum Americans were world leaders in intellectual piracy. They were notorious for simply reprinting the work of English writers and not paying royalties to either them or their publishers. On his 1842 American tour, Charles Dickens, the best-known victim of this practice, vociferously advocated for the passage of an international copyright measure. Although Americans flocked to catch a glimpse of Boz, creator of Oliver Twist and Nicholas Nickleby, no one was much interested in what he had to say about the pirating of English fiction and nonfiction. Accusations of money-grubbing and worse were flung his way—as a wounded Dickens wrote a friend, the invective turned his "blood to gall." Whatever he and his compatriots may have thought of having their writing shanghaied, Jeremiah Hamilton, and hordes of American book-buyers, benefited from cheaper prices for pirated editions of their work. In the case of Hamilton's library, an important two-volume edition of *The Works of Lord Bacon,* including a lengthy introductory essay, had been published in London in 1838. An eight-volume edition of Bolingbroke's works had appeared in 1809. Knockoff versions of both had been printed on the other side of the Atlantic—for instance, Carey and Hart, a Philadelphia firm, published a multivolume edition of Bolingbroke's works in 1841. Over the years there had been innumerable English editions of *Paradise Lost,* although probably Hamilton owned an American one, such as that published in Boston in 1831. Similarly, the quarterly *Edinburgh Review,* the foremost nineteenth-century journal of opinion, had been plagued by piracy. Up until the early 1840s, or about the time the inventory of Hamilton's library was taken, almost all copies of the *Edinburgh Review* sold in America were unauthorized (and were easily identified by a distinctive page layout with "double columns of print").[8] In all likelihood, the vast majority of the books and magazine issues on Hamilton's shelf were knockoffs, printed in the United States.

There was a bookish quality to the pioneering black broker. Although little about Jeremiah Hamilton's formative years can be established with any certainty, the most authoritative obituary, published in the *New York Daily Tribune,* insisted that Hamilton received a "good education" in Puerto Rico. Clearly, this entailed something more inspiring than mere rote learning, for the young boy developed a fondness for study, a habit "which he continued throughout his life." Indeed, the writer made a point of emphasizing that Hamilton "was thoroughly conversant with the best English and Spanish authors, and devoted much time to the study of moral philosophy and history."[9] And there is certainly the self-improving air of someone trying to educate himself to Hamilton's library. A thinker such as Francis Bacon, for example, was much more influential throughout the nineteenth century than he is today, and his writings remained a staple among autodidacts. In England, after the 1870 legislation that extended elementary schools to the relatively small proportion of the population without access to formal education, publishers rushed to bring out cheap school editions of several central authors, and their number included Bacon.[10]

Especially interesting in this respect is the last book on the inventory. It is likely that this was *The Treasury of Knowledge and Library of Reference,* the sixth edition of which was published in New York in 1836 and the seventh in 1839,[11] although both of these editions were three volumes, and the inventory noted only two. These volumes were an autodidact's dream. As well as a dictionary and a "compendious English grammar," they contained lists of the principal mountains in the world, populations of European cities and the British ministries for the previous quarter of a century. There was also a decided American inflection to the volumes: not only was the frontispiece an engraving of George Washington, but most of the third volume was an appendix consisting of biographical sketches of those who had signed the Declaration of Independence, the Declaration itself, Washington's Farewell Address, a list of colleges and universities in the United States and much, much more.

The *Edinburgh Review,* on the other hand, was a window into the sophistication of the British intellectual elite. Founded in 1802, by the late 1830s and early 1840s the quarterly was renowned for its lengthy reviews, often running to dozens of pages, of books covering an eclectic range of subjects. While the politics were broadly whiggish, the *Review* in these years displayed opinionated and lively writing. If, as seems likely, Hamilton's ten copies of the quarterly were recent, he may well have seen, in the October 1839 issue, a scathing assessment of Captain Maryatt's account of his travels in America, some twenty-five pages of relentlessly devastating prose. Perhaps he even browsed through the review of Tocqueville's *Democracy in America,* in which he could have read about the recent depredations in his own city: "The people of New York and Philadelphia sacked and destroyed . . . the schools and churches of their black fellow-citizens, while numbers who took no share in the outrage amused themselves with the sight."[12] For the most part, though, the *Review* steered clear of American subjects and concentrated on British concerns. It was a shrewd vehicle for someone without the benefit of an extensive education to get up to speed on the books and issues animating the Anglo-Atlantic world of letters.

Although there was a strain of self-help running through the works Hamilton had collected, it would be misleading to emphasize too much this side to his library. Just like the writers for the *Edinburgh Review,* authors such as Aristotle, Bacon, Bolingbroke and Milton were complex political and philosophical thinkers. And, in fact, Hamilton's library was anything but a random collection of books.

In a strange way, these texts, written by three Englishmen and a Greek, were as American as the maps of New York City and the United States of America that Hamilton had hanging on his wall. The strain of thought they developed was associated with a loose grouping of coffeehouse radicals and opposition politicians who were enormously influential in the American colonies, probably more so than they were back in England. As the leading historian of the intellectual origins of the Revolution wrote, "more than any other single group of writers they shaped the mind of the American Revolutionary generation."[13]

These writers are viewed as the antecedents or intellectual godfathers of the liberal state in part because they thought deeply about self-interest. There is a pessimistic side to these thinkers, one that American historians have tended to elide. Writers such as Bolingbroke, Bacon, and Milton held an extraordinarily dark view of human nature. The notion that human nature is depraved was hardly new to moral philosophy. It was a particularly strong theme in the writings of Augustine, and the reason most classical moralists such as Cicero, or Renaissance philosophers such as Machiavelli, believed in the importance of learning virtue was because they knew that humans are not naturally virtuous.[14] In the seventeenth and eighteenth centuries, however, following the wars of religion, thinkers such as Bacon, Milton, and Bolingbroke increasingly came to bleak conclusions regarding the prospects for virtue.[15] They portrayed the world about them as dangerous and corrupt, a world in which virtue could destroy a man. This was a place where when the prince laughed you laughed, when he cried you cried, and when he sweated you sweated, a world so nakedly without morals that it allowed full rein to the imagination of a Milton, and, come to that, a Shakespeare or a Ben Jonson. Francis Bacon too was a master of this realm. In such an environment, individuals must focus on their own survival rather than employing virtue to devote themselves to the common good. As a result, these philosophers, poets, and politicians came to think more deeply about what self-preservation entailed, and they concluded, at first reluctantly, that self-interest, which for Renaissance moralists was simply corruption, was a necessity. As Bacon wrote in the essay "Styx and Treaties," princes always break their promises, so "there is adopted therefore but one true and proper pledge of faith; and it is not any celestial divinity. This is Necessity (the great god of the powerful), and the peril of state, and communion of interest. Now Necessity is elegantly represented under the figure of Styx; the fatal river across which no man can return."[16] Once self-interest was set free, subsequent generations of moral philosophers, most importantly, Bernard Mandeville and Adam Smith, would begin to theorize the capitalist and opportunistic world that Jeremiah Hamilton inhabited and thrived in. It comes as no surprise, then, that Jeremiah Hamilton would have taken such a keen interest in the moral foundations of the place where he was making his mark.

There were two main ways in which these writers spoke to Jeremiah Hamilton's unusual position. First, they described the New York and particularly the Wall Street in which he lived. From the 1790s, and more so after the opening of the Erie Canal, Wall Street, with its position close to the trading port, was a center of capital exchange driven by the triumph of interest in public affairs. The intellectual scaffolding of modern capitalism had been established within living memory, but the authors on Hamilton's shelves had laid the foundations. They had explained that to survive in such a world it was necessary to take on its qualities, even if that meant behaving in a corrupt fashion. A reader who was black and trying to make his way on Wall Street must have had a heightened identification with such a message of survival in a dangerous world. If an individual was going to engage in this world, then it was necessary to act in such a way that would be regarded by many as corrupt. Hamilton's whole life was one long example of a black man beating white New Yorkers at their own game, ruthlessly—and the devil take the hindmost.

Second, running through the prose of these writers was a pastoral theme, a longing for a sylvan retreat from the city that would be picked up by Thomas Jefferson, among a host of American thinkers.[17] From Virgil's "Eclogues" through the eighteenth century, the pastoral genre was used to contrast the corruption of the city with the simplicity of the country. For authors such as Bacon, an alternative way of dealing with the dominance of interest in the city was to remove oneself to the countryside. Either one must master interest and corruption or one must retreat from it. Hamilton would try both solutions. For him the city was even more dangerous, because New York was not just a site of the corruption of commerce, but a place where, at any moment, vicious outbreaks of violence directed at a black man, particularly one married to a white woman, could erupt.

Jeremiah Hamilton had already demonstrated a willingness to distance himself from New York City's corruption, no matter how inconvenient such a move was for a man earning his living on Wall Street. In 1836, as we have seen, he resided in Bloomingdale, then well outside the city and a carriage ride of nearly ten miles from the financial district. The following year he turned his eye even farther afield and made extensive preparations to move up the Hudson River to Poughkeepsie, some five or six hours by water from New York City. He invested heavily in wharves, land and buildings, including what was known as the Mansion House. The grandness of his new property gave the game away. Hamilton was setting himself up to become a player in the thriving town's affairs, but it all came to naught, his empire crumbling to dust in the aftermath of the panic of 1837. He was left stranded in the city.

It took five years for the economy to recover fully from the recession that followed the panic. It took Hamilton even longer. His experience of hard times culminating in the humiliation of bankruptcy, let alone the indignity of being ridiculed by lawyers and journalists in a notorious libel case and blackballed by one of the city's stock exchanges, can hardly have endeared New York life to the still-young businessman. And the practical problems and perils of being black, having a white wife and raising a family in a Gotham never too far from racial conflagration must have weighed heavily on his mind. Hamilton was more than willing, indeed eager, to confront—even literally to go toe to toe in the case of Justice Merritt—any white businessmen or establishment figures who got in his way or insulted him. Understandably, he was more cautious and protective about any potential threat to the well-being of his wife and young children. For all the drawbacks to city living, though, Wall Street still offered him his last best chance of making money. During most of the decade after 1837 Hamilton could only dream about living anywhere but New York. Nothing was possible until he had reestablished his finances.

By the time a tempting opportunity did present itself in 1846 or 1847 his fortunes were on the rise, signaled only a few years later by James McCune Smith's sneer in *Frederick Douglass' Paper* that the broker was now "the only black millionaire in New York." Hamilton, hearing of a troubled owner willing to let go of his property at a bargain price, bought what was known as the Glover House or the Glover Farm. This time he was relocating not to a bustling Poughkeepsie rapidly becoming a manufacturing town, but to the comparative solitude of the New Jersey countryside. The Glover House was located near Denville and about thirty miles from Manhattan. As had been true with his earlier purchase of the Mansion House, Hamilton, craving the spotlight, bought the best property for miles around. A traveler in the region a few years later, being much taken by the "fine, large aristocratic mansion," asked some of the older inhabitants about the history of the well-known landmark. Apparently, in the 1820s, a South Carolinian planter named Glover walked into a New York millinery store, fell in love instantly with a beautiful girl working there, and soon after married her. She was not well born and was scandalously younger than Glover; he knew "his wife would not be well received in his aristocratic circle at the South." Consequently, Glover built the large house at Denville, furnished it extravagantly and "installed his interesting wife as its mistress." Together "they lived in very elegant style, and reared a family of children."[18] Now Jeremiah Hamilton also wanted to install his much younger wife as Glover House's mistress and rear their children, all in the most elegant style possible.

The dwelling and setting could hardly have been improved upon. Glover House was "splendidly situated in the midst of a beautiful valley on a commanding eminence, and can be seen at a great distance in every direction." In 1841, a Scotsman considering purchasing the estate for his daughter rode out to examine the property. He found the mansion, built of stone and brick, to be excellent. It contained "a hall, two large public rooms and eight or ten bedchambers" and reminded him of nothing so much as "a gentleman's house in Scotland." Glover House was located on some 270 acres, 169 arable and the rest in wood. As a working farm, it was a lackluster proposition. The light and gravelly soil was not particularly fertile. Wheat, Indian corn, and clover yielded only unimpressive crops. Although a handful of dairy cows grazed in the thirty acres of meadow, they were the only livestock.[19] No one was going to make much money out of farming Glover House.

But its agricultural shortcomings did not blind Hamilton to the splendors of the property as a gentleman's country seat, a retreat from the city. Looking down on his acres from the house, he could see, less than a quarter of a mile away, a clear stream "well supplied with trout." There were, as well, two ponds stocked with fish. Most jarring of all, though, the estate contained "plenty of quail, woodcock, snipe, and other game."[20] Needless to say, the arresting image of a black millionaire strolling through the terraced garden in front of his mansion, surveying the splendors of his New Jersey estate, let alone the startling idea of him fishing for trout or shooting quail for sport, does not fit well with our usual understanding of the way African Americans lived in the antebellum North.

It would be fascinating to know how the Morris County gentry, indeed any locals, reacted to what must have been the disquieting presence of Hamilton and his family. New Jersey had ended slavery only a few months before the black man moved to Glover House, and most slaves in the state had toiled on farms not unlike the one he had just purchased.[21] The world was turning upside down. Unfortunately, if anyone did write down his or her impressions of the unusual newcomers, I have been unable to find them. Traces of their presence, however, can be found in the more mundane records kept by the various levels of government. On August 5, 1850, only months before their rural idyll ended, the federal census-taker visited Glover House. He valued the property at $5,000, about half of what it would have fetched on the market, and then listed the members of the household. When the Hamiltons arrived in New Jersey they already had three daughters—Miranda, born in 1837 or 1838; Evelina, born in 1842 or 1843; and Josephine, born in 1845. While the couple lived in New Jersey they had two more children—Adelaide in 1847 and Theodore in 1849. Young Theodore was also included in a list of Morris County births for that year—the entry for him notes that he was born on August 13, 1849. As well, the census-taker recorded that in 1850 the household contained two young Irish domestics: Mary Gebban, aged twenty-four, and Brigit Gebban, aged nineteen, and an Irish eighteen-year old, Martin Burleigh. The young man probably worked on the farm. There were also several men living close by, designated as property-less laborers by the official, who may well have been in Hamilton's employ.[22]

The census-taker also scrawled down on his sheet that Jeremiah Hamilton was a farmer. Whether this was just an assumption—he lived on a farm and therefore must have been a farmer—is unclear. A year earlier, the Morris County official recording Theodore's birth listed Hamilton's occupation as merchant. Wall Street was certainly a trek from Glover House, involving a carriage trip of twenty-four miles to Newark, six miles on a train to Jersey City, and then a ferry to Manhattan. For all the impressiveness of his estate, Hamilton was isolated from the New York financial district. He continued to play the market, even if, probably, he visited Manhattan at irregular intervals.

The Hamiltons' rural sojourn ended in November 1850, and its dramatic denouement was also of a piece with everything we know of the black broker's business career. Jeremiah Hamilton always sailed close to the wind. He was little concerned with the law, never liked to pay the full price for anything, and did his best to arrange matters so that, in any venture, someone else bore the risk while he pocketed the profits. As it turned out, Hamilton had bought the Glover House cheaply from a man who possessed what turned out to be a bad title to the property. This was not the first time he had gambled and lost by buying questionably documented real estate—more than a decade earlier he had burnt his fingers speculating in Williamsburgh's unimproved lots. In this case, the bibulous ne'er-do-well who sold Hamilton the property was estranged from his wife and "partly deranged"; as soon as he died the family brought a suit of ejectment against Hamilton. All that we know of the court proceedings in Morristown is that, in late November 1850, they stretched out over a week and a half—an intriguingly long time—and that, after retiring for four hours, the jury ruled against Hamilton and he lost Glover House.[23] By then, anyway, the charms of the countryside had faded, and he was prepared to cope once more with the travails of city living. Hamilton and his family promptly returned to New York.

The New Jersey hiatus had a postscript, one that also echoed strangely what had happened in the 1830s. Back then an opposing lawyer had bought Hamilton's Hallet Landing investment for a bargain-basement price. In the ejectment suit one of his lawyers had been A. C. M. Pennington, an already-prominent attorney who went on to become a member of Congress in 1853. Hamilton made a point of hiring the best lawyers. In early 1857, Pennington purchased Glover House for $10,000 and was expected to take up residence in the spring.[24] Hamilton may not always have had the best of luck with real estate, but he knew good property when he saw it. Unfortunately for him, members of the legal profession profited more handsomely from his real estate dealings than Hamilton ever did.

At least moving back to New York City allowed Eliza Jane Hamilton to see more of her family, particularly her mother, who was having her own legal difficulties. In 1845 Margaret Morris had taken a ten-year lease on 648 Broadway and then spent $2,000 fitting out the premises, converting them into what was called a boardinghouse. The term is slightly misleading; her business more closely resembled what we might call a boutique hotel. Her son-in-law had been an investor in Morris's similar if smaller venture in the late 1830s, and probably Jeremiah Hamilton had put up at least some of the money in 1845 as well. By May 1850, she had thirty-eight boarders and was making a handsome quarterly profit of $800. In April 1850, new tenants, on a ten-year lease, had moved into the neighboring Constitution Hall at 650 Broadway, previously a public hotel and a dancing school, converting the lower floors into a multistory stable and carriage house. The noise from the moving around of animals and vehicles at all hours of the day and night and the smell of horse sweat and excrement was unbearable.

Her business ruined, Margaret Morris sued for $5,000 damages according to one newspaper account, $10,000 by another. At the trial, the defendant asserted his "perfect right to keep a livery stable, and denies that there is anything in his doing so to injure the adjoining premises." Morris responded that Broadway, the city's boulevard and showpiece, was an entirely unsuitable location for such an activity. She then listed the names of the thirty boarders who had fled her establishment on account of the noisome livery stable. Her once-thriving enterprise was reduced to a rump of eight guests. The judge instructed the jury that if boarders had in fact left because of the "bad air" it must be a nuisance and Morris was entitled to damages. After hours of deadlock, the jury could not reach a verdict and the judge discharged them. Details of their confidential deliberations soon leaked. The vote had been eleven to one in Morris's favor. Indeed, the *New York Sun*'s man-on-the-spot was able to report matter-of-factly that "the dissenting juror keeps a livery stable up town."[25] No one seemed too surprised at such a flagrant conflict of interest—that was just New York.

Jeremiah Hamilton and his family moved into a house at 68 East Twenty-Ninth Street, close to the Lexington Avenue intersection. The 1851–1852 city directory listed him as a merchant with an office at 80 Broadway and his home on East Twenty-Ninth. According to the 1852 city assessment this residence was valued at $9,000—these valuations, used for tax purposes, were always low.[26] As the city expanded, this precinct was becoming more fashionable. One reporter in 1851, describing Madison and Fifth between Thirtieth and Thirty-Fourth, or the area beginning little more than a block to the west and a block to the north of Hamilton's house, had been surprised by the "very unusual number of first class dwellings." In contrast to the older buildings downtown, structures "of greater beauty and durability are fast rising, and offer in addition to their more attractive exterior, a combination of the modern improvements for the supply of water, light and heat, and personal comfort not dreamed of by our forefathers." These brownstones, resplendent with large plate glass windows and fitted out with the best internal finishes, were, at this time, the height of modernity and "readily sell, some of them before they are finished, at 15 to 18 thousand dollars each."[27]

A self-made man, Jeremiah Hamilton, whenever he had money—indeed, even when he did not—never stinted himself. He displayed a grand style that a Vanderbilt or any other American tycoon would have appreciated. Be it lawyers, houses or cigars, Hamilton insisted on only the best. As one of his obituarists shrewdly summed up, the black broker "deemed that as by his own exertions he had won wealth and a reputation he was entitled to enjoy them, and he did so." Although by the time of his death, Hamilton and his family had moved a few houses down to 122 East Twenty-Ninth Street, he described this residence as comfortable and elegant.[28] That was precisely how this black man had intended to live his whole life.

Even the charitable acts of the Hamiltons fitted in nicely with their new neighborhood's sensibility. Their model was the Benjamin Day household, located only four blocks away at 55 East Twenty-Fifth Street. The two families were close—when Eliza Jane Hamilton gave birth to her second daughter, she and Jeremiah named the child Evelina Shepard Hamilton. Evelina Shepard was the name of Benjamin Day's wife. Evelina Day's grandson fondly remembered her as only having one fault: "She was too tender-hearted to turn any one away from the door." Even before the Day children grew up, "old women began to seep in, and pay her long visits." At any one time there were usually two or three such women resident in the upper bedrooms of the house. Benjamin Day was unenthusiastic and seemed "as though he would sometimes have liked to put them out of the house." But he never did, because, as his grandson explained, "I suppose he felt sorry for them." In any event, Day realized that success in moving along the women would only cause his wife to replace them with other deserving charity cases.[29]

Although quite possibly there were others, traces survive of only one such woman living for lengthy periods in the Hamilton household. This arrangement had commenced soon after they moved into their new house on East Twenty-Ninth Street—and the woman in question was impossibly exotic. IsabellaGanneclift, born in Gibraltar in 1793, had married a Spaniard at twelve years of age and by the time she was seventeen had borne four children, only one of whom survived. Her husband, after an argument with another Spaniard over Isabella, was killed in the subsequent duel. In 1815 she married an American, a Captain G. W. Walker. Until his death in 1854, "she courted fashionable society, and no gathering of importance was complete at either Saratoga, Newport, Boston or Washington without the presence of Mrs Walker." A strikingly attractive woman when younger, she later boasted: "I knew Clay and Webster, and Benton and Calhoun, and Randolph, and all the great men of the day. I knew them very well." After her second husband's death, then in her sixties, she married Abijah Smith, a businessman from Kingston, New York. He died in 1879, and Eliza M. Smith, the name by which she was known in the final decades of her life, died in 1880.

All three of Smith's marriages were miserable affairs. For the most part reporters were reticent about publicizing marital discord; nevertheless, according to one account, she lived for forty years with her second husband even "though severe domestic storms visited the home of Captain Walker and his wife." Soon after Eliza Smith's third wedding her new husband became an invalid and relations between the couple became so unpleasant that they agreed to live apart. As a consequence of her turbulent marriages, for long periods Eliza Smith sheltered with Eliza Jane and Jeremiah Hamilton. Everything came out in the early 1880s in a series of legal proceedings over Smith's disputed will. As one reporter noted dryly, Mrs. Smith "seemed to have a mania for making wills"—there were at least four, possibly more. In one of the earlier documents the bulk of her estate, worth somewhere around $10,000, was left to Eliza Hamilton, but she was excluded from the last one signed just before Smith died. Eliza Hamilton challenged the validity of this final will in the Surrogate's Court in Kingston, New York. The case hinged on such matters as whether Eliza Smith's speech was intelligible with her false teeth out and if it was strange for her to be walking down a corridor wearing neither shoes nor stockings in the days following a bad fall that had caused her almost to choke on her own blood. Eliza Hamilton lost her suit when the judge declined to find either that Eliza Smith was incompetent or that there was undue influence involved in the signing of the new will.[30]

Things may well have gone sour at the very end, but for some three decades the two women had been close. In her testimony in March 1881, Eliza Hamilton remembered that she "had known Mrs Smith between thirty-two and thirty-three years." Most likely, they met soon after the Hamiltons returned to New York in late 1850. Initially, what probably happened is that Eliza Hamilton offered Eliza Smith (as she later became) shelter from what looks to have been an abusive marriage with Captain Walker. For all her exotic showiness, Smith was not wealthy. Misapprehensions about how much money the other party possessed played a large role in the bitter disintegration of her final marriage. As Eliza Hamilton testified, Smith was "a guest at intervals" in her house over the ensuing decades. What had started off as an act of charity, similar to those for which Evelina Day was known, developed into friendship—Hamilton told the court in March 1881 that they were "very intimate." Indeed, Eliza Hamilton was not the only member of the household who became close to Eliza Smith. In a final twist to this story, the will that removed Eliza Hamilton from the list of Smith's beneficiaries bequeathed to her son, Walter Scott Hamilton, all of the old lady's Lake Shore Railroad stock. Walter, born about 1852, had been the baby of the household when Eliza Smith first started staying with the Hamiltons.[31]

There is no record of what Jeremiah Hamilton thought of Smith's sojourns in his house, or indeed of those of any other charitable cases who may have stayed. Perhaps he was as wryly phlegmatic about any inconvenience as his friend Benjamin Day. Hamilton, though, was very well aware that none of his behavior went unobserved. As far back as 1840, James Gordon Bennett pointed out in the *New York Herald,* the broker was "a 'highly respectable' colored gentleman, of some celebrity in Wall street."[32] Although the scare marks signaled a sarcastic view of Hamilton's respectability, there still can be no doubting the Prince of Darkness's celebrity. How then did New Yorkers, both black and white, deal with a black man who was not only prominent but also increasingly obviously wealthy?

Jeremiah Hamilton's relations with other African Americans were strained. One obituarist did record that although Hamilton was "possessed of capacity and wealth far above his race in general he never frowned them down."[33] And that is probably true—he was not one for displaying airs or graces and had acquaintances from all strata of New York society. For the most part, though, Hamilton lived apart from other African Americans. His wife and friends were white; he made money in a white world. He employed Irish immigrants as servants. Even the objects of his charity were white. These things were noticed. Black leaders certainly knew of Hamilton, and they approved neither of him nor of what he had achieved.

A passing reference to Hamilton published in an African American newspaper just after he had returned to the city laid bare the disdainful opinion of several of the black community's most prominent spokesmen. In early 1852, James McCune Smith, the black intellectual, canvassed the relationship between wealth and race in several letters to Frederick Douglass. As intended, these wide-ranging essays were published in *Frederick Douglass' Paper*. In the first piece, Smith contemplated what would occur if every free black man received $100,000 and owned a "brownstone front and a pair of greys in the avenues." He concluded that little would change: "Our habits of thought, of expression, and of action would be the same." Not only would African Americans remain in thrall to whites and their ideas, but, most importantly, they would relinquish their role as activists: "Gold freezes up the humanities and all their surroundings. The wealthy are never a progressive class; they are by necessity conservatives." Smith concluded: "Hundred thousand dollar black men would be no better than hundred thousand dollar white men."[34] This was never a context in which Jeremiah Hamilton was going to be assessed generously.

In his third letter, Smith argued that the position of African Americans "can only be bettered by a nobler ideal." And he knew "money is not that nobler ideal; but liberty, equality, human brotherhood, in a word—manhood—is that nobler ideal." He went on: "I take it that Alexander Crummell [an antislavery activist and early pan-Africanist] has done more for the advancement of our people by his true manhood, than any colored man could do by amassing gold." Smith continued: "Compare Sam Ward [another antislavery activist] with the only black millionaire in New York, I mean Jerry Hamilton; and it is plain that manhood is a 'nobler ideal' than money." According to Smith, Ward "has illustrated his people and his country." Jeremiah Hamilton, on the other hand, "has fled from his identity . . . like a dog with a tin kettle tied to his tail!"[35]

James McCune Smith and Frederick Douglass were the two most important African American intellectuals of the nineteenth century. But their treatment of Hamilton—Smith writing about him in such a fashion, Douglass printing his friend's calumny—was not the proudest moment in either man's illustrious career. Several issues of the paper later, William Wilson, writing under the name Ethiop, responded to Smith's essay. Wilson, a teacher and later principal at Colored Public School No. 1 in Brooklyn, was another correspondent of *Frederick Douglass' Paper*. Often he differed sharply from Smith over significant issues in black life and was noted particularly for his advocacy of the importance of black business. Wilson deplored the lack of an African American monied elite who might galvanize black economic development. Toward the end of his letter, "Ethiop" made a more measured comment than Smith about Hamilton. He began: "You also make mention of the recreancy to principle of Jerry Hamilton, and all such who slip out of identity." And then pointed out, reasonably, that "this sliding out [of identity], is usually done, not 'with tin kettle and noise' behind, (as you have more elegantly expressed it than I did,) but in a most clandestine manner."[36]

James McCune Smith's and William Wilson's exchange about Jeremiah Hamilton raises the issue of racial passing.[37] As we saw in Chapter Two, by this time, Hamilton was letting people know he came from the West Indies and not, as he had claimed earlier, from Richmond, Virginia. His origins remained a mystery, one that Hamilton himself hardly tamped down, and there were always whispers about his past. One of the nastier of the Hamilton obituaries dredged up some of this gossip: "He did his best to pass off for a Spaniard, but did not succeed."[38]

Interestingly, for the statistical purposes of the federal government Jeremiah Hamilton was not a black man. In the 1850, 1860 and 1870 censuses he was counted as a white individual. The reasons for this, in my view at least, are caught up in the issue of how a white man, a clerk with scores of houses to visit and catalogue, dealt with the oddity of an obviously wealthy black man. Census-takers listed each individual in a household, including children, and then, across the page, filled in columns for the person's age, sex, occupation, place of birth and other categories. In all three of these censuses, the official was supposed to mark down in column six if the individual was white, black or mulatto (in 1870 the categories of Chinese and Indian were added). In practice, at least in the neighborhoods in which Jeremiah Hamilton lived, he left this column blank for everyone (or in 1860 put a diagonal slash through each and every box). Individuals were assumed to be, and counted as, white unless the census-taker made the effort to mark down a B in column six. Examples of the writing of a B can be found in all three censuses by turning over a page or two from the entries for Hamilton's family members. The circumstances under which the individual entries were entered in the schedule are not at all clear. Perhaps Jeremiah Hamilton was away at work and, when his white wife answered the census-taker's questions, the official assumed that the businessman, like everyone else around, was white. Or perhaps in each case the official, after walking up the drive to Hamilton's impressive mansion in Morris County, New Jersey, or knocking on the doors of the substantial houses at 68 East Twenty-Ninth Street or 122 East Twenty-Ninth Street, and in deference to wealth, omitted to mark down a B on the broker's schedule. Something similar occurred at Hamilton's death. The doctor had visited Hamilton in his home several times in the days before pneumonia and exhaustion killed him on May 19, 1875. The doctor filled out the death certificate meticulously, including detail unmentioned anywhere else, such as that Hamilton's parents were born in Port au Prince, but left blank the space where "Color" was supposed to be inserted.[39] It seems that, neither for the first nor the last time in American history, money lightened the color of an individual's skin.

By contrast, when Jeremiah and Eliza Hamilton's son Theodore, born in Denville on August 13, 1849, was included in the Morris County, New Jersey, record of births, the official marked down quite clearly that the baby was "Col^d," or colored. Not only that, but there was no category for skin color—he had volunteered this information and squeezed it in next to Theodore's name. Thirty-eight other children were listed on this page of the record—none were treated in the same fashion as Theodore Hamilton.

For all the ambiguity of Hamilton's race as recorded in government statistics, no one who read a New York newspaper or who saw him on the street was in any doubt about his color. Even James McCune Smith seemed more concerned about Hamilton's lack of identification with and support for African Americans than any suggestion he was claiming to be white. The activist was most interested in damning Hamilton for his successful pursuit of money. As well, unlike other successful and wealthy blacks such as Thomas Downing, Hamilton had nothing to do with African Americans and did not write checks to underwrite the activities of the early civil rights activists.

Perhaps the most telling point in all of this was Ethiop's quietly sensible reminder that any "sliding out" from being black was usually done "in a most clandestine manner."[40] Simply put, too many people knew who Jeremiah Hamilton was for him ever to be categorized as white. As I argued earlier, the stories of Hamilton being born in the Caribbean—in Haiti, Cuba, Puerto Rico or Jamaica— made it easier for his children, despite the fact that at least one or two of them were dark complexioned, to maintain their whiteness. Their lives, much quieter than their father's, did not feature in either newspapers or courtrooms. And in this at least they were successful—no one, it seems, even questioned that they were white.

In the end, Jeremiah Hamilton made his peace with the idea of living in the city. He had tried to remove himself, but it had not worked out. The pull of New York was too strong. And, like Duke Ellington, he had to learn not to knock himself out thinking about Jim Crow. To a considerable extent, money insulated him from the worst of the city's racial problems. He could live in his nice house on East Twenty-Ninth Street, looking back down to the city, and feel he and his family were relatively safe. Never completely, though. Hamilton knew very well that when New York eventually erupted into a racial firestorm, a black man as prominent as he was had to become invisible—quickly.

TWELVE

MAKING MONEY

rying to establish any sort of accounting of Jeremiah Hamilton's business dealings after he reestablished himself in the mid-1840s following his bankruptcy and up until his death in 1875 is difficult. It does seem likely that during this thirty-year period the broker made the bulk of his money by accumulating smaller commissions and profits rather than from infrequent, if more spectacular, market coups—but maybe not. The only traces of his business practices are buried in the frequently opaque files of a few court cases, material that occasionally can be fleshed out with newspaper stories. Unhelpfully, while the standard of financial and legal reporting of the black broker's career up to 1843 was impressive, often surprisingly so, the coverage throughout the last three decades of his life was never as comprehensive nor of a similar quality. Ironically, then, as Hamilton became less the celebrity broker, no longer a black whiz kid flashing across the sky, and more an established, eventually senior, Wall Street figure, he also became more elusive. Not that this transformation in his status occurred overnight or was ever complete—Hamilton did not become a stranger to New York's legal system. Of course, the problem with relying on court cases is that they usually focus the spotlight on business failures. Although he lost several of these suits, read carefully, they still reveal something of Hamilton's complex ambivalence toward the business world. Uniquely, he was both a black man on Wall Street and someone who remained familiar with the fulminations of Bacon, Bolingbroke and Milton about the corruption of commerce. At the big end of town Jeremiah Hamilton may have continued to be a recognized identity, and even found himself treated with some degree of respect as he aged, but he never could be a Wall Street insider. Two cases, one from the 1840s involving the Poughkeepsie Silk Company and the other, a decade later, in which Hamilton took Cornelius Vanderbilt's Accessory Transit Company to court, are particularly instructive.

The origins of the first suit lay in the flush times of the early 1830s. In April 1832, the New York legislature incorporated the Poughkeepsie Silk Company and revised and amended the act of incorporation three years later.[1] At this time in antebellum America corporations were becoming a common form of business organization. Their big advantage was that they were treated as "legal persons" separate from their shareholders, who, as a result, had only a limited liability.[2] Key individuals in the Silk Company were associated with the Improvement Party, a local booster organization with ambitions to make the village of Poughkeepsie a showpiece of commercial and manufacturing development. Every November shareholders elected seven directors to oversee the running of the business, and they in turn elected one of their number as president. Prominent directors such as Henry Tallmadge, Benjamin Tallmadge and John Delafield constituted the corporation's public face. Capitalized at $200,000, with 2,000 shares at a par value of $100 each, the Poughkeepsie Silk Company had broad authority to pursue the "culture and manufacture of silk in all its various branches." The company quickly bought up valuable real estate, including waterpower rights, and invested in machinery as well as paper assets such as notes, bonds, and mortgages. According to a report in the *Poughkeepsie Telegraph,* an extensive silk factory was completed by June 1834.[3] Initially, business flourished and "the affairs of said Company were for some time in a prosperous condition."

The panic of 1837 brought everything to a shuddering halt. Not only did demand for silk shrink to negligible levels and the company's assets plummet in value, but also almost all of the directors and stockholders were very soon either insolvent themselves or financially embarrassed. In that respect at least, Jeremiah Hamilton was a typical shareholder. Later, in 1845, Hamilton filed a statement of claim assailing the company's directors for their passivity during the crisis of 1837 and in the years since. They had failed "to aid or energetically sustain its business operations," standing idly by as the factory languished and declined. Hamilton elaborated that the company's "affairs became embarrassed; its liabilities increased, its business diminished until it was finally through the neglect, carelessness or the indifference of those to whose care and management it had been entrusted, discontinued and suspended altogether." Indeed, with their attention elsewhere, the firm's leadership simply had abandoned "all hope or expectation or intention" of managing the enterprise, and "it has so remained for almost seven years past." For some time now, the Poughkeepsie Silk Company had been a wreck.

Jeremiah Hamilton's interest in the company dated back to 1835 or 1836, probably to the time when he had made up his mind to leave New York and relocate to Poughkeepsie. He had bought shares in the new silk factory on behalf of a John S. Crary of New York. But something went awry—possibly the problem resulted from Crary's death, and likely the economic crunch was involved as well. When Hamilton declared bankruptcy in 1842, his assets included a claim against Crary's estate "for real estate & stock of the Silk Co of Poughkeepsie sold him in January 1837," totaling some $10,500. This obligation, which was unlikely ever to be met, was part of Hamilton's $20 bargain-basement buyback of debts owed to himself at the general assignee's auction in October 1842. Possibly he had bought shares of his own back in 1836, or maybe he had ended up holding Crary's never-paid-for shares. In either case, there were no Poughkeepsie Silk Company shares listed in the official accounting of his bankruptcy.[4] Nevertheless, at the beginning of 1845 Hamilton owned 133 shares, or roughly 6 percent of the company's stock. As with the other investors, he had not paid the par value of $100 but had taken "calls upon each share of said stock to the sum of seventy five dollars." What this meant was that the initial offering of shares had been at, say, $10 each, and then, as the Poughkeepsie Silk

Company required more capital for its activities, it had issued "calls" on its investors for, say, $25, calls that would cease when they had paid the share's full face value of $100. In this case, Hamilton had had to ante up a total of $75 a share, and his entire outlay to the company was $9,975. This was a substantial sum of money, about $2.35 million in today's dollars.

Now, in 1845, Hamilton decided to see if he could rescue something of his investment, for which he would only get pennies on the dollar in the unlikely event he could find a buyer. Hamilton commenced an action against the Poughkeepsie Silk Company in the Chancery Court, meaning that he was seeking a remedy in equity (or something other than damages—in this case, appointment of a receiver). Nominally, his suit was filed on behalf of Poughkeepsie's stockholders and creditors, although clearly Hamilton was motivated by self-interest. He and his lawyers took a shotgun approach in the statement of claim—they included everything. Under the terms of the company's act of incorporation, there had to be elections of directors and a president on the first Tuesday of every November. None had been held in 1844, and Hamilton was skeptical of the legitimacy of some of the other recent elections. The corporation's business was supposed to be located in Poughkeepsie, but there was no office there, and Henry Tallmadge, president for at least the past five years, lived in New York City. All the corporation's papers and books were in a box that Hamilton presumed was held by Tallmadge in his New York premises. Hamilton had managed to learn that the Poughkeepsie Silk Company's properties were still earning in excess of $2,000 a year. Tallmadge received all revenue, and for years the absentee president had been paying himself an annual salary of $1,000 for doing, as far as his black accuser was concerned, absolutely nothing. And no one seemed to know where the rest of the income was going.

Hamilton wanted to examine the books in order to establish the exact financial position of the corporation. Clearly, he suspected that some questionable accounting was occurring. For at least the past year or two, the corporation's assets had been deteriorating in value, and none of its obligations had been paid. As far as he could tell, the Poughkeepsie Silk Company's dwindling assets, and the income they produced, were about to be swamped by the accumulating interest on its debts. Tallmadge was pocketing his substantial fee and running what was left of the corporation into the ground. Although Hamilton's views of such a cavalier approach can be inferred easily enough, it is not obvious whether Tallmadge's actions, or lack thereof, were deliberate or simply the result of indifference. Regardless, the result was inevitable. If events meandered on for much longer, then the still-productive assets would "be wasted or consumed and all lost to the creditors of said corporation and to its stockholders." Indeed, shareholders, already denied any income from their investments for almost a decade, were also going to "lose all the money by them invested in the stock of said Company."

Hamilton's desired outcome from the court case was straightforward. Dissolve the corporation, appoint a receiver and let him liquidate all the assets as best he could in order to pay off the outstanding debts. Once he had completed this, the receiver should make a "distribution of the residue among the stockholders." Indeed, "in equity and good conscience" Tallmadge and his accomplices on the board should have pursued such a course many years earlier. But it was not to be. The court ruled against Hamilton and ordered him to pay costs of $73.48 to Tallmadge and the Silk Company. Although there was no explanation for the decision, the defendant's lawyers had made most of their running on technical grounds, attacking Hamilton's standing in making the case and arguing that such a suit should have been pursued in a court of law rather than an equity venue.

When placed in the context of Hamilton's life up until 1845, a number of features of this case stand out. First, there was his eagerness to take on members of the establishment, be they Wall Street brokers or the business leaders of Poughkeepsie. In this instance, the desire for revenge added an edge to the proceedings. Hamilton and Delafield's earlier business dealings in the 1830s had ended up in court and cost the black man a considerable amount of money. Second, Hamilton emphasized his outsider's position. As a black man he was never going to be admitted to the establishment and thus had no investment in maintaining the authority or prestige of that establishment. If they were going to have a series of rules, be they rules of the stock exchange or rules about the running of a corporation, then, if it was to his advantage, he would hold them to those rules: when they ignored blithely their own regulations he would drag them into court and insist that they be held accountable. Last, the suit was informed by Hamilton's experience of bankruptcy. He knew that, far from being the result of individual moral failing, financial reversals and setbacks were simply part of the business cycle. Moreover, having attended a general assignee's sale at which he had picked through the detritus of his and other men's insolvency and even purchased a bargain or two, he knew that someone always profited from other people's misfortune. In the years after the panic of 1837, Americans were learning how to exploit business failure, to make money out of the inevitable downturns, disasters and mistaken ventures that were part and parcel of a large and dynamic market economy.[5] By trying to dissolve the Poughkeepsie Silk Company and then break up and sell off the assets of the corporation from under the noses of a complacent set of directors, Hamilton was attempting to recoup whatever he could of his original investment. Without quite realizing what he was doing, he was also a pioneer in the early stages of the development of what would later be known as vulture capitalism.

As it turned out, Hamilton's aggressive lawsuit against the Poughkeepsie Silk Company was a trial run for the biggest case of his business career. In the mid-1850s, Jeremiah G. Hamilton sued "the Accessory Transit Company, Cornelius Vanderbilt, Charles Morgan and others." Twenty years later, Vanderbilt's obituarist in the *National Republican* mentioned briefly his subject's involvement in what he termed "the Nicaraguan transit business," before relegating the whole affair to "a matter of history and court records."[6] While true enough, the obituarist neglected to add that, in this case at least, neither history nor court records are transparent. The events surrounding the suit, and indeed the suit itself, are complicated; much of the story is probably unknowable.

It began in 1848 with the spectacular discovery of gold at Sutter's Mill in California. Even President Polk waxed enthusiastic in his annual message to Congress: "The accounts of the abundance of gold in that country are of such extraordinary character as would scarcely command belief were they not corroborated by the authentic reports of officers in the public service." Scores of thousands of people set out for the west. Some trekked overland, but the majority went by sea. In the year following Polk's message, some 762 vessels left North American ports for California. Even before 1848 American steamship entrepreneurs had been interested in opening up a passage to California through Central America, cutting months and thousands of miles of expensive travel off the trip around Cape Horn. The allure of California gold gave added impetus to their efforts. Some proposed a railroad over the narrowest point, the Isthmus of Panama. Cornelius Vanderbilt favored an even shorter route that took advantage of Nicaraguan geography by steaming 120 miles up the San Juan River to Lake Nicaragua and then 110 miles across the lake itself, leaving only a dozen or so miles of land left to traverse to reach San Juan del Sur on the Pacific Ocean. Necessarily such a scheme entangled Americans in the tumult of Central American politics.[7] In August 1851, the Nicaraguan conservative government chartered the Accessory Transit Company, awarding it a monopoly on steamboats in the country in return for 10 percent of the profits and $10,000 a year. Within a short time Vanderbilt reputedly was making $1 million a year from ferrying people to California and, on the return journey, gold back to New York.[8]

Born in 1794, Cornelius Vanderbilt, as T. J. Stiles, his most recent biographer, aptly claimed, was "the first tycoon." A self-made man who started off as a boatman, amassed a fortune from running a fleet of steamships and then made even more money out of the railroad boom, Vanderbilt dominated New York's financial sector in the decades in which Jeremiah Hamilton, younger by some thirteen years, was active as a broker. Although not enamored with the day-to-day running of businesses, Vanderbilt loved putting together the deal, delighted in the kill and in breaking anyone who stood in his way. New York society may have had difficulty warming to the frequently boorish man, but in the middle decades of the nineteenth century he was an economic colossus bestriding the city.[9]

The Commodore, an honorific that gave him pleasure, treated his companies as personal playthings. This was particularly the case with the Accessory Transit Company, for Vanderbilt not just a moneymaking enterprise but a venture of vision. The proposed interoceanic canal would allow him to leave his mark on the world. For all that, he dealt out some very rough treatment to the business. Indifferent to the interests of shareholders, Vanderbilt deliberately drove up or down the price of Accessory Transit stock to suit his own purposes. After falling out with his former confederate Joseph L. White, most of whose money was tied up in the company, the tycoon acted quickly and brutally. He announced that henceforth his vessels would steam to Panama before proceeding to Nicaragua, making for a much lengthier passage to San Francisco than rival ships underwent. Accessory Transit's price on the exchange nearly halved, dropping from $40 to $24. This cost Vanderbilt too, but the losses hurt White much more. According to a large shareholder in the company, "Vanderbilt declared that he would rather sink his ships at the dock than that White should make money." After the plunge in price, a catastrophic fall that led to the holdings of many of those investing on the margin, or with borrowed money, being sold out from under them, Vanderbilt and his family bought more company stock—cheaply.[10]

Although the route through Nicaragua proved to be a goldmine, the politics of the country continually threatened its smooth running. The long-running struggle between the conservative elite based in Granada and their liberal antagonists from León degenerated into civil war, and once the American filibuster William Walker backed the liberals they gained control of much of the country. Accessory Transit, it turned out, had negotiated its deal with the conflict's losers. In February 1856 the provisional president of the Republic of Nicaragua, Patricio Rivas, who was essentially a puppet of William Walker, issued a decree dissolving the Accessory Transit Company. Vanderbilt would expend a considerable amount of money and effort to ensure the demise of the Walker regime, but in the short term the company did its best to carry on business as usual, more or less pretending the decree had not occurred. In May 1856 the company proceeded with its regular election of directors, and they duly appointed Cornelius Vanderbilt to its presidency.[11]

Jeremiah Hamilton saw opportunity and seized it. Very quickly after the Nicaraguan government had acted, he initiated legal proceedings in New York (where the company was listed on the stock exchange) against Vanderbilt and Accessory Transit demanding that notice be taken of the dissolution and the company wound up, creditors paid off, and the surplus distributed to shareholders. In essence, he was attempting again what he had tried with the Poughkeepsie Silk Company, only this time, seemingly, he was taking on Cornelius Vanderbilt. The first public airing of the case was in October 1856 at a preliminary hearing for an injunction and the immediate appointment of a receiver. Pedro de Silva, secretary of the legation from Nicaragua in the United States, testified that he had been present in Granada's public square at the promulgation of the decree dissolving the Accessory Transit Company. He also detailed how since the ascension to power of William Walker, who had replaced Rivas, neither the legislature nor the Courts of Justice had met, and that "what is known as martial law" held sway throughout the Republic. For reporters and anyone else present, this and subsequent hearings in New York courtrooms provided an education in Central American history and politics.[12]

They also revealed something of Vanderbilt's dominion over the Accessory Transit Company. Apparently, the company did not even have its own bank account—monies were paid directly to Vanderbilt, and he then took care of the company's debts. Accessory Transit's assets, including everything from docking facilities to the steamers *Northern Light* and *Star of the West,* were not in the company's name but in Vanderbilt's. As well, the Pacific Mail Steamship Company was paying Accessory Transit $40,000 a month, money that Vanderbilt had been accepting as agent of the company.[13] Vanderbilt treated the company as his personal realm.

At every opportunity Hamilton, or his lawyers, hammered away at the fact that the authority that had constituted the company— the Nicaraguan government—had revoked its charter. Vanderbilt and others named in the suit had "possessed themselves of a large amount of property of the said company & are using the same without regard to the said decree of dissolution or the rights of the stockholders consequent thereon." Hamilton sought the appointment of a receiver and instructions to the defendants not to sell or transfer any property of any sort. He also wanted to have the books scrutinized, demanding an accounting from Vanderbilt of any monies received from the Pacific Mail Steamship Company and the company's agents in San Francisco, New Orleans and New York. In all fairness, the black man suggested, Accessory Transit's debts should be paid off, the remaining property liquidated and the proceeds distributed among stockholders.[14]

There is something puzzlingly quixotic about Hamilton's David and Goliath–style confrontation with Vanderbilt. For all the tycoon's cavalier indifference to shareholders, the result of the case can hardly have been surprising to anyone. Certainly, the New York Supreme Court judge hearing the application for the injunction had no difficulty in distinguishing this case from other company dissolutions. Nicaragua, after all, was not the United States of America. "There is scarcely, in the varied and blood-stained history of mankind, a more sad example than Spanish America affords of the instability of power and the fickleness of the multitude, when once let loose from traditional respect and reverence for law and custom." The judge continued in much the same vein, arguing: "In that unhappy country one military adventurer succeeds another in the possession of the supreme power with almost as much rapidity as the fleeting images of the magic lantern." Indeed, "the rule of each successful usurper is notoriously evanescent; what is done to-day will be undone to-morrow." Such capricious instability should never be allowed to wreck American enterprise.[15]

This judge, who heard the actual case a few weeks later as well, also did not like the David and Goliath aspect of it. Hamilton owned 200 shares in Accessory Transit. Although he claimed to have been acting on behalf of other shareholders he was the only one applying for relief. On this point, and several others, the judge accepted what was put to him by the defendant's lawyers. "The owners of 58,857 shares strenuously remonstrate against it, and express their dissent to this application for the appointment of a receiver in this action, 'preferring that the affairs of the Company shall continue under the present management, unless changed by the votes of a majority of the stockholders.'" This turned out to be crucial, for by the time of the hearing of the full case, the judge, no matter how skeptical he was of the legitimacy of any Nicaraguan regime, had accepted that the government had dissolved Accessory Transit. But he refused to utter one word about any legal consequences of this dissolution "for the reason that only one stockholder applies for it." The perplexed *Herald*'s court reporter thought the judge's reasoning "extraordinary," a judicial flexing of power that did not belong to the judiciary. It was akin to denying "justice or legal rights to one man because other men do not demand them."[16] Although things dragged on for a while, Hamilton's legal challenge had failed.

Or did it? Who was really pulling the strings in this case, and to what end, remains anything but clear. Twenty years later, in the wake of Vanderbilt's death, at least two writers canvassed the issue of "the Nicaragua transit business." According to one, in the *New York Tribune,* Vanderbilt had engaged in "a fierce struggle with Jeremiah Hamilton for control of the Nicaragua Transit Company." Although Hamilton was "beaten on 'the Street,'" he "took refuge in the courts, and an interminable litigation was the result." The other reference was in a front-page obituary of Vanderbilt in the *National Republican,* in which the reporter stated: "There was only one man who ever fought the Commodore to the end, and that was Jeremiah Hamilton." He explained: "Hamilton fought him in the courts until he got a settlement." And then he recorded a remarkable admission: "The Commodore respected him [Hamilton]," although "he did not fear him because he never feared anybody." Very similar wording had been used a few months earlier in "Wall Street Reminiscences," a piece published in various newspapers. The anonymous writer of this memoir had also included the detail that Vanderbilt "respected Hamilton's persistency in fighting him." He summed up the affair thus: "That Nicaragua business has never been settled yet. It is a curious thing that nobody has ever followed it up."[17]

Thirty months earlier Jeremiah Hamilton had died. Hardly surprisingly, the black millionaire's demise was marked by nowhere near the same quantity of newsprint as would be expended on the first American tycoon's. Nevertheless, Hamilton's death did receive wide notice: many newspapers ran often-brief obituaries. The *New York Herald* published one of the more considered and revealing pieces, featuring a sentence that, in slightly reworked form, was also included in the *New York Tribune*'s obituary: "In 1848 he [Hamilton] was intimately connected with Mr. Vanderbilt in the Nicaragua

Steamship line and by his shrewd management he made the investment a paying one."[18]

Details such as "interminable litigation," the parties to the suit
settling, and particularly the cooperation between Vanderbilt and
Hamilton to make a success of the Nicaraguan venture jar with the
admittedly not very revealing newspaper stories or court records
that I have used in piecing together my account. Of course, newspapers make mistakes—often very sloppy ones—all the time, and
maybe these obituary writers simply got things wrong. Maybe. Still,
these loose ends exacerbate my nagging sense that when it comes
to the "Nicaragua business," I have missed something. The details
of what happened may be superficially correct, but somehow my
take on these events is not quite right. Here, perhaps, a suggestion
from a steamboat enthusiast, Ernest A. Wiltse, is of some help. Some
seventy-five years ago he wrote of the case *Jeremiah G. Hamilton
v. Accessory Transit Company* that "it was generally believed that
Commodore Vanderbilt was behind this latter suit." As he went on
to add, several "Vanderbilt henchmen appeared as witnesses for the
plaintiff." This was also the context in which he reported that Hamilton "was said in the press to be a son-in-law of Vanderbilt."[19] The
author was not a historian, and his book contained no footnotes or
references. My use of digital search engines and reading of newspapers has not turned up any evidence supporting his claims. For all
that, my hunch is that he was right. Such deviousness would fit in
with my understanding of the character of both men.

Was there any sort of relationship between Cornelius Vanderbilt
and Jeremiah Hamilton? Hamilton may have earned the tycoon's
"respect" by being the only person to struggle with him "to the end"
in a fight on Wall Street, but anyone reading any of the biographies
of Vanderbilt will discover that Jeremiah Hamilton is an invisible
man. Although some of these tomes are lengthy, the black man is
nowhere mentioned in them. It seems clear now that the pair knew
of one another from the mid-1850s. Probably Vanderbilt had been
aware of him at least since the mid-1830s, when Hamilton, along
with his steamship, was trying to establish himself in Poughkeepsie.
For all the lack of evidence about this, what still remain striking
are the similarities between New York's richest African American

and its richest man. Indeed, the way Hamilton began in shipping, owned steamships, and then moved on to dealing almost exclusively in railroad shares, as well as his keenness to use the courts as part of normal business practice, all suggest a willingness to emulate the example of the older man.

There was one other similarity between the two men. Each had a large family—Vanderbilt with thirteen children, Hamilton with ten—and attached symbolic meaning to the naming of at least some of their children. As we have already seen, Jeremiah and Eliza Jane Hamilton called their second daughter Evelina Shepard Hamilton after the maiden name of Benjamin Day's wife. According to Vanderbilt's most recent biographer, his "heroes can be identified by the names he gave to his sons: William Henry (after General William Henry Harrison, hero of the War of 1812), George Washington—and Cornelius."[20] What is interesting here is that in order to emphasize his point, the author has excised the younger Cornelius's second name. His full name was Cornelius Jeremiah Vanderbilt. Jeremiah was not a particularly common name. Corneil, as he was later known, was born in 1830. This was only a year or two after Jeremiah Hamilton's unsuccessful expedition to deliver counterfeit coin to Haiti, an illegal venture funded and organized by a group of prominent but anonymous New Yorkers. The conspirators were never named—Hamilton kept his mouth shut, and they owed him for that. Perhaps Vanderbilt's "respect" for Jeremiah Hamilton predated the "Nicaragua business" by nearly three decades? For all my searching, I have turned up no evidence of any such link. But the idea still gnaws at me. Historians should never admit to their febrile imaginings, and, in truth, this one probably should have been left on the cutting room floor or, at best, interred quietly in a footnote. However, if I was a novelist or a scriptwriter trying to make sense of the relationship between Hamilton and Vanderbilt, I know what my "Rosebud" would be.

Be that as it may, what does remain certain is that Jeremiah Hamilton, in a suit that resembled closely his action again the Poughkeepsie Silk Company, took on the Accessory Transit Company and Cornelius Vanderbilt in a prominent trial. If Vanderbilt was engaged in some Machiavellian maneuvers with Hamilton, then they probably failed. In 1858, an unpaid creditor, Pennsylvania Coal Company, succeeded in what Hamilton had at least ostensibly been trying to do a couple of years earlier—having a court appoint a receiver.[21] Vanderbilt had lost control of Accessory Transit.

Nothing else in the last three decades of Jeremiah Hamilton's career came close to garnering the attention focused on the Accessory Transit Company imbroglio. His more typical everyday transactions often followed the pattern the broker had established much earlier in his business life of having someone else underwrite his speculations. Sometime early in 1854, Hamilton instructed Timothy T. Merwin, a partner in a firm of Wall Street brokers, to purchase one hundred shares of New York and Erie Railroad Company at $69 ⅜. Sixty days later, when it was time to settle the account, the stock's price had almost halved. Hamilton, wanting nothing more to do with such a disastrous transaction, refused to accept delivery or pay for the shares. Several months later his broker, out of pocket some $7,000, gave up waiting for his money, sold the shares and sued Hamilton for the consequent loss of $3,573.36. Although the lower courts came down in Hamilton's favor because of very narrow technical shortcomings in the way his broker had acted, eventually common sense prevailed, and the Superior Court reversed those earlier decisions. The legal proceedings stretched out over nearly eighteen months, and at no stage did Erie's price reach any more than two-thirds of the level it had been at when the broker had filled the order. As an investment, it was a dead loss. Hamilton, though, was uninterested in taking responsibility for his own bad call. Needless to say, if the shares had gone up, there would have been no problem—he would have paid for the shares, sold them and walked away with the profit.[22]

Hamilton appears to have had ready access to large sums of cash—apparently both his own and credit—and, at a price, made this available to others to speculate on the stock market. This was a form of margin lending—a speculator would lodge other stock, bonds, or even cash with Hamilton as security and then borrow more than the security was worth to purchase shares. It was a way for an individual not only to use money he had tied up in other assets, but also to leverage it. He could, for example, put down $2,000 worth of security and borrow $4,000 to gamble on shares. In a bull market,

everything worked fine—the shares went up in value and the speculator sold them for a profit, returned what he had borrowed with
interest and, in turn, received back whatever assets he had lodged
as security. A bear market, or when prices fell, was another matter.
Then it was the losses rather than the profits that were leveraged.

Although lending money in this fashion can be very lucrative—particularly as novices and higher-risk borrowers, who can be
charged higher rates, are drawn in—defaults are inevitable in flat or
falling markets. On occasion during the 1850s Hamilton had to pursue recalcitrant clients through the court system. In one instance the
defendant, George Barker, claimed that $30,000 worth of mortgage
bonds of the Western Vermont Rail Road Company he had put up
for security had been sold out from under him, but to no avail, as the
judge ordered him to pay Hamilton $18,273.77.[23]

The black broker also bought paper, or legal promises to pay
money, from others who had lent to gamblers playing the market. In
another case that wound up in court, Joseph L. White had given a
note to Charles Morgan in return for shares. Morgan had then sold
the note, and Hamilton eventually picked it up at a discount. White
either refused to, or could not, pay up on the due date and, in a move
that Hamilton should have appreciated, challenged the legality of
his original contracts with Morgan, which "were made as wagers or
speculations," contravening the provisions of a New York state law
against stockjobbing. Accepting this argument would have resulted
in every subsequent transaction in the chain having to be ruled void.
The Supreme Court rejected out of hand such tendentious reasoning
and ordered that the defendant pay Jeremiah Hamilton $9,564.71.[24]

This case, as well as showing something of Hamilton's business
practices, was also intriguing because of the people involved. The
transactions had occurred in 1856 as the Accessory Transit case
came to a head. Joseph L. White, the defendant, was Vanderbilt's
former confederate, whom, throughout the 1850s, the tycoon had
gone to extraordinary lengths to try to crush financially. Morgan,
though earlier linked to the Commodore, had also fallen out with
Vanderbilt. It seems, then, that very soon after the Accessory Transit
court case, Jeremiah Hamilton pursued Vanderbilt's sworn enemy
through the legal system and won a substantial judgment against

him. It would be fascinating to know if Hamilton originally bought the paper simply to make money or with the intention of harassing Joseph White, perhaps even on someone else's behalf—or, of course, for both reasons.

The most revealing insights into Hamilton's business come from a series of court cases originating in several share purchases that occurred in 1864. Although the details were not uncommon in litigation about stock purchases or sales—disputes about a transaction's timing, and thus who was to profit, or lose money, from it—what was rather more unusual was the amount of recorded testimony generated by the various court appearances and appeals.[25]

Wentworth Butler, by profession a librarian, knew Hamilton initially through his job at the New York Society Library, an institution frequented by the African American, but later as a client, and had introduced him to his brother, Josiah Butler, who had expressed an interest in also making money on the stock market. Someone had passed on a tip to the tyro speculator telling him to buy Michigan Southern Railroad stock. Bumping into Hamilton on the street, Butler inquired of the company's prospects. An encouraging Hamilton said: "I am going to buy 500 shares for myself, and I will buy you 100 if you wish." But, he explained, "I do not trust to brokers," adding, not entirely honestly, that when dealing with them, "I buy for cash." One hundred shares would cost about $10,000. Although Hamilton reassured his eager client "that he would let [him] have six or eight thousand dollars," he required Butler to raise the rest of the money. That would take him at least a few hours to sort out. Butler caught the Brooklyn ferry and visited his brother-in-law, Charles Stewart, who agreed to put up $2,500, on the understanding that he and Butler would divide equally any profit.

The price of Michigan Railroad, as low as 92 on that Friday, shot up to 101 on Monday and by Tuesday had reached 105. Hamilton claimed not to have had time to buy on Friday. He had to ensure the $2,500 check was not going to bounce and to secure the additional money. On Monday morning Hamilton "found the stock market was what they called rampant," or rising sharply, and thought he "would refrain from buying anything." By Tuesday, Stewart had cold feet and insisted that Butler retrieve his money from Hamilton.

Although Hamilton was willing to give him stock he refused to hand over the desired certified check. Butler protested that Hamilton was breaking his word. "I only promised that," Hamilton replied, "to see if you would be mean enough to take it." By Wednesday, tempers had frayed further. When a panicky Butler demanded a refund Hamilton told him: "You leave my office or I will kick you out." Not long after, the matter was in the hands of the lawyers. In addition to the refund of his $2,500, Charles Stewart insisted he was entitled to $1,100 compensation for the profit he and Butler would have realized if only Hamilton, as he had agreed to, had bought Michigan Railroad on the Friday. Although it is not certain, there was at least a suggestion around the courtroom that Hamilton had managed to buy shares on that Friday and, when they increased in value, had appropriated the transaction for his own benefit.

The transcript of this case makes it clear that Hamilton was running what was termed a "pool." This resembled a modern hedge fund. In this case investors were "pooling" their money—Wentworth Butler had put in $1,000, and presumably others had contributed similar sums. The benefit of such an arrangement was that the pool's contents were used as the margin, or security, to borrow more money so that a much larger sum was available to play the market. What stocks were purchased was left entirely to Hamilton's discretion, but the entire point of a pool, as with a hedge fund, was to take aggressive and therefore more hazardous positions in the market. In effect, Hamilton was risking other people's savings in order to speculate in the market.

We only know about this pool from an instance of failure, which is slightly misleading. Jeremiah Hamilton had established a reputation for predicting the market successfully. After hearing of his ability, people were desperate to reap the benefit of the black broker's advice. Josiah Butler testified that Hamilton "told my brother if I would send up a basket of champagne I will give you some points; I am in the pool." The gift was a necessary "acknowledgment of his kindness." On re-examination, Butler elaborated to the court that Hamilton had let it be known that "I should send him a basket of champagne and a box of segars." Furthermore, he made it absolutely clear that "he did not want any but the very best." After all, "he was to give me some points." The box of 600 cigars cost $16, and the bottles of champagne totaled some $41.

It is worth pausing at this point to consider this moment in the city's history. Three years into a Civil War of almost unimaginable carnage in which the central issue was the existence of racial slavery, less than twelve months after the Draft Riots, New York's own cataclysm, in which the mutilated bodies of African Americans were hanged from lampposts, an unapologetic wealthy black man let it be known that he was willing to receive cigars and champagne—mind you, only the very best—as acknowledgment of his "kindness." In order to gain privileged access to this African American's wisdom about the market prospects of listed corporations, modern entities beyond most Americans' understanding, that were laying thousands of miles of railroad track and steaming huge iron vessels across oceans, some white New Yorkers were willing almost to grovel. Hamilton could get away with such behavior—just—on Wall Street; on any other city street he too would have been strung up from a lamppost. His chutzpah was remarkable.

Participation in modern hedge funds is very limited. They are designed specifically for institutions and very wealthy individuals— in short, sophisticated investors. And Hamilton's experience in this case demonstrates the wisdom of such a restrictive approach. Charles Stewart and Josiah Butler were neophytes, with only a little money that they were extremely nervous about losing. They changed their minds daily. In Hamilton's defense, when Butler first visited him in his office, he told him he was not interested in accepting his money and referred him to Jerome and Co., a broker with a seat on the exchange. Whether feigned or not, initially Hamilton seemed reluctant to let Butler get involved—with good reason, as it turned out. Similarly, Wentworth Butler visited Hamilton's office repeatedly, pestering him about what was happening. He testified: "I was personally interested to the amount of $1,000, which is of some consequence to me." That "of some consequence to me" was the kicker. Although he had a spare $1,000 to invest, and by most standards he was comfortably well off, he was the sort of jumpy speculator who often is more trouble than he is worth.

There was also always something a little too sharp about the way Jeremiah Hamilton conducted his business. Nowadays, although hedge funds charge very high fees, there is, thanks to government regulation, a reasonable degree of transparency to the process. At the time of the Civil War there was no oversight, other than private legal action (a clumsy and not very practical remedy), and the potential for unscrupulous brokers running a "pool" to fiddle the books or add hidden charges was almost limitless. The file for *Charles Stewart v. Jeremiah G. Hamilton* in the New York County Clerk's Office contains a copy of the printed transcript of the Superior Court proceedings compiled for the subsequent appeal.[26] On it there are pencil annotations that must be contemporary—I doubt anyone else has looked at this thirty-odd-page pamphlet in the 150 years since it came off the press. At one point Hamilton told the court: "I said I would charge nothing for my services." In the margin someone has contradicted his testimony with a neatly written: "Yes he did!" It would have taken an accountant some time poring over the (now nonexistent) books to work out whether this was so or not.

Relations between Jeremiah Hamilton and both Butlers became very messy at the end of April 1864. It turned out that Hamilton claimed he had used $1,000 from Wentworth Butler as the margin to buy Michigan Railroad at 105. When the stock price fell, Hamilton demanded the rest of the money for the shares. Butler refused to pay. In early May, Hamilton sold the shares and sued to recover his loss of $1,550.60. Butler was annoyed at having the shares sold out from underneath him in such a peremptory fashion, particularly when he discovered that Hamilton had bought Michigan Railroad at 93 before the run on the stock drove the price up to 105. As his disgruntled client elaborated, Hamilton had "falsely and fraudulently concealed said purchase and denied the same for the purpose of defrauding and cheating this defendant and has retained said stock and converted the same to his own use to the damage of this defendant of twelve hundred dollars." Hamilton's claim to have bought for Butler at 105, or at the market's peak, just rubbed salt in the wound. Now much wiser in Wall Street subterfuges, Butler realized that Hamilton intended "when stocks should advance in price to represent to the defendant that he had not purchased for him and when the market price should fall to allege and claim that he had purchased at the highest price and that the defendant's deposit was lost." Working out the rights and wrongs of these cases is difficult. On the one hand, there was a characteristic silky glibness to Hamilton's behavior, probably indistinguishable from the slipperiness displayed by most men jobbing on Wall Street. On the other hand, the Butler brothers demonstrated an almost-willful combination of naiveté and unreasonableness. Probably, as was the case in one or two earlier suits against Hamilton, they all deserved one another. And perhaps the New York courts recognized this in the way they cut the Gordian knot. The judicial solution to the two separate cases essentially was that Hamilton had to reimburse Josiah Butler and Wentworth Butler their initial investments, neither brother was to be compensated for the profits they alleged were their due, and Hamilton had to pick up the bill for costs.

THIRTEEN

TO THE DRAFT RIOTS

All his working life as a butcher Thomas F. De Voe had risen early. It was no surprise, then, that five o'clock on a Sunday morning in August 1859 found the forty-eight-year-old historian of the city's markets strolling through the bustle of Catharine Market as its butchers and fishmongers set up for business. Down near the water, in front of two or three closed stores, were several of "the last of the 'Long Island negroes,' some of which had for the last fifty years visited this market on Sunday mornings." The oldest had spread out her roots and herbs on top of a cellar door. De Voe asked her: "How many of the old colored persons (once slaves) are there now left, who yet come here?" She replied: "There was only about *four* who occasionally came—*the rest are all dead*." De Voe observed, "The last five words came forth with a good deal of feeling." Now she had grown old and those she had lived with and loved were dead, but the woman still remembered them. Soon, other than in a line or two of De Voe's book, they would be forgotten.

The woman's recollections were of Long Island Negroes. Commonly they had tied their hair in cues with dried eel-skin or sometimes combed it about their shoulders to resemble the then-fashionable wigs, sold their fish and oysters and clams in Catharine Market and danced for eels on raised shingles, hunks of wood or planks in competition with the Jersey Negroes, mostly from Tappan and whose forelocks were plaited and tied with tea-leads.[1] But, for all the particularity of her compatriots, the woman's point about diminishing numbers and the times a-changing had a broader relevance, applying to the city as a whole. By the 1850s, the generation that had negotiated the end of slavery in and around New York City was dying out. Cato Alexander, impresario of Cato's on the main road out of town near Fifty-Second Street, where for decades fashionable whites had stopped for a drink while out riding or sleighing, died in 1858; Pete Williams, who "for many years kept *the* dance-house of the Five Points, which was a great resort for strangers from abroad who were anxious to see the 'sights,'" had died in 1852; even the black patriarch Thomas Downing would die in 1866.[2] And these were only the well-known African American entrepreneurs noticed with obituaries in the white press. Most of this generation had been slaves, although some were born free, but these were the pioneers who overcame considerable white hostility and established what freedom meant, how New York would work without the institution of slavery. They were remarkable men and women, and the once-enslaved woman who spoke to De Voe was right to lament, in pained voice, their passing.[3]

If the end of slavery had given an impetus and vibrancy to African American life and culture in the 1820s, 1830s, and even into the 1840s, things seemed rather different by the 1850s. In part, this was a matter of demography. The black population of New York reached 16,358 in 1840, its highest level before the end of the Civil War. Thereafter the number of African Americans declined to 13,815 in 1850 and 12,574 in 1860. At the same time the city's total population was increasing at an astonishing rate—from 515,547 in 1850 to 813,669 in 1860. Tens of thousands of Irish and German migrants were making New York their home. In 1860, there were slightly more New Yorkers born in Prussia than there were blacks living in the city. For every African New Yorker in that year, there were about ten inhabitants who came originally from one of the German states. Blacks were becoming a very small minority of the city's population. In the 1830s, roughly one in every eighteen New Yorkers was black; by 1860 that ratio had plummeted to one in every sixty-seven.[4] Inevitably, such a dramatic change affected both African American life and that of the city itself.

In the 1830s and down into the 1840s, an effusion of African American culture had seemed to be occurring everywhere and made its mark on New York. Although a black popular culture still existed in the 1850s, it and indeed African Americans were nowhere near as obviously present on the city streets as they had been in earlier decades. This change was readily apparent in the New York newspapers, many of which were now printed on larger sheets of paper and had more pages but devoted much less space to blacks. Editors still ran stories about African Americans and carried on sending their reporters to haunt the courts, but reading the press it seems as if the writers were describing another world from that existing only a decade or two prior.

Although there were fewer African Americans in New York and aspects of black culture may not have received the attention of earlier years, in the 1850s black activists of various sorts seem to have attained a higher profile and to be better organized. As has only recently been reestablished convincingly, hundreds of former slaves came through New York on the Underground Railroad, an enterprise run by black and white abolitionists.[5] None of this black organizing or politics was of any particular interest to Jeremiah Hamilton. There were, however, aspects of the black struggle for recognition of their rights in the 1850s that had the potential to affect the black broker's everyday life in New York City. This was most obviously the case with Jim Crow segregation. For all Jeremiah Hamilton's distancing of himself from other African Americans, he was in much the same position as any number of respectable blacks in New York City—something as simple as catching an omnibus or train uptown could all too easily end in public humiliation or violence.

Throughout the 1850s, the exclusion of African Americans from public transport or their segregation in separate carriages remained a running sore. In 1850, an anonymous black man firmly reminded everyone of one simple fact—trouble did not occur on Brooklyn om-nibuses, but only in New York City. There, he insisted, "the objec-tion is *not* with the passengers, but with the proprietors; and too often with the drivers alone, without any prohibition from the pro-prietors."[6] Things may well have been worse in the city, but every day African Americans continued to ignore the regulations, and the drivers, as they had back in the early 1840s, and ride on the vehicles. Inevitably, a continual stream of incidents made the newspapers, and some ended up in court.[7]

The best known of these cases involved Elizabeth Jennings, a black teacher and the daughter of a black abolitionist who was try-ing to get to church on a July afternoon in 1854. According to her later statement, she and her friend Sarah Adams walked to the cor-ner of Pearl and Chatham streets to catch one of the horse-drawn Third Avenue cars. The driver told her to wait for the vehicle behind, which "had my people in it, that it was appropriated for that pur-pose." But she was running late. Jennings informed the conductor that she was "a respectable person born and raised in New York"—as she well knew, this was a point of distinction from the Irish-born employee with whom she was battling. Few things were as irritating to many African Americans as the way newcomers were automati-cally accorded rights, for instance, to ride public transport, denied to those whose families had lived in the United States for generations. Jennings continued to lambast the driver for being "a good for noth-ing impudent fellow for insulting decent persons while on their way to church." Soon the driver and the conductor were grappling with Jennings, but, after a minute or two, they gave up trying to put her off. The driver proceeded along his route some six blocks until he saw a policeman. Summoned over, the policeman promptly dragged Jennings off the car, gave her a push "and tauntingly told me to get redress if I could."[8] This she did, suing and eventually winning dam-ages of $225 and the right to ride.

Though hailed as a triumph, this decision hardly settled mat-ters. It had been filed in a Brooklyn court, a place where a jury was much more likely to be amenable to such a cause, and seems to have had limited impact on what occurred in New York City. Certainly, clashes carried on occurring regularly.[9] The most revealing of these incidents involved Thomas Downing—it is the sequel to what had happened to him fifteen years prior.

Early on a Monday evening in September 1855, a black woman slipped into Thomas Downing's oyster cellar at the intersection of Broad and Wall streets. She had come into town from Flushing out on Long Island to deliver two letters for her employer to 45 Thirty-Eighth Street. The sixty-four-year-old Downing agreed to accompany her uptown. They walked across to the corner of Park Place and Church Street and caught car No. 27 on the Sixth Avenue Railroad. As soon as he noticed them, the conductor commenced complaining about their presence, and when the vehicle reached Chambers Street, he ordered the driver to stop. It was about eight o'clock in the evening. The disgruntled railroad employee placed his hands on Downing's shoulders and told him to get off. At this point, the black man later remembered, several white passengers urged him and his companion "to sit still, as the conductor had no right to put us out, as we had as much right to ride as they had." Stymied, the conductor reluctantly instructed the driver to proceed, all the while threatening to summon the police. After listening to the official for a moment or two, Downing retorted sharply that he should do just that, "as the officers were placed for the purpose of keeping peace, and he was disturbing me." Never known for his retiring manner, the oysterman was getting more belligerent in his old age. Taken aback, the conductor replied defensively:

> "Well, my orders are to put you out."
> "My dear sir, I would not take a business if I had to break the law to carry it out."

At the corner of Canal and Varick, the car stopped again. Several whites came and loomed over Downing, announcing that they were also conductors and were about to eject him. "No you won't—I don't leave this car till I get to the end of my journey." As they advanced on him, one of them mistook the brass key in Downing's hand for a weapon and yelled: "Don't use your knife!" Everyone backed away and looked apprehensive. Downing then spoke: "Gentlemen, if I have violated or committed a breach of the law, here is my card, and you know where to find me." Although the conductor was not about to accept a black man's card, several other passengers, curious about this crusty character carrying calling cards, came over and helped themselves to one. After a minute or two of whispers, everyone in the carriage had found out his name, and most knew who he was. Pleasure at being recognized suffused Downing's account. Now, several told him: "Don't get out." Another said: "I will sit with you. I have known you for the last thirty years in Broad-street."[10]

By this time, quite a large crowd had gathered in the street surrounding the stationary car, and, as a *New York Times* reporter eloquently put it, "a muss was brewing." He continued: "It appeared that the conductor was trying to eject from the car everybody's excellent friend, MR THOMAS DOWNING, whose oysters, as served up at Nos. 3 and 5 Broad-street, and the praise of them, are in everybody's mouth." Later Downing remembered a stray voice demanding, "Put him out," but for the *Times* man, the current of public opinion went entirely the other way: "The outside people did anything but sympathize with the struggling conductor." Even the African American admitted that whatever complaint he had noticed was drowned out by shouts of "Stay in Downing." When the car remained immobile, members of the mob put their shoulders to the vehicle and began pushing it forward regardless of "brakes, driver or horses." The conductor gave up trying to hold back the tide, and the crowd erupted in approval. As the car started up again, the black oysterman could hear reverberating white voices: "Three cheers for DOWNING. Hurra, hurra, hurra." This was another unusual moment in the history of race relations in New York City.

As car No. 27 proceeded up Sixth Avenue, Downing, observing the furtive conversations between the conductor and the driver, knew that they had no intention of stopping and allowing him and his companion to alight. Consequently, when the vehicle approached Thirty-Eighth Street Downing asked his newfound friend now sitting next to him: "Will you be kind enough to ring the bell for me?" He did, and the driver, looking back into the car and seeing the white gentleman standing ready to disembark, brought the vehicle to a halt, and Downing and his companion were able to get off safely.[11]

If, back in 1841, much of the New York press had been critical of the need for segregation, by 1855 some of the newspapers,
particularly the *New York Tribune* and the *New York Times,* were
simply scathing. The *Times* reporter began his account of the Downing incident by suggesting that the Sixth Avenue Railroad had "made
sacrifice sufficient to appease any fancied prejudice that exists in the
community against the decent treatment of black people." Even the
"most prejudiced" had to be satisfied with the railroad's attempt
to keep the races separate. But continuing for any longer in such
a fashion was pointless. "The other Railroads, more wisely, treat
negroes as if they were no worse than drunken men and prostitutes,
and their sense is appreciated." He concluded by pointing out to the
Sixth Avenue Railroad that, on this issue, its lack of sense "grows
too apparent."[12]

There can be no doubt that sentiment about how relations between whites and African Americans should be conducted had
changed. The support that Downing had garnered on car No. 27
would have been unthinkable in 1841. Some white New Yorkers, at
least, were discovering that all blacks were not the same, that in fact
they could differentiate African Americans by class and respectability. What had happened on the Sixth Avenue Railroad turned on the
victim's identity as a famous restaurateur catering to the white elite.
He was also wealthy. Decisions about who could or could not ride on
railroads did not affect most ordinary African Americans unable to
afford the fare—whenever they needed to go somewhere in the city
they walked.

As well, the *Times* reporter's enjoyment in flaying the stubborn
backwardness of the railroad led him to underestimate seriously how
deep-seated the prejudice against African Americans remained in
New York. Even blacks catering to a white clientele still had to acknowledge the power of Jim Crow. A few days after the Sixth Avenue
Railroad incident, a black man, Joseph R. Rolin, asked Downing in
the press why he and another black proprietor of an eating establishment "object[ed] to colored men taking seats in their saloons,
at the side of Wall-street bankers and brokers." As a *Times* writer
commented: "The question is really one of interest, and pertinent."[13]

Downing's experience made it clear that whether or not African Americans could use railroads and omnibuses in New York City was undecided. On September 4, 1856, some 2,000 members of the Independent Order of Odd Fellows, one of the largest fraternal black organizations, met in New York. Just for the day, the Sixth Avenue Railroad lifted its ban on black passengers, and James McCune Smith took advantage. "It was real fun," he wrote, "on the way thither, to see the tables turned in the cars; the inside filled with well-dressed colored people, and the outside front and rear crowded with equally well-dressed white people." As he noted, the absence of any disturbance on the day showed "the downright absurdity, as well as sinfulness, of excluding decently dressed persons from any of our city cars. The second, third, and fourth avenue cars make no such exclusion." But the Sixth Avenue Railroad remained notorious among African Americans. In late 1858 a white passenger objected when a black man got onboard one of its cars. According to the report in the *New York Tribune,* "about one-half of the passengers shouted, 'Let the man ride—let the man ride;' while the other half in a most violent and noisy manner, objected." Eventually, he was allowed to travel, but the division of opinion was more telling of the racial climate.[14] By the end of the decade, many well-dressed and respectable African American men and women did use New York's public transport with no trouble. But there was always a chance that something could go wrong and a humiliating incident, ranging from racial abuse to violence, erupt out of nothing.

In fact, Thomas Downing's experiences provide an interesting barometer of race relations in late antebellum New York City. For decades he had been the genial host catering to a white clientele who reveled in his "humility and modesty" and expected him to fend off black customers. My impression is that by the time he reached his mid- to late sixties this was wearing rather thin. His irritation with segregation, obvious enough in 1855, became even more evident, particularly after the *Dred Scott* ruling of the Supreme Court in 1857 laying down that African Americans, whether slave or free, were not American citizens and had no legal standing in a federal court. Indeed, he, with good reason, was becoming a very angry old man, eager to confront officialdom and lecture its representatives, to tell them what he thought of the government. Early in 1860 Downing, at the time experiencing some financial setbacks, was subpoenaed to appear in court. The black man informed the judge that, because of *Dred Scott,* he would not answer any questions: "As a negro, he had no rights, and was subject to no responsibilities." The unimpressed judge insisted that he testify. Later in the year, when the census-taker came knocking on Downing's door he was in for a memorable few minutes. Although the black man answered his initial questions readily enough, when asked to state the value of his property he "positively refused." Indeed, according to a *Herald* reporter, Downing "lectured the marshal rather sharply on the subject." He went on to explain to the bemused official "that as the government at Washington regarded him as a chattel, he could not own chattels," or "property . . . cannot own property." The net result, as the *Herald* recorded, was that "the Census Department so far remains ignorant of the value of the property of the most celebrated oysterman in America."[15]

It was not just that Downing was increasingly cantankerous. In the years before the Civil War, relations between blacks and whites were deteriorating, notwithstanding the fact that African Americans were becoming a much smaller minority in the city. The oysterman— aged, wealthy, and well-known—could display his contempt for, say, the *Dred Scott* decision in ways that were not safe for other African Americans. There was a reason that New York was a stop on the Underground Railroad and not the destination. For decades now, African Americans, both escaped slaves and free blacks, had been kidnapped and returned to, or sold into, a life of slavery in the South. This too was a contributing factor in the city's declining black population. Even though African Americans were a less prominent feature of the cityscape, individuals still had to contend with an element of danger when they walked down the street.[16] As well, the openly pro-southern sympathies of substantial numbers of New York's political and commercial elite, their willingness, and indeed eagerness, to hand back fugitive slaves, must have given pause to many African Americans. The future looked anything but promising.

New York's prosperity had depended on the slave South. For decades now, its banks had financed the cotton crop and the purchase of land and slaves; its merchants had dominated the shipping of cotton across the Atlantic; its manufacturers and middlemen had dispatched clothing, shoes, and hats, as well as hoes and axes, to southern planters for their slaves. Although there was a slight diminishing of the importance of this relationship after the panic of 1857, J. B. D. De Bow, whose *De Bow's Review* was a leading voice of southern opinion, still considered New York in 1860 as being "almost as dependent upon Southern slavery as Charleston itself."[17] In the presidential election of that year, Abraham Lincoln may have carried New York State, but in New York City he only managed to garner about one-third of the vote. For a while in April 1861, some in the city, including its mayor, flirted with the idea of secession or withdrawing from the Union and becoming a free port of some sort or other.[18]

There was a precariousness to living in New York as a free black, and things only became more dangerous when the Civil War began. For all the distance Jeremiah Hamilton had managed to place between himself and other African Americans, he too had to be prepared to cope with the continuing threat of mob violence. Dreams of citizenship and equality in New York had been deferred and would carry on being deferred for a long time to come. The question, as Langston Hughes framed it so eloquently nearly a century later, was simply: Would it all explode? This time the answer was yes—and the resulting conflagration, known as the Draft Riots, was one of the worst weeks in the city's history.

Congress had passed the federal Conscription Act in March 1863 in an effort to help spark the North's flagging military fortunes. All men aged between twenty and thirty-five and unmarried men between thirty-five and forty-five were liable for military service. Each congressional district had to hold a lottery to determine who would fight for the Union. Those drafted could avoid service by finding an "acceptable substitute" or paying $300. The burden thus fell disproportionately on the poor, particularly families dependent on the wages of the young male conscripts. This measure thrust the federal government into working-class life in an unprecedented fashion.

One other aspect of the Conscription Act contributed disproportionately to turning New York City into a tinderbox. The law applied to "able-bodied male citizens of the United States," meaning that only white men would be drafted. There was already racial tension in the labor market, but the new law raised the specter of African Americans, especially newly emancipated freedmen, taking jobs from white men who were away fighting for the Union. As Iver Bernstein, the leading historian of the Draft Riots, observed: "It is not hard to see, then, how the Conscription Act—biased against the poor, magnifying white racial fears, and involving the federal government as never before in local affairs—galvanized ongoing conflicts in the city."[19]

On the morning of Saturday, July 11, 1863, the first lottery in New York City was held. By the end of the day, blindfolded clerks had selected 1,236 names from out of a hollow drum of polished wood mounted on a stand. Calm prevailed. On Monday morning, July 13, the second drawing was held at the Provost Marshall's Office at Forty-Seventh Street and Third Avenue, and things played out differently. Violence broke out, and the disturbance spread across the city like a wildfire. Crowds poured out into the streets, and rioters cut down telegraph poles, pulled up railway track, and committed acts of mayhem and looting. Peace was not restored fully until the next weekend, and only after regiments were ordered north from Gettysburg and some 6,000 soldiers occupied the city. By the end of the Draft Riots at least 119 individuals had lost their lives. Many were killed as troops subdued the city, but twelve were African Americans, murdered, often in the most gruesome fashion, by white rioters.[20]

Initially, rioters, reflecting their hatred of the draft itself, directed their attacks at government and military buildings. Very quickly, though, African Americans became the targets of mob violence. A *New York Herald* reporter wrote of the eleventh ward that "the laboring classes there appear to be of the opinion that the negroes are the sole cause of all their trouble, and many even say that were it not for the negroes there would be no war and no necessity for a draft."[21] This sentiment was hardly confined to the eleventh ward. As had been true of most outbreaks of anti-black violence in New York for decades, a surly white resentment of anything that could represent black achievement, be it particular individuals or an institution, soon bubbled to the surface.

The Colored Orphan Asylum was a four-story building on Fifth Avenue between Forty-Third and Forty-Fourth Streets. According to an official associated with the institution, at about four o'clock on Monday afternoon, the first day of the riots, "the children numbering 233, were quietly seated in their school rooms, playing in the nursery, or reclining on a sick bed in the Hospital when an infuriated mob, consisting of several thousand men, women and children, armed with clubs, brick bats etc. advanced upon the institution."[22] The children were spirited away through a back entrance while voices howled: "Kill the monkies." After sacking the institution of anything of value, members of the mob fired the building. Although firefighters were present, rioters cut hoses and damaged hydrants in order to ensure the building was destroyed—and it was, in not much more than twenty minutes. As one historian has argued, the riot as a whole was an attempt, "no less thorough for its being relatively unplanned and uncoordinated, to annihilate 'black life' in New York City."[23]

The overall intention of the rioters may well have been to erase the African American presence from what they thought of as their city. For the most part, however, rioters exhibited some caution, avoiding areas with the heaviest concentration of blacks, notably the Five Points, and focusing on African Americans who were more isolated from their compatriots. Opportunism was involved too. Events at the neighborhood level often were tinctured by local resentments and grudges. The Draft Riots were a great opportunity to settle scores and put any uppity black in his place. That certainly appeared to be the case with the way things panned out on East Twenty-Ninth Street. It started late on Tuesday evening, July 14, the second day of the riots.

Daniel Murray worked as a clerk for the druggist at the corner of Fourth Avenue and Twenty-Ninth Street. He was understandably jumpy that night. A few minutes before ten o'clock some nearby shouts prompted him immediately to close the store. Once outside and hurrying home, he heard a strange bustling noise. He also noticed the sounds of knocking on doors and hushed voices saying, "Send down that nigger" and "Fetch him down." A small neighborhood mob was gathering, mostly consisting of the Irish or local-born sons of the Irish. Mary Flannery saw them heading toward Fourth Avenue, "hallowing as they passed." The intention of mob members was certainly no secret. Flannery had "asked a small boy where they were going and he said they were going to Hamiltons to break in." She admitted, "I was afraid of them," and had retreated inside.[24]

At nearly a quarter past ten, Eliza Jane Hamilton watched "a number of men and boys" approach the house, marching down Twenty-Ninth Street while chanting menacingly, "68, 68, 68." That was the number where she lived. The couple had anticipated trouble. All the doors, she recalled, "were well secured," but they lived in a house, not a fortress. When the mob arrived at their destination, one of the young men "rang the door bell violently." No one answered. Immediately, a few individuals went to the basement entrance, kicked in a panel of the door and forced their way inside. The intruders then rushed up the internal steps from the basement. As Eliza Jane Hamilton later calmly related to the authorities: "I met them at the head of the stairs."[25]

This was Eliza Jane Hamilton's moment, and she was magnificent. Eliza Hamilton has featured so little in this book simply because of her invisibility in the sources. At the time of the Draft Riots she was forty years old and had given birth to ten children, two of whom had died at a very young age. For a quarter of a century this white woman had been married to the much older black "celebrity." Living in New York as part of an interracial couple, no matter how much money they had, must have been a bruising education. There was steel in her character, and, on the night of July 14, she faced down a mob bent on bloodshed. Afterwards, she had to tell the authorities what had happened, and they recorded her testimony. As far as I can tell, this is the only surviving trace of her words.[26] Interestingly, she made no mention of whether, during the home invasion, any of her children or the servants were present or had been sent away.

Four or five men and seven or eight boys broke their way into 68 East Twenty-Ninth Street. At the top of the basement stairs Eliza Hamilton asked them what they wanted. One of the men answered that "they were looking for Mr Hamilton as they wanted to kill him." "Why?" she asked. He replied that her husband "had injured his mother and he wanted to be revenged." She neither had seen this man before nor had any idea who he was. His cryptic utterance was never explained. The intruders pushed past Eliza Hamilton and swarmed over the house searching for Jeremiah Hamilton or anything to steal. After a while some of the men came back downstairs and asked for liquor and cigars. "I told them I had no liquor, but gave them cider and segars," Eliza Hamilton later recalled.

She recognized one of the trespassers, a thirteen-year-old named John Leary Jr., born in New York, the son of an Irishman. "I had seen the boy Leary pass our house frequently; I supposed he lived in the neighborhood but did not know where." Perhaps for this reason, Eliza Hamilton concentrated on him out of the fifteen or so persons in the house, following the young man from floor to floor of what, to the intruders, seemed an impressively opulent residence: "I saw the boy Leary almost all the time he was in the house." When Leary went into the front room on the second story, he helped himself to a bundle of clothing on the table. Just delivered from D. Devlin and Co., the decidedly modern and large retail clothing store on Broadway near City Hall, it included two suits of new clothes, six pairs of socks and some suspenders, items intended for Eliza Hamilton's son Walter, who was almost the same age as Leary. No one else was in the room, and she "told the boy Leary to give me the things, and I took them out of his hands; he made no resistance." A quarter of an hour later, Leary and Eliza Hamilton were alone again in a hall on another story, and the boy asked if her children had any old clothes or pantaloons to spare. She blurted out that she knew him and asked where he lived. He answered in Fortieth Street. That was a lie; he lived at his father's blacksmith shop farther down East Twenty-Ninth Street. She deflected his request for cast-off apparel: "I told the boy Leary, when he asked for clothes, that it was no time to hunt up clothes."[27]

The men had made themselves comfortable on the ground floor drinking cider and smoking cigars while the boys roamed the house. They scattered things around and made a mess in a room on the third story, stealing $25 in cash and a few other items valued at about $40. Similarly, a few drawers had been tipped upside down in the basement, but nothing seemed to be missing.

A minor incident occurred just before everyone left. Leary was rummaging around in the parlor extension off the back of the ground floor when he found the Hamiltons' son Theodore's gun on a sofa. Eliza Hamilton and John Leary struggled over the weapon. "I told him to give me up the gun. He tried to hold it, and resisted giving it up." Although they were less than ten feet distant from the men, who had their backs turned and were smoking and drinking, she succeeded in reclaiming her son's gun. At this point everyone stood up to leave. As they filed past Eliza Hamilton, leaving the way they had come in, via the basement stairs, she watched, backed into a corner with the gun concealed behind her. Last to leave was Leary. As he passed Hamilton he reached around her and grabbed hold of the weapon, and the pair wrestled over it again. Leary said, "Here is a gun!" but only loudly enough for the last person leaving to hear. A large Irishman with "two murderous looking weapons in his hands" came back up the stairs and confronted her. For the first time, Hamilton remembered, "I was frightened and the man took the gun from me in a forcible manner." He muttered to her that she "was damned lucky to escape so well." Leary stood there, watching the exchange. By Eliza Hamilton's account at least, there was something decidedly unsettling about Leary's behavior while he was in her house.[28]

The mob was inside the Hamilton residence for maybe forty-five minutes. Everyone in the neighborhood seemed to know what was going on, even before it happened, but the street outside remained eerily empty. People were keeping their distance. It seems that only one person was concerned enough to see if he could assist in any way.

William James, a shipbroker who lived at the corner of Fourth Avenue and Twenty-Ninth Street, had left work that day well ahead of his usual quitting time—everyone in the city was on edge because of the disturbances. He had been home with his family since early afternoon. Just before ten o'clock he walked across to the northwest corner of the intersection and bought himself a pitcher of ale. While he stood in the street a neighbor informed him "there was trouble down at Hamiltons, and the purport of it was that they were going to burn him out, and hang him." James queried: "Will you go down?" The answer was a firm no. James then went inside his house, put down his pitcher, came back out and asked his neighbor again to accompany him. He could only recollect half of the reply.

> "I would not put myself in the hands of that crowd for. . . ." I forget what else he said.
>   "You won't stop here and see a man murdered without going to assist him?"

James set off alone down East Twenty-Ninth Street "to lend any assistance if I could, to prevent the rioters doing any injury." At that point he had never spoken to Jeremiah Hamilton in his life. James did his best to look like someone out for a casual evening stroll. When he had almost reached the lamppost in front of number 68, a sentinel stepped out from the shadows and accosted him. The nineteen-year-old guard pulled a pistol from his pocket, cocked it, poked James in the breast with the barrel, and demanded: "What the hell are you doing here?" James patted the young man on the shoulder and said:

> "What the devil are you going to do with that. Take that away."
>   "You're one of us."
>   "Tell me what this is all about."
>   "There is a nigger living here with two white women, and we are going to bring him out, and hang him on the lamp-post, and you stop and see the fun."
>   "How are you going to get him."
>   "There is a lot of our fellows in the house now, and they are going to bring him out."

At this point, the men and boys, "carrying various things wrapped up," began emerging from the basement door and made their way up to the street. According to James, one lad asked the sentinel: "Why don't you go in the basement and get what you want?" He replied that "he had been in and had his fill." Everyone disappeared quickly into the night.[29]

The Hamiltons were probably well aware of how "damned lucky" they had been. What occurred the following afternoon only four or five blocks away, on the corner of Seventh Avenue and West Twenty-Eighth Street served to remind them of how ugly things so easily could have become if the mob had caught Jeremiah Hamilton at home. Rioters, led by George Glass, an Irish laborer, burst into a house on the corner of Twenty-Seventh Street and Seventh Avenue. They seized Abraham Franklin, a crippled black coachman, and his sister Henrietta, drove the pair out onto the street and beat them up. The mob then kicked and herded Franklin along for a block to the corner of West Twenty-Eighth Street, where they hanged him from a lamppost. Passing troops rescued Henrietta and cut down her brother's body, but as soon as they had departed, the rioters hung him back on the lamppost and cheered loudly for Jeff Davis. Later, a sixteen-year-old Irish butcher named Patrick Butler grabbed hold of Franklin's corpse by the genitals and dragged him along the street to hurrahs and yells from the crowd.[30] The world had gone mad.

Where was Jeremiah Hamilton on the evening of July 14? Judging from the case file in the District Attorney's Indictment Papers, he was simply somewhere else. The mob may have been looking for him, but no one mentioned where the hunted black man was at ten o'clock that night. Here a letter written nine days later by one of Hamilton's neighbors is of some help. Camilla Davis Leonard's son was away serving in the Union Army, and she kept him up to date with local news: "You have doubtless heard of our disgraceful riots in New York." After bemoaning the city's "warlike appearance"— Gramercy Park overflowed with tents and horses—she detailed that "a large number of the rioters assailed neighbor Hamiltons with loud cries for the 'Nigger.'" Mrs. Hamilton's protestation that "there were no colored persons there" only inflamed passions. By this time, according to Leonard, Jeremiah Hamilton "had already made his way over the fence into 28th St."[31]

If Leonard was correct and Hamilton had in fact decamped by scrambling over his back wall, then that magnified the importance of the role his wife had played. Presumably the fifty-six-year-old Jeremiah Hamilton only would have used such an undignified method of egress if it had been the sudden approach of the vengeful mob, shouting the number of his house, that had compelled him to leave. Earlier in the evening he could have slipped out of his front door and no one would have noticed. Eliza Hamilton's heroic action in mollifying the intruders, dispensing cigars and cider while they searched the house, distracted his pursuers for some thirty minutes or more. The delay gave Jeremiah Hamilton ample time to get out of the neighborhood, away from the men and boys intent on hanging him from the lamppost in front of his house.

Where did Hamilton flee? This is not certain. William James, the man who had walked down Twenty-Ninth Street to see what was happening at number 68, said that "it was after I had been at the station house that I spoke to him [Jeremiah Hamilton] for the first time." The timing of this is unclear—most likely it was on the night of July 14, but maybe it was at a later date. Quite possibly, Hamilton had scaled his back fence and headed to the nearest police station. According to Camilla Leonard, "he was persuaded to leave town till the excitement was over," but that would not have happened until the following Wednesday morning. A few days later, he and his family returned to Twenty-Ninth Street, though doubtless not without trepidation. His neighbor reported to her son: "They are all back again but the blinds are closed and not a face to be seen." How welcome they felt in their neighborhood on their return was another matter. Leonard confessed that "I felt a little anxious about our house fearing theirs would be burned and ours be destroyed with it."[32]

Camilla Leonard also worried about what might still happen: "It is thought by many that they will organize and that this is only the beginning of fearful strife." African Americans were even more apprehensive. Concerns about their future combined with the sheer horror of what had occurred during the four days of rioting convinced many to depart. Writing in early August, a few weeks after the riot, a *New York Tribune* writer reported that "a large number of colored families have left the city with the intention of never returning to it again."[33] By the time of the 1865 census the city's African American population had dropped below 10,000 individuals for the first time since the mid-1810s. Back then, the total population had been under 100,000, less than one-seventh of what it was in 1865.[34] In the immediate aftermath of the Draft Riots, New York City became the "whitest" it had been since the seventeenth century.

The events of the night of July 14 were a terrifying experience for Jeremiah and Eliza Jane Hamilton. They had been "damned lucky to escape so well." Moving back into a house that intruders had broken into and pillaged must have been difficult. Almost certainly there was a sense of violation. Within a year or two the couple and their family had moved—even if just down the street—to a slightly grander residence.[35] But were they shocked or surprised when an angry white mob targeted their genteel retreat from the city? Probably not. Doubtless they had hoped to be left alone, but far from being unexpected, the home invasion was the realization of the constant threat the couple had prepared for and learned to live with for three decades of married life. Although in the next few years they would spend more time traveling overseas and going on summer vacations, the couple seems to have had no thoughts of moving away from the city. They had tried that in the 1830s and again in the 1840s and, seemingly, had made their peace with living in New York and everything that that entailed. For the rest of his life Jeremiah G. Hamilton would live at 122 East Twenty-Ninth Street.

EPILOGUE

A LION IN WINTER

L ate one afternoon in the fall of 1866, a twenty-three-year-old Irishman named John Murphy tried to look inconspicuous as he loitered near St. Paul's Church on Broadway. He watched the street intently. Even back then New York never stopped rebuilding itself, and some recent "improvement" had created pedestrian and traffic chaos between Vesey and Fulton streets. Later, a *Herald* reporter marveled at the "opportunities afforded the light fingered and fleet footed gentry for plying their vocation." The bottleneck was like an artificial reef, a sunken wreck in the Hudson River—it concentrated prey. Pickpockets and purse snatchers "ever on the alert, have not been slow to appreciate the opportunities thus offered."

Perhaps the aging man looked frail. Maybe it was because he was the only black man on the sidewalk. Certainly he appeared prosperous. Who knows why Murphy picked him out as his mark—but he did. "In the confusion among the cars, carts, stages, coaches and half maddened horses," Murphy closed in briskly on Jeremiah Hamilton, bumping and jostling him. But Murphy had miscalculated. Hamilton was a lot quicker and stronger than he looked. Feeling his watch being pulled out of his vest pocket, he grabbed Murphy in a vise-like grip and did not let go until a policeman from the Broadway squad arrived on the scene. The young Irishman was locked up in a police cell overnight, and the following day he would be taken to the Tombs, where "Mr. J. G. Hamilton, the well known broker, will appear and make a formal complaint against him."[1]

Even though he had failed as a pickpocket, Murphy had demonstrated a discerning eye for timepieces. Hamilton's gold watch was valued at $200, and the gold chain attaching it to his vest was worth $150. The gentleman's expensive accoutrements would have made a nice haul. Watch and chain were one of Hamilton's prized possessions. At his death, some eight and a half years later, he bequeathed "my gold watch and chain" to Theodore, his eldest son. His eldest daughter, Miranda, was left "my diamond ring." These were the first bequests detailed in his will, mentioned before he shared out any real estate or other property.[2] The watch's significance derived from more than just its monetary value. Perhaps Hamilton's father had given it to him, or perhaps it had marked some event, maybe even had been engraved with his full name, spelling out what the mysterious G. stood for. Or perhaps all biographers believe that, just out of reach, there is a key that will unlock their subject.

An attempted robbery on a New York street was a commonplace, but there is something endearingly human in the idea of Hamilton hanging on, with such tenacity, to an object he valued so highly. The incident itself was replete with reversals. Seemingly Hamilton could not help himself. Even when a stranger tried to rob him, he ended up puncturing all-too-familiar stereotypes. More typically in such affairs, at least in newspaper accounts, the victim was a white man and the robber a young African American. There was a well-known con—it was called "burning" and the perpetrators "burners"—that usually ended with a black man snatching a white man's money and running off. Sometimes the mark was alert enough to grab hold of the young African American. More often the robber escaped and the streets echoed to futile cries of "Stop thief!" As well, next day at the Police Office John Murphy stated sullenly, "I am not guilty" and then made his mark with a crude-looking X. The very literate black man gave a brief and assured account of what had happened and affixed to the document his beautifully elaborate signature, curlicues and all.[3] John Murphy was going to prison; Jeremiah G. Hamilton got on with the rest of his life.

This incident was also the last occasion during his lifetime that Hamilton's actions featured in the newspapers. Obituary writers depicted these final years fleetingly, hinting at a novel mellowness to them. According to the *Herald*, "his advise was regarded by some of the most substantial men on the street as exceptionally sound," a verdict echoed in the *Tribune*, which said that "his judgment in banking business was highly esteemed, and he was often consulted by prominent bankers." Another pointed out that Hamilton "was, with one exception, the oldest Wall street speculator in that city."[4] Perhaps he was getting old, a little bit respectable and no longer interesting. But, after the incident with the pickpocket, reporters would not write about him again until his death. All that is left in the record of these final years is his name on various lists or documents.

Identification becomes a problem and it can be difficult to confirm exactly who is the person on a particular list. In December 1865, a J. G. Hamilton was included among dozens of New York merchants and businessmen in an advertisement in the *New York Tribune*. The signatories were searching for economy and fidelity in city administration and supporting Marshall Roberts for mayor, Murray Hoffman for corporation counsel. If this was Jeremiah Hamilton, it was the first time he was linked to anything remotely political. Maybe his newfound respectability drew him more fully into city affairs. Nine years later, a J. G. Hamilton was one of a handful of people named in a story about the New Jersey legislature as being involved in a proposed scheme for a million-dollar railroad bridge to Staten Island.[5] In neither case is it at all certain that this was Jeremiah G. Hamilton.

In May 1864 Eliza J. Hamilton had purchased, for $200, a lot in Green-Wood Cemetery in Brooklyn. A few months later two of the Hamiltons' daughters—Camilla and Cora—were removed from other sites in the graveyard and reinterred in the new family plot. These daughters must have died very young—Cora had been first buried on April 5, 1857, and Camilla on December 31, 1863, and yet there is no trace of either in any census schedule. On December

4, 1868, Margaret Morris, Eliza's mother, aged seventy-five, was buried there as well. Her grave was marked with an obelisk—it still stands, though the inscription is unreadable, erased by more than a century of weathering. On March 14, 1873, Eliza's brother, George H. Morris, died in London. The Hamiltons arranged to bring the body back across the Atlantic, and on April 16 he too was buried in the family plot.[6]

In the years after the home invasion, the Hamiltons traveled more frequently. They joined much of New York society and fled the city in the summer—Jeremiah and Eliza Hamilton went to Saratoga. Needless to say, the resort was better known for African American domestics and servants than African American guests. During the 1870s they spent several weeks each summer with a Professor Otto Von Below and his wife. In June 1872, according to the *New York Evening Post,* "among those now enjoying Saratoga life are well-known men from all parts of the country." The piece included J. G. Hamilton in a list of names, "all of New York and booked for the season."[7] The Hamiltons also went abroad, which, given the size of the family and the costs of first-class travel, must have been an expensive enterprise. In November 1864, a brief notation in the *Herald* listed that "J.G. Hamilton, wife, and nine children" had departed on the steamship *Golden Rule* en route for Greytown.[8] The figure of nine children was incorrect—either someone miscounted (there were only six alive in 1864) or mistakenly included the servants as children. This Nicaraguan port was the first stop in Cornelius Vanderbilt and Accessory Transit's route to the Pacific Ocean. Almost certainly, the listing in the *Herald* meant that Hamilton and his family went to the West Coast and spent some time in San Francisco.

But most intriguing of all are two fleeting mentions of Hamilton and his family in the *New York Herald* in September 1870. The first noted that, among many others, "J.G. Hamilton and family" and, separately, "Theodore A. Hamilton" were "at the Paris Office for the week ending August 23 1870." Sixteen days later, the *Herald* included their names in a list of New Yorkers then in London.[9] There are no other details. We have no idea if before arriving in Paris they had spent weeks touring the Continent, or if they had gone straight there from New York. What we do know is that, with impeccable timing, Hamilton and his family turned up in the City of Light as the Franco-Prussian War was reaching its conclusion. On August 18, probably about the time the Hamiltons set foot in the city, the French forces were defeated at the Battle of Gravelotte, and, as a leading historian of these events has written, "a Prussian siege of Paris now seemed inevitable."[10] The capital was in an uproar. Elihu Washburne, the American minister to France, noted in his remarkable diary on September 2: "I am depressed and sad at the scenes of misery, suffering and anguish." In the six weeks since Napoleon III's declaration of war on July 19, the American legation had helped more than 3,000 Americans flee Paris.[11] Whether this number included the Hamiltons, or whether they made their own escape, is unclear. But by early September 1870 they were safe in London. What impact, if any, the drama of events in Paris, or indeed Europe, had on Jeremiah Hamilton and his family is unknown. There is, however, a coda to the Hamiltons' European tour. In 1879, Adelaide Morris Hamilton married Alphonse Krizek in New York.

Adelaide Morris Hamilton Krizek

The couple moved to Geneva, Switzerland, and lived out their lives in Europe. She was the only one of the eight known children of Jeremiah and Eliza Hamilton not buried in the family plot in Green-Wood Cemetery.

Books and reading remained an important part of Jeremiah Hamilton's life. One indication of this was that he and Eliza named their second son, born in 1852, Walter Scott Hamilton. Another was that on May 22, 1856, about the time he commenced his legal action against Accessory Transit and Cornelius Vanderbilt, Hamilton bought from the estate of Andrew Gray one share in the New York Society Library, entitling him, for the payment of an annual fee, to borrow books. Before the founding of the New York Public Library in 1895, the Society Library was the most important library in the city, containing in 1856 some 35,000 volumes. At this time the premises of the elite institution were located on University Place between Twelfth and Thirteenth streets. As was acknowledged frankly in the 1870 annual report, "this is not a library to which the laboring classes readily have access." In fact, "its associations have tended to confine it to the wealthier portion of society."[12]

The New York Society maintained charging ledgers, a record of the borrowings of individual members. Over the two decades of Hamilton's membership, the librarian, or his clerk, made some 236 entries under his name. Some were for multivolume titles, and occasionally a notation was as vague as "select novels," but the African American member carried to his homes on East Twenty-Ninth Street in excess of 250 books. More than 150 of the entries were made in the 1870s during the last five years of his life.[13]

The range of Hamilton's reading was truly impressive. Most of the volumes were nonfiction. He continued his earlier interest in the English coffeehouse radicals who had so stirred the eighteenth-century American colonists. He borrowed different (if unspecified) volumes of Bacon on multiple occasions. As well, in May 1858, after losing his suit against Vanderbilt, Hamilton took home, as the entry detailed, "Hobbes Works (folio)"—Thomas Hobbes had an even grimmer view of the natural state of man than Bolingbroke or Bacon, and he anatomized the understanding of self-interest that would, in time, be foundational to the development of capitalism. Hamilton also checked out of the library volumes of Plato, Cicero, Tacitus, and Plutarch; as well, there were entries for Montaigne, Grotius, and Carlyle. He read individual numbers of the *Edinburgh Review,* various collections of sermons and Mary Wollstonecraft's *Vindication of the Rights of Woman.* Hamilton was fond of history: he borrowed several volumes of Macaulay's *History of England* and a few books whose titles are indecipherable but contain "history" in them, and he appears to have read at least two biographies of Napoleon. One title that stood out in his reading was Joel Cook's *The Siege of Richmond* (1862). What was striking about this was that only a handful of books in Hamilton's long list of borrowings were about the United States. Perhaps his unusually specific interest in the fate of the Confederate capital adds a little bit of weight to the case for Jeremiah Hamilton having spent at least some of his youth in Richmond.

Other books raise similarly intriguing questions about the link between Hamilton's reading and his life. In March 1864, he borrowed Sir Gardner Wilkinson's *On Colour and on the Necessity for a General Diffusion of Taste Among All Classes with Remarks on Laying Out Dressed or Geometrical Gardens* (1858) and a week later "Chevreul on Color," presumably *The Principles of Harmony and Contrast of Colors* (French edition 1854, translated into English in 1855). This was a few months after the mob had broken into his house and probably about the time he and his wife were contemplating buying a new residence and moving. Perhaps he was using these books as a primer in house decoration. If so, he learned well—after his death one impressed individual described the new Hamilton residence as "a model of comfort and elegance" that "shows in every feature the taste of a man of intellect and refinement."[14] Or perhaps he was educating himself about art. Translations of Chevreul were influential and popular: reading his work would have allowed Hamilton to talk knowledgeably about, for example, chiaroscuro, or the painted contrasts between light and shade. As well, I suspect he was in the market to buy paintings. A couple of years earlier he had read *Art Studies: The "Old Masters" of Italy; Painting* (1861) by James Jackson Jarves, one of the first Americans to collect Italian paintings.

Hamilton also appreciated imaginative literature. He read *Abelard and Heloise,* Boccaccio's *Decameron* and Goethe's *Faust.*

Within a few days in 1861, he took home to peruse at his leisure two different translations of Dante. He also borrowed a few novels, including Henry Fielding's *Tom Jones,* Thackeray's *Vanity Fair* and Dickens's *Pickwick Papers* and *Our Mutual Friend.* What did a black broker who had spent most of his life in avid pursuit of the dollar on Wall Street make of Dickens's often-caustic commentary on the role of money in Victorian London? Did Hamilton reflect on his own past as he turned the pages of *The Adventures of Gil Blas,* an early-eighteenth-century picaresque novel about the son of a stablehand and a chambermaid forced by circumstances to flout the law and meet all sorts of disreputable people who, thanks to a sly quickness and wit, succeeds in life, ending up enjoying his fortune and retiring to a castle? There is a temptation to make simplistic and reductive connections between what he read and his life. But he did borrow *Gil Blas* twice, once in 1857 and again in 1872. My own view is that much of what he read, from Plato to Dickens, did, in the most general terms, help prepare him for his unusual existence as a black man living in New York and making money on Wall Street. Above all, some writers such as, most obviously, Bolingbroke, Bacon and Hobbes provided him with the philosophical underpinnings that enabled him to understand the fundamental importance of self-interest in a capitalist society and justified his existence. He must have been a fascinating conversationalist—perhaps a writer in *Harper's Bazaar* hinted at that by describing Hamilton as "an intelligent, gentlemanly man."[15] Finally, perhaps some of the many pages he read even helped prepare him for his death.

The end came quickly. In mid-May 1875 the Hamiltons were making preparations to travel to Saratoga for the summer when Jeremiah Hamilton fell ill and took to bed. A few days later, at about six o'clock in the morning on May 19, 1875, he died from pneumonia and exhaustion. According to the death certificate Hamilton was sixty-seven years, eleven months and twenty-two days old. His final request was that "he should be laid by the side of a daughter who was buried in Greenwood a few years ago." The funeral took place three days later, at nine o'clock in the morning in the Hamilton's capacious house at 122 East Twenty-Ninth Street. Professor Von Below and his wife came down from Saratoga to attend. The Reverend

Dr. Sabine conducted the service, paying "a glowing tribute to his memory." A "large concourse of his friends" then escorted the coffin to Green-Wood, and Jeremiah G. Hamilton was interred in the family plot.[16]

Dozens of newspapers from one end of the country to the other printed brief notices of his death, often captioned "The Richest Colored Man in the Country," "A Colored Speculator" or some such. He was acknowledged in the *Albany Evening Journal* as the "wealthiest colored man in the United States," in the *Galveston Daily News* as "the colored millionaire of New York," and in the *Commercial Advertiser* as someone "who has long been identified with commercial enterprises in this City."[17] Most of the coverage had a cloying air of respectability to it. Even the *New York Herald,* of all papers, ended an appreciative 500-word obituary by noting that Hamilton had left "a large circle of friends, who recognize no caste when death calls." It was not, however, all sweetness and light. A notice that ran in the *Cincinnati Enquirer,* although reprinted from a New York newspaper, began: "The notorious colored capitalist long identified with commercial enterprises in this city is dead and buried." Meanspiritedly, the writer went on to claim that Hamilton "did his best to pass off for a Spaniard, but did not succeed," and had "married a white lady of very respectable family, poor and handsome." He concluded that the "would-be descendant of the De Cordovas was a nuisance, and the ladies are happy now that he has departed."[18] Hamilton might well have been relieved that not everyone wanted to relegate him to the category of venerable old man and irrelevance. Someone still considered him dangerous, worth a final slur or two.

Eliza Jane Hamilton lived for another thirty years, residing in the family home at 122 East Twenty-Ninth Street until almost the end, dying in 1904. She was buried in the plot she had chosen in Green-Wood, next to her husband and their eldest daughter, Miranda, who had died in 1895. All bar one of the other Hamilton children were interred there in Brooklyn as well: Theodore in 1911, Walter in 1913, Josephine in 1926 and finally Evelina in 1927. As best as I can tell, none of the Hamiltons who remained in the United States had any children. Adelaide Morris Krizek, however, had a boy named Alphons Morris Hamilton Krizek, born in Geneva in 1880. He was known as Allie von Krizek, and all of Jeremiah and Eliza Hamilton's descendants alive today can trace their ancestry back to him.[19]

And what happened to the money? Eliza Jane Hamilton and Evelina Hamilton were appointed executors and charged with distributing his estate. He left the house at 122 East Twenty-Ninth Street, along with "all the furniture, bedding, books, paintings, engravings, statuary, silver, silver plate and bronzes," to his four daughters, although Eliza was to have use of the house during her lifetime. Perhaps the wording describing the contents was formulaic, but it does sound as if he had collected artworks. In 1874, the house was valued in the city's annual assessments, which were always low, at $12,000. He also left "Real Estate in Greenwich and Albany Streets," and the rents from them, to be divided up among his children. In the 1874 assessments for the first ward, three houses were listed as being owned by Hamilton, at 124, 124 ½, and 126 Greenwich Street, today on the edge of the World Trade Center site. They were all three-story buildings and valued at a total of $36,000. There were also several individual bequests: $2,000 to an Anna Graham, who appears to have lived in Poughkeepsie; $500 to a Hamilton Phelps; $500 to Mary Gibbons, "my faithful servant"; and $100 to her sister, Bridget, "formerly in my employ." Probate was granted, but the space in the document for the total value of the estate was left blank. In his will, then, Jeremiah Hamilton only mentioned his New York City real estate, the contents of his house, some individual items and $3,100 in small bequests. Any other property, real or personal, was to be shared between his children. This must have included bank accounts, cash on hand, and, particularly for someone who worked on Wall Street, shares, bonds and other financial instruments, none of which are mentioned specifically in the will. The family retained possession of the East Twenty-Ninth and Greenwich Street houses into the twentieth century. None of his sons or daughters appears to have been under any necessity to make their own way in the world— Jeremiah Hamilton had provided more than enough for Eliza Jane Hamilton and her children to enjoy comfortable lives.[20]

It was an anticlimactic end to what had been by any standards an extraordinary trail-blazing life. That it should all vanish after one generation was not surprising—dynasties in American life are the exception, not the rule. What remains more puzzling is that Jeremiah Hamilton's story disappeared even quicker than did the money. He challenges still-received ideas about New York black life and particularly our understanding of black economic life.

In one of the seminal texts of the African American canon, James Weldon Johnson's *Autobiography of an Ex-Coloured Man* (1912), the protagonist twice experiences New York City. When he first arrives, identifying himself as a black man, the narrator plunges into an underground world of gambling in the Tenderloin district, a world in which gamblers passively accept the fact that fate, something beyond their control, determines the outcome of their endeavors. On his return, now as a white, the ex-colored man jumps with even more enthusiasm into the marketplace, opening a savings account, investing in real estate, and carefully calculating the increase in his fortunes. No longer acquiescent, but now actively shaping his own destiny, he delights in his new entrepreneurial guise, exclaiming, "What an interesting and absorbing game is money making!" In Johnson's telling, the allegedly value-free marketplace was marked by racial and cultural barriers, obstacles that prevented his protagonist from becoming a bourgeois economic man until he had shucked off his black skin.[21]

And yet, right from the moment of freedom in New York City, there were blacks shouldering aside the barriers placed in their path and jumping with enthusiasm into the marketplace. They did not always thrive, but they most certainly tried—and very occasionally they succeeded beyond any possible expectation. But this history of excited black participation in the economy, of doing something other than huckstering on the street, has been ignored, erased from the story of black New York. Even James Weldon Johnson, well-read and knowledgeable about the history of African Americans in New York, publishing a few years later the classic *Black Manhattan* (1930), clearly never came across the Prince of Darkness—and in this he was hardly alone. Three-quarters of a century before Johnson published the fictional *Autobiography of an Ex-Coloured Man* in 1912, the real-life figure of Jeremiah G. Hamilton could well have uttered: "What an interesting and absorbing game is money making!" This black man did not just open a savings account; he himself behaved like a bank, lending thousands of dollars to whites. He owned ships, he traded in shares, he bought and sold real estate, and he was Wall Street's first black millionaire. James McCune Smith, Frederick Douglass and others suggested that Hamilton paid too high a price for business success, had indeed shucked off his skin and become an ex-colored man. But that was not how most New Yorkers viewed him.

It was not just that Jeremiah Hamilton succeeded on Wall Street, but more the large style he exhibited as he cut a swath through the big end of town. There was nothing timid or deferential about him. He never believed in turning the other cheek, and that is one of his most appealing features. Hamilton always gave better than he got. When Justice Merritt struck Hamilton with his cane, the black broker swung back at him with a rung seized from a passing cart. When two white men had him arrested late at night, he retaliated, arranging to have the police drag his accusers out of bed before dawn and held in a cell until they could raise a hefty sum for bail. You crossed Hamilton at your peril. To be sure, very occasionally he did have to defer to the madness of New York's racial situation. When the mob came banging on his front door looking to hang him, he hightailed it over the back fence. Mostly, though, he met any challenge head on. We have no idea how much, if any, pleasure Hamilton took from his behavior, but the choking resentment and disgust with which the antiquarian Charles Haswell related the black broker's ostentatious desegregation of Delmonico's and his brazen insistence on being treated the same as a white man while he went about his business suggest it must have involved moments of intense satisfaction. He reminds me of nothing so much as some of the Pantheon of Black Heroes, folk figures who emerged at the end of the nineteenth century and who reversed the normal structures of American power and prestige. Often these hard men were killers, merciless as they destroyed their white adversaries.[22] Hamilton used the fine print in legal documents instead of a razor, but his intent and attitude were much the same. Doubtless, the man himself would have hated such a comparison. He would have preferred that I liken him to a Vanderbilt, a Carnegie or an Astor. And he would have had a point. In the end, Jeremiah Hamilton took New Yorkers on at their own game and beat them at it.

What, then, is left to say? For mine, the particular combination of words used in one of the notices of Hamilton's death—"The notorious colored capitalist long identified with commercial enterprises in this city is dead and buried"—remains as astonishing as anything published in New York in the nineteenth century. It should stand as his epitaph. Although unfriendly, this testimony still says something important about Jeremiah Hamilton, and, by hinting at a now-forgotten history, it reveals something surprising about Gotham itself. Has there ever been another occasion when someone has considered a black man to be synonymous with New York commerce? The Prince of Darkness was indeed a remarkable man, and it would be some time before New York City would see his like again. Perhaps it never has.

ACKNOWLEDGMENTS

Sydney is a long way from New York—about 10,000 miles, some 24 hours traveling from the moment the plane's wheels leave the ground in the southern hemisphere. I loathe the flying. Most trips, as the plane bounces all over the sky above Nadi or Denver, I end up wondering why the hell I can't write a book where an archival trip means a half-hour bus ride. But I know the answer, even as I sit white-knuckled in a metal coffin at 38,000 feet. Although it is a minority position, (mind you, still handy for needling both Australian and American colleagues), writing about the society in which I live would lead me to a very quick intellectual death. Perversely, then, I also am fond of all that distance between New York and Sydney.

For all that, living on the other side of the world from the sources does create the odd logistical problem. Money helps to overcome them. For the last quarter of a century, the Australian Research Council has funded me in an extremely generous fashion. An ARC Professorial Fellowship for "The Making of Black Manhattan" and an ARC Discovery grant for "The Prince of Darkness" paid for research trips, computers, and relief from teaching. I am extremely grateful. I shudder to think how much longer this book would have taken and how different it would have ended up looking without this support.

For some time as I pursued Jeremiah G. Hamilton I was uncertain whether this could be a book or should be simply an essay. A

dinner at Leon and Rhoda Litwack's house in Berkeley where they as
well as Dick Hutson, Cornelia Levine, Ann Litwack, Waldo Martin,
and Kathy Moran convinced me it had to be a book. Conversation
moved on very quickly to the more interesting issue of how to cast
the movie.

As with just about every word I have published, this book was
written in Sydney. Most of the research, though, was carried out in
the United States, and I must thank a number of libraries and repositories for their gracious help. The Municipal Archives of the City of
New York is a treasure trove of the city's history; for thirty years
now Ken Cobb and his staff have gone out of their way to facilitate
my research and I am extremely grateful for their help. I have been
frequenting the New-York Historical Society for even longer. Reading the original newspapers in their library is so much more pleasant
than going blind staring at out-of-focus microfilm and the NYHS's
holdings of New York newspapers are terrific. I thank the staff in the
library for their help and kindnesses over decades. I also thank the
staff at the Dutchess County Clerk's Office, Poughkeepsie, Green-
Wood Cemetery Archives, the newspaper section in the Library of
Congress, National Archives and Record Administration, Northeast
Region, New York City, New York County Clerk's Office, New York
Society Library, New York Public Library, the Beinecke Library at
Yale University and the Widener Library at Harvard University.

My department at the University of Sydney can be an exhilarating place to work and I am grateful to all my colleagues. In particular I would like to thank Thomas Adams, Barbara Caine, Marco
Duranti, Andrew Fitzmaurice and Glenda Sluga for commenting on
chapters. Mike McDonnell took time out from the finishing off of
his own manuscript to read critically the first half of this book. Iain
McCalman, a great friend and supporter, commented astutely on
three chapters. I owe Andrew Fitzmaurice a very large debt—conveniently, his office is next door to mine, and he helped me consider-
ably as I tried to figure out the importance of Jeremiah Hamilton's
library and reading habits. It's nice having smart and generous colleagues. Similarly, Jennifer Milam, my friend in Art History, as well
as getting me lost driving all over Virginia (how two people with as
many degrees as we have between us, as well as a GPS system, could

miss Montpelier by 60 miles still beggars my mind), helped me understand the significance of some of Hamilton's reading. And while on the subject of my university colleagues: it is reassuring to work at a place where the Dean, Duncan Ivison, not only values and supports research, but also is still a very active scholar himself.

Elsewhere Clare Corbould, Chris Dixon, Tim Minchin, Michael Ondaatje, Trevor Burnard, and in England Nick Gebhardt, have substantially contributed to the intellectual environment in which I work. The same is also true of Richard Bosworth, even if he has now fled to Oxford, David Goodman, Ian Tyrrell and Richard Waterhouse. All four have been terrific friends for well over a quarter of a century. Unfortunately two other long-term friends, John Salmond and Graham White, both of whom were stalwart supporters of my work, and in the case of Graham a collaborator on three books, died while this book was being written. Their deaths have made my world a much less pleasurable place.

I have also had help from the United States. Ira Berlin read several chapters with his customary sharp eye and gave his usual generous encouragement. George A. Thompson Jr. supplied me, very kindly, with several stories from New York newspapers that I had not seen. Over the last few years Jim Grossman, Earl Lewis, Lynda Kaplan, Richard Rabinowitz, Joyce Seltzer, Ben Urwand, David Waldstreicher and Matt Wittmann have suffered through too many stories about Jeremiah Hamilton. For a decade Stephen Robertson was my friend, colleague and collaborator at the University of Sydney; now he is my friend, colleague and collaborator at George Mason University. Conversations with him have shaped significantly everything I have written for nigh on a decade and a half. Not only is David Blight a font of wisdom on nineteenth century America and a great dinner conversationalist, but he has also been responsible, very generously, for lining me up with both my agent and my New York research assistant. I am very grateful to all of these colleagues.

As well as smart colleagues my university has allowed me to work with smart students, usually much more so than I am. But I am not stupid—I employ them as research assistants. Ivan Coates, Sarah Dunstan and Deirdre O'Connell, as I expected, have been creative and imaginative as well as diligent. In New York, Chris McKay has been a wonderful researcher. She managed to find things in places I had no idea existed. I am very fortunate to have Wendy Strothman as my agent. Ably assisted by Lauren MacLeod, she has been impressively effective and a pleasure to deal with. From the moment she read the proposal, my editor, Elisabeth Dyssegaard, has championed this book. I am grateful to her and Laura Apperson, Donna Cherry and Sarah Vogelsong at St. Martin's Press for converting my manuscript into a book.

I very seldom speak in the United States. As a result there is an idiosyncratic Commonwealth tinge to the audiences on whom I have inflicted my thoughts on Jeremiah Hamilton. I have given talks about him at the University of Sydney, the University of Auckland, Cambridge University and Oxford University. I would like to thank Jennifer Milam, Paul Taillon, Barry Reay, Michael O'Brien, Tony Badger and Stephen Tuck for organizing those occasions and the audiences for their comments.

And now, a slightly more idiosyncratic paragraph: For years I have spent much of every April and October on the Upper West Side doing research. The Milburn Hotel, near 76th and Broadway, has been a home away from home. I'd like to thank the staff, particularly Adam usually manning the front desk as I stagger in late at night after 24 hours of traveling from Sydney, for making me welcome. More often than not, I end up eating across Broadway at Viand, another place that treats me well, and where at the weekend, if you are lucky, you can find David Blight eating breakfast. Near a quarter of a century ago, I admitted in the acknowledgments that my first book "could never have been completed without the aid of various drugs, among which nicotine, caffeine, and Springsteen must be named." Now I have grown older and, although laying no claim to being much wiser, am probably more sensible. I no longer smoke cigarettes—or anything else, come to that. I still drink copious quantities of coffee, though rather less than used to be the case. And I remain a Springsteen addict. Unusually perhaps, I write with headphones on, music playing at not quite sonic boom levels. I listen to an eclectic range of music, everything from Puccini to Miles Davis and Kendrick Lamar. But Springsteen is the constant, the artist I turn to when the blank screen terrifies me the most.

This book is dedicated in part to three friends. Glenda Sluga's intellectually lively presence, her willingness to gossip and talk about our different projects, has been a vital part of my life for more years than either of us care to mention. I have known Stephen Garton for even longer. My erstwhile golfing partner before he became dean and then provost may be off running the joint, but still finds time for his aging friend (thanks to his assistant Darren Burdon—my life would be so much more pleasant if I too could have a Darren to organize things for me). Stephen read every chapter within days of it being finished and saved me from any number of excesses. So too did Chris Hilliard. Chris also patiently untangled messy paragraphs and discreetly eliminated some of my more egregious infelicities in passages I e-mailed to him late at night when I was at my wits' end. I am grateful to all three and have no idea how I could manage without them.

Finally—yes, Virginia, there is an end to these acknowledgments and it is in sight—there are those who have never read a sentence of my prose. And never will. There are things more important than books as they remind me most days. Lexie Macdonald has put up with me, particularly me writing books, for a long time. Her shrewd judgments on all manner of things have influenced me much more than she realizes; I thank her for years of patient support and love. And lastly, there is our son, Macdonald White, the apple of the eye of both of his parents. Watching him grow up over the last decade and a half has been a real pleasure. I envy the elegance and power of his golf swing, tolerate his attempts to convince me that the travails of Manchester United are of earth-shattering importance, and am grateful for his presence in our lives. This book is for Mac as well.

NOTES

INTRODUCTION: INVISIBLE MAN

1. *New York Herald,* January 6, 1841.
2. *Times Picayune,* August 8, 1839; Herman Melville, "Bartleby," in *Billy Budd, Sailor and Other Stories* (Harmondsworth: Penguin Books, 1970), 60. "Bartleby" was first published in 1853.
3. *New York Herald,* January 6, 1841.
4. *Morning Courier and New-York Enquirer,* March 27, 1830 (supplement).
5. *Frederick Douglass' Paper,* March 18, 1852.
6. *Pacific Appeal,* July 31, 1875. According to one historian: "*Millionaire* was a term coined about 1845 to describe the wealth of John Jacob Astor and about ten others who qualified. By 1860, there were over a hundred persons deserving the title." See Steve Fraser, *Every Man a Speculator: A History of Wall Street in American Life* (New York: HarperCollins, 2005), 79. It was used a bit earlier than that to describe Astor. See, for example, *New York Spectator,* September 25, 1837. As well, following Hamilton's death editors sometimes used the word in their captions on the story. See "Death of a Colored Millionaire," in *Hudson Evening Register,* May 20, 1875; "Death of a Millionaire Colored Man," in *Daily British Colonist* (British Columbia), June 12, 1875.
7. *Courier and New-York Enquirer,* August 5, 1836; *New York Herald,* December 9, 1840; *New York Sun,* August 5, 1843.
8. *Subterranean,* August 12, 1843.
9. *New York Herald,* October 10, 1836; *New York Sun,* October 10, 1843.
10. *Sunday Flash,* October 3, 1841; *New York Herald,* December 22, 1843.
11. Ernest A. Wiltse, *Gold Rush Steamers of the Pacific* (Lawrence, MA: Quarterman Publications, Inc., 1976 [1938]), 203.
12. Adrian Cook, *The Armies of the Streets: The New York City Draft Riots of 1863* (Lexington: University Press of Kentucky, 1974), 134; Iver Bernstein, *The New York City Draft Riots: Their Significance for American Society and Politics in the Age of the Civil War* (New York: Oxford University Press, 1990), 35–36.
13. John Stauffer, ed., *The Works of James McCune Smith: Black Intellectual and Abolitionist* (New York: Oxford University Press, 2006), 90.

14. Henry Louis Gates Jr. and Evelyn Brooks Higginbotham, eds., *African American National Biography*, 8 vols. (New York: Oxford University Press, 2008).

15. *Commercial Advertiser,* June 19, 1828; *New York Herald,* December 22, 1843; *New York Morning Express,* December 22, 1843; *True Sun,* December 22, 1843.

16. *Cincinnati Enquirer,* May 30, 1875; *Harper's Bazaar,* June 19, 1875, p. 395.

17. *New York Herald,* July 14, 1836; *Harper's Bazaar,* June 19, 1875, p. 395.

18. I have been influenced by the approach taken in such classic books as Natalie Zemon Davis, *The Return of Martin Guerre* (Cambridge: Harvard University Press, 1983); Alfred F. Young, *The Shoemaker and the Tea Party: Memory and the American Revolution* (Boston: Beacon Press, 1999); Alfred F. Young, *Masquerade: The Life and Times of Deborah Sampson, Continental Soldier* (New York: Knopf, 2004); Linda Colley, *The Ordeal of Elizabeth Marsh: A Woman in World History* (New York: Pantheon Books, 2007). In all these cases, though, there was some sort of memoir or oral history of the central figure published almost contemporaneously. Nothing of the sort exists for *Prince of Darkness.* In that respect, this book bears a resemblance to some of the archivally rich work that has been done on slavery. See James H. Sweet, *Domingo Alvares, African Healing, and the Intellectual History of the Atlantic World* (Chapel Hill: University of North Carolina Press, 2011); Rebecca J. Scott and Jean M. Hébrard, *Freedom Papers: An Atlantic Odyssey in the Age of Emancipation* (Cambridge: Harvard University Press, 2012).

19. See, for example, Shane White, "The Gold Diggers of 1833: African American Dreams, Fortune-Telling, Treasure-Seeking and Policy in Antebellum New York City," *Journal of Social History* 47 (Spring 2014): 673–95; Shane White, "Freedom's First Con: African Americans and Changing Notes in Antebellum New York City," *Journal of the Early Republic* 34 (Fall 2014): 385–409.

20. *Joseph Vargas v. Jeremiah G. Hamilton,* Equity Case Files of the U.S. Circuit Court for the Southern District of New York, 1791–1846, National Archives Microfilm Publications M884, Roll 15, x-116.

21. "Master of the Universe" was used famously in Tom Wolfe, *The Bonfire of the Vanities* (New York: Farrar, Straus and Giroux, 1987).

CHAPTER ONE: HAITI, 1828

1. *Commercial Advertiser,* June 24, 1828.

2. Rayford W. Logan, *The Diplomatic Relations of the United States with Haiti 1776–1891* (Chapel Hill: University of North Carolina Press, 1941), 194; Charles Mackenzie, *Notes on Haiti, Made During a Residence in That Republic,* 2 vols. (London: Henry Colburn and Richard Bentley, 1830), 2:179.

3. Laurent Dubois, *Haiti: The Aftershocks of History* (New York: Metropolitan Books, 2012), 19.

4. Dubois, *Haiti,* 21.

5. The scholarship on the Haitian Revolution has mushroomed in recent years. I have been most informed by Laurent Dubois, *A Colony of Citizens: Revolution and Slave Emancipation in the French Caribbean,*

1787–1804 (Chapel Hill: University of North Carolina Press for the Omu-
hundro Institute, 2004); Laurent Dubois, *Avengers of the New World:
The Story of the Haitian Revolution* (Cambridge: Harvard University
Press, 2004); Jeremy Popkin, *You Are All Free: The Haitian Revolution
and the Abolition of Slavery* (New York: Cambridge University Press,
2010); Ashli White, *Encountering Revolution: Haiti and the Making of
the Early Republic* (Baltimore: Johns Hopkins University Press, 2010);
Thomas Bender, Laurent Dubois, and Richard Rabinowitz, eds., *Revolution!: The Atlantic World Reborn* (London: Giles, 2011).

6. Quoted in David Brion Davis, *Inhuman Bondage: The Rise and Fall of
Slavery in the New World* (New York: Oxford University Press, 2006),
169.

7. Logan, *Diplomatic Relations,* 152–53.

8. Chris Dixon, *African America and Haiti: Emigration and Black Nation-
alism in the Nineteenth Century* (Westport, CT: Greenwood Press, 2000),
39–46. See also Sara Fanning, *Caribbean Crossing: African Americans
and the Haitian Emigration Movement* (New York: New York University
Press, 2015).

9. J[ohn] Benwell, *An Englishman's Travels in America: His Observations
of Life and Manners in the Free and Slave States* (London: Binns and
Goodwin, 1853), 195.

10. Logan, *Diplomatic Relations,* 195.

11. Mackenzie, *Notes on Haiti,* 1:4, 7; James Franklin, *The Present State
of Hayti* (London: John Murray, 1828), 274–75. For Mackenzie being a
black man, see Fanning, *Caribbean Crossing,* 13–14.

12. *Commercial Advertiser,* June 19, 1828.

13. Franklin, *Present State of Hayti,* 274; Mackenzie, *Notes on Haiti,* 1:31.

14. *Commercial Advertiser,* June 24, 1828; *Freedom's Journal,* November 14,
1828.

15. Stephen Mihm, *A Nation of Counterfeiters: Capitalists, Con Men, and
the Making of the United States* (Cambridge: Harvard University Press,
2007); St. Clair McKelway, "Mister 880," in *Reporting at Wit's End:
Tales from* The New Yorker (New York: Bloomsbury, 2010), 138.

16. Mihm, *Nation of Counterfeiters,* 3, 289; Michael O'Malley, "Specie and
Species: Race and the Money Question in Nineteenth-Century America,"
American Historical Review 99 (April 1994), 369–95 at 374; Michael
O'Malley, "Rags, Blacking, and Paper Soldiers," in *Face Value: The En-
twined Histories of Money & Race in America* (Chicago: University of
Chicago Press, 2012), 105. See also David Henkin, *City Reading: Written
Words and Public Spaces in Antebellum New York* (New York: Columbia
University Press, 1998), 137–65.

17. Mihm, *Nation of Counterfeiters,* 239. On this point, see also O'Malley,
"Specie and Species," 374–75.

18. Allan Pinkerton, *Thirty Years a Detective* (St. Louis: Historical Publishing Company, 1884), 518; quoted in Mihm, *Nation of Counterfeiters,*
233.

19. *New York Evening Post,* June 25, 1828.

20. Dubois, *Haiti,* 102.

21. *Commercial Advertiser,* June 24, 1828.

22. *Commercial Advertiser,* June 24, 1828. As well, a month or two earlier a
Boston "artist" had been asked "to make dies for striking Haytien coin."

The engraver refused, and "information of the proceedings of these men was forthwith sent to Hayti." See *Commercial Advertiser*, July 3, 1828.

23. Mihm, *Nation of Counterfeiters*, 66–102.

24. *National Advocate*, January 18, 1828; *Commercial Advertiser*, June 24, 1828.

25. *New York Evening Post*, July 31, 1827; *New York Evening Post*, May 13, 1826; *New York Spectator*, June 13, 1828. There are many ways to estimate the value of 1828 dollars in today's dollars. Throughout this book, I have employed a commonly used indicator based on the unskilled wage. See http://www.measuringworth.com/uscompare/index.php.

26. *Commercial Advertiser*, June 24, 1828.

27. *Freedom's Journal*, November 14, 1828; *Commercial Advertiser*, June 24, 1828.

28. *Freedom's Journal*, November 14, 1828.

29. *Commercial Advertiser*, June 24, 1828.

30. *Commercial Advertiser*, June 19, 1828.

31. *New York Evening Post*, June 21, 1828; *New York Morning Courier*, June 23, 1828; *Commercial Advertiser*, June 24, 1828.

32. On Hewlett, see Shane White, *Stories of Freedom in Black New York* (Cambridge, MA: Harvard University Press, 2002), 131–34, 153.

33. *Commercial Advertiser*, June 24, 1828.

34. *New York Gazette and General Advertiser*, June 27, 1828; *New York Evening Post*, June 25, 1828; *New York Spectator*, July 1, 1828.

35. *Commercial Advertiser*, July 3, 1828; *Daily Advertiser*, reprinted in *Freedom's Journal*, June 27, 1828; *Commercial Advertiser*, June 19, 1828; *National Gazette*, June 26, 1828.

36. *Freedom's Journal*, March 16, 1827. On *Freedom's Journal* more generally, see Jacqueline Bacon, Freedom's Journal: *The First African-American Newspaper* (Lanham, MD: Lexington Books, 2007); Winston James, *The Struggles of John Brown Russwurm: The Life and Writings of a Pan-Africanist Pioneer, 1799–1851* (New York: New York University Press, 2010).

37. James, *Struggles of John Brown Russwurm*, 19–21, 131–34.

38. *Freedom's Journal*, March 16, 1827; *Freedom's Journal*, March 23, 1827.

39. *Freedom's Journal*, June 27, 1828; *Freedom's Journal*, July 4, 1828.

40. *Freedom's Journal*, August 29, 1828.

41. *Freedom's Journal*, November 14, 1828.

42. *Freedom's Journal*, December 5, 1828.

43. *Morning Courier and New-York Enquirer*, June 27, 1829.

44. *Freedom's Journal*, January 31, 1829.

45. Chas. H. Haswell, *Reminiscences of an Octogenarian of the City of New York (1816 to 1860)* (New York: Harper & Brothers, 1896), 490–91; *Morning Courier and New-York Enquirer*, August 5, 1836; *New York Herald*, December 10, 1839; *New York Herald*, December 9, 1840.

CHAPTER TWO: MOVING TO NEW YORK

1. Frederick Douglass, *My Bondage and My Freedom* (1855) in *Frederick Douglass: Autobiographies* (New York: Library of America, 1994), 140.

2. For the best account of New York City in these years, see Edwin G. Burrows and Mike Wallace, *Gotham: A History of New York City to 1898*

(New York: Oxford University Press, 1999), 409–586. On traveler accounts, see Bayrd Still, *Mirror for Gotham: New York as Seen by Contemporaries from Dutch Days to the Present* (New York: Fordham University Press, 1994 [1956]), 78–124.

3. See, for example, *Theophilus Peck v. Jeremiah Hamilton,* filed July 12, 1830, Common Pleas, 1830-#771, New York County Clerk's Office, New York (henceforth NYCC); *Augustus A. Cammann, Nathaniel R. Hosack and Henry Bohlen v. Jeremiah G. Hamilton,* filed October 23, 1833, Superior Court, 1833-#147, NYCC; *Thomas Woodward v. Jeremiah G. Hamilton,* filed July 25, 1834, Chancery Court, BM W-2307, NYCC; *Theophilus Peck v. Jeremiah Hamilton,* filed December 4, 1833, Chancery Court, BM P439, NYCC; *Lois H. Judson v. Jeremiah Hamilton,* filed October 24, 1834, Supreme Court, 1834 H-107, NYCC.

4. *New York Daily Tribune,* May 22, 1875; *Jonathan Leech v. Jeremiah G. Hamilton,* filed February 23, 1836, Chancery Court, BM 555-L, NYCC.

5. *New York Evening Post,* February 15, 1833; *New York Passenger Lists, 1820–1957* at ancestry.com.

6. *Freedom's Journal,* July 4, 1828; *Commercial Advertiser,* June 19, 1828; *American Mercury,* July 1, 1828.

7. *Freedom's Journal,* November 14, 1828.

8. *Pacific Appeal,* July 31, 1875.

9. *Leech v. Hamilton; New York Herald,* August 10, 1836.

10. *People v. James Bergen, Jeremiah G. Hamilton & Richard Sutton,* filed August 13, 1843, District Attorney's Indictment Papers, Municipal Archives of the City of New York, New York; *Daily Plebeian,* August 5, 1843.

11. *Daily Advertiser,* July 23, 1829; *National Advocate,* July 14, 1826.

12. *Morning Courier and New-York Enquirer,* March 15, 1833. For background on the New York African American population in these years, see Shane White, *Stories of Freedom in Black New York* (Cambridge: Harvard University Press, 2002), 7–67.

13. On Downing, see John H. Hewitt, "Mr. Downing and His Oyster House: The Life and Good Works of an African-American Entrepreneur," *New York History* 74 (July 1993): 229–52; George T. Downing, "A Sketch of the Life and Times of Thomas Downing," *A. M. E. Church Review* (April 1887): 402–10.

14. Abram C. Dayton, *Last Days of Knickerbocker Life in New York* (New York: George W. Harlan, 1882), 101–4; Martin Robison Delany, *The Condition, Elevation, Emigration, and Destiny of the Colored People of the United States* (Philadelphia: Published by the Author, 1852), 103–4.

15. *New York Evening Post,* September 26, 1855.

16. *Chicago Defender,* July 29, 1922, p. 14; *New York Amsterdam News,* February 22, 1928, p. 3.

17. *New York Tribune,* October 7, 1845.

18. *New York Tribune,* February 20, 1852; *New York Tribune,* September 27, 1853.

19. *New York Herald,* July 14, 1836; *New York Sun,* August 6, 1836.

20. Rockaway, Morris, New Jersey, *1850 United States Federal Census,* ancestry.com; New York Ward 21, *1870 United States Federal Census,* ancestry.com.

21. New York Death Certificate 206996, Municipal Archives of the City of New York; Lot 14972, Section 158, Green-Wood Cemetery Archives, Brooklyn, New York.

22. *Philadelphia Inquirer,* May 20, 1875; *Cincinnati Enquirer,* May 30, 1875.

23. *New York Daily Tribune,* May 22, 1875; *Albany Evening Journal,* May 30, 1875; *Albany Evening Journal,* June 5, 1875.

24. New York City, *1880 United States Federal Census,* ancestry.com.

25. Record for Evelina Shepard Hamilton, May 15, 1895, *U.S. Passport Applications, 1795–1925,* ancestry.com; Record for Evelina Shepard Hamilton, January 17, 1898, *U.S. Passport Applications, 1795–1925,* ancestry. com.

26. Manhattan, New York, *1900 United States Federal Census,* ancestry. com; Orangetown, Rockland, New York, *1910 United States Federal Census,* ancestry.com; Orangetown, Rockland, New York, *1920 United States Federal Census,* ancestry.com.

27. Laurent Dubois, *Haiti: The Aftershocks of History* (New York: Metropolitan Books, 2012), 93–94; *National Advocate,* June 20, 1828.

28. Arthur and Elizabeth Odell Sheehan, *Pierre Toussaint: A Citizen of Old New York* (New York: P. J. Kennedy & Sons, 1955); Douglas Walter Bristol Jr., *Knights of the Razor: Black Barbers in Slavery and Freedom* (Baltimore: Johns Hopkins University Press, 2009), 34–39; Thomas L. Nichols, *Forty Years of American Life,* 2 vols. (London: John Maxwell and Company, 1864), 2:240; Thomas J. Shelley, "Toussaint, Pierre," in Henry Louis Gates Jr. and Evelyn Brooks Higginbotham, eds., *African American National Biography,* 8 vols. (New York: Oxford University Press, 2008), 7:623–24.

29. Although it may very well look like I am trying to have it both ways, in the end I think he came from Haiti, that he and his family fled, and that he spent a number of years in Richmond, Virginia.

30. On barbering, see Bristol, *Knights of the Razor,* 32–33, 77, 104.

31. Tom Reiss, *The Black Count: Glory, Revolution, Betrayal, and the Real Count of Monte Cristo* (New York: Crown Publishers, 2012), 36–40; Rebecca J. Scott and Jean M. Hébrard, *Freedom Papers: An Atlantic Odyssey in the Age of Emancipation* (Cambridge: Harvard University Press, 2012), 20–23.

32. See Scott and Hébrard, *Freedom Papers,* 47–50.

33. Record for Evelina Shepard Hamilton, May 15, 1895, *U.S. Passport Applications, 1795–1925;* Record for Evelina Shepard Hamilton, January 17, 1898, *U.S. Passport Applications, 1795–1925; Philadelphia Inquirer,* May 20, 1875.

34. *New York Tribune,* May 22, 1875; *Albany Evening Journal,* June 5, 1875.

35. *Lois H. Hudson v. Jeremiah Hamilton,* filed October 24, 1834, Supreme Court, 1834 H-107, NYCC; *Augustus A. Cammann, Nathaniel R. Hosack and Henry Bohlen v. Jeremiah G. Hamilton,* filed October 23, 1833, Superior Court, 1833 #147, NYCC; *Eugene Grosset v. Jeremiah G. Hamilton,* filed March 19, 1834, Superior Court, 1834-368, NYCC.

36. *New York Herald,* June 25, 1836; *Arthur Tappan v. Jeremiah G. Hamilton,* filed October 30, 1834, Chancery Court, BM T-103, NYCC.

37. Margaret G. Myers, *The New York Money Market* (New York: Columbia University Press, 1931), 41.

38. Jonathan Levy, *Freaks of Fortune: The Emerging World of Capitalism and Risk in America* (Cambridge: Harvard University Press, 2012), 2. As well, I have benefited from Sharon Ann Murphy, *Investing in Life: Insurance in Antebellum America* (Baltimore: Johns Hopkins University Press, 2010); Eric Wertheimer, *Underwriting: The Poetics of Insurance in America, 1722–1872* (Stanford: Stanford University Press, 2006).

39. C. Bradford Mitchell, *A Premium on Progress: An Outline History of the American Marine Insurance Market, 1820–1970* (New York: Newcomen Society in North America, 1970), 7–18.

40. Marcus Rediker, *The Slave Ship: A Human History* (New York: Viking, 2007), 240–41.

41. *New York Spectator,* June 13, 1828.

42. *New York Spectator,* June 13, 1828. The report in the *Spectator* was taken from the *Commercial Advertiser.*

43. *New York Spectator,* June 13, 1828.

44. *Jeremiah G. Hamilton v. American Insurance Co.,* filed June 8, 1830, Chancery Court, BM 408-H, NYCC; *Theophilus Peck v. Jeremiah Hamilton,* filed December 4, 1833, Chancery Court, BM P439, NYCC; *Arthur Tappan v. Jeremiah G. Hamilton,* filed October 30, 1834, Chancery Court, BM T-103, NYCC.

45. Mitchell, *Premium on Progress,* 18; *New York Spectator,* October 24, 1836.

46. *Morning Courier and New-York Enquirer,* October 19, 1836; *The Sun,* October 19, 1836; *Journal of Commerce,* October 22, 1836; *New York Spectator,* October 24, 1836. See also *Joseph Tinkham & Simeon Hart v. The Sea Insurance Company,* filed November 3, 1836, New York Superior Court, NYCC.

CHAPTER THREE: THE GREAT FIRE, 1835

1. As with a frightening number of subjects in nineteenth-century New York history, by far the best short account of the fire is Edwin G. Burrows and Mike Wallace, *Gotham: A History of New York City to 1898* (New York: Oxford University Press, 1999), 596–601. As well, my account draws heavily on the *Journal of Commerce* and *Mercantile Advertiser,* reprinted in *Albany Evening Journal,* December 19, 1835; *New York Spectator,* December 21, 1835; *Commercial Advertiser,* reprinted in *Albany Evening Journal,* December 22, 1835; *Commercial Advertiser,* reprinted in *Boston Courier,* December 21, 1835; *Courier and Enquirer,* reprinted in *Daily National Intelligencer,* December 22, 1835. For other studies of fire, see Greg Bankoff, Uwe Lübken, and Jordan Sand, eds., *Flammable Cities: Urban Conflagration and the Making of the Modern World* (Madison: University of Wisconsin Press, 2012); Meredith Henne Baker, *The Richmond Theater Fire: Early America's First Great Disaster* (Baton Rouge: Louisiana State University Press, 2012); and, most of all, the exemplary Jane Kamensky, *The Exchange Artist: A Tale of High-Flying Speculation and America's First Banking Collapse* (New York: Viking, 2008).

2. *Commercial Advertiser,* reprinted in *The Globe,* December 21, 1835; Allan Nevins, ed., *The Diary of Philip Hone: 1828–1851,* 2 vols. (New York: Dodd, Mead and Company, 1927), 1:185–90.

3. Nevins, *Diary of Philip Hone*, 1:186; Burrows and Wallace, *Gotham*, 598; *Courier and Enquirer*, reprinted in *Daily National Intelligencer*, December 22, 1835.

4. *Journal of Commerce*, reprinted in *Albany Evening Journal*, December 19, 1835; *Commercial Advertiser*, reprinted in *Albany Evening Journal*, December 22, 1835.

5. Nevins, *Diary of Philip Hone*, 1:185–86; *Journal of Commerce*, reprinted in *Albany Evening Journal*, December 19, 1835; *Commercial Advertiser*, reprinted in *Albany Evening Journal*, December 19, 1835.

6. *New York Spectator*, December 24, 1835; *New York Herald*, May 17, 1836.

7. *Commercial Advertiser*, reprinted in *Albany Evening Journal*, December 19, 1835; *Albany Evening Journal*, December 21, 1835; Burroughs and Wallace, *Gotham*, 598. The best study of the transformation of real estate in New York City remains Elizabeth Blackmar, *Manhattan for Rent, 1785–1850* (Ithaca, NY: Cornell University Press, 1989).

8. Nevins, *Diary of Philip Hone*, 1:189–90; Graham Russell Gao Hodges, *New York City Cartmen, 1667–1850* (New York: New York University Press, 2012 [1986]), 151–52.

9. *Commercial Advertiser*, reprinted in *Daily National Intelligencer*, December 22, 1835; *New York Spectator*, December 21, 1835.

10. Nevins, *Diary of Philip Hone*, 1:189–90.

11. *New York Sun*, March 29, 1839.

12. Bayrd Still, *Mirror for Gotham: New York as Seen by Contemporaries from Dutch Days to the Present* ([orig. pub. 1956] New York: Fordham University Press, 1994), 97.

13. Allan Nevins and Milton Halsey Thomas, eds., *The Diary of George Templeton Strong*, 4 vols. (New York: Macmillan Company, 1952), 1:8, 44, 126, 196.

14. *New York Herald*, March 15, 1836; *New York Mirror*, reprinted in *New York Herald*, June 13, 1836.

15. William Bradford, *An Enquiry How Far the Punishment of Death Is Necessary in Pennsylvania* (Philadelphia: T. Dobson, 1793), 31–32.

16. See, in particular, the excellent Jeremy Popkin, *You Are All Free: The Haitian Revolution and the Abolition of Slavery* (New York: Cambridge University Press, 2010), 2–3, 217–45. The quote is on 244.

17. See Jill Lepore, *New York Burning: Liberty, Slavery, and Conspiracy in Eighteenth-Century Manhattan* (New York: Alfred A. Knopf, 2005).

18. The main source for the Albany fire is "Examination of Bet, Slave of Philip S. Van Rensselaer," November 18, 1793, New York State Library, Albany, New York. The fire and executions received extensive newspaper coverage. See *Albany Register*, November 18, 1793; January 27, 1794; February 3, 1794; February 10, 1794; *American Minerva*, January 6, 1794; January 17, 1794; January 20, 1794. See also Don R. Gerlach, "Black Arson in Albany, November 1793," *Journal of Black Studies* 7 (1977): 301–12.

19. Virtually every issue of New York newspapers in these months carried news of these fires. See, for example, *New York Journal*, November 22, 1796; December 16, 1796; December 27, 1796; December 30, 1796; *Centinel of Freedom*, December 21, 1796; *American Minerva*, December 15, 1796; *Minerva*, September 2, 1797. See also Sara E. Johnson, *The Fear*

of French Negroes: Transcolonial Collaboration in the Revolutionary Americas (Berkeley: University of California Press, 2012).

20. Lewis Morris to his son, December 29, 1796, New York State Library.

21. On freedom, see Shane White, *Stories of Freedom in Black New York* (Cambridge: Harvard University Press, 2002); David N. Gellman, *Emancipating New York: The Politics of Slavery and Freedom, 1777–1827* (Baton Rouge: Louisiana State University Press, 2006).

22. The New York Manumission Society pursued an unprecedented number of owners in court for treating their slaves cruelly in these years. See White, *Stories of Freedom*, 16–20, 39–42.

23. Here I only raise arson, but young blacks were also involved in poisoning or tampering with their owners' food. See White, *Stories of Freedom*, 23.

24. *The People v. Jemima a slave of William Wright,* filed June 21, 1810, District Attorney's Indictment Papers, Municipal Archives of the City of New York (DAIP); *The People v. Charlotte, a Black Girl,* filed June 7, 1811, DAIP; *The People v. Rose, a Black Girl,* filed December 4, 1811, DAIP.

25. Leslie Harris, *In the Shadow of Slavery: African Americans in New York City, 1626–1863* (Chicago: University of Chicago Press, 2003), 113–15; John Stanford, *An Authentic Statement of the Case and Conduct of Rose Butler, Who Was Tried, Convicted, and Executed for the Crime of Arson* (New York: Broderick and Ritter, 1819); *New York Evening Post,* June 11, 1819; Thomas F. De Voe, *The Market Book* (New York: Burt Franklin, 1969 [1862]), 481.

26. *New York Spectator,* January 17, 1823.

27. *The Transcript,* April 13, 1835. On Slam as a slum landlord, see *New York American,* August 15, 1823; *The People v. William Slam,* filed August 16, 1826, DAIP.

28. *Commercial Advertiser,* May 18, 1832.

29. *True Sun,* June 13, 1845; *True Sun,* June 14, 1845. Eugene Sue (1804–1857) was a French novelist whose *Mysteries of Paris* (1843) sold 15,000 copies in New York within weeks of publication. The book pioneered the "mystery and miseries" genre, with panoramic accounts of various cities revealing, often in voyeuristic fashion, "low life." See *Journal of Commerce* (semi-weekly), November 4, 1843.

30. *New York Herald,* September 27, 1839.

31. *Journal of Commerce,* reprinted in *Albany Evening Journal,* December 19, 1835; *Journal of Commerce,* December 23, 1835; George T. Downing, "A Sketch of the Life and Times of Thomas Downing," *A.M.E. Church Review* 408 (April 1887).

32. *Journal of Commerce,* January 1, 1841.

33. *New York Herald,* July 14, 1836.

34. *New York Herald,* July 20, 1836. As we saw in Chapter One, the reward for Hamilton's head in Haiti was only $300, not $10,000.

35. Although not printed until July 20, the letter is dated July 15, the day after Bennett published his attack on the Prince of Darkness. The letter is signed H—in my view Hamilton was its author.

36. *New York Herald,* July 20, 1836.

37. Burrows and Wallace, *Gotham,* 598–99; Nevins, *Diary of Philip Hone,* 1:232–33; *New York Herald,* October 19, 1837.

38. See, for example, *New York Daily Tribune*, July 26, 1864. For twentieth-century black press stories, see *Chicago Defender*, July 29, 1922, p. 14; *New York Amsterdam News*, February 22, 1928, p. 3.

CHAPTER FOUR: BUSINESS

1. *New York Herald*, August 8, 1836.
2. Most of the details included in my reconstruction of the events in this case are taken from the initial court case and a story in the *Sun*. See *Jonathan Leech v. Jeremiah G. Hamilton*, filed February 23, 1836, Chancery Court, BM 555-L, New York County Clerk's Office, New York; *New York Sun*, August 8, 1836.
3. *New York Sun*, August 8, 1836.
4. *Leech v. Hamilton*; *New York Sun*, August 8, 1836.
5. *Leech v. Hamilton*. The *Herald* reported that the *Sandusky*, bound for Havana, had returned for a refit. See *New York Herald*, December 16, 1835.
6. *Leech v. Hamilton*; *New York Sun*, August 8, 1836; *New York Evening Post*, August 19, 1836.
7. T. J. Stiles, *The First Tycoon: The Epic Life of Cornelius Vanderbilt* (New York: Alfred A. Knopf, 2009), 238.
8. *Morning Courier and New-York Enquirer*, August 5, 1836; *Journal of Commerce*, August 6, 1836.
9. *People v. William Thompson*, filed March 12, 1841, District Attorney Indictment Papers, Municipal Archives of the City of New York, New York; John Stauffer, ed., *The Works of James McCune Smith: Black Intellectual and Abolitionist* (New York: Oxford University Press, 2006), 89. For details of the perjury case against Downing, also see *New York Daily Tribune*, February 20, 1852.
10. *New York Times*, August 10, 1836. The editor of the *Journal of Commerce*, the other paper that printed the notice of Hamilton's arrest, specifically stated that the item was not delivered to them by any of the police officers involved in arresting Hamilton. See *Journal of Commerce*, August 10, 1836. Undoubtedly, though, Leech and Johnson were responsible for the story being published.
11. *Morning Courier and New-York Enquirer*, August 5, 1836.
12. *New York Herald*, August 8, 1836.
13. Frank M. O'Brien, *The Story of the Sun: New York: 1833–1928* (New York: D. Appleton and Company, 1928), 1–11. More generally on the advent of the penny press, I have been instructed by Frank Luther Mott, *American Journalism, A History: 1690–1960*, 3rd ed. (New York: Macmillan, 1962); Andie Tucher, *Froth and Scum: Truth, Beauty, Goodness, and the Ax Murder in America's First Mass Medium* (Chapel Hill: University of North Carolina Press, 1994); Matthew Goodman, *The Sun and the Moon: The Remarkable True Account of Hoaxers, Showmen, Dueling Journalists, and Lunar Man-Bats in Nineteenth Century New York* (New York: Basic Books, 2008); Isabelle Lehuu, *Carnival on the Page: Popular Print Media in Antebellum America* (Chapel Hill: University of North Carolina Press, 2000); Christopher B. Daly, *Covering America: A Narrative History of a Nation's Journalism* (Amherst: University of Massachusetts Press, 2012).

14. *New York Sun,* September 2, 1933; *New York Times,* December 22, 1889.
15. O'Brien, *Story of the Sun,* 1–10; *New York Times,* December 22, 1889.
16. O'Brien, *Story of the Sun,* 1–10, 18–19; Daly, *Covering America,* 59–62.
17. Shane White, *Stories of Freedom in Black New York* (Cambridge: Harvard University Press, 2002), 48; O'Brien, *Story of the Sun,* 19.
18. *The American,* June 6, 1820; O'Brien, *Story of the Sun,* 17. For mention of the full-time court reporters employed by the *Morning Courier* and the *Journal of Commerce,* see *Morning Courier and New-York Enquirer,* November 30, 1829.
19. *New York Sun,* September 5, 1833.
20. *New York Sun,* August 21, 1835.
21. O'Brien, *Story of the Sun,* 37–57. On the hoax, see in particular, Goodman, *Sun and the Moon.*
22. *New York Herald,* May 6, 1835. On the *Herald,* see Daly, *Covering America,* 63–64. See also *Memoirs of James Gordon Bennett and His Times by a Journalist* (New York: Stringer & Townsend, 1855).
23. *New York Herald,* February 28, 1837.
24. Allan Nevins, *The Diary of Philip Hone: 1828–1851,* 2 vols. (New York: Dodd, Mead and Company, 1927), 1:195.
25. Goodman, *Sun and the Moon,* 83; quoted in O'Brien, *Story of the Sun,* 62.
26. *New York Sun,* August 6, 1836; *Morning Courier and New-York Enquirer,* August 6, 1836.
27. *New York Sun,* August 6, 1836.
28. *New York Sun,* August 8, 1836.
29. *New York Daily Advertiser,* August 10, 1836; *New York Herald,* August 10, 1836; *New York Times,* August 10, 1836.
30. *Morning Courier and New-York Enquirer,* August 10, 1836; *New York Sun,* August 10, 1836.
31. *New York Herald,* August 10, 1836.
32. *New York Sun,* August 11, 1836.
33. *New York Evening Post,* August 15, 1836.
34. *New York Evening Post,* August 18, 1836; *New York Evening Post,* August 19, 1836.
35. *New York Times,* August 24, 1836; *New York Herald,* August 24, 1836; *New York Spectator,* August 26, 1836; *New York Sun,* August 24, 1836.
36. *New York Spectator,* August 26, 1836.

CHAPTER FIVE: JIM CROW NEW YORK

1. *Freedom's Journal,* April 20, 1827; *Freedom's Journal,* April 27, 1827. On this event see Shane White, "'It Was a Proud Day': African Americans, Festivals, and Parades in the North, 1741–1834," *Journal of American History* 81 (June 1994): 13–50.
2. *Freedom's Journal,* July 6, 1827; *New York Daily Advertiser,* reprinted in *Long Island Star,* July 12, 1827; *Freedom's Journal,* July 13, 1827.
3. *A Memorial Discourse by Reverend Henry Highland Garnet with an Introduction by James McCune Smith, M. D.* (Philadelphia, 1865), 24–26.

4. On the broader process of emancipation in these years, see Shane White, *Stories of Freedom in Black New York* (Cambridge: Harvard University Press, 2002), 7–67.

5. *New York Enquirer,* August 10, 1827. For a similar complaint, see *Morning Courier and New-York Enquirer,* March 27, 1830 (supplement). For an account of the importance of black street life in these years, see Shane White and Graham White, *Stylin': African American Expressive Culture from Its Beginnings to the Zoot Suit* (Ithaca, NY: Cornell University Press, 1998), 85–124.

6. *National Advocate,* June 21, 1823.

7. *New York Herald,* October 29, 1835.

8. *Montreal Gazette,* reprinted in *New York Evening Post,* July 22, 1829; Henry Bradshaw Fearon, *Sketches of America: A Journey of Five Thousand Miles Through the Eastern and Western States of America* (London: Longman, Hurst, Rees, Orme, and Brown, 1818), 58–60; J. S. Buckingham, *The Slave States of America,* 2 vols. (New York: Negro Universities Press, 1968 [1842]), 2:112.

9. For white disruption of services, see, for example, *Journal of Commerce,* March 3, 1840; *Journal of Commerce,* April 28, 1840; *New York Sun,* February 21, 1842.

10. [Thomas Hamilton], *Men and Manners in America,* 2 vols. (Edinburgh: William Blackwood and London: T. Cadell, 1834), 1:96–101.

11. *New York Daily Express,* January 26, 1843.

12. *New York Courier,* reprinted in *New York Morning Express,* September 4, 1846.

13. *New York Herald,* August 26, 1843; *New York Herald,* February 23, 1839.

14. Ira Rosenwaike, *Population History of New York City* (Syracuse, NY: Syracuse University Press, 1972), 36.

15. Edwin G. Burrows and Mike Wallace, *Gotham: A History of New York City to 1898* (New York: Oxford University Press, 1999), 565; *New York Daily Express,* September 2, 1840; quoted in Burrows and Wallace, *Gotham,* 565.

16. *New York Times,* May 26, 1837; *Colored American,* June 10, 1837.

17. *Journal of Commerce,* November 19, 1840; *Journal of Commerce,* January 1, 1841.

18. See Craig D. Townsend, *Faith in Their Own Color: Black Episcopalians in Antebellum New York City* (New York: Columbia University Press, 2005). Historians have barely mentioned the incident involving Thomas Downing, for reasons that elude me. For a more general account of segregation on public transport, see Blair L. M. Kelley, *Right to Ride: Streetcar Boycotts and African American Citizenship in the Era of* Plessy v. Ferguson (Chapel Hill: University of North Carolina Press, 2010).

19. *Journal of Commerce,* December 31, 1840; *Commercial Advertiser,* December 31, 1840; *New York Daily Express,* December 31, 1840; *New York Sun,* February 11, 1841. See also *People v. William Skirving,* January 13, 1841, District Attorney's Indictment Papers, Municipal Archives of the City of New York, New York.

20. *New York Daily Express,* December 31, 1840; *Commercial Advertiser,* December 31, 1840; *Journal of Commerce,* January 1, 1841; *New York Herald,* December 31, 1840.

21. *New York Daily Express,* January 4, 1841.

22. *New York Daily Express,* February 11, 1841; *Journal of Commerce,* February 11, 1841; *New York Sun,* February 11, 1841.

23. *New York Daily Express,* February 11, 1841; *Journal of Commerce,* February 11, 1841; *New York Sun,* February 11, 1841.

24. *New York Herald,* September 14, 1845.

25. *New York Daily Tribune,* June 5, 1847.

26. Addresses taken from *Longworth's American Almanac, New-York Register, and City Directory for Sixty-Third Year of American Independence* (New York: Thomas Longworth, 1838), 297.

27. Eliza Hamilton gave her birth date as October 1822 in the 1900 census. This fits in with how old she told the census-taker she was in 1870 and 1880. For this and all the material in this paragraph, see Rockaway, Morris, New Jersey, *1850 United States Federal Census,* ancestry.com; New York Ward 21, 1855, *New York State Census,* ancestry.com; New York Ward 21, *1870 United States Federal Census,* ancestry.com; Enumeration District 279, New York City, *1880 Federal Census,* ancestry.com; Enumeration District 690, New York City, *1900 Federal Census,* ancestry.com.

28. *New York Herald,* July 14, 1836.

29. *New York Herald,* March 6, 1842. On interracial sex, see Leslie M. Harris, "From Abolitionist Amalgamators to 'Rulers of the Five Points': The Discourse of Interracial Sex and Reform in Antebellum New York City," in Martha Hodes, ed., *Sex, Love, Race: Crossing Boundaries in North American History* (New York: New York University Press, 1999), 191–212; Peggy Pascoe, *What Comes Naturally: Miscegenation Law and the Making of Race in America* (New York: Oxford University Press, 2009). On black dance in New York, see Shane White, "The Death of James Johnson," *American Quarterly* 51 (December 1999): 753–96.

30. See, for example, a long account of an expedition of a *Herald* reporter and several southern gentlemen, escorted by a police officer, in *New York Herald,* May 14, 1846.

31. On Hewlett, see White, *Stories of Freedom,* 68–184; George A. Thompson Jr., *A Documentary History of the African Theatre* (Evanston, IL: Northwestern University Press, 1998); Marvin McAllister, *White People Do Not Know How to Behave at Entertainments Designed for Ladies & Gentlemen of Colour: William Brown's African and American Theater* (Chapel Hill: University of North Carolina Press, 2003).

32. *New York Evening Post,* March 29, 1837; *New York Herald,* March 29, 1837.

33. White, *Stories of Freedom,* 176–77.

34. *New York Herald,* June 6, 1839; *New York Sun,* June 8, 1839; *Journal of Commerce,* June 8, 1839; *Morning Courier and New-York Enquirer,* June 10, 1839.

35. *Morning Courier and New-York Enquirer,* June 10, 1839. I have preferred this account of the end of the case as more likely than the other ones, which have Ann Hewlett held until bail could be made.

36. *Journal of Commerce,* July 1, 1840; *New York Daily Express,* July 1, 1840.

37. *Journal of Commerce,* August 3, 1838. See also, for example, *Commercial Advertiser,* June 6, 1832; *New York Herald,* March 2, 1836; *Journal*

of Commerce, October 24, 1838; *Commercial Advertiser,* August 21, 1845.

38. *New York Herald,* July 6, 1839.

CHAPTER SIX: REAL ESTATE

1. Scott Reynolds Nelson, *A Nation of Deadbeats: An Uncommon History of America's Financial Disasters* (New York: Alfred A. Knopf, 2012), 115–16; Alasdair Roberts, *America's First Great Depression: Economic Crisis and Political Disorder after the Panic of 1837* (Ithaca: Cornell University Press, 2012), 32–33.

2. Glyn Davies, *A History of Money: From Ancient Times to the Present Day* (Cardiff: University of Wales Press, 1994), 480–81.

3. The observation is based on my reading of the first fifty years of the District Attorney's Indictment Papers, Municipal Archives of the City of New York, New York (DAIP)—people who had had money stolen commonly listed the denominations and the banks that had issued the notes.

4. Richard Doty, *America's Money, America's Story: A Chronicle of American Numismatic History,* 2nd ed. (Atlanta: Whitman Publishing, 2008), 98.

5. John Kenneth Galbraith, *Money: Whence It Came, Where It Went* (London: Andre Deutsch, 1975), 88–89.

6. Charles R. Geisst, *Wall Street: A History from Its Beginnings to the Fall of Enron* (New York: Oxford University Press, 2004), 21; *New York Herald,* September 2, 1835.

7. Stuart Banner, *American Property: A History of How, Why, and What We Own* (Cambridge: Harvard University Press, 2011), 19–20.

8. Edwin G. Burrows and Mike Wallace, *Gotham: A History of New York City to 1898* (New York: Oxford University Press, 1999), 576.

9. Allan Nevins, *The Diary of Philip Hone: 1828–1851,* 2 vols. (New York: Dodd, Mead and Company, 1927), 1:156.

10. *New York Daily Advertiser,* August 27, 1835.

11. *New York Herald,* March 3, 1836; *New York Herald,* March 4, 1836; *New York Herald,* June 15, 1836.

12. Leslie M. Harris, *In the Shadow of Slavery: African Americans in New York City, 1626–1863* (Chicago: University of Chicago Press, 2003), 117–19.

13. Rhoda Golden Freeman, "The Free Negro in New York City in the Era before the Civil War" (unpublished Ph.D. diss., Columbia University, 1966), 122–23. Historians have not spent much time considering African American property ownership. But see Leonard P. Curry, *The Free Black in Urban America, 1800–1850: The Shadow of the Dream* (Chicago: University of Chicago Press, 1981), 37–48; Jacqueline Jones, *A Dreadful Deceit: The Myth of Race from the Colonial Era to Obama's America* (New York: Basic Books, 2013), 97–144; Judith Wellman, *Brooklyn's Promised Land: The Free Black Community of Weeksville, New York* (New York: New York University Press, 2014), 13–48.

14. See, for example, an editorial in the *New York Morning Express,* March 18, 1846, arguing that freedom was "almost a curse" to African Americans. "Negroes are in an anomalous condition in the free States, and in a

condition, which, with all due deference to others who think differently from us, ought not to exist."

15. *Journal of Commerce* (semi-weekly), August 10, 1847. Conceivably this was Weeksville, although I have seen no other reference to any of the landholders out there being blind.

16. *Richmond Whig,* reprinted in *National Era,* October 6, 1859.

17. *National Era,* October 6, 1859.

18. *New York Herald,* December 10, 1840; *New York Daily Express,* December 11, 1840; *New York Daily Express,* January 5, 1841.

19. *People v. William Thompson,* November 25, 1840, DAIP; *People v. Eliza Adams,* April 20, 1839, District Attorney Indictment Papers, Municipal Archives of the City of New York.

20. *People v. William Thompson; New York Daily Express,* December 11, 1840.

21. Timothy J. Gilfoyle, *City of Eros: New York City, Prostitution, and the Commercialization of Sex, 1790–1920* (New York: Norton, 1992), 43–46.

22. *New York Transcript,* March 7, 1836; *The Sun,* March 7, 1836; *New York Herald,* July 14, 1836; *The Sun,* July 14, 1836.

23. Roy Rosenzweig and Elizabeth Blackmar, *The Park and the People: A History of Central Park* (Ithaca, NY: Cornell University Press, 1992), 64–73; Leslie M. Alexander, "Community and Institution Building in Antebellum New York: The Story of Seneca Village, 1825–1857," in Angel David Nieves and Leslie M. Alexander, eds., *"We Shall Independent Be": African American Place Making and the Struggle to Claim Space in the United States* (Boulder: University Press of Colorado, 2008), 23–46; Leslie M. Alexander, *African or American? Black Identity and Political Activism in New York City, 1784–1861* (Urbana: University of Illinois Press, 2008), 154–73. See also, for example, the student-produced film titled *Seneca Village: An Oasis in the Time before Central Park,* at http://vimeo.com/5275662.

24. Rosenzweig and Blackmar, *Park and the People,* 64–73.

25. *New York Transcript,* August 25, 1835; *New York Daily Advertiser,* August 26, 1835; *People v. Robert Ritter,* September 17, 1835, DAIP.

26. *People v. Robert Ritter.*

27. *Jeremiah G. Hamilton v. James B. Taylor,* filed June 20, 1837, Chancery Court, D CH 115-H, New York County Clerk's Office, New York (NYCC).

28. *New York Herald,* July 14, 1836.

29. *People v. William Thompson,* March 12, 1841, DAIP. For the perjury case against Downing, see *New York Daily Tribune,* February 20, 1852. For a brief comment on the case by James McCune Smith, see John Stauffer, ed., *The Works of James McCune Smith: Black Intellectual and Abolitionist* (New York: Oxford University Press, 2006), 89.

30. *Joseph Vargas v. Jeremiah G. Hamilton,* Equity Case Files of the U.S. Circuit Court for the Southern District of New York, 1791–1846, National Archives Microfilm Publications M884, Roll 15 x-116; *Long Island Farmer and Advertiser,* June 12, 1840.

31. *Poughkeepsie Journal,* October 19, 1836.

32. See, for example, *Poughkeepsie Telegraph,* August 10, 1836; *Poughkeepsie Journal,* October 19, 1836; *Poughkeepsie Telegraph,* October 19, 1836; *Poughkeepsie Telegraph,* March 1, 1837.

33. *Vargas v. Hamilton; Commercial Advertiser,* April 12, 1837. In the court case Hamilton claimed the Poughkeepsie and Hallet Cove Landing cost $27,000. However, in the deeds filed in Dutchess County, the cost of the Union Landing purchase was $30,000. See Indenture, Liber 60, 567-68, Dutchess County Clerk's Office, Poughkeepsie, New York.

34. *John Delafield v. Jeremiah G. Hamilton,* filed September 15, 1837, Chancery Court, BM 451-D, NYCC; *Commercial Advertiser,* April 12, 1837. Again, the deeds for this real estate specify $30,000 and not $20,000. See Liber 59, 398-400, Dutchess County Clerk's Office.

35. *Commercial Advertiser,* January 18, 1837.

36. *New York Sun,* July 13, 1837.

37. *Commercial Advertiser,* April 12, 1837.

38. *New York Sun,* July 13, 1837.

39. Nevins, *Diary of Philip Hone,* 1:253.

CHAPTER SEVEN: BANKRUPTCY

1. Edwin G. Burrows and Mike Wallace, *Gotham: A History of New York City to 1898* (New York: Oxford University Press, 1999), 615. On the panic, see Jessica M. Lepler, "1837: Anatomy of a Panic" (Ph.D. diss., Brandeis University, 2008); Jessica M. Lepler, *The Many Panics of 1837: People, Politics, and the Creation of a Transatlantic Financial Crisis* (New York: Cambridge University Press, 2013); Scott Reynolds Nelson, *A Nation of Deadbeats: An Uncommon History of America's Financial Disasters* (New York: Alfred A. Knopf, 2012), 95–125; Alasdair Roberts, *America's First Great Depression: Economic Crisis and Political Disorder after the Panic of 1837* (Ithaca, NY: Cornell University Press, 2012); Burrows and Wallace, *Gotham,* 603–18.

2. Allan Nevins, ed., *The Diary of Philip Hone: 1828–1851,* 2 vols., (New York: Dodd, Mead and Company, 1927), I: 228, 254, 257.

3. *New York Daily Express,* February 14, 1838.

4. *New York Daily Express,* August 9, 1837.

5. *Joseph Vargas v. Jeremiah G. Hamilton,* Equity Case Files of the U.S. Circuit Court for the Southern District of New York, 1791–1846, National Archives Microfilm Publications M884, Roll 15 x-116. On Cuban clayed sugars, see Roland T. Ely, "The Old Cuba Trade: Highlights and Case Studies of Cuban-American Interdependence during the Nineteenth Century," *Business History Review* 38 (Winter 1964): 456–78 at 457, 471. Hamilton's 500 boxes of white and brown sugar arrived in New York in early April. See *Commercial Advertiser,* April 12, 1837.

6. *Vargas v. Hamilton.*

7. *John Delafield v. Jeremiah G. Hamilton,* filed September 15, 1837, Chancery Court, BM 451-D, New York County Clerk's Office, New York (NYCC).

8. *Vargas v. Hamilton.*

9. *New York Herald,* December 22, 1843; *Morning Courier and New-York Enquirer,* December 22, 1843; *True Sun,* December 22, 1843; *New York Tribune,* December 22, 1843.

10. *New York Herald,* January 13, 1838.

11. *New York Herald,* January 17, 1838.

12. Shane White, *Stories of Freedom in Black New York* (Cambridge: Harvard University Press, 2002), 201–2.

13. *New York Herald,* January 31, 1838; *New York Herald,* February 3, 1838.

14. See, for example, *New York Herald,* October 26, 1839, in which a story ran under the caption "THE NIGGER PENNY PAPER."

15. *Longworth's American Almanac, New-York Register, and City Directory for Sixty-Third Year of American Independence* (New York: Thomas Longworth, 1838), 297.

16. *Vargas v. Hamilton.*

17. *Vargas v. Hamilton.*

18. Quoted in Elizabeth Blackmar, *Manhattan for Rent, 1785–1850* (Ithaca, NY: Cornell University Press, 1989), 213; Frances Trollope, *Domestic Manners of the Americans,* ed. Donald Smalley (New York: Alfred A. Knopf, 1949 [1832]), 349–50. On May Day, or moving day, see Blackmar, *Manhattan for Rent,* 213–16; Graham Russell Gao Hodges, *New York City Cartmen, 1667–1850* (New York: New York University Press, 2012 [1986]), 162–66.

19. *New York Daily Express,* May 7, 1838.

20. *Joseph Vargas v. Jeremiah G. Hamilton,* filed April 12, 1839, Chancery Court, BM V-757, NYCC.

21. *New York Sun,* September 14, 1841.

22. Frank M. O'Brien, *The Story of the Sun: New York: 1833–1928* (New York: D. Appleton and Company, 1928), 77–88. The interview with Day was published in *New York Sun,* September 2, 1933.

23. O'Brien, *Story of the Sun,* 89–91; *New York Sun,* September 2, 1833.

24. *Vargas v. Hamilton.*

25. *New York Daily Express,* December 9, 1840; *New York Herald,* December 9, 1840.

26. *Long Island Farmer and Advertiser,* June 12, 1840.

27. *New York Herald,* December 22, 1843; *Colored American,* July 13, 1839.

28. *New York Herald,* December 22, 1843; *Morning Courier and New-York Enquirer,* December 22, 1843; *True Sun,* December 22, 1843; *New York Tribune,* December 22, 1843.

29. *Albany Evening Journal,* February 26, 1840; *New York Sun,* February 29, 1840.

30. Quoted in Edward J. Balleisen, *Navigating Failure: Bankruptcy and Commercial Society in Antebellum America* (Chapel Hill: University of North Carolina Press, 2001), 13.

31. Balleisen, *Navigating Failure,* 1, 2, 102, 124.

32. *New York Sun,* February 2, 1842.

33. Balleisen, *Navigating Failure,* 2; Case file Jeremiah G. Hamilton, No. 953, Entry 117, Bankruptcy Records, Act of 1841, U.S. District Court of the Southern Federal District of New York, National Archives and Record Administration, Northeast Region, New York City; *New York Sun,* February 8, 1842; *Vargas v. Hamilton; Morning Courier and New-York Enquirer,* June 27, 1842; *New York Evening Post,* September 29, 1842.

34. *Wealth and Wealthy Citizens of New York City Comprising an Alphabetical Arrangement of Persons Estimated to Be Worth $100,000 and Upwards* (New York: Sun Office, 1842); Edward Pessen, "Moses Beach Revisited: A Critical Examination of His Wealthy Citizens Pamphlets,"

Journal of American History 58 (September 1971): 415–26. See also Edward Pessen, "The Wealthiest New Yorkers of the Jacksonian Era: A New List," *New York Historical Society Quarterly* 54 (April 1970): 145–72.

35. Pessen, "Moses Beach Revisited," 418–20.
36. *New York Herald,* December 22, 1843; *Morning Courier and New-York Enquirer,* December 22, 1843; *True Sun,* December 22, 1843; *New York Tribune,* December 22, 1843.
37. *Wealth and Wealthy Citizens of New York,* 7–8.

CHAPTER EIGHT: STARTING OVER

1. *New York Herald,* December 14, 1842.
2. Case file, Jeremiah G. Hamilton, No. 953, Entry 117, Bankruptcy Records, Act of 1841, U.S. District Court for the Southern Federal District of New York, National Archives and Record Administration, Northeast Region, New York City.
3. Edward J. Balleisen, *Navigating Failure: Bankruptcy and Commercial Society in Antebellum America* (Chapel Hill: University of North Carolina Press, 2001), 139, 151–57.
4. *New York Evening Post,* September 29, 1842; Record of Sales (Sales Book), Entry 127, Bankruptcy Records, Act of 1841, October 1842, U.S. District Court for the Southern District of New York, National Archives and Records Administration, Northeast Region, New York City.
5. *New York Sun,* January 20, 1843.
6. *New York Sun,* June 16, 1842. The paper unconvincingly partly retracted the story the next day. See *New York Sun,* June 17, 1842; *New York Herald* (weekly), June 18, 1842. More than 2,000 New Yorkers went through the bankruptcy system over the thirteen months of its operation. Hamilton was hardly about to publicize the fact that he was a petitioner, and the main place where notices were printed was page 4 of the *Morning Courier.* This page—jammed full of legal, government and official notices in small, often smudged, print—makes for very difficult reading (a judgment based on decades of experience). Those in court could easily have missed news of Hamilton's impending bankruptcy.
7. Lunar's name is given as either Jose or Joseph in the sources. I have used the former, other than within quotes. For the original case, see *Atlantic Insurance Company v. Jose Lunar,* filed March 30, 1843, Chancery Court, BM A-114, New York County Clerk's Office, New York.
8. *Journal of Commerce,* December 22, 1835; *Morning Herald,* April 28, 1838; Case file, James Bergen, No. 168, Entry 117, Bankruptcy Records, Act of 1841, U.S. District Court for the Southern Federal District of New York, National Archives and Record Administration, Northeast Region, New York City.
9. Initially, Sutton remembered it as Clark and Brown's, but later on, when questioned by the defense counsel, he corrected himself. The actual term used in the source was "dinner," which meant the midday, not the evening, meal.
10. *New York Herald,* August 5, 1843.
11. *Morning Courier and New-York Enquirer,* January 14, 1843; *New York Herald,* August 5, 1843; *New York American,* March 9, 1843.

12. *Wealth and Wealthy Citizens of New York City Comprising an Alphabetical Arrangement of Persons Estimated to Be Worth $100,000 and Upwards* (New York: Sun Office, 1842), 7–8; *New York Sun,* June 24, 1843.

13. *New York Herald,* August 5, 1843.

14. *New York Herald,* August 5, 1843.

15. *New York Herald,* August 5, 1843.

16. *New York Herald,* August 5, 1843.

17. *Daily Plebeian,* August 5, 1843; *Fredonia Censor,* August 11, 1843; *Commercial Advertiser,* August 5, 1843.

18. *Daily Plebeian,* August 5, 1843; *New York Evening Post,* August 5, 1843.

19. *New York Herald,* August 8, 1843.

20. *New York Herald,* August 5, 1843; *Daily Plebeian,* August 5, 1843.

21. *New York Sun,* August 10, 1843.

22. *New York Herald,* August 10, 1843. Little is known of Driggs, but for items outlining that he too had had financial problems and had fraudulently sued an insurance company, see particularly *New York Sun,* June 30, 1838; *Morning Courier and New-York Enquirer,* June 30, 1838. For an earlier incident, see *New York American for the Country,* September 27, 1836. I have spent many an hour trying to find any trace of this supposed murder attempt in the legal records in the Municipal Archives, obviously without success.

23. Sean Wilentz, *Chants Democratic: New York City and the Rise of the American Working Class, 1788–1850* (New York: Oxford University Press, 1984), 327–35, quote at 331; Edwin G. Burrows and Mike Wallace, *Gotham: A History of New York City to 1898* (New York: Oxford University Press, 1999), 635. See also Donna Dennis, *Licentious Gotham: Erotic Publishing and Its Prosecution in Nineteenth-Century New York* (Cambridge: Harvard University Press, 2009).

24. *The Subterranean,* August 12, 1843.

25. *The Subterranean,* August 26, 1843.

26. *Sunday Bulletin,* quoted in *True Sun,* August 28, 1843; *True Sun,* August 28, 1843.

27. *Daily Plebeian,* August 8, 1843.

28. *New York Evening Post,* September 2, 1843; *Morning Courier and New-York Enquirer,* September 4, 1843.

29. *New York Herald,* August 29, 1843; *New York Herald,* August 30, 1843; *New York Herald,* August 31, 1843; *New York Herald,* September 2, 1843; *New York Herald,* September 8, 1843; *New York Herald,* September 11, 1843; *New York Herald,* September 17, 1843; *New York Herald,* September 20, 1843; *New York Herald,* September 21, 1843. For details of Thompson's later career, see *New York Herald,* July 12, 1844. In a court case, he claimed: "I am a sort of constabulary force in myself"; "I act in detecting robbers, partly from generosity, and partly from pay"; "I am a sort of thief catcher"; and even "I am great at hunting up conspiracies." See also *National Police Gazette,* March 27, 1847.

30. *New York Evening Post,* September 23, 1843; *New York Morning Express,* September 23, 1843; *True Sun,* September 23, 1843; *New York American,* September 23, 1843; *New York Morning Express,* October 17, 1843; *True Sun,* October 17, 1843; *New York Tribune,* February 6, 1844; *True Sun,* February 6, 1844.

CHAPTER NINE: THE TRIAL

1. *New York Sun*, August 5, 1843; *New York Sun*, August 7, 1843.

2. *True Sun*, March 20, 1843; *True Sun*, March 21, 1843.

3. *Abstract of the Decisions of the Chancellor, From March 5, 1844 to March 4, 1845*, IV (Saratoga Springs, NY: Wilbur & Rice, 1844–1845), 4:29; *New York Sun*, April 29, 1843; *New York Sun*, May 1, 1843.

4. *True Sun*, May 26, 1843.

5. *New York Sun*, February 10, 1843; *The People v. Moses Y. Beach*, filed February 28, 1843, District Attorney's Indictment Papers, Municipal Archives of the City of New York, New York; *True Sun*, June 3, 1843; *True Sun*, June 7, 1843.

6. Timothy J. Gilfoyle, "'America's Greatest Crime Barracks': The Tombs and the Experience of Criminal Justice in New York City, 1838–1897," *Journal of Urban History* 29 (July 2003): 525–54; Charles Sutton, *The New York Tombs: Its Secrets and Its Mysteries* (Montclair, NJ: Patterson Smith, 1973 [1874]), vi, 48–49; Charles Dickens, *American Notes* (Koln, Germany: Konemann, 2000 [1842]), 101; quote about abortion in Gilfoyle, "The Tombs," 528.

7. *New York Herald*, May 11, 1849.

8. Gilfoyle, "The Tombs," 528–29; Dickens, *American Notes*, 102; *True Sun*, December 20, 1843.

9. *New York Herald*, December 22, 1843. On libel law, see Norman L. Rosenberg, *Protecting the Best Men: An Interpretive History of the Law of Libel* (Chapel Hill: University of North Carolina Press, 1986).

10. *New York Herald*, December 22, 1843.

11. *New York Herald*, December 22, 1843.

12. The best account of the flash press is the excellent Patricia Cline Cohen, Timothy J. Gilfoyle, and Helen Lefkowitz, *The Flash Press: Sporting Male Weeklies in 1840s New York* (Chicago: University of Chicago Press, 2008). See also Donna Dennis, *Licentious Gotham: Erotic Publishing and Its Prosecution in Nineteenth-Century New York* (Cambridge, MA: Harvard University Press, 2009), 43–92.

13. *New York Herald*, December 22, 1843.

14. *True Sun*, December 22, 1843.

15. *New York Herald*, December 22, 1843.

16. *Sunday Flash*, October 3, 1841.

17. *Sunday Flash*, October 17, 1843; Cohen, Gilfoyle, Lefkowitz, *Flash Press*, 198–205.

18. Cohen et al., *Flash Press*, 3–5. The largest collection of these newspapers is located in the American Antiquarian Society.

19. Orlando Patterson, *Slavery and Social Death: A Comparative Study* (Cambridge: Harvard University Press, 1982), 60–61.

20. *New York Sun*, December 27, 1843. For an excellent account of racial ideas, see Bruce Dain, *A Hideous Monster of the Mind: American Race Theory in the Early Republic* (Cambridge: Harvard University Press, 2002).

21. Robert C. Toll, *Blacking Up: The Minstrel Show in Nineteenth-Century America* (New York: Oxford University Press, 1974), v, 30–31. There is an extensive historiography of minstrelsy. I have found most useful Eric Lott, *Love and Theft: Blackface Minstrelsy and the American Working*

Class (New York: Oxford University Press, 1993); W. T. Lhamon Jr., *Raising Cain: Blackface Performance from Jim Crow to Hip Hop* (Cambridge: Harvard University Press, 1998).

22. *New York Herald,* December 22, 1843.

23. *New York Sun,* August 10, 1843.

24. *New York Herald,* December 22, 1843.

25. *New York Herald,* December 22, 1843.

26. *New York Tribune,* December 22, 1843. See also *True Sun,* December 22, 1843; *Daily Plebeian,* December 22, 1843; *Journal of Commerce,* December 23, 1843.

27. *New York Herald,* December 22, 1843.

28. *New York Sun,* December 22, 1843.

29. *New York Sun,* December 22, 1843; *True Sun,* December 23, 1843.

30. *Daily Plebeian,* December 23, 1843; *True Sun,* December 25, 1843.

31. *True Sun,* December 25, 1843.

32. *True Sun,* December 25, 1843.

33. *True Sun,* December 25, 1843.

34. *True Sun,* December 25, 1843. As we saw in Chapter Two, back in 1836 Hamilton had mentioned the possibility of taking a mercantile voyage to Calcutta in the following spring. That is the only other mention of India I have found.

35. *True Sun,* December 25, 1843; *New York American,* December 23, 1843.

36. *New York Tribune,* December 25, 1843; *Commercial Advertiser,* December 26, 1843.

37. *New York Herald,* December 23, 1843. On Sue's sales, see *Journal of Commerce* (semi-weekly), November 4, 1843; Ned Buntline, *The Mysteries and Miseries of New York* (New York: Berford & Co., 1848). The best account of Buntline remains Peter George Buckley, "To the Opera House: Culture and Society in New York City, 1820–1860" (unpublished Ph.D. diss., State University of New York at Stony Brook, 1984), 431–47.

38. *Subterranean,* December 30, 1843.

39. *Daily Plebeian,* December 24, 1843. Even this "nominal" sentence was suspended until the following year, when the court could hear evidence "improper for the public ear" that the defense considered would satisfy them that the fine should be much less than $50.

40. *New York Sun,* December 25, 1843.

41. *New York Sun,* December 26, 1843.

42. See, for example, *Rome Sentinel,* May 14, 1844.

CHAPTER TEN: WALL STREET

1. *The New World; A Weekly Family Journal of Popular Literature, Science, Art,* August 12, 1843.

2. Charles R. Geisst, *Wall Street: A History from Its Beginnings to the Fall of Enron* (New York: Oxford University Press, 2004), 33. On Wall Street, see also Steve Fraser, *Every Man a Speculator: A History of Wall Street in American Life* (New York: HarperCollins, 2005); Steve Fraser, *Wall Street: America's Dream Palace* (New Haven, CT: Yale University Press, 2008). By far the most useful book, though, simply because the authors are not desperate to get to the twentieth century, has been Walter Werner and Steven T. Smith, *Wall Street* (New York: Columbia University Press, 1991).

3. William Worthington Fowler, *Twenty Years of Inside Life on Wall Street* (New York: Orange Judd Company, 1880), 25.

4. J. Benwell, *An Englishman's Travels in America: His Observations of Life and Manners in the Free and Slave States* (London: Binns and Goodwin, 1853), 11–16; *New York Herald,* November 2, 1838; [William Armstrong], *A Reformed Stock Gambler, Stocks and Stock-Jobbing in Wall Street with Sketches of the Brokers and Fancy Stocks* (New York: New-York Publishing Company, 1848), 8, 18; *New York Herald,* December 3, 1835. At times writers almost suggested the weather shaped the market: "The weather continued unpleasant yesterday, and business appeared to feel the influence of it"; *New York Sun,* March 26, 1840. Or "the Weather and the stock market were yesterday alike—dismal"; *New York Sun,* February 20, 1840.

5. *True Sun,* October 26, 1843. For a story about male and female children in Wall Street, up to forty at a time, entering "counting rooms and offices" and stealing "every kind of merchandize that is exposed, for a moment, to their depredations," see *New York Herald,* January 27, 1841.

6. *True Sun,* December 29, 1843; *True Sun,* December 31, 1845. See also the recorder's charge to the grand jury about the "evils and frauds" resulting from the system of stockjobbing in *New York Sun,* February 9, 1842.

7. Benwell, *An Englishman's Travels,* 30.

8. Benwell, *An Englishman's Travels,* 16; *New York Morning Express,* January 31, 1846.

9. Benwell, *An Englishman's Travels,* 19–20.

10. Werner and Smith, *Wall Street,* 20–34; *True Sun,* October 22, 1845. According to this last article, there were "some 200 brokers, of whom probably 90 take their seats daily." My lower figure in the text is taken from my reading of nearly two decades of stock exchange minutes, particularly from the votes on new members. See *New York Stock and Exchange Board Minutes, 1833–50,* New York Stock Exchange Archives.

11. *True Sun,* October 22, 1845.

12. *New York Stock and Exchange Board Minutes.* For the resolution about hats, see June 25, 1836. See also Werner and Smith, *Wall Street,* 20–34.

13. *New York Stock and Exchange Board Minutes,* May 8, 1837–March 1, 1838. Myer Levy was the broker whose profile replaced Jeremiah Hamilton's in the *Sunday Flash* newspaper, as detailed in the last chapter, leading to a libel suit. See *Sunday Flash,* October 17, 1843.

14. Werner and Smith, *Wall Street,* 30.

15. *New York Herald,* October 19, 1837.

16. *New York Sun,* June 8, 1838.

17. Abram C. Dayton, *Last Days of Knickerbocker Life in New York* (New York: George Harlan, 1882), 64–74.

18. Fowler, *Twenty Years of Inside Life on Wall Street,* 53.

19. Werner and Smith, *Wall Street,* 55–57.

20. *New York Stock and Exchange Board Minutes.* For the "Black Book" for defaulters, see, for example, the entry for December 13, 1838.

21. *New York Herald,* December 12, 1836; *Jeremiah G. Hamilton v. John Wood,* filed July 10, 1837, Chancery Court, BM-413-H, New York County Clerk's Office, New York (NYCC); *New York Herald,* February 15, 1838; *New York Herald,* November 21, 1838.

22. *New York Sun,* June 27, 1837.

23. *New York Spectator,* April 2, 1838; *Hamilton v. Wood;* Bankruptcy Case File of Jeremiah G. Hamilton, #953, filed February 5, 1842, Entry 117, Bankruptcy Records, Act of 1841, U.S. District Court for the Southern Federal District of New York, National Archives and Record Administration, Northeast Region, New York City; *New York Herald,* February 15, 1838.

24. *New York Herald,* December 10, 1839; *Journal of Commerce,* December 11, 1839.

25. *New York Morning Express,* December 22, 1843; *True Sun,* December 22, 1843.

26. *New York Sun,* November 20, 1841; *New York Sun,* November 29, 1841.

27. Bankruptcy Case File of Jeremiah G. Hamilton, #953, filed February 5, 1842; *New York American,* October 25, 1841.

28. *New York Sun,* June 16, 1842; *New York Herald* (weekly), June 18, 1842.

29. *New York Evening Post,* May 1, 1843; *New York Stock Exchange and Board Minutes,* November 14, 1843. Ephraim Stimson became the third partner on November 1, 1843. *New York Evening Post,* November 7, 1843.

30. *Jeremiah G. Hamilton v. Sidney C. Genin,* filed November 23, 1844, Chancery Court, BM 409-H, NYCC.

31. *New York Herald,* March 9, 1845; *New York Herald,* March 10, 1845.

32. *New York Morning News,* March 10, 1845.

33. *Times-Picayune,* March 19, 1845; *Baltimore Sun,* March 13, 1845; *Charleston Courier,* March 13, 1845; *Maine Cultivator and Hallowell Gazette,* April 5, 1845.

CHAPTER ELEVEN: LIVING WITH JIM CROW

1. Richard O. Boyer, "The Hot Bach," in Henry Finder, ed., *The 40s: The Story of a Decade* (New York: Random House, 2014), 388.

2. Bankruptcy Case File of Jeremiah G. Hamilton, #953, filed February 5, 1842, Entry 117, Bankruptcy Records, Act of 1841, U.S. District Court for the Southern Federal District of New York, National Archives and Record Administration, Northeast Region, New York City; "J. G. Hamilton," *United States IRS Tax Assessment Lists, 1862–1918,* ancestry.com.

3. *New York Sun,* December 6, 1843. See also *New York Sun,* December 7, 1843.

4. [William] A. Armstrong, *Reformed Stock Gambler, Stocks and Stock-Jobbing in Wall Street with Sketches of the Brokers and Fancy Stocks* (New York: New-York Publishing Company, 1848), 30.

5. *New York Sun,* December 30, 1839.

6. Chas H. Haswell, *Reminiscences of an Octogenarian of the City of New York (1816 to 1860)* (New York: Harper & Brothers, 1896), 490–92.

7. Frederick Douglass, *Narrative of the Life of Frederick Douglass, An American Slave* (1845) in *Frederick Douglass: Autobiographies* (New York: The Library of America, 1994), 42.

8. Michael Slater, *Charles Dickens* (New Haven, CT: Yale University Press, 2009), 180–96. On international copyright, see Christopher Hilliard, "Publishing," in *The Fin-de-Siècle World,* ed. Michael Saler (New York: Routledge, 2014), 367–79. *The Works of Lord Bacon,* 2 vols. (London: William Ball, 1838); *The Works of the Late Right Honourable Henry St. John,*

Lord Viscount Bolingbroke, 8 vols. (London: J. Johnson et al., 1809); *The Works of Lord Bolingbroke with a Life,* 4 vols. (Philadelphia: Carey and Hart, 1841); *Paradise Lost: A Poem, in Twelve Books* (Boston: Langdon Coffin, 1831); Joanne Shattock, *Politics and Reviewers: The Edinburgh and The* Quarterly (London: Leicester University Press, 1989), 97–100.

9. *New York Daily Tribune,* May 22, 1875.

10. Jonathan Rose, *The Intellectual Life of the British Working Classes* (New Haven, CT: Yale University Press, 2001), 33.

11. *The Treasury of Knowledge and Library of Reference,* 3 vols. (New York: Conner & Cooke, 1836); *The Treasury of Knowledge and Library of Reference,* 3 vols. (New York: Collins, Keese & Co., 1839).

12. "Captain Maryatt's *Diary in America,*" *Edinburgh Review* 70 (October 1839): 123–49; "Democracy in America," *Edinburgh Review* 71 (October 1840): 1–47, quote at 23.

13. Bernard Bailyn, *The Ideological Origins of the American Revolution* (Cambridge: Harvard University Press, 1967), 35. See also the perceptive Daniel T. Rodgers, "Republicanism: The Career of a Concept," *Journal of American History* 79 (June 1992): 11–38.

14. See Quentin Skinner, *The Foundations of Modern Political Thought,* vol. 1 (Cambridge: Cambridge University Press, 1978); J. G. A. Pocock, *The Machiavellian Moment: Florentine Political Thought and the Atlantic Republican Tradition* (Princeton, NJ: Princeton University Press, 2003).

15. Richard Tuck, *Philosophy and Government 1572–1651* (Cambridge: Cambridge University Press, 1993); M. M. Goldsmith, "Liberty, Luxury and the Pursuit of Happiness," in *The Languages of Political Theory in Early Modern Europe,* ed. Anthony Pagden (Cambridge: Cambridge University Press, 1987), 225–52.

16. Quoted in Tuck, *Philosophy and Government,* 109.

17. The classic statement of this remains Leo Marx, *The Machine in the Garden: Technology and the Pastoral Ideal in America* (New York: Oxford University Press, 1964). See also Annabel M. Patterson, *Pastoral and Ideology: Virgil to Valéry* (Berkeley: University of California Press, 1987); John F. Kasson, *Civilizing the Machine: Technology and Republican Values in America, 1776–1900* (New York: Hill and Wang, 1999 [new ed.]).

18. *Frederick Douglass' Paper,* March 18, 1852; *New York Evangelist,* July 28, 1859.

19. *The New World; A Weekly Family Journal of Popular Literature, Science, Art and News,* March 4, 1843, p. 262.

20. *The New World; A Weekly Family Journal of Popular Literature, Science, Art and News,* March 4, 1843, p. 262.

21. See James J. Gigantino II, *The Ragged Road to Abolition: Slavery and Freedom in New Jersey, 1775–1865* (Philadelphia: University of Pennsylvania Press, 2014).

22. Rockaway, Morris, New Jersey, *1850 United States Federal Census,* ancestry.com; Return of Births in Rockaway, Morris County, from First of May 1849 to First of May 1850, New Jersey State Archives, Trenton, New Jersey.

23. *The New World; A Weekly Family Journal of Popular Literature, Science, Art and News,* March 4, 1843, p. 262; *Newark Daily Advertiser,* November 20, 1850; *Newark Daily Advertiser,* November 30, 1850.

24. *Newark Daily Advertiser,* February 14, 1857.

25. *Commercial Advertiser,* December 5, 1850; *New York Sun,* December 6, 1850; *New York Sun,* December 12, 1850; *New York Sun,* December 14, 1850. On horses in the city more generally, see Clay McShane and Joel A. Tarr, *The Horse in the City: Living Machines in the Nineteenth Century* (Baltimore: Johns Hopkins University Press, 2007); Catherine McNeur, *Taming Manhattan: Environmental Battles in the Antebellum City* (Cambridge: Harvard University Press, 2014).

26. Charles R. Rode, *New York City Directory, for 1851–52* (New York: Doggett & Rode, 1851), 235; Record of Assessment Manhattan, 1852, 18th Ward, 29th St., Cross Lexington Ave., Municipal Archives of the City of New York, New York.

27. *New York Sun,* August 9, 1851.

28. *New York Herald,* May 20, 1875.

29. *New York Sun,* September 2, 1933.

30. *New York Sun,* October 7, 1880; *Kingston Daily Freeman,* March 11, 1881; *Kingston Daily Freeman,* February 16, 1883.

31. *New York Sun,* October 7, 1880; *Kingston Daily Freeman,* March 11, 1881.

32. *New York Herald,* December 9, 1840.

33. *New York Herald,* May 20, 1875.

34. *Frederick Douglass' Paper,* February 12, 1852. On Smith, see John Stauffer, ed., *The Works of James McCune Smith: Black Intellectual and Abolitionist* (New York: Oxford University Press, 2006).

35. *Frederick Douglass' Paper,* March 18, 1852.

36. *Frederick Douglass' Paper,* April 8, 1852.

37. Passing has long been an important issue in the writing of African American history. See, most recently, Daniel J. Sharfstein, *The Invisible Line: Three American Families and the Secret Journey from Black to White* (New York: Penguin Press, 2011); Allyson Hobbs, *A Chosen Exile: A History of Racial Passing in American Life* (Cambridge: Harvard University Press, 2014). For an exemplary study of one unusual case, see Martha A. Sandweiss, *Passing Strange: A Gilded Age Tale of Love and Deception across the Color Line* (New York: Penguin Press, 2009).

38. *Cincinnati Enquirer,* May 30, 1875.

39. Rockaway, Morris, New Jersey, *1850 United States Federal Census,* ancestry.com; New York Ward 21, *1860 United States Federal Census;* New York Ward 21, *1870 United States Federal Census,* ancestry.com; New York Death Certificate 206996, Municipal Archives of the City of New York, New York.

40. *Frederick Douglass' Paper,* April 8, 1852.

CHAPTER TWELVE: MAKING MONEY

1. My account of this case is derived almost entirely from *Jeremiah G. Hamilton v. The Poughkeepsie Silk Company,* filed June 17, 1845, Chancery Court, CH-465-H, New York County Clerk's Office, New York (NYCC).

2. On corporations, see G. Edward White, *Law in American History: From the Colonial Years through the Civil War* (New York: Oxford University Press, 2012), 263–70.

3. *Poughkeepsie Telegraph,* July 13, 1836.

4. Bankruptcy Case File of Jeremiah G. Hamilton, #953, filed February 5, 1842, Entry 117, Bankruptcy Records, Act of 1841, U.S. District Court of the Southern Federal District of New York, National Archives and Record Administration, Northeast Region, New York City.

5. This point is developed well by Edward J. Balleisen, *Navigating Failure: Bankruptcy and Commercial Society in Antebellum America* (Chapel Hill: University of North Carolina Press, 2001).

6. *Semi-Weekly Courier and New York Enquirer,* October 13, 1856; *National Republican,* January 5, 1877.

7. By far the best account of Vanderbilt and Nicaragua is T. J. Stiles, *The First Tycoon: The Epic Life of Cornelius Vanderbilt* (New York: Alfred A. Knopf, 2009), 163–331, Polk quote on 172. See also Stephen Dando-Collins, *Tycoon's War: How Cornelius Vanderbilt Invaded a Country to Overthrow America's Most Famous Military Adventurer* (New York: Da Capo Press, 2008).

8. Edwin G. Burrows and Mike Wallace, *Gotham: A History of New York City to 1898* (New York: Oxford University Press, 1999), 652.

9. Stiles, *First Tycoon.*

10. Stiles, *First Tycoon,* 217–20.

11. Stiles, *First Tycoon,* 253–97. For an incisive account of the implications of the Walker regime, see Walter Johnson, *River of Dark Dreams: Slavery and Empire in the Cotton Kingdom* (Cambridge: Harvard University Press, 2013), 366–94.

12. *New York Daily Tribune,* October 14, 1856.

13. Ernest A. Wiltse, *Gold Rush Steamers of the Pacific* (Lawrence, MA: Quarterman Publications, 1976 [1938]), 203–4; *Jeremiah G. Hamilton v. Accessory Transit Company,* filed January 27, 1858, Supreme Court, 1858 H-33, New York County Clerk's Office, New York.

14. *Hamilton v. Accessory Transit Company.*

15. *New York Daily Times,* October 9, 1856.

16. *New York Daily Times,* October 9, 1856; *New York Herald,* November 4, 1856.

17. *New York Daily Tribune,* January 5, 1877; *National Republican,* January 5, 1877; *Troy Daily Times,* August 8, 1876.

18. *New York Herald,* May 20, 1875; *New York Daily Tribune,* May 22, 1875. The *Tribune*'s shortened version of this sentence was: "In 1848 he became associated with Mr Vanderbilt in the Nicaragua Steamship Company."

19. Wiltse, *Gold Rush Steamers,* 203–4.

20. Stiles, *First Tycoon,* 70–71.

21. Stiles, *First Tycoon,* 315.

22. John Duer, *Reports of Cases Argued and Determined in the Superior Court of the City of New York* (Albany: W. C. Little and Company, 1858), 6:244–53.

23. *Jeremiah G. Hamilton v. George Barker,* filed January 28, 1857, Supreme Court, 1857 B-727, NYCC.

24. *Jeremiah G. Hamilton v. Joseph L. White,* filed November 14, 1857, Superior Court, 1857-#932, NYCC.

25. I have pieced together my account from *Charles Stewart v. Jeremiah G. Hamilton,* filed March 15, 1865, Superior Court, 1865-#455, NYCC; *Charles Stewart v. Jeremiah G. Hamilton,* filed June 28, 1865, Superior

Court, 1865-#475, NYCC; *Wentworth Butler v. Jeremiah G. Hamilton,* filed November 20, 1865, Superior Court, 1865-#232, NYCC.

26. *Charles Stewart v. Jeremiah G. Hamilton,* filed June 28, 1865, Superior Court, 1865-#475, NYCC.

CHAPTER THIRTEEN: TO THE DRAFT RIOTS

1. Thomas F. De Voe, *The Market Book* (New York: Burt Franklin, 1969 [1862]), 369–70, 345.

2. *New York Herald,* February 17, 1858; *New York Daily Times,* November 29, 1852; George T. Downing, "A Sketch of the Life and Times of Thomas Downing," *A.M.E. Church Review* (April 1887): 402–10.

3. I have written about this generation elsewhere. See, for example, Shane White, *Stories of Freedom in Black New York* (Cambridge: Harvard University Press, 2002); Shane White, "Freedom's First Con: African Americans and Changing Notes in Antebellum New York City," *Journal of the Early Republic* 34 (Fall 2014): 385–409.

4. Ira Rosenwaike, *Population History of New York City* (Syracuse: Syracuse University Press, 1972), 36, 42–45.

5. Eric Foner, *Gateway to Freedom: The Hidden History of the Underground Railroad* (New York: W. W. Norton & Company, 2015). Throughout this book, I have made very little mention of black activists or black thought. These subjects had very little to do with Jeremiah Hamilton's world, and other historians have dealt with them very well. See, for example, the excellent Patrick Rael, *Black Identity and Black Protest in the Antebellum North* (Chapel Hill: University of North Carolina Press, 2002).

6. *New York Tribune,* September 16, 1850.

7. By far the best work on this subject is Darryl M. Heller, "The Poor Man's Carriage: Street Railways and Their Publics in Brooklyn and New York, 1850–96" (unpublished Ph.D. diss., University of Chicago, 2012), 69–112. Unfortunately I came across this dissertation too late, reading it only days before sending this manuscript to the press.

8. *New York Tribune,* July 19, 1854.

9. Heller, "Poor Man's Carriage," 87.

10. *New York Daily Times,* September 26, 1855. Downing's statement was printed in a number of papers, and, indeed, the *Times'* copy was taken from the *New York Evening Post.* See also *New York Daily Tribune,* September 26, 1855.

11. *New York Daily Times,* September 26, 1855.

12. *New York Daily Times,* September 26, 1855.

13. *New York Daily Times,* October 31, 1855.

14. *Frederick Douglass' Paper,* reprinted in John Stauffer, ed., *The Works of James McCune Smith: Black Intellectual and Abolitionist* (New York: Oxford University Press, 2006), 161–62; *New York Tribune,* August 25, 1858.

15. *Charleston Courier,* March 24 1860; *New York Herald,* January 25, 1861.

16. See Graham Russell Gao Hodges, *David Ruggles: A Radical Black Abolitionist and the Underground Railroad in New York City* (Chapel Hill: University of North Carolina Press, 2010); Foner, *Gateway to Freedom.*

17. David Quigley, "Southern Slavery in a Free City: Economy, Politics, and Culture," in Ira Berlin and Leslie M. Harris, eds., *Slavery in New York* (New York: New Press, 2005), 263–88, De Bow quote at 283.

18. Foner, *Gateway to Freedom,* 9, 219.

19. Iver Bernstein, *The New York City Draft Riots: Their Significance for American Society and Politics in the Age of the Civil War* (New York: Oxford University Press, 1990), 7–14, quote at 8. This book remains by far the best study of the Draft Riots, and I have relied on it. See also Iver Bernstein, "Securing Freedom: The Challenges of Black Life in Civil War New York," in *Slavery in New York,* ed. Berlin and Harris (see note 17), 289–324.

20. Adrian Cook, *The Armies of the Streets: The New York City Draft Riots of 1863* (Lexington: University Press of Kentucky, 1974), 55; Bernstein, *New York City Draft Riots,* 18–20; Bernstein, "Securing Freedom," 291.

21. Quoted in Bernstein, *New York City Draft Riots,* 36.

22. Quoted in Leslie M. Harris, *In the Shadow of Slavery: African Americans in New York City, 1626-1863* (Chicago: University of Chicago Press, 2003), 280.

23. Bernstein, "Securing Freedom," 295.

24. Statement of Daniel Murray, *People v. John Leary and John Leary Junior,* filed October 28, 1863, District Attorney's Indictment Papers, Municipal Archives of the City of New York, New York (DAIP); Statement of Mary Flannery, *People v. John Leary,* DAIP.

25. Statement of Eliza Jane Hamilton, *People v. John Leary.*

26. There were a few words, paraphrases more than direct quotations, in newspaper articles about the 1880 court case cited in Chapter Eleven. Her statement in *People v. Leary,* though, was of a completely different order, being slightly more than seven pages of the clerk's handwriting.

27. Statement of Eliza Jane Hamilton, *People v. John Leary.*

28. Statement of Eliza Jane Hamilton, *People v. John Leary.*

29. Statement of William James, *People v. John Leary.* One of the two white women known to be in the house was Eliza Hamilton. Conceivably the other was their servant, Mary Gibbons, or Eliza Smith, the woman who often stayed with the Hamiltons. Or possibly it was one of the Hamiltons' daughters.

30. Cook, *Armies of the Streets,* 143.

31. "Letter from Camilla Davis Leonard to Her Son, Robert Woodward Leonard, Dated Rockaway, July 23, [1863]," April 22, 1863, Correspondence: 1861–1865, 019-0192, Robert Woodward Leonard Collection, New-York Historical Society.

32. Statement of William James, *People v. John Leary;* "Camilla Davis Leonard to Her Son."

33. "Camilla Davis Leonard to Her Son"; *New York Tribune,* August 3, 1863.

34. Rosenwaike, *Population History of New York City,* 8, 18, 36, 77.

35. *Trow's New York City Directory for the Year Ending May 1 1868* (New York: John F. Trow, 1868), 431.

EPILOGUE: A LION IN WINTER

1. *New York Herald,* October 31, 1866.

2. *The People v. John Murphy,* filed November 13, 1866, District Attorney's Indictment Papers, Municipal Archives of the City of New York, New

York; Will and Probate Petition of Jeremiah G. Hamilton, File #1875-0004, Surrogate Court of New York Archive, New York.

3. *People v. John Murphy.* On burning, see Shane White, "Freedom's First Con: African Americans and Changing Notes in Antebellum New York City," *Journal of the Early Republic* 34 (Fall 2014): 385–409.

4. *New York Herald,* May 20, 1875; *New York Daily Tribune,* May 22, 1875; *Albany Evening Journal,* June 5, 1875.

5. *New York Daily Tribune,* December 4, 1865; *New York Daily Tribune,* February 19, 1874.

6. Details of Lot 14972, Green-Wood Cemetery Archives, Brooklyn, New York; *New York Herald,* December 3, 1868; *New York Herald,* April 15, 1873. Camilla, "youngest daughter of J.G. and Eliza J. Hamilton," died of congestion of the brain on December 29, 1863. See *New York Times,* December 31, 1863.

7. *Daily Saratogian,* May 24, 1875; *New York Evening Post,* June 25, 1872. See also Myra B. Young Armstead, *"Lord Please Don't Take Me in August": African Americans in Newport and Saratoga Springs, 1870–1930* (Urbana: University of Illinois Press, 1999).

8. *New York Herald,* November 15, 1864.

9. *New York Herald,* September 10, 1870; *New York Herald,* September 26, 1870.

10. John Merriman, *Massacre: The Life and Death of the Paris Commune* (New York: Basic Books, 2014), 1–8, quote at 5.

11. Michael Hill, ed., *Elihu Washburne: The Diary and Letters of America's Minister to France during the Siege and Commune of Paris* (New York: Simon & Schuster, 2012), 39–40. See also David McCullough, *The Greater Journey: Americans in Paris* (New York: Simon & Schuster, 2011).

12. Quoted in Austin Baxter Keep, *History of the New York Society Library* (New York: De Vinne Press, 1908), 492. Jeremiah G. Hamilton's share certificate is held by the New York Society in New York.

13. See Charging Ledger 1856–1858, 529, New York Society Library, New York; Charging Ledger 1856–1858, 526; Charging Ledger 1858–1860, 560; Charging Ledger 1860–1863, 983; Charging Ledger 1864–1865, 421; Charging Ledger 1865–1866, 444; Charging Ledger 1866–1869, 429; Charging Ledger 1869–1872, 460; Charging Ledger 1872–1875, 460; Charging Ledger 1872–1875, 473.

14. *New York Herald,* May 20, 1875.

15. *Harper's Bazaar,* June 19, 1875, 395.

16. New York Death Certificate 206996, Municipal Archives of the City of New York, New York; *New York Tribune,* May 22, 1875; *New York Herald,* May 21, 1875; *Daily Saratogian,* May 24, 1875; *Baltimore Sun,* May 24, 1875.

17. *Philadelphia Inquirer,* May 20, 1875; *North Carolinian,* June 30, 1875; *Albany Evening Journal,* June 5, 1875; *Galveston Daily News,* June 2, 1875; *Commercial Advertiser,* May 22, 1875. For other notices, see, for example, *Nashville Union and American,* May 20, 1875; *Decatur Weekly Republican,* May 20, 1875; *Atlanta Constitution,* May 22, 1875; *Indianapolis News,* May 22, 1875; *Gallipolis Journal,* May 27, 1875; *Warrenton Gazette,* June 25, 1875.

18. *New York Herald,* May 20, 1875; *Cincinnati Enquirer,* May 30, 1875.

19. Details of Lot 14972, Green-Wood Cemetery Archives.

20. Will and Probate Petition of Jeremiah G. Hamilton, File #1875-0004; Assessments of the First Ward of the City of New York, 1874, Municipal Archives of New York, New York.

21. James Weldon Johnson, *The Autobiography of an Ex-Coloured Man* (New York: Hill and Wang, 1960 [1912]), 103–25, 192–96. I have been strongly influenced by Ann Fabian's reading of this novel. See Fabian, *Card Sharps, Dream Books, and Bucket Shops: Gambling in Nineteenth-Century America* (Ithaca, NY: Cornell University Press, 1990), 108–13.

22. The term "Pantheon of Heroes" is from Lawrence Levine. See Lawrence W. Levine, *Black Culture and Black Consciousness: Afro-American Folk Thought from Slavery to Freedom* (New York: Oxford University Press, 1977), 367–440.

INDEX